Living
With Godly Passion

Daily Readings for those with a Passion to Share Jesus

By J. David Eshleman, DMin.

LIVING WITH GODLY PASSION

Daily Readings for those with a Passion to Share Jesus

Copyright © 2010
by **J. David Eshleman**

Scripture quotations marked AMP: "Scripture quotations taken from the New American Standard Bible®, Copyright © 1960, 1962, 1963, 1968, 1971, 1972, 1973, 1975, 1977, 1995 by The Lockman Foundation. Used by permission." (www.Lockman.org)

Scripture quotations marked CEV are taken from the Contemporary English Version® Copyright ©1995 American Bible Society. All rights reserved.

Scripture quotations marked KJV are from the Holy Bible, King James Version (Authorized Version). First published in 1611. Quoted from the KJV Classic Reference Bible, Copyright ©1983 by The Zondervan Corporation.

Scripture quotations marked Msg. are taken from The Message. Copyright ©1993, 1994, 1995, 1996, 2000, 2001, 2002, 2003 by Eugene H. Peterson. Used by permission of NavPress Publishing Group.

Scripture quotations marked NIV are taken from the Holy Bible, New International Version®. NIV®. Copyright ©1973, 1978, 1984 by International Bible Society. Used by permission of Zondervan. All rights reserved.

Scripture quotations marked NLT are taken from the Holy Bible, New Living Translation, copyright © 1996, 2004, 2007. Used by permission of Tyndale House Publishers, Inc. Carol Stream, IL 60188. All rights reserved.

Scripture quotations marked LB are taken from The Living Bible copyright ©1971. Used by permission of Tyndale House Publishers, Inc., Carol Stream, IL 60188. All rights reserved.

No part of this work may be reproduced or copied in any form or by any means—graphic, electronic, or mechanical, including photocopying, recording, taping, or information—without the written permission of the author's family.

Library of Congress Number: 2010931889
International Standard Book Number: 978-1-60126-243-1

Printed 2010 at
Masthof Press
219 Mill Road
Morgantown, PA 19543-9516

DEDICATION

To my wife
Helen
whose passion for sharing Jesus
along with her gift of intercession
greatly encourages and empowers me
to share the Good News.
Her zeal, in spite of her physical limitations,
and often because of them,
has inspired multitudes to walk closely with Jesus
and to share his love with their friends.

PREFACE

The Apostles could not help but speak about what they had seen and heard. (See Acts 4:20.) They joyfully shared the Good News. Some Christians would rather have a root canal than share their faith. Why are we so hesitant? If we had the cure for cancer and did not share it, we would be guilty of a criminal offense. We have the cure for the world's ailments but so often we are hesitant to share it. As our culture becomes more secular, the need to share the Good News of Jesus increases.

Eight-five percent of the churches in the United States have either plateaued or are in decline. Many have already closed. Unless Christians renew their first love, they will be indifferent to sharing the Good News and many more churches will close.

These daily readings are an effort to reverse that trend. They help equip Christians with Godly courage and confidence as they realize the resources and the priority Jesus places on our need to be a witness, and the confidence, boldness and joy he gives us via his Holy Spirit. Jesus, in his final words, just before he ascended to heaven gives us both the authority (see Matthew 28:18-20) and the power to be his witnesses (see Acts 1:8).

When we share Jesus' invitation of love and forgiveness, and it is accepted, heaven throws a party. (See Luke 15.)

Begin reading wherever you find yourself in the calendar year. There is no advantage to waiting until the New Year to begin.

I have included a prayer at the conclusion of each reading. You are encouraged to wait on the Lord to hear his voice instructing your heart for the next steps of your day.

I pray the following prayer daily. I commend it to you for your consideration.

> *Father, you gave your only Son for me, I don't have that passion for others, give me your passion. Jesus, you gave your life for me, I don't*

have that level of compassion, give me your compassion. Holy Spirit, you left heaven in all its splendor to come and dwell in my sinful heart, now made holy by your work, give me your passion and power to share your love and compassion for the lost. Amen.

Mother Teresa is reported as saying, "Anyone who imitates Jesus to the full, must also share in his passion."

Due to the general focus of this book, the Lord's Commission (Matthew 28:18-20) and the final words of Jesus (Acts 1:8) appear in several readings. As learning occurs by way of repetition, you will find some truths intentionally repeated.

In the 1,000+ Scripture references included, I have used several different translations for the purpose of making God's word more understandable in our culture. Their abbreviations are:

AMP	*Amplified Bible*
CEV	*Contemporary English Version*
LB	*Living Bible*
KJV	*King James Version*
Msg.	*Message Bible*
NIV	*New International Version*
NLT	*New Living Translation*

At times I inserted words to the Biblical text for clarification. These words appear in parenthesis in the text.

Join me in praying for the Lord to restore the passion of introducing people to Jesus who brings hope, purpose, and abundant life to all who open their lives to him. You and I are exceedingly privileged to be involved in the most exciting and joyful adventure you can imagine—seeing lives transformed by the powerful name of Jesus!

Without the loving support of my wife, Helen, this project would not have been possible. Her prayers, loving counsel, and encouragement were vital. Ray Greer gave many hours correcting my misspelling and punctuation, Janet Kreider and Martha Nissley assisted in proof reading. Lois Ann Mast and her staff at Masthof enabled this work to be completed in record time. Finally the glory and praise goes to Jesus who made it all possible.

- July 2010

January 1

Joy in Heaven

Luke 15:3-24

When a shepherd finds a lost sheep, he calls together his friends and neighbors and says, "Rejoice with me; I have found my lost sheep." Jesus says, "I tell you that in the same way there will be more rejoicing in heaven over one sinner who repents than over ninety-nine righteous persons who do not need to repent" (Luke 15:6-7 NIV).

When the woman finds her lost coin she says, "Rejoice with me, I have found my lost coin." Jesus says, "In the same way, I tell you, there is rejoicing in the presence of the angels of God over one sinner who repents" (Luke 15:9-10 NIV).

Notice how the father rejoices when the lost son returns: "The father said to his servants, 'Quick! Bring the best robe and put it on him. Put a ring on his finger and sandals on his feet. Bring the fattened calf and kill it. Let's have a feast and celebrate. For this son of mine was dead and is alive again; he was lost and is found.' So they began to celebrate" (Luke 15:22-24 NIV).

I find it interesting that the only time the Bible informs us that we can bring joy in heaven is when a sinner is born again. I expect there is joy in heaven whenever God's people walk in faithfulness to their Lord but the only time the Bible explicitly states we cause rejoicing in heaven is when a person repents and accepts Jesus as their Lord and Savior.

What a privilege we have to bring joy to the angels in heaven. Let's witness with both our words and our deeds. Francis of Assisi said in essence, "Witness 24/7, if necessary use words." That's like saying, "Be sure to wash, if necessary use water." We need to employ both deeds and words. If Jesus would have come and not informed us with words we would still be lost.

Share Jesus so others can be transferred from the kingdom of darkness to the Kingdom of God's dear Son. (See Colossians 1:14.)

Father, I thank you for sending your Son who lived a perfect life and informed us how we can enter the family of God. Lord, help me to be a faithful and fruitful witness. Amen.

January 2

Seated With Christ

Ephesians 2:6

"He raised us from the dead along with Christ, and we are seated with Christ in the heavenly realms all because we are one with Christ Jesus" (Ephesians 2:6 NLT).

Paul is in prison. He has suffered horrendous persecution and yet he says that God has raised him up to sit beside him in the heavenly places. We too are seated in the heavenly realms. Paul prays:

"I pray that you will begin to understand the incredible greatness of his power for us who believe him. This is the same mighty power that raised Christ from the dead and seated him in the place of honor at God's right hand in the heavenly realms. Now he is far above any ruler or authority or power or leader or anything else in this world or in the world to come" (1:19- 21 NLT).

Paul understood where he was seated. If you understand where you are seated you will know you are far above any ruler, authority, power, or any situation now or in your future. No situation you will face will be able to remove you from that seat beside Jesus.

I officiated at 150 funerals in my ministry. I just participated in a memorial service for a man age 51. Some of you lost a child. Some of you are battling cancer, pain, and depression. Some are in bondage to nicotine, or jealousy, or to a spirit of criticism. Ask God to open your eyes to see where you are seated. You are beside Messiah Jesus above all those situations!

The Hebrew root word for "to heal" is "relax." If we learn to rest and relax in the seat Jesus provides for us beside him we will experience a peace, and joy beyond our imagination. Ask him to open your eyes to see where you are seated today. Thank him for the victory that is yours because of where you sit.

Father, I thank you for my seat beside Jesus. Thank you for a place to rest and relax especially in the difficult situations of life. Thank you for the victory that is ours because of where we sit. Amen.

January 3

Fullness of Joy

Psalm 16:11

"In your presence is fullness of joy and at thy (your) right hand are pleasures forever more" (Psalm 16:11 JKV).

Everyone wants fulfillment and joy. This verse promises not only joy but fullness of joy. When the disciples returned from their first missionary journey they were joyful because of the power Jesus gave them to drive out demons. Jesus informed them they were to rejoice not because of the power to cast out demons but because their names were written in heaven. Joy comes from a right relationship with Jesus. (See Luke 10:20.)

We are a pleasure-seeking society. At God's right hand are pleasures forever. Living in his presence brings joy. Think of David's problems. His own son wanted to kill him. The king wanted to kill him. He had to run for his life. His infant son died in spite of his fasting and prayers. Yet he writes: "I have set the Lord always before me… I will not be shaken. Therefore my heart is glad and my tongue rejoices;… You have made known to me the path of life; you fill me with joy in your presence" (Psalm 16:8-11 NIV).

Paul reminds us that we are seated at God's right hand beside Jesus. (See Ephesians 2:6.) He is above all the problems we can ever imagine. Paul also writes: "We are close to death, but here we are still alive. We have been beaten within an inch of our lives. Our hearts ache, but we always have joy. We are poor, but we give spiritual riches to others. We own nothing, and yet we have everything" (II Corinthians 6:9-10 NLT).

Jesus said, "God blesses those who are persecuted because they live for God, for the Kingdom of Heaven is theirs. God blesses you when you are mocked, persecuted and lied about because you are his followers. Be happy about it! Be very glad! For a great reward awaits you in heaven. And remember, the ancient prophets were persecuted, too" (Matthew 5:10-12 NLT).

Lord Jesus, help me to make your presence the priority in my life today. Thank you for the joy you give me. Amen.

January 4

Thirsty for God

Psalm 42:1-2

"As the deer pants for streams of water, so I long for you, O God. I thirst for God, the living God" (Psalm 42:1-2a NLV).

David was feeling separated from God. He was desperate to find God. He had a burning passion to draw close to God.

The writer of Hebrews says he will reward us if we earnestly or diligently seek him. (See 11:6)

Jeremiah expresses it this way, "If you will look for me in earnest you will find me when you seek me. I will be found by you" (29:13-14 NLT).

Jesus said: "If you are thirsty come to me! If you believe in me, come and drink! For the Scriptures declare that rivers of living water will flow out from within" (John 7:37-38 NLV).

Why does God seemingly make it hard to find him at times? He wants us to be sincere in our desire for him. He must be first. He demands our allegiance. He will not share his glory with another. If he was easy to find we would take him for granted.

When you got up this morning were you thinking about all the things you need to do today? Did you say, "Good God morning! Or Good morning God? If you love the Lord with all your heart, your heart was panting and burning for the streams of Living Water—panting for more of Jesus.

Ask God to give you a single-minded focus—a focus of desiring to please him and walk with him. He will be sure to answer your sincere prayer. You will see the difference and rejoice in it. Practice spiritual breathing: exhale any thought or images that appear in your mind that would be displeasing to him and inhale his love, forgiveness, grace and power. Drink from the stream of Living Water. Notice the difference as you walk with him today.

Father, I confess that I need a greater passion to love you and serve you. Draw me to yourself today. Amen.

January 5

Love of God's Word

Psalm 119:20

"I am overwhelmed continually with a desire for your laws" (Psalm 119:20 NLT). "My soul is consumed with longing for your laws at all times" (NIV). "My soul is starved and hungry, ravenous!—insatiable for your nourishing commands" (Msg). "What I want most of all and at all times is to honor your laws" (CEV).

Do you love the Word of God? Is it more precious than your newspaper? When you get up in the morning, which do you choose, the morning paper or the living word?

"Oh, how I love your law! I meditate on it all day long" (Psalm 119:97 NIV). Is your mind focused on the news or on the Good News? David was a man after God's own heart. He loved the Lord and he loved his word. He writes: "Your commands make me wiser than my enemies for they are ever with me. I have more insight than all my teachers, for I meditate on your statutes. I have more understanding than the elders, for I obey your precepts" (Psalm 119:97-100 NIV).

I have found that I need to ask God to give me a love for his word. If we cry out to him he will answer that prayer. In answering that prayer your life will be transformed. You will move from one degree of glory to another. (See II Corinthians 3:18 KJV.)

It is almost always something good that will keep us from the word of God, something good but not what is best. Beware of the barrenness of a busy life! God's word is a lamp and light throughout the day. (See Psalm 119:105.)

In our love of God's word we must remember that it is the word that points us to Jesus the Living Word. We don't worship the word, we worship Jesus. "You diligently study the Scriptures because you think that by them you possess eternal life. These are the Scriptures that testify about me, yet you refuse to come to me to have life" (John 4:39-40 NIV).

Father, give me a fresh love for your word so I can know you more intimately. Thank you. Amen.

January 6

Eyes to See

Psalm 119:37

"Divert my eyes from toys and trinkets, invigorate me on the pilgrim way" (Psalm 119:37 Msg). The NIV reads, "Turn my eyes away from worthless things; preserve my life according to your word."

"Your eye is a lamp that provides light for your body. A pure eye lets sunshine into your soul. But an evil eye shuts out the light and plunges you into darkness" (Luke 11:34 NLT). "Dear Lord, I only have eyes for you. Since I've run for dear life to you take good care of me" (Psalm 141:8 Msg).

Children are drawn to toys and trinkets in the store. As adults most of us have a lot of childishness in us. The average person in the U.S. watches TV several hours a day plus spends another hour or two on the internet. How many commercials promote "worthless toys and trinkets?" How many TV programs are "worthless toys and trinkets?" Someone said TV is chewing gum to the eyes. Some programs are downright evil. They are full of violence, immorality and filthy language.

When we watch these programs, our eyes plunge us into darkness. Set your mind on things that are, "true and honorable and right. Think about things that are pure and lovely and admirable. Think about things that are excellent and worthy of praise" (Philippians 4:8 NLT).

David wrote in Psalm 23, that since the Lord is his Shepherd, he would not lack any good thing. Then he lists good things the Lord provides beginning with green pastures. Green pastures provide satisfying nourishment. Cows lie down in contentment when they feed on the green pastures. They chew their cud, which is a picture of meditation. Are we chewing on God's nourishing word throughout the day? Remember to feed first in the green pastures.

Did you take time to feed on the Word this morning?

Father I commit my eyes and my heart to focus on your word and to do your will. Give me a love for your word like David who said, "My soul is consumed with a longing for your word." Help me to love your word. Amen.

January 7

The Great Commission

Matthew 28:18-20

"All authority in heaven and on earth has been given to me. Therefore go and make disciples of all nations, baptizing them in the name of the Father and of the Son and of the Holy Spirit, and teaching them to obey everything I have commanded you. And surely I am with you always, to the very end of the age" (Matthew 28:18-20 NIV).

God has given us the authority to make disciples. We cannot make disciples unless we are disciples ourselves. As the disciples returned from their first mission they were joyful because they cast out demons. Jesus reminded them that they need to rejoice because of their relationship with him. (See Luke 10:17-20.)

The key to fulfilling the Great Commission is always our relationship to him. Do I know the risen Lord? If I know him I will be fruitful. "I am the Vine, you are the branches. When you're joined with me and I with you, the relation intimate and organic, the harvest is sure to be abundant" (John 15:5 Msg).

The needs of the people about us are enormous. We will be overwhelmed by them unless Jesus is the most important reason for our ministry. It is he who gives us the authority and the power to meet those needs. (See Acts 1:8.) "Apart from me you can do nothing" (John 15:5b NIV). We have the mind of Christ. (See I Corinthians 2:16.) It is not human wisdom or human sympathy that will make disciples.

Jesus said, "When I am lifted up from the earth I will draw all men unto me" (John 12:32 NIV). Only those who know him can lift him up. Paul's supreme goal in life and our goal must be: "I want to know Christ and the power of his resurrection and the fellowship of sharing in his suffering, becoming like him in his death" (Philippians 3:10-11 NIV). The Greek word for "knowing" is experiential knowledge: a personal intimate relationship with Jesus.

Jesus must be your Lord, your friend, your life. When your life is lost in his, he will use you to make disciples in Jerusalem (at home), and even to the ends of the earth.

Lord, I give myself completely to you today. Use me to be a disciple-maker for you. Amen.

January 8

You Have an Older Brother!

Proverbs 17:17

"A brother is born for adversity" (Proverbs 17:17). "A real friend sticks closer than a brother" (Proverbs 18:24b NLT).

Anyone who obeys God is my brother or sister or mother. Anyone who obeys my Father in heaven is my brother or sister or mother. (See Mark 3:33-35.)

While we appreciate our natural families let's remember that Jesus is our brother, and God is our Father.

"So now Jesus and the ones he makes holy have the same Father. That is why Jesus is not ashamed to call them his brothers and sisters. For he said to God,

"I will declare the wonder of your name to my brothers and sisters.

I will praise you among all your people."

He also said, "I will put my trust in him." And in the same context he said, "Here I am - together with the children God has given me" (Hebrews 2:11–13 NLT).

Jesus is not ashamed to call us his sibling. With our older brother, Jesus, on our side nothing can defeat us! Can I remember Jesus is my older brother today and walk in that reality? Praise His Name!

One thing that will help us walk in that reality is to remember that others who name the name that is above every name, are our brothers and sisters. They have experienced the same blood washed cleansing from the Lamb who was slain before the foundation of the world. Let's build bridges to all God's children. Then the world will know that Jesus is God's Son. (See John 17:21.)

Lord Jesus, I can't comprehend how you can be my brother or how your Father can be my Father, but by faith I claim that relationship today. Amen.

January 9

Everyone is a Worshipper!

Jeremiah 29:13

"You will worship me with all your heart and I will be with you and accept your worship" (Jeremiah 29:13 CEV).

Everyone worships something or someone. For those who don't know God or have a longing to know and please God, their worship is focused on themselves. It's all about them and their needs and wants.

Jesus said, "The true worshippers will worship the Father in spirit and truth, for they are the kind of worshipers the Father seeks" (John 4:24b NIV).

The dictionary defines worship as expressions of reverence toward God or extravagant respect or admiration of God. How wonderful it is that we have a God who is worthy to receive our worship. The false gods of materialism, or power, or pleasing people will never satisfy. Jesus alone satisfies. He hears our every plea and knows our every thought, as well as our joys and disappointments. Let's thank him for his greatness, his compassion and faithfulness which are new every morning. (See Lamentations 3:23.)

Are they new to you? If not, take time to see Him. See him in creation, in your circumstances. Take time to hear his voice. He is there whether we discern his presence or not. Psalm 139:7 NLT, "I can never get away from your presence!"

Thank God from your heart that he is with you. That is worship! Pray for grace to recognize him in each person you meet today. He is there. Remember we work with God rather than for God. He is at work in every situation and in every person. As the Spirit gives you eyes to see and ears to hear, thank him and worship Him! As you focus on Jesus, he will put a spring in your step, a smile on your face and a joy in your heart.

Lord, I love you, I give myself to you, I worship you. I praise you. You are all I want. You alone satisfy. Thank you Jesus! Amen.

January 10

You are Greater Than . . .

Matthew 11:11

One of the most unbelievable verses in the Bible is Matthew 11:11 NLT, "I assure you, of all who have ever lived, none is greater than John the Baptist. Yet even the most insignificant person in the Kingdom of Heaven is greater than he is!"

I have never heard a sermon on this verse. It almost sounds irreverent and blasphemous to say that I am greater than Abraham, Jacob, Moses, David, Isaiah, Jeremiah or Daniel. How can that be? According to Luke 10:23-24 and I Peter 1:10-11 the kings and prophets longed to see our day. "It is all so wonderful that even the angels are eagerly watching these things happen" (I Peter 1:12 NLT).

How can this be possible? The resurrection of Jesus changed everything! We have a new DNA, a new nature (See I Peter 1:4.) "If anyone is in Christ, he is a new creation; the old has gone the new has come" (II Corinthians 5:17 NIV). "He has given us his very great and precious promises, so that through them you may participate in the divine nature and escape the corruption in the world caused by evil desires" (II Peter 1:4 NIV). No wonder Paul writes that the gift of Jesus is too wonderful for words. (See II Corinthians 9:15.)

Moses' glory faded when he left God's presence. Our glory increases continually as we walk with Jesus. "All of us have had that veil removed so that we can be mirrors that rightly reflect the glory of the Lord. And as the Spirit of the Lord works within us, we become more and more like him and reflect his glory even more" (II Corinthians 3:18 NLT). What a privilege!

If you meditate on these verses there is no way you can feel discouraged or depressed. As you meditate on Matthew 11:11 you will be transformed into the image of our Lord!

Lord, help me to grasp what your resurrection has done for me. It's really all about you. Apart from you I am nothing. Praise be to your wonderful name! Amen.

January 11

Scale a Wall!

Psalm 18:29

Are you up against a wall? "With my God I can scale any wall" (Psalm 18:29b NLT).

Is your life filled with discouragement, frustration, and seeming impossible circumstances? David writes: "With my God"—notice the three secret code words. "With my God" I can scale a wall! With God I can do anything. Paul writes from prison, "I can do everything with the help of Christ who gives me the strength I need" (Philippians 4:13 NLT). "Don't be discouraged, defeated or feel dejected, for the joy of the Lord is your strength" (Nehemiah 8:10). The Lord's strength and joy was there for Nehemiah and for David. It can be your strength too!

Jesus reminds us that when we abide in him and obey him our joy is full.

You say, "No one understands how high my walls are! Remember that the temptations that come into your life are no different from what others experience. God is faithful. He will keep the temptation from becoming so strong that you can't stand up against it. When you are tempted, he will show you a way out so that you will not give in to it" (I Corinthians 10:13 NLT).

I try to remember to thank the Lord for his blessings—more than I can perceive. One of my closest friends was an unwanted child, shuffled from one foster home to another. Many children have no living parents or relatives to care for them. They roam the streets at a very young age, eating from garbage dumps. Many become slaves of evil men. Why wasn't I born in poverty?

We must bring the light of Jesus into these lives so they too can have hope enabling them to rise above their indescribable circumstances. With my God I can scale any wall!

Lord, help me to remember today that you are with me and living your life through me. Therefore no wall is too high for you to overcome. Thank you. Amen.

January 12

In the Desert/Wilderness

Psalm 6:6-7

Earlier we focused on Psalm 18:29 NLT, "With God I can scale a wall." David did not feel this way every day. "I am worn out from sobbing. Every night tears drench my bed; my pillow is wet from weeping. My vision is blurred by grief; my eyes are worn out because of all my enemies" (Psalm 6:6-7 NLT).

Then in the next verses he says, "The Lord has heard my crying and my plea; the Lord will answer my prayer." David is realistic. He is honest. He owns his feelings.

David said, "My whole world is coming unglued" (Psalm 82:5c Msg), and then he adds in v. 8, "You've got the whole world in your hands!" What a contrast!

In Psalm 42:3-4 Msg he writes: "Day and night I have only tears for food…, My heart is breaking as I remember how it used to be: I walked among the crowds of worshipers, leading a great procession to the house of God, singing for joy and giving thinks - it was the sound of a great celebration!"

He tells us the solution to his depression: v. 5, "I will put my hope in God! I will praise him again—my Savior and my God!" Continuing with this psalm: he talks about his tears, his enemies, running from Absalom his son, and running from Saul, the King.

Don't be afraid to confess your pain and anguish before God. Even Jesus did in Gethsemane. "…he began to be filled with anguish and deep distress. He told them, My soul is crushed with grief to the point of death…" (Matthew 26:37-38 NLT).

Father, look upon my pain and my sorrow. Grant me faith to believe you are with me in this valley of testing. Help me to keep my eyes fixed on you. "Get me out of this mess and up on my feet." (Psalm 71:2 Msg). Amen.

January 13

Good and Bad

Matthew 22:10

Both good and bad are to be invited to the banquet. "So the servants went out into the streets and gathered all the people they could find, both good and bad, and the wedding hall was filled with guests" (Matthew 22:10 NIV).

"The servants went out on the streets and rounded up everyone they laid eyes on, good and bad, regardless. And so the banquet was on—every place filled" (Msg).

I was fascinated by the word "bad." The Greek word is *poneros*. It appears 76 times in the N.T. Matthew uses this word 25 times. In the King James Version it is translated "evil" 17 times and "wicked" seven times. This is the only place it is translated "bad."

Do we see ourselves as "bad" or "good?" We may think we are pretty good especially as we compare ourselves with the neighbor who is abusing his wife and children, or the criminals who are serving time in prison. Apart from Jesus we are "bad," even, "wicked." As Jeremiah 17:9 NLT says, "The human heart is most deceitful and desperately wicked, who really knows how bad it is?" I need to frequently pray, "Lord deliver me from self-absorption." Adam and Eve's sin of rejecting God's way is at the root of all our wickedness. Pray, "Lord, help me to understand that I must confess my selfishness and run to the cross." With Paul we say, I am crucified with Christ and it is not me who lives but Christ in me. (See Galatians 2:20.)

One of the biggest problems for Christians is unconsciously thinking God got a bargain when he got us! Any such attitude cuts us off from the Holy Spirit's power and cuts us off from our unchurched friends. We are Pharisees/hypocrites to the core. We must pray to see ourselves as Jesus see us in our unrepentant state. There is only one remedy for that: repent and receive the cleansing blood of our Lord Jesus. We are made pure again! Hallelujah!

Father, you saw my wicked heart and yet you loved me. I can never thank you enough for your love. Cleanse me and make me pure. Thank you. Amen.

January 14

Persistence

Luke 11:8-10

Some years ago I read that 97% of people believe in prayer. In fact in my 50 years of pastoral ministry, I could count on my fingers the times I regretted praying with someone. Most people, especially older people are still respectful when you pray with them and for them. Once they express a need, there is usually an open door to pray to meet that need.

Jesus taught us about prayer with an illustration of a man who comes late at night to get some food for his visiting friends. "But I tell you this—though he won't do it as a friend, if you keep knocking long enough, he will get up and give you what you want so his reputation won't be damaged." Or as the footnote says, "because of your persistence" (Luke 11:8 NLT). "So I tell you, keep on asking, and you will be given what you ask for. Keep on looking, and you will find. Keep on knocking, and the door will be opened. For everyone who asks, receives. Everyone who seeks, finds. And the door is opened to everyone who knocks" (vv. 9-10).

Jesus says that everyone receives an answer if they are persistent. Don't give up! Sometimes the answer is not what we like to hear but God will answer. He knows best. A wonderful gift he has promised is the gift of peace: "I am leaving you with a gift—peace of mind and heart. And the peace I give isn't like the peace the world gives. So don't be troubled or afraid" (John 14:27 NLT).

Paul expressed it in these words: "I've learned by now to be quite content whatever my circumstances. I'm just as happy with little as with much, with much as with little. I've found the recipe for being happy whether full or hungry, hands full or hands empty. Whatever I have, whatever I am. I can make it through anything in the One who makes me who I am" (Philippians 4:11-13 Msg).

Lord, forgive me for giving up so quickly when my prayers are not answered immediately. Thank you for being patient with me. Grant me a greater faith in you. Amen.

January 15

Incomparable Riches

Ephesians 2:7

Paul prays that we might know the incomparable great power for us who believe. This power is like the power he exerted when he raised Jesus from the dead. (See Ephesians 1:19.) Then in Ephesians 2:6-7 NIV, Paul says, "God raised us up with Christ and seated us with him in the heavenly realms in Christ Jesus, in order that in the coming ages he might show the incomparable riches of his grace, expressed in his kindness to us in Christ Jesus."

God's power is incomparable.

I asked a scientist why we don't drop our most powerful bomb in the midst of a hurricane and dissipate much of its strength. His response is that our strongest bomb would not even affect a hurricane. God's power is incomparable. His grace abounds (Romans 5:20) or becomes more abundant!

If you are in a valley today, focus on God's power and God's grace. Pray, "Lord, open my eyes and my heart to see and understand more of your power and grace in my situation." Don't live in guilt—his incomparable grace is there for you. Don't live in weakness of spirit—his incomparable strength is there for you. Remember, there is nothing too difficult for Him! He will never leave you. (See Matthew 28:20.) God said, "I will never fail you. I will never forsake you" (Hebrews 13:5b).

If you are not going through a valley pray for your friend who is in the valley. You can use Paul's words in Ephesians 3:16 NLT, "I pray that from his glorious, unlimited resources he will give you mighty inner strength through his Holy Spirit." Tell them you are praying for them and show your love with an act of kindness to encourage them. Someone said, "People need three things: encouragement, encouragement, and encouragement. If that doesn't work, try encouragement!

Lord Jesus, you have incomparable riches. Help me to grasp them and live in them so others can be encouraged and desire these riches as well. Amen.

January 16

How Big is Your Faith?

Psalm 2:8

"Ask of me, and I will make the nations your inheritance, the ends of the earth your possession" (Psalm 2:8 NIV). While this is speaking prophetically of Jesus, Paul reminds us, "Since we are his children, we will share his treasures—for everything God gives to his Son, Christ, is ours, too" (Romans 8:17 NIV).

"Ask for the nations." Some people don't even ask God for the salvation of their next door neighbor. Few Christians feel little responsibility for their neighbors or peers. When we get to the judgment day and see our friends who have not given their life to Jesus, can you picture them turning to you, as they cry in desperation, "Why didn't you tell me I needed to be born into God's Kingdom? I saw you and talked with you hundreds of times. You never once told me about Jesus?" What will we say?

Jesus said, "As the Father sent me I am sending you into the world" (John 17:18 and 20:21). Why did the Father send Jesus—"to seek and save the lost" (Luke 19:10). Just as Jesus was sent we are sent!

You are sent to your office, to your classroom, to your neighbors. How is it that we can work at the same place, live beside the same neighbors for years and go to school for a whole semester, sit beside or work beside these people and not pray for them or share the Good News with them?

Ask God to give you a compassion for your unchurched friends. He will open the door for you to share the Good News if you earnestly ask him to do so. The apostles were bold. They went everywhere preaching the word. The Holy Spirit will give you the same boldness if you cry out to God for a fresh anointing of his Spirit. Don't let guilt overwhelm you for not sharing Jesus. He will forgive you. However, repentance means we will change our ways. We can't change except through his power. Trust him. He will surprise you today as you seek to be a witness for him.

Lord, forgive me for not proclaiming your Good News to my neighbor. Empower me by your Holy Spirit to witness for you today. Amen.

January 17

Do You Want More Faith?

Matthew 9:29

When the blind man came to Jesus for healing, Jesus said, "According to your faith it will be done to you" (Matthew 9:29). Perhaps we don't have faith because our concept of Jesus is not big enough. Remember, he knows the hairs on our head. (See Matthew 10:30.) He knows our thoughts. (See Psalm 139:2.) He counts the stars and calls them by name. (See Psalm 147:4.)

"The sun is one of 100 billion stars in our galaxy, the Milky Way… there are 100 billion galaxies!"[i] That's 10 trillion stars for every one of the 7 billion people on planet earth. That's 10 trillion, not million! Some say when God told Abraham, "I will multiply your descendants into countless millions, like the stars of the sky and the sand of the seashore" (Genesis 22:17 NLT), He was saying that there are as many stars as there are grains of sand on the sea shore. God is incomprehensible. To say God transcends us is the understatement of history.

Does that help you to believe what David writes: "You keep track of all my sorrows. You have collected all my tears in your bottle. You have recorded each one in your book" (Psalm 56:8 NLT). If he can call the stars by name it's nothing for him to collect all our tears in a bottle. The longer we walk with Jesus, the fewer questions we have because we learn to trust our all-knowing Father even though we can't understand or comprehend his ways. (See Isaiah 55:8-9.)

As I was writing the phone rang with the news that a godly man whom scores of people had prayed for was just admitted to intensive care. While I have experienced many direct and dramatic answers to prayer and scores of answers to physical healing, this man is in God's care just as much, or even more so than the person who experienced dramatic physical healing.

Jesus never leaves us nor forsakes us. (See Hebrews 13:5). He never makes a mistake. He always does what is right. (See Genesis 18:25.) Greater is he that is within us than he that is in the world. (See I John 4:4.) You can trust him!

Father, increase my faith today. Amen

January 18

Is Your Church Relevant?

Ephesians 1:23

"The church...is not peripheral to the world; the world is peripheral to the church. The church is Christ's body, in which he speaks and acts, by which he fills everything with his presence" (Ephesians 1:23 Msg).

Many people have found the church to be a huge disappointment. There are many books today that speak of the irrelevancy of the church. I went on a college campus and interviewed students asking them two questions: What do you think of Jesus, and what do you think of the church? Most are respectful of Jesus but see the church as irrelevant. Many don't see the church making an impact on our society.

There are times I agree with these youth. Would your community miss the church if it would close its doors? That's basically what happened in Europe where only five percent of the people relate to the church. Having said that, the church is the best we have. The government certainly will not get our world out of the mess we are in. The military, the community clubs, and even the Red Cross cannot provide the answers. There is only one person who can transform lives. That is Jesus. He lives in his body, the church.

Do you pray for and support your church or do you criticize it? Does your church serve and meet the needs of the surrounding community?

Jesus promised that the "power of hell (gates of Hades) will not conquer it" (See Matthew 16:18 NLT.) People in our communities need more than words they need to see Jesus in action. We are Christ's ambassadors which means we do what Jesus did. Jesus was appointed to preach Good News to the poor. He was sent to proclaim release for the captives and those in oppression. He gave freedom for prisoners and recovery of sight to the blind. (See Luke 4:18.) When we follow Jesus' example we will no longer be irrelevant.

Lord, help me to be Jesus to my neighbors. Help me to make my church relevant to the needs of the people I meet. Thank you. Amen.

January 19

Would You Like to Meet Jesus — You Can!

Matthew 25:37-40

"These righteous ones will reply, 'Lord, when did we ever see you hungry and feed you? Or thirsty and give you something to drink? Or a stranger and show you hospitality? Or naked and give you clothing? When did we ever see you sick or in prison, and visit you?' And the King will tell them, "I assure you, when you did it to one of the least of these my brothers and sisters, you were doing it to me" (Matthew 25:37-40 NLT).

Can Jesus make it any clearer? When we serve the needy we are serving him? When we welcome a little child on behalf of Jesus we welcome him. (See Luke 9:48.) Jesus said, "Anyone who accepts your message is also accepting me. And anyone who rejects you is rejecting me" (Luke 10:16 NLT). In Acts 9:14 NLT, Jesus calls from heaven to Saul and says, "Saul, Saul, why are you persecuting me?" Notice how closely Jesus identifies with you. If you want to get close to Jesus, serve others.

Ask Jesus to open your eyes to someone today who is sick—go visit them, call them, send them a card or an encouraging email. Do you know someone who lost their job or who is discouraged? Maybe someone comes to mind who is hungry- physically or spiritually. Jesus said when you minister to them you serve Him. You may remember he said a cup of cold water given because you love him will be rewarded. (See Matthew 10:42.)

"God is love" (I John 4:8, 16). "If anyone has enough money to live well and sees a brother or sister in need and refuses to help—how can God's love be in that person?" (I John 3:17 NLT). When you serve these people by meeting their needs you are serving Jesus. Remember you can meet Jesus today! What a privilege. Jesus reminds us when we obey his commands we will be blessed and rewarded. (See John 13:17.)

Father I want to meet you today. Help me to be a servant. Open my eyes and give me courage to serve you today. Amen.

January 20

Worship

John 4:24

Jesus said we are to worship him in spirit and in truth. (See John 4:24.) What does it mean to worship God in spirit? I think it is similar to Jesus command to love God with all our heart. (See Matthew 22:37.) The heart is the executive center of our lives.

If I were writing John 4:24, I would want to place truth before spirit. We who are cultural products of the western world emphasize the rational. Jesus seems to be more concerned about our spirits. He said he will send the spirit to guide us into all truth. I find the translation of John 4:24 given in the *Contemporary Bible* quite helpful. "God is Spirit and those who worship God must be led by the Spirit to worship him according to the truth." "When he, the Spirit of truth, comes, he will guide you into all truth" (John 16:13 NIV).

The Spirit and truth are both essential. But many Christians, including myself, have emphasized the letter of the word and neglected hearing the Spirit's interpretation and intent of the word. Jesus came to fulfill the law. (See Matthew 5:17.)

When we emphasize the letter and neglect the spirit our worship becomes legalistic and dead. It's the Spirit that brings life. Are we afraid of the Spirit? We can't control the Spirit. Jesus said it is like the wind. (See John 3:8.) Of course our worship must be founded on the truth and lined up with the truth. But one reason Christians lack the joy of the Lord is that we grieve the Spirit by our ritualistic and formal worship. We like to worship with our mind more than our heart. Let's not be afraid to follow our heart and of course check to see that our actions do not contradict the foundational word of truth which "teaches us what is true and makes us realize what is wrong in our lives. It straightens us out and teaches us to do what is right" (II Timothy 3:16-17 NLT).

Father, I thank you for the joy of worshipping from our spirit. May we be led by the Spirit to worship you according to the truth. Amen.

January 21

Hidden with Christ

Colossians 3:3

"For you died and your life is now hidden with Christ in God" (Colossians 3:3 NIV). My life is hidden with Christ in God, therefore I am not only in Christ but also in God. "Your old life is dead. Your new life, which is your real life—even though invisible to spectators—is with Christ in God. He is your life. When Christ (your real life, remember) shows up again on this earth, you'll show up, too—the real you, the glorious you. Meanwhile, be content with obscurity, like Christ" (Colossians 3:3-4 Msg).

Admittedly this is beyond the natural mind. Therefore we must accept it by faith. Activating our faith is not always easy. If I am hidden with Christ in God I do not need to worry. He will never let me fall. He will give me wisdom for every decision. He will give me strength to do what he wants me to do. I am secure in Him.

In Acts 24:27, Paul was kept in prison because Felix wanted to gain favor with the Jewish leaders. Imagine being in prison for two years because the governor wants to please a political group. But Paul never wasted his life in prison. He writes in Philippians 1:12-13 NLT, "I want you to know,...that everything that has happened to me here has helped to spread the Good News. For everyone here, including all the soldiers in the palace guard, knows that I am in chains because of Christ. And because of my imprisonment, many of the Christians here have gained confidence and become more bold in telling others about Christ."

When our life is hidden with Christ in God we will linger in his presence so we recognize his voice. (See John 10:3.) We go only where he wants us to go, do only what he wants us to do, say only what he wants us to say. Is such a life possible? Yes. But only if we walk in obedience to his will. (See John 14:15.) "If we walk in the light, God himself being the light, we also experience a shared life with one another, as the sacrificed blood of Jesus, God's Son, purges all our sin" (I John 1:7 Msg).

Thank you Father, for placing me in Christ which means Jesus is with me. Help me Lord, to live in that reality. Amen.

January 22

In Christ

Romans 8:1

"Therefore, there is now no condemnation for those who are in Christ Jesus" (Romans 8:1 NIV). One hundred sixty-some times, the New Testament informs the Christian that he or she is in Christ. Why this constant repetition? Is it because we don't remember our position or is it because we don't get it? Galatians 2:20 NIV, "I have been crucified with Christ and I no longer live, but Christ lives in me. The life I live in the body, I live by faith in the Son of God, who loved me, and gave himself for me." The Msg says, "Christ lives in me. The life you see me living is not 'mine', but it is lived by faith in the Son of God, who loved me and gave himself for me." I no longer live since Christ lives his life in or through me."

There is only one person who can live the Christian life and that is Christ. I have been a Christian sixty years and am still trying to live in that reality. When I do, life has purpose and meaning. As we live in this reality we discover we are a new creation. (See II Corinthians 5:17.) Hallelujah! No more struggling except the struggle of faith. That's what Paul meant when he said we are to fight the good fight of faith. The fight is to have the faith to believe it is Christ's life lived in us and not our life lived in the power of the flesh, or power of our old nature.

The old nature lets us down every time. The new nature is God in us! What could be better! Thank him for living in you and through you. He changes our "want to." We no longer want to get revenge. We no longer have jealous feelings when others get promoted ahead of us, even though we were in the office longer than they were. We show love to those who would be our enemies. Only Jesus by his Holy Spirit abiding in us can give us this life of victory.

Father, thank you for making it possible for me to invite you to live through me. I can never thank you enough. Amen.

January 23

Why Did Jesus Come?

Luke 19:10

Many times in the Gospel we are told why Jesus came and how he spent his time.

- He came to seek and save those who are lost. (See Luke 19:10 TEV.)
- His very name, Jesus, means "The Lord saves." (See Matthew 1:21 NIV footnote.)
- Jesus came not to condemn the world but to save it. (See John 3:17 Free Translation.)
- Jesus came to give sight to the blind and to show those who think they see that they are blind. (See John 9:39b and 12:47-48 Free translation.)
- He says, "I have not come to call the righteous, but sinners" (Mark 2:17 NIV).
- "The Spirit of the Lord…has anointed me to preach good news to the poor. He has sent me to proclaim freedom for the prisoners and recovery of sight to the blind, to release the oppressed, to proclaim the year of the Lord's favor" (Luke 4:18-19 NIV).
- "He had great pity for the crowds that came, because their problems were so great and they didn't know where to go for help" (Matthew 9:36 NLT). "As he approached Jerusalem and saw the city, he wept over it" (Luke 19:41 NIV). (See also Luke 13:34-35.)
- Mark 1:38 NLT, Jesus said, "We must go on to other towns as well, and I will preach to them, too, because that is why I came."
- In Acts 10:38, NIV, Luke sums up Jesus' activities: ". . . He went around doing good and healing all who were under the power of the devil, because God was with him." (Compare Matthew 9:35.)

We don't need to wonder why Jesus came. These many scriptures make it clear he came to save the lost and minister to the needs of those who were marginalized. Since he sends us, John 17:18 and 20:21, just as the Father sent him, we don't need to wonder what our assignment is today. Pray for the courage to do it!

Lord Jesus, give me courage to do what you did: seeking the lost. Help me to follow in your steps as your disciple. Amen.

January 24

Where Are Our Evangelists?

Ephesians 4:11

When Jesus ascended he gave gifts to the church: "apostles, prophets, evangelists, pastors and teachers" (Eph. 4:11 free translation).

One doesn't need to be a rocket scientist to understand that unless God turns things around, many churches will become extinct as young adults are dropping out in many of our more traditional churches.

Where are our evangelists? Gift questionnaires (questions that reveal our spiritual gifts) indicate that ten percent of Christians have the gift of evangelist. We affirm librarians, ushers, secretaries, administrative assistants, Sunday school teachers, small group leaders, pastors, etc. Why don't we call and affirm evangelists? The Ethiopian Church calls evangelists before they call pastors. What would happen if we empower ten percent of our members as evangelists? Let's pray, affirm, and empower them for the ministry of evangelism. This change will be a major step in turning our churches from decline to growth.

You may say, "Shouldn't everyone be a witness, not just a certain few?" Of course. Acts 1:8 says that God gives us power when the Holy Spirit comes upon us to be witnesses in Jerusalem—that means we witness to those we rub shoulders with. It's helpful to ask, "Shouldn't everyone be a teacher, a giver, or an intercessor?" Of course, but some have the gift of teaching, the gift of giving, or the gift of intercession. To some, God has given the gift of evangelism even though everyone is to be a witness for the Lord.

I believe if you have a sister in your congregation who has a special gift of relating to her unchurched neighbors, and you free her by taking care of her children from time to time or clean her house so she can minister to her neighbors, you will receive the same reward she will receive for witnessing to her neighbors. Let's recognize and empower our evangelists.

Lord Jesus, thank you for the gift of evangelist in our churches. Help me to encourage them. Empower me to use my gift of evangelism as a faithful and fruitful witness for you. Amen.

January 25

Let's Empower Our Youth!

Mark 3:17

"These are the twelve he (Jesus) appointed:...James son of Zebedee and his brother John (to them he gave the name Boanerges, which means Sons of Thunder)" (Mark 3:16-17 NIV).

How old were the disciples when Jesus called them? I believe Jesus called John when he was in his teens and the other disciples probably in their twenties. In their culture, one was not recognized as a teacher until you were age thirty. (See Luke 3:23.) Jesus broke the cultural traditions by calling these young men. Let's call and empower our youth.

Youth will do things differently. Jesus referred to James and John as "Sons of Thunder" (Mark 3:17 NLT) or "thunderbolts" as the *Contemporary English* Version states. That can be frightening, but Jesus took the risk. We too must take the risk. Empowering youth and young adults will bring new life to our traditional congregations.

We need their enthusiasm. Ask God to open your eyes to see these potential young men and women who have a passion to see people come to Jesus and who relate well with people. Tap them on the shoulder. Believe in them, listen to their concerns. Bless and affirm them in their gifts. Tell them you believe God has gifted them for ministry in extending his Kingdom. As we mentor, pray, and walk with them, they will lead us in our church revitalization.

Most people who become Christians accept Christ when they are in their teens or even before. Pray for eyes to see the potential in each youth/young adult and invite them to hear the call of the Lord upon their lives.

The ball is in our court. Jesus said we are to pray to him to send workers into the harvest. Are we praying? When we pray he will open our eyes to see these young people. Don't be surprised that many of our Christian workers will be found among our youth and young adults. It happened in Jesus' day. It can happen in ours.

Lord Jesus, make me an encourager for these youth to step out in evangelistic and church planting ministry for you. Amen.

January 26

Let's Empower Our Senior Citizens

Psalm 92:14-15

"They will still bear fruit in old age, they will stay fresh and green, proclaiming, The Lord is upright; he is my Rock, and there is no wickedness in him" (Psalm 92:14-15 NIV).

Many churches have a disproportional number of senior citizens. Let's empower them for effective ministry. I observed another pastor bring on staff a man in his fifties who had just retired with a sizeable pension. He willingly served the church with token financial remuneration. His gift of service to the church was an important factor in helping his church reach into the community in a powerful way. Many people came to know Jesus and are being discipled. Many older persons have free time to give in serving the Lord if we provide them with meaningful opportunities.

In *Taking Back the Good Book*, Andrew Krolls writes: "Seniors feel the church has been stolen from them. All that was familiar to them has been taken away. We force them to stand for long periods of time as we repeatedly sing praise choruses with which they are unfamiliar. When the church does provide a program for its seniors, the program is often condescending, designed to keep them busy but denying them vital ministry. They feel like they've been shoved aside and so they simply drop out of church." [ii]

Some of the most important lessons of my life, I learned from older persons. My mind goes to an older blind person who suffered a stroke that left her paralyzed on one side. Her first response was to thank God it was on the side she used less. She could still feed herself with her right hand.

One reason we are to honor our parents is that we will be blessed with a long life. (See Ephesians 6:2-3.) Because of their many years of experience, they usually have greater wisdom. Moses prayed: "Teach us to make the most of our time, so that we may grow in wisdom" (Psalm 90:12 NLT). I pray that prayer most every day, "Lord, help me to not waste time today. Give me a heart of wisdom."

Jesus, I thank you for older people who have enriched my life. Help me to honor them and encourage them today. Amen.

January 27

We Are Fruit Bearers!

John 15:16

"You didn't choose me, remember; I chose you, and put you in the world to bear fruit, fruit that won't spoil. As fruit bearers, whatever you ask the Father in relation to me, he gives you" (John 15:16 Msg).

Approximately a dozen times in the first several verses of John 15, we are told to remain in Jesus and then he will remain in us. We are to be proactive. We are to draw near to God and he will draw near to us. (See James 4:8.) Fruit bearing is first of all about our relationship to Jesus. With that relationship in sync we are to love one another. (See vv.12,13,17.)

One of my favorite books is brother Lawrence's, *The Practice of the Presence of God*. Brother Lawrence had learned the most essential element of the Christian life: how to remain in the daily presence of God.

If we are not remaining in Jesus, we can do many things but they amount to nothing of eternal value. (See 15:5.) We need to maintain our appointments to meet with God each day. Meeting with him in the morning will help us cultivate a consciousness of His presence throughout the day.

Remaining or abiding means we need to make a conscious decision to keep the relationship up to date. Paul put it in different terms by telling us to "Pray continually" (I Thess. 5:17). One aid is to practice spiritual breathing: we confess or exhale our sins and inhale God's forgiving grace. Even though we are servants of Jesus, he reminds us that we are also friends. (See v.15.) Fruitfulness begins as we remain in Jesus.

Lord, help me to remember you throughout the day. May your Holy Spirit speak deep within my spirit reminding me of your presence, then I will be a channel of blessing to others as the fruit of your Spirit lives in and through me. Amen.

January 28

God's Ways Are Not Always Easy to Understand

Luke 13:4

"What about the eighteen men who died when the Tower of Siloam fell on them" (Luke 13:4 NLT)?

In Luke 13:1-5, Pilate murdered several people as they were offering sacrifices at the Temple in Jerusalem. There was also a tower that fell killing 18 people. Perhaps Jesus did not give the full answer why these things happened but he said we are to learn a lesson from the tragedies of life. They are meant to cause us to repent lest we also perish. Repentance is a "politically incorrect" word today. Jesus makes it clear we need to repent. "Unless you repent you will perish." (See vv. 3 & 5.)

God promised Paul he would witness in Rome. Why did God allow 276 passengers on the boat to survive? (See Acts 27:24 & 37.) The 276 survived because Paul was to bring the gospel to the capital of the world.

In Acts 12:4 &19 Peter was spared while James (v.2) was put to death. When God miraculously released Peter from prison sixteen guards were executed because of Peter's "escape". No one can fully explain God's ways. James gave his life, Peter "escaped" and sixteen men had to die because of Peter's "escape." Oswald Chambers writes: "One life totally devoted to God is of more value to Him than one hundred lives which have been simply awakened by His Spirit." [iii] In the Old Testament the death angel killed 185,000 in one night. (See II Kings 19:35.)

God would have spared the entire city of Sodom if he could have found ten righteous persons. (See Genesis 18:32.) Lot and his two daughters escaped as the city of Sodom was destroyed. Lot's wife was destroyed because she was disobedient and looked back to the city. (See also Jeremiah 5:1.) Ultimately it was the "fall" in the Garden of Eden that caused all pain, judgment and death. Thank God for Jesus and the blessed hope he has provided for everyone through his sacrifice on the cross and his victorious resurrection providing grace to repent and receive eternal life.

Jesus, help me to see the tragedies of life as warnings to repent. Help me by the power of your Holy Spirit to call others to repentance. Amen.

January 29

The Generosity of God

John 4:10

In John 4, Jesus being tired stopped to rest at Jacob's well in Samaria. The disciples went to town to buy food. A Samaritan woman came to the well to draw water. In those days Jews and Samaritans did not talk together, but Jesus asked her for a drink of water. She was shocked that Jesus spoke to her. She asked him, "Why are you asking me for a drink?" (v.9). "Jesus answered, "If you knew the generosity of God and who I am, you would be asking me for a drink, and I would give you fresh, living water" (v.10 Msg).

Jesus says to you and me, "If you but knew the generosity of God you would ask me for living water for yourself as well as to give to others." Why are we so often running on empty? Where is the living water?

Jesus promised in John 7:37-38 Msg, "If anyone thirsts, let him come to me and drink. Rivers of living water will brim and spill out of the depths of anyone who believes in me this way, just as the Scripture says."

Do we believe in the generosity of God? The generosity of God is for the prebelievers like this Samaritan woman as well as for you and me! No wonder Paul writes in Ephesians 3:16 NLT, "I pray that from his glorious, unlimited resource he will give you mighty inner strength through his Holy Spirit." Do you believe God has unlimited resources?

Let's pray as Paul suggests, that he will give us mighty inner strength through his Holy Spirit and whatever you pray believing you shall have. "We can be confident that he will listen to us whenever we ask him for anything in line with his will. And if we know he is listening when we make our requests, we can be sure that he will give us what we ask for" (I John 5:14-15 NLT).

Father, I thank you for your unlimited resources. I repent of any self-centeredness. Fill me with your Holy Spirit so I can share the water of life with others today. Amen.

January 30

Rejoice in Suffering

Habakkuk 3:17-19

"Though the fig tree does not bud and there are no grapes on the vines,
Though the olive crop fails and the fields produce no food,
Though there are no sheep in the pen and no cattle in the stalls,
yet I will rejoice in the Lord, I will be joyful in God my Savior.
The Sovereign Lord is my strength; he makes my feet like the feet of a deer, he enables me to go on the heights" (Habakkuk 3:17-19 NIV).

The Message Bible reads:
"Though the cherry trees don't blossom and the strawberries don't ripen,
Though the apples are worm-eaten and the wheat fields stunted,
Though the sheep pens are sheepless and the cattle barns empty,
I'm singing joyful praise to God. I'm turning cartwheels of joy to my Savior God.
Counting on God's Rule to prevail, I take heart and gain strength.
I run like a deer. I feel like I'm king of the mountain!"

How can this be? Again and again I hear of our many brothers and sisters suffering in prison who ask us to pray not for their deliverance but that they may be faithful. Remember Stephen's victorious death. (See Acts 6:15 and Acts 7.) Read the *Martyrs Mirror* or *Foxes Book of Martyrs* and take courage as you read of their joy in the midst of persecution.

I recently went to hear the testimony of one of the leaders of the house church movement in China. He has been imprisoned three different times because of his faith in Christ. He has suffered much over the years. One time he could have escaped with another person, but the Holy Spirit told him to stay and witness to the other prisoners. God used him in a mighty way to bring the good news to many in prison. Now that he is released he continues to be an effective witness for our Lord.

Lord Jesus, empower me to rejoice in suffering. Thank you for suffering joyfully for me on the cross. Help me to take up my cross and follow you today. Amen.

January 31

Real Happiness!

Luke 15:5-7

In Luke 15 Jesus makes it clear that all of heaven is joyful when one sinner returns home. The Shepherd leaves the ninety-nine and searches for the one lost sheep. If you pray and ask the Lord to open your eyes to the lost sheep in your sphere of influence, he will reveal to you who that sheep is. Pray for that person. Tell God you will be willing to do anything to bring that person into the fold. If you lack that passion or zeal, ask God to give it to you.

Moses and Paul both illustrate that passion with the prayer: "Please forgive their sin—and if not, then blot me out of the record you are keeping" (Exodus 32:32 NLT). Paul writes in Romans 9:2-3 NLT, "My heart is filled with bitter sorrow and unending grief for my people, my Jewish brothers and sisters. I would be willing to be forever cursed—cut off from Christ!—if that would save them."

What would happen if you and I would have the zeal of Moses and Paul? Pray for God to give you a heart of compassion. For most Saturdays of my 48 years of pastoral ministry, I visited with one or more unchurched families in the community inviting them to church or to consider the claims of Christ.

Whenever you see a U-Haul coming to your area you don't need to pray about going to see them and extend a welcome to them. You can pray about what to say or what to take along as a welcoming gift or pray about when to go. Jesus commissioned you to go and be a witness in "Jerusalem." Welcome them to the community. Offer to help them unload the truck. Show them around town. There is no end to the possibilities including inviting them to church and introducing the children to their new Sunday school teacher or the adults to a small group that has been praying for a new family moving to that address. You will experience joy as you relate to new people and invite them to church and to the Lord Jesus.

Jesus, give me a passion like Moses and Paul. Give me courage to take the initiative to invite new people to worship and to meet you. Amen.

February 1

Live with Passion and Compassion

Matthew 9:36

"He felt great pity for the crowds that came, because their problems were so great and they didn't know where to go for help. They were like sheep without a shepherd" (Matthew 9:36 NLT).

When I get up in the morning, I frequently thank God for his passion in giving his only Son for me. Then I thank Jesus for his willingness to leave heaven and live among sinful men and die a cruel death on the cross. I thank the Holy Spirit for leaving heaven and being willing to live in my sinful heart now made holy by his transforming power. That morning prayer has made a profound difference in my life.

If we but have a fraction of God's passion for sinful humanity, we could turn the world right side up. The primary emotional response of Jesus for our world was compassion. Jesus was perfect. If anyone could be turned off by the sin in our world it was Jesus. Instead of looking or reacting with disdain at problem people, he reacted with compassion. Jesus saw people as sheep that had been bruised, beaten and confused. They needed a shepherd.

Jesus was perfect yet sinners crowded around him. The more mature we are spiritually the more sinners should feel comfortable with us. It was true with Jesus. His love showed. He was approachable. Both sinners and children were drawn to him. They could tell he was genuine. They felt loved.

Ask God to give you the heart of Jesus toward those who are lost and have no understanding of God's indescribable love for them. He will answer that prayer.

Lord, you came not to condemn the world but to save it. Help me to see people as you see them—sheep without a shepherd. Fill me with the same love and compassion you have for them. Amen.

February 2

Wisdom Proverbs

Proverbs 19:27

"If you stop learning you will forget what you already know" (Prov. 19:27 CEV).

"Wisdom is sweet to your soul. If you find it, you will have a bright future, and your hopes will not be cut short" (Prov. 24:14 NLT).

One of my definite joys in life is when I gain a new insight. This was true for David as well. Consider these verses from Psalm 119 NLT: verse 20, "I am overwhelmed continually with a desire for your laws" verse 39b, "Your laws are all I want in life," verse 77b. "Your law is my delight," verse 97. "I have more insight than my teachers, for I am always thinking of your decrees," verse 99. "Oh how I love your law! I think about it all day long," verse 111. "Your decrees are my treasure; they are truly my heart's delight," verse 131. "I open my mouth, panting expectantly, longing for your commands." Once David started talking about God's Word, he couldn't get stopped.

Ask God to give you a love for his word. I often get up in the morning thinking what a privilege it is to read and feast on God's eternal word. Ask God for a holy passion for his word, especially the living word, who is Jesus, and thank him as he answers that prayer.

Paul prayed for wisdom more than anything else. There is a huge difference between wisdom and knowledge. "While knowledge may make us feel important, it is love that really builds up the church. Anyone who claims to know all the answers doesn't really know very much. But the person who loves God is the one God knows and cares for" (I Corinthians 8:1b-3 NLT). Let's keep prayers for wisdom and love at the top of our prayer list.

James gives us the wonderful promise that if we lack wisdom we need to ask God but we dare not waver or we will not receive it. (See James 1:3-4.)

Father, I need your wisdom. I ask in faith believing you will grant it. Thank you. Amen.

February 3

Prayer and Passion

Luke 19:10

I believe there is a direct relationship between fervent prayer and passion. When Eastern Mennonite Mission Board representatives asked our mission organization in Ethiopia why they took a day each week to pray and fast they said, when they stopped this practice the church stopped growing. Their churches no longer planted daughter congregations. However when they gave a day each week to prayer and fasting the work was blessed by God. Lives were changed, churches were planted and God's Kingdom expanded.

Paul instructs us: "Devote yourselves to prayer, being watchful and thankful. And pray for us, too, that God may open a door for our message, so that we may proclaim the mystery of Christ, for which I am in chains. Pray that I may proclaim it clearly, as I should. Be wise in the way you act toward outsiders; make the most of every opportunity. Let your conversation be always full of grace, seasoned with salt, so that you may know how to answer everyone" (Colossians 4:2-6 NIV).

Do you find your zeal for the Lord lagging? Come to him in repentance, asking him to light the fire in your heart for his mission which is to seek and save the lost. (See Luke 19:10). Our zeal for the lost must come from a heart of obedience to the Great Commission of our Lord. (See Matthew 28:18-20). We are told to go, to baptize, to teach and make disciples. It is not primarily the need to see people educated or lifted out of poverty that will keep us giving sacrificial service. It is obedience to Christ's command and the power of the Holy Spirit in us that enables us to serve faithfully and fruitfully without burnout.

Cry out to him first in repentance for your indifferent attitude or flagging zeal and tell him you want to put him ahead of everything else—to love him with all your heart, soul, mind and strength and he will give you a burning passion to reach a lost world beginning with your peers.

Jesus, forgive me for my indifference. Cleanse me and give me a passion to love you with all my heart. Send me into my world to witness for you today. Amen.

February 4

Facing a Mountain?

Mark 11:27

"Humanly speaking, it is impossible. But not with God. Everything is possible with God" (Mark 11:27 NLT).

As a youth I stuttered. I knew what it was to be humiliated, to be laughed at, to feel inferior. As a boy, life was often discouraging. At age 15, I developed a heart condition that caused me to miss five months of school. It was during that time that I read missionary stories, listened to gospel preachers on the radio and grew in my faith. I felt God wanted to use me in his Kingdom work but I was frustrated because of my poor self image and poor health. How could God use me with my stuttering tongue?

It didn't happen overnight—it took years—many years. I'm embarrassed to say, as a pastor I prayed more frequently, "Lord help me talk," than, "Lord give me something to say." In fact my stuttering is not 100% cured. There are times in certain situations where I pray for grace to speak without stuttering. As I walk with the Lord, pray and do my part in accepting every opportunity to serve him, gradually over the years he has helped me overcome this handicap. This is one of the greatest miracles of my life.

Interestingly when the Lord called me to my first pastorate, their former pastor had a very noticeable speech impediment. While we certainly do not rejoice in other's handicaps, it made it easier for me to accept that pastoral position. God allows all things for a purpose.

Paul prayed for the Lord to remove his "thorn in the flesh." God's grace was sufficient for Paul. If you live with a "thorn in the flesh" do your part to overcome it, but if God does not see fit to remove it, he will use you in spite of it. In fact he may even use you to a greater advantage than if you did not have that "thorn."

Oswald Chambers wrote: "No sin is worse than the sin of self pity, because it removes God from the throne of our lives, replacing Him with our own self-interests. [iv]

Lord Jesus, thank you for the painful difficulties of life. They have helped me to lean on you more. Use me, refine me, and mold me for your glory. Amen.

February 5

God Can Do More Than We Can Imagine!

Ephesians 3:20-22

Our key scripture at Capital Christian Fellowship was Ephesians 3:20-21 NIV, "Now to him who is able to do immeasurably more than all we ask or imagine, according to his power that is at work within us, to him be glory in the church and in Christ Jesus throughout all generations, for ever and ever! Amen."

The amazing aspect of this scripture is not that God can do more than we can ask or imagine, after all, he is Lord of the cosmos; the amazing thing is that he does more than we can imagine through you and me. Apparently the Ephesians had to be reminded of God's mighty power in them. "Finally, be strong in the Lord and in his mighty power" (6:10 NIV).

The young minister Timothy was timid so Paul reminds him, "God did not give us a spirit of timidity, but a spirit of power, of love, and of self-discipline" (II Timothy 1:7 NIV). *The Message* Bible says, "God doesn't want us to be shy with his gifts, but bold and loving and sensible."

When Jesus met the disciples in the upper room after his resurrection, "He breathed on them and said, Receive the Holy Spirit" (John 20:22 NIV). A few days later the Holy Spirit came. Peter was an empowered man as he preached with boldness. Three thousand people repented and received Christ. Throughout the book of Acts, the apostles and the early Christians were bold for our Lord. That same power and boldness is there for each of us. Let's walk in it.

The late Bill Bright, wrote: "It is my strong conviction that it is impossible to ask God for too much if our hearts and motives are pure and if we pray according to the Word and will of God. Remember, it is a basic spiritual principle that whatever we vividly envision, ardently desire, sincerely believe and enthusiastically act upon will come to pass assuming, of course, that there is scriptural authority for it. It is this principle that is the foundation of praying supernaturally." [v]

Jesus, sometimes I forget your promise. I claim by faith your promise to do through me more than I can ask or imagine. Thank you, Jesus. Amen.

February 6

My Blind Friend

Luke 4:18

I have a friend who is blind. He walks with a white cane. I marvel how he can "see." He loves to travel to "see" many new and wonderful scenes. How is that possible? Lois, his wife, is his eyes, describing everything for him.

You and I have many blind friends, at least we should have. Like Lois we need to open blind eyes. In fact Jesus says that's why he came. Luke 4:18 NLT, "He has sent me to proclaim…that the blind will see."

"The Lord opens the eyes of the blind" (Psalm 146:8 NLT). When he (God) comes, he will open the eyes of the blind and unstop the ears of the deaf" (Isaiah 35:5 NLT). These scriptures point to a new day when all God's children who are blind will see. In the meantime we must open the minds and the eyes that the devil has blinded. "Satan, the god of this evil world, has blinded the minds of those who don't believe, so they are unable to see the glorious light of the Good News that is shining upon them" (II Corinthians 4:4 NLT).

Helen Keller said, "The most pathetic person in the world is someone who has sight, but has no vision." Some people have no apparent vision, no goals, no enthusiasm or passion. Life to them is a treadmill of work and sleep.

Jesus created us to live with a purpose—to fellowship with him. As God came in the garden looking for a relationship with Adam and Eve he comes knocking on our heart's door to relate to us. Ask him to open your eyes to see him in nature, in other people, in your situation, and to hear his voice. He is there.

David prayed: "O Lord, you have examined my heart and know everything about me. You know when I stand up. You know my every thought when far away. You chart the path ahead of me. And tell me where to stop and rest. Every moment you know where I am. You know what I am going to say even before I say it, Lord. You both precede and follow me. You place your hand of blessing on my head" (Psalm 139:1-5 NLT). Amen.

February 7

Our Blessed Hope

Titus 2:13

"Looking for that blessed hope, and the glorious appearing of the great God and our Savior Jesus Christ" (Titus 2:13 KJV).

"Be joyful in hope, patient in affliction, faithful in prayer" (Romans 12:12 NIV).

Yesterday I was talking with a friend who told me he spent most of his day with a person who did not believe in life after death. "When you're dead, you're dead." The apostle Paul had a different view. He says, "We are confident,… and would prefer to be away from the body and at home with the Lord" (II Corinthians 5:8). How could he say that? He had seen the Lord. He was caught up to paradise and heard things so astounding that they cannot be told (II Corinthians 12:4). Paul was sure of life after death.

Stephen saw the Lord calling him home when he was dying. (See Acts 6.)

Jesus said, "Don't be troubled. You trust God, now trust in me. There are many rooms in my Father's home and I am going to prepare a place for you. If this were not so, I would tell you plainly. When everything is ready, I will come and get you. So that you will always be with me where I am" (John 14:1-3 NLT).

"For our present troubles are quite small and won't last very long. Yet they produce for us an immeasurably great glory that will last forever! So we don't look at the troubles we can see right now; rather, we look forward to what we have not yet seen. For the troubles we see will soon be over, but the joys to come will last forever" (II Corinthians 5:17-18 NLT).

"Let us exult in the hope of the divine splendor that is to be ours" (Romans 5:2 NEB). Paul again says in I Corinthians 2:9 (Free Translation), "No one has heard or imagined what God has arranged for those who love him."

Lord, I thank you for the blessed hope where we will be with you forever. Amen.

February 8

Compel Them to Come!

Luke 14:23 and Mark 2:1-12

Jesus gave this parable in response to the man who said that it would be great to share in God's Kingdom. A Master prepared a great feast and invited guests but they all made excuses: one bought a field, another bought oxen and another just got married. This upset the Master so he told his servant to invite the poor, the crippled, the lame and the blind. The servant reported there is still room. The Master said make anyone you find come, so that the house will be full. (See v. 23.)

The word for "make" in the Greek means "this is absolute necessity". I checked 17 versions or paraphrases. Six said, "make them come in," five "compel," three "urge," two "force," and one "drag them in."

Do we make/compel people to come to the heavenly banquet?

In Mark 2 Jesus came to his home town. The home town people heard he was home, so they packed out the house where he was. Four men brought a paraplegic on a stretcher so Jesus could heal him. Because of the crowd they were unable to get to Jesus, so they went up on the roof and removed the tiles and lowered the man down in front of Jesus.

Imagine going to your neighbor's house and taking off part of the roof! These men meant business! They had faith that Jesus would heal this man. They were determined to have him meet Jesus.

How determined are we to have our neighbors meet Jesus? Jesus said we are to compel them to come to the heavenly banquet. Jesus suffered on the cross to make it possible for us to come to him for healing, both spiritual and physical.

Do you have this kind of passion? Ask Jesus to give you the passion and the faith of these four men who brought the paraplegic to Jesus.

Lord, give me a greater passion for the lost. You loved me and proved your love for me by dying for me. Help me to love as you loved. Amen.

February 9

You Are Sent

John 20:21-23

Jesus said, "Peace be with you! As the Father has sent me, I am sending you" (John 20:21 NIV). As he was praying he said to the Father, "As you sent me into the world, I am sending them into the world" (John 17:18 NLT). These statements of our Lord are addressed to the disciples but they include you and me. Notice the word "as." This implies that there is no difference between the Father sending Jesus and Jesus sending us. Does that mean we have the same authority?

The next verses in John say, "And with that he breathed on them and said, 'Receive the Holy Spirit. If you forgive anyone his sins, they are forgiven, if you do not forgive them, they are not forgiven" (vv. 22-23 NIV).

As the Holy Spirit leads you, there will come a time when you can invite your friends to receive the forgiveness that Jesus has already provided for them. Instead of condemning them for what they are doing, ask them if they are ready to receive the forgiveness Jesus has provided. You may say, "Jesus forgives you, I forgive you. Please accept the forgiveness he offers to you."

Some will say, "Who needs forgiveness? What did I do to need forgiveness?" Share with them that you need forgiveness every day. Sometimes I have thoughts or actions of pride, jealousy, envy, irritability, lust or hate. God says these are all sin. He forgives me if I sincerely ask him.

The Bible says in the letter of I John 1:8-9 NLT, "If we say we have no sin, we are only fooling ourselves and refusing to accept the truth. But if we confess our sins to him, he is faithful and just to forgive us and to cleanse us from every wrong. If we claim we have not sinned, we are calling God a liar."

Lord, I thank you for your forgiveness. Help me to extend that forgiveness to my friend who does not yet understand that forgiveness of Jesus is there for him or her as well. Amen.

February 10

Grow in Grace

II Peter 3:18

"Grow in grace and knowledge of our Lord and Savior Jesus Christ" (II Peter 3:18 NIV). How can you grow in grace? One way is to understand how sinful we really are. Our heart is hopelessly dark! When we see ourselves as God sees us outside of Christ we are hopeless. Knowing we are hopeless we come to Christ and he gives us pardon and restoration into God's family. What an absolutely incredible transfer! Such love demands our everything!!!

How can we grow in grace? The longer Paul lived as a Christian and the more mature he became, the more he understood his sinful heart. He said, "I am less than the least of all God's people" (Ephesians 3:8 Msg). Again he said, "I am the least of the apostles and do not even deserve to be called an apostle..." (I Corinthians 15:9 NIV). Paul saw himself in need of God's marvelous grace. In Romans 7:14 and 18 NIV he says, "I am unspiritual, sold as a slave to sin," and "I know that nothing good lives in me, that is, in my sinful nature."

Although Adam and Eve were created in God's image, in the Garden of Eden they defied God by eating of the forbidden fruit. That defiance was passed down to us. As Paul writes: "All have sinned and fall short of the glory of God" (Romans 3:23 NIV). Sin separates us from God but Jesus bridges the gap in bringing us back to God. What marvelous grace!

Jeremiah reminds us: "The heart is deceitful above all things and beyond cure. Who can understand it" (Jeremiah 17:9 NIV)? "The heart is hopelessly dark and deceitful, a puzzle that no one can figure out." (Msg). If we understand that we are utterly sinful by nature we will cry out to God for his grace. If we understand that we all have the old nature in us it will help us grow in grace.

Lord you are absolutely incredible. Thank you for your grace. Help me to love you more, to serve you with all my passion, prayer, intelligence and energy. Amen. (See Mark 12:30 Msg.)

February 11

Endless Treasures

Ephesians 3:8, 16

"I was chosen for this special joy of telling the Gentiles about the endless treasures available to them in Christ" (Ephesians 3:8 NLT). *The Message* Bible speaks of the "inexhaustible riches and generosity of Christ." The NIV says, "The unsearchable riches of Christ." In v. 16 NLT Paul writes: "I pray that from his glorious, unlimited resources he will give you mighty inner strength through His Holy Spirit."

Can you remember hunting for something and experiencing the joy of finding it? Maybe it was your wallet, your car keys, or a passport. When you read the Word of God do you find treasures? David did. Jeremiah, the weeping prophet, also saw the endless riches in God even before Jesus came.

"The thought of my suffering and homelessness is bitter beyond words. I will never forget this awful time, as I grieve over my loss. Yet I still dare to hope when I remember this: The unfailing love of the Lord never ends! By his mercies we have been kept from complete destruction. Great is his faithfulness; his mercies begin afresh each day. I say to myself, 'The Lord is my inheritance; therefore, I will hope in him!' The Lord is wonderfully good to those who wait for him and seek him. So it is good to wait quietly for salvation from the Lord. And it is good for the young to submit to the yoke of his discipline" (Lamentation 3:19-27 NLT).

Have you discovered that Jesus has endless treasures available for you? They are there. All you have to do is claim them. Cry out to Jesus for the fullness of the Holy Spirit (see Ephesians 5:18) and he will give it to you. You will need to do this again and again because our hearts grow cold. We need his fullness every moment. Learn to operate in this fullness. "In His presence is fullness of joy" (Psalm 16:11 KJV).

That's the secret. Don't go another moment without operating in his endless treasures or his inexhaustible riches! It's there for your taking!

Father, thank you for your endless treasures in your Son Jesus and the treasures in your Word. Open my eyes to see them and open my heart to live in them. Amen.

February 12

Increase My Faith

Ephesians 3:20-21

When Paul comes to the end of the doctrinal section in Ephesians 3:20-21 NLT, he writes: "Now glory be to God! By his mighty power at work within us, he is able to accomplish infinitely more than we would ever dare to ask or hope. May he be given glory in the church and in Christ Jesus forever and ever through endless ages, Amen."

The thing that astounds me is not the mighty power of God doing more than I can possibly imagine, but the fact that he wants to do it through you and me! I can think and imagine a lot, but God says he can do infinitely more through me. Oh Father, increase my faith!

Is this what Jesus had in mind when he taught us to pray: "May your kingdom come soon. May your will be done on earth just as it is in heaven" (Matthew 6:10 NLT).

Different times Jesus rebuked the disciples for their lack of faith. When they couldn't heal the demon-possessed boy, Jesus said, "You stubborn, faithless people! How long must I be with you until you believe? How long must I put up with you? Bring the boy to me" (Matthew 17:17 NLT).

When Peter got out of the boat he walked on the water, but seeing the waves he began to sink. He shouted for Jesus to save him. Jesus grabbed him and said, "You don't have much faith. Why did you doubt me" (Matthew 14:31 NLT)? When the disciples and Jesus were in the storm they woke Jesus. "Jesus rebuked the wind and the raging waves. The storm stopped and all was calm! Then he asked them, Where is your faith" (Luke 8:24-25 NIV)?

Jesus cursed the fig tree. Peter was surprised when he saw it had withered. Jesus said, "I assure you that you can say to this mountain, May God lift you up and throw you into the sea, and your command will be obeyed. All that's required is that you really believe and do not doubt in your hearts. Listen to me! You can pray for anything, and if you believe, you will have it" (Mark 11:23-24 NLT).

Lord, increase my faith! Amen.

February 13

You are God's Masterpiece!

Ephesians 2:10

"We are God's masterpiece. He has created us anew in Christ Jesus, so that we can do the good things he planned for us long ago" (Ephesians 2:10 NLT).

"God in heaven appoints each person's work" (John 3:27 NLT).

God is in the process of telling his story through our lives. In Ephesians 2:10, *Poiema* is the Greek word we translate workmanship. This is the root word for poem. God weaves us into his poem. *Poiema* is God's awesome plan to conform us to the image of his Son. (See Romans 8:29.) He has every intention to carry it on to completion (See Philippians 1:6.) God is the great craftsman and storyteller who loves to tell his story through our lives as we are being restored and redeemed. He does not neglect any area of our lives.

God speaks to you, his child and says, "My child, don't ignore it when the Lord disciplines you, and don't be discouraged when he corrects you. For the Lord disciplines those he loves. And he punishes those he accepts as his children" (Hebrews 12:5b-6 NLT).

Jesus said, "He (God) cuts off every branch that doesn't produce fruit, and he prunes the branches that do bear fruit so they will produce even more" (John 15:2 NLT).

One of our biggest challenges in life is to willingly submit to God's discipline. We are a diamond in the rough. God has to keep chiseling off the rough spots so we can shine like stars in the universe. (See Philippians 2:15 NIV.)

We are God's masterpiece in the making. Know that whatever God allows in your life is for your benefit. He is transforming you from one degree of glory to another. (See II Corinthians 3:18.)

Lord, help me to accept with joy whatever comes into my life today. Give me a faithful heart of love and trust as you continue to make me your masterpiece in the midst of this evil world. Amen.

February 14

I am Shocked...

Galatians 1:6

"I am shocked that you are turning away so soon from God who in his love and mercy called you to share the eternal life he gives through Christ" (Galatians 1:6 NLT).

With one exception, Paul began all of his letters to the churches thanking them for their faithfulness to our Lord. Why this one exception? Why was Paul so upset with the Galatian Church? He hated hypocrisy.

When it comes to sins of the flesh the Corinthian church tops them all. Paul writes in II Corinthians 12:20b-21 NLT, "I am afraid that I will find quarreling, jealousy, outbursts of anger, selfishness, backstabbing, gossip, conceit, and disorderly behavior. Yes, I am afraid that when I come, God will humble me again because of you. And I will have to grieve because many of you who sinned earlier have not repented of your impurity, sexual immorality, and eagerness for lustful pleasure."

We would be embarrassed to be a member of this church.

Why was Jesus more upset with the Pharisees than with those in the world living in overt sin such as the woman at the well, or the rich man not willing to give up his riches?

Both Paul and Jesus hated hypocrisy. Jesus said in Matthew 23 NLT, "How terrible it will be for you teachers of religious law and you Pharisees, for you cross land and sea to make one convert, and then you turn him into twice the son of hell as you yourselves are," (v 15). "You are careful to tithe even the tiniest part of your income, but you ignore the important things of the law—justice, mercy, and faith" (v 23). "You are so careful to clean the outside of the cup and the dish, but inside you are filthy—full of greed and self-indulgence!" (v 25). "Snakes! Sons of vipers! How will you escape the judgment of hell?" (v 33). The Lord hates hypocrisy.

Lord, help me to remove my mask and be authentic in all I do and in all I say. Amen.

February 15

What Greater Cause?

I Peter 4:10

Our great purpose is to bring glory to God and to serve others. "Each one should use whatever gift he has received to serve others" (I Peter 4:10 NIV). How do we serve them?—by sharing the love and grace of Jesus with them.

When I was a child we had a motto in our living room that made a huge impression on me. It read, "Your life will soon be past, only what's done for Christ will last." Although I have come to believe the motto would have been more theologically correct if it read, "Your life will soon be past, only what's done with Christ will last," it still made an impact on my life.

In Luke 15, Jesus tells us three stories: the lost sheep, the lost coin and the lost son. That which is important to Jesus is what is lost. The lost need to be found. Believers need to hear and be challenged to do all they can to help others who are lost find hope in Jesus. Jesus came to seek and to save the lost. (See Luke 19:10.)

Jesus modeled serving (see Philippians 2:5-7). When He left heaven he came to serve and to rescue you and me from our sins and give us his very life. His life was a life of service. "Jesus went around doing good and healing all who were oppressed by the devil, for God was with him" (Acts 10:38b NLT).

Jesus washed the disciples' feet - the job of the slave. (See John 13.) The church must be involved in our local communities. What concerns the people of the community concerns us. Sometimes we need to be a voice for the voiceless, whether they are abused children, those without healthcare, orphans, unwed mothers or those caught in human trafficking. Let's help to clean up our schools. We cannot be silent.

Celebrate the joys of serving. When we serve others, our faith is made stronger. When I help those in need, my needs look smaller. Jesus says in serving the "least of these"—we are serving Him. You're never closer to Jesus than when you're serving, loving and engaging the poor and hurting.

Lord Jesus, I dedicate my life to serving you by serving others. Amen.

February 16

Fickle Praise

Luke 4: 14-32

"He (Jesus) taught in their synagogues and was praised by everyone" (Luke 4:15 NLT).

Jesus came to his home town and as was his custom he went to the synagogue. The leaders gave him the Isaiah scroll to read. He chose to read Isaiah 61:1-2: "The Spirit of the Lord is upon me, for he has appointed me to preach Good News to the poor. He has sent me to proclaim that captives will be released, that the blind will see, that the downtrodden will be freed from their oppressors, and that the time of the Lord's favor has come" (Luke 4:18-19 NLT).

Following this reading Jesus reminded them that during the time of famine, Elijah was sent not to Israel but to the widow of Zaraphath. He also reminded them that Elijah healed Naaman, a Syrian, rather than the lepers in Israel. (See vv. 25-27.) This angered these good church people to the point they wanted to kill him but he slipped away through the crowds.

Why did their praise turn so quickly to rage? Jesus was accepting people they didn't accept—the widow of Zaraphath and the Syrian, Naaman. To them the Messiah was coming to benefit only the Jews. People who were far from God are ones Jesus came to serve. Jesus had great compassion for those who were needy.

Jesus remembered that God promised Abraham that through his family all the families of the earth would be blessed. The more spiritually mature we are, the more approachable we need to be to those who the Pharisees saw as far from God. We need to be accepting of others no matter what nationality or what needs they have. At times we are like the Pharisees who reeked of self-righteousness and judgment.

How many friends do we have in these categories? How many of these people are in our congregation? Do I have compassion like Jesus did for those who are hurting? How many immigrants are in our circle of friends? How many are in our congregation?

Dear Lord, give me a heart of compassion like you had for those who are oppressed and needy. Amen.

February 17

Perseverance

I Timothy 4:16

"Watch your life and doctrine closely. Persevere in them, because if you do, you will save both yourself and your hearers" (I Timothy 4:16 NIV).

"May the Master take you by the hand and lead you along the path of God's love and Christ's endurance" (II Thessalonians 3:5 Msg).

Human nature wants immediate action, immediate results. We get frustrated when the fast food restaurant order is delayed more than ten seconds. We want high speed internet. Some red lights test my patience when I have to wait what seems to me like fifteen minutes.

Paul says we are to persevere in our character and our teaching because perseverance results in salvation or deliverance. James writes, "Consider it pure joy…whenever you face trials of many kinds, because you know that the testing of your faith develops perseverance. Perseverance must finish its work so that you may be mature and complete, not lacking anything" (James 1:2-4 NIV). Perseverance is a characteristic of maturity. There is no such thing as instant maturity.

Life is not a 100-yard dash; it's a marathon. Paul writes: "I discipline my body like an athlete, training it to do what it should. Otherwise, I fear that after preaching to others I myself might be disqualified" (I Corinthians 9:27 NLT). Paul is not implying that he will lose his salvation but he is concerned that he will not be qualified to preach to others. Paul needs to practice what he preaches. He needs to persevere. My neighbor prayed for more than thirty years for her parents to come to Christ. What joy she expressed in reporting their conversion. Moses was on the back side of the desert for forty years before God called him to deliver his people. Joseph waited seventeen years before he was raised to a position of leadership.

Paul says in II Corinthians 4:17 NLT, "For the light, momentary afflictions that we bear are producing in us an eternal weight of glory far beyond all comparison." We endure as we focus on the eternal perspective rather than our current situation. Some of you are praying for a member of your family to turn their life over to Christ. God will answer even though we may not see the answer in our lifetime. He is faithful.

Lord, help me to persevere. Amen

February 18

Hidden Treasures

Colossians 2:3

"In Christ are hidden all the treasures of wisdom and knowledge." (Colossians 2:3 Free Translation).

Why does God seem to hide from us? Why are there times when the Scriptures do not speak to us?

"You will seek me and find me when you seek me with all your heart" (Jeremiah 19:13 NIV). "Yes, when you get serious about finding me and want it more than anything else, I'll make sure you won't be disappointed" (Jeremiah 29:13 Msg).

Eight times the Psalmist writes: "Do not hide your face from me." Moses instructs Aaron and his sons to bless the people: "The Lord make his face shine upon you and be gracious to you; the Lord turn his face toward you and give you peace" (Numbers 6:25-26 NIV).

When God seems far away we need to seek him with all our hearts. We need to ask him to search our hearts to see if there is anything displeasing to him. (See Psalm 139:23-24.) We need to pray, "Lord open my blind eyes to see anything that displeases you and I will do whatever you say." If God still seems to hide, we must accept the silence and praise him for who he is and thank him knowing he is there and will never abandon us. (See Hebrews 13:5.)

When something is hidden, the longer we search, the greater the joy when we find it. Isn't this true when we discover the reality of Jesus for our immediate situation? As we search the Scriptures and find hidden treasures, our faith grows. We experience joy and thanksgiving. As we share these new discoveries, and once hidden treasures with others, they too can rejoice.

I remember when my eyes were opened as I read Romans 5:1 where we stand in his grace. I don't need to struggle to get there. Jesus has placed me there. What a treasure! It's neat to know this wonderful truth that came alive to me in a fresh way.

Jesus, I thank you for revealing these hidden treasures to me. They give me great joy. Amen.

February 19

All the Families of the Earth

Genesis 12:3

"All the families of the earth will be blessed through you" (Genesis 12:3b NLT).

John R.W. Scott writes: "I pray that these words, 'all the families of the earth,' may be written on our hearts. It is this expression more than any other that reveals the living God of the Bible to be a missionary God. It is this expression too that condemns all our petty parochialism and narrow nationalism, our racial pride (whether white or black), our condescending paternalism and arrogant imperialism.

How dare we adopt a hostile or scornful or even indifferent attitude to any person of another color or culture if our God is the God of 'all the families of the earth'? We need to become global Christians with a global vision, for we have a global God." [vi]

One of the more negative weaknesses of the American Church is that Sunday morning is the most segregated hour of the week. Jesus prayed four times in John 17 (verses 11, 21, 22, and 23) that we would be one. Jesus knew that unity would be a great challenge for us. He taught us to pray that his Kingdom would be realized on earth just as it is in heaven. In heaven we will be one. In Revelation John saw, "a crowd, too great to count, from every nation and tribe and people and language, standing in front of the throne and before the Lamb" (Revelation 7:9 NLT).

One of my greatest joys was pastoring Capital Christian Fellowship in Lanham, Maryland, with 30 or more nationalities represented throughout the congregation and in all levels of leadership. Whenever a church through the power of the gospel breaks down the dividing walls of hostility, the Gospel is a beacon light of healing to the community.

Lord, help me to love people of all classes and cultures and to demonstrate that love with practical acts of God's generosity. Amen.

February 20

You Are Sent

John 17:18 and John 20:21

Most dedicated disciples of our Lord believe they are called by God to serve others. After all Jesus came to serve, not to be served. (See Mark 10:45.) Jesus was very conscious of being sent by the Father. Many times in John's Gospel he refers to the Father sending him. He says in John 17:18 NLT, "As you sent me into the world, I am sending them into the world." And again 20:21 NLT, "As the Father has sent me, so I send you."

Are you conscious of being sent? When you get up in the morning do you realize that Jesus is sending you today to a lost world? We have a responsibility to represent the One who sends us. We need to hear and then obey what he has outlined for our day. Not only are we to be faithful we are to be fruitful: "This is to my Father's glory, that you bear much fruit, showing yourselves to be my disciples" (John 15:8 NIV).

Jesus then adds: "You didn't choose me. I chose you. I appointed you to go and produce fruit that will last, so that the Father will give you whatever you ask for, using my name" (John 15:16 NLT). We are sent and also chosen to produce fruit that will last for eternity. We must ask in Jesus name for the fruit.

What is the fruit that will remain? Is it the fruit of the Spirit: "Love, joy, peace, patience, kindness, goodness, faithfulness, gentleness, and self-control" (Galatians 5:22-23 NLT)? Or is it the fruit of people coming to Christ? "When the Holy Spirit has come upon you, you will receive power and will tell people about me everywhere—in Jerusalem, throughout Judea, in Samaria, and to the ends of the earth" (Acts 1:8 NLT).

It is both character and witness, character and souls. Both are necessary. Both bring glory to the Father.

Lord, help me to realize that just as you were sent by the Father, you sent me into the world to be a light and a witness for you. Amen.

February 21

All I Want

Psalm 16:5

"You Lord are all I want! You are my choice and you keep me safe" (Psalm 16:5 CEV).

"Your laws are all I want in life" (Psalm 119:39b NLT).

"You're all I want in heaven! You're all I want on earth" (Psalm 73:15 Msg)!

David wanted one thing more than anything—the presence of God. People want a lot of things. The credit card craze is proof. For Christians, earthly things need to take a back seat. The Lord must be first. In fact Jesus said, "If anyone comes to me and does not hate his father and mother, his wife and children, his brothers and sisters—yes, even his own life- he cannot be my disciple" (Luke 14:26 NIV). We know we are not to hate anyone so what does Jesus mean? Some of the modern paraphrases take the liberty to interpret Jesus' words: "Anyone who comes to me but refuses to let go of father, mother, spouse, children, brothers, sisters—yes, even one's own self—can't be my disciple" (Luke 14:26 Msg).

Paul writes, "Everything else is worthless, when compared with the priceless gain of knowing Christ Jesus my Lord. I have discarded everything else, counting it all as garbage, so that I may have Christ and become one with him" (Philippians 3:8-9a NLT).

David said, "This one thing I ask of the Lord—the thing I seek most—is to live in the house of the Lord all the days of my life, delighting in the Lord's perfections and meditating in his Temple" (Psalm 27:4 NLT). Do you desire to live in his presence each moment?

Jesus promised, If we keep his Kingdom ahead of everything else the "everything else" will be given to us. (See Matt. 6:33.) Paul writes, "I want to know Christ and the power of his resurrection and the fellowship of sharing in his sufferings, becoming like him in his death" (Philippians 3:10 NIV). Have you and I come to the place where we can say? Lord, you are all I want?

Lord, I surrender my all to you. I give you my time, my allegiance, my family, my job, my will. It is yours to use as you see fit. So help me Lord. Amen.

February 22

The Kingdom of God is Near

Luke 10:9,11

"If a town welcomes you, eat whatever is set before you and heal the sick. As you heal them, say, 'the Kingdom of God is near you now.' But if a town refuses to welcome you, go out into its streets and say, 'We wipe the dust of your town from our feet as a public announcement of your doom.' And don't forget the Kingdom of God is near" (Luke 10:8-10 NLT).

Are you aware of the difference between working with God and working for God? Working for God can get very tiring. Working with God is the conscious recognition that God is already working in the situation or working with the person(s) we are finding so difficult. Since the Holy Spirit has come, we are not working for God as much as we are working with God. "The Kingdom of God is within you" (Luke 17:21 NLT).

Knowing God is already working in us and in the people we are relating to, takes the pressure off of us to see results and gives us a new confidence, a boldness as we begin to see Jesus in them. Jesus says we are to remind them the Kingdom of God is near. This phrase can also be translated, "the Kingdom of God is here." If we pray for their healing and they reject our witness Jesus said that we are to remind them that the Kingdom of God is at their doorstep. (See Msg).

What happens if we pray and they are not healed? I encourage you to pray and see what happens. Watch God at work and trust him for the results. Later Jesus said we are to visit the sick (Matthew 25:36). In that situation he did not tell us to heal the sick. Let's be faithful to pray for the sick as James instructs us and let the results up to God. (See James 5:13-16.)

You are working, "with God?" He is in charge. He will help us be faithful and fruitful. With this perspective your life's work will take on fresh power and joy as you minister in his sufficiency.

Jesus, thank you for bringing the Kingdom of God to us and placing it in us. Amen.

February 23

Not in Danger

Luke 10:3-4,19

Jesus says to the 70 disciples, "Go now, and remember that I am sending you out as lambs among wolves. Don't take along any money, or a traveler's bag, or even an extra pair of sandals. And don't stop to greet anyone on the road." Then by way of contrast, Jesus says in verse19. "I have given you authority over all the power of the enemy, and you can walk among snakes and scorpions and crush them. Nothing will injure you" (Luke 10:3-4, 19 NLT).

What do wolves do with baby lambs? Devour them!

Why did Jesus make these contrasting statements? Jesus sends us out but that does not mean we will find it comfortable and easy. He sent the disciples in a boat and a furious storm came. Jesus was driven by the Spirit into the wilderness and temptations came.

A person who was about to be martyred for their faith is reported as saying, "I am near death, but I'm not in danger." Is this what Jesus meant when he said that nothing can harm you? (See also v. 19.)

Do we believe our security is in Christ even though the wolves may eat us alive? Are we at peace with the thought of going home to be with Jesus even though it involves suffering before we arrive there? If there is hesitance because of unfinished business with making things right with others then we need to make our peace now. If our hesitance is that we believe our work on earth is not finished, then we need to tell God and let the results in his hands.

I believe this is what Paul describes in Philippians 1:21-25 NLT, "To me, living is for Christ, and dying is even better. Yet if I live, that means fruitful service for Christ. I really don't know which is better. I'm torn between two desires: Sometimes I want to live, and sometimes I long to go and be with Christ. That would be far better for me, but it is better for you that I live. I am convinced of this so I will continue with you so that you will grow and experience the joy of your faith."

Lord, help me to live today so that if this is the last day of my life I will hear: "Well done, good and faithful servant, enter into the joy of the Lord." Amen.

February 24

A Plentiful and Ripe Harvest

Luke 10:1-12, John 4:35

Jesus informs the disciples in Luke 10:2, that the harvest is plentiful. Do you and I experience a plentiful harvest? If the harvest is not plentiful Jesus says we are to pray for more workers. Do we pray for more workers? Do our children and the children in our church know we pray for them to be workers? Or, are we hoping our children will prepare themselves with a lucrative position so they can have plenty of money, make a name for themselves and have a comfortable nest egg for retirement.

Jesus said the harvest is ripe. John 4:35 NIV, "Do you not say, 'Four months more and then the harvest'? I tell you, open your eyes and look at the fields! They are ripe for harvest. Even now the reaper draws his wages, even now he harvests the crop for eternal life, so that the sower and the reapers may be glad together." Jesus is saying there is an urgency. Bring in the harvest while it is ripe. In Luke 10:4 Jesus instructs the 70 to not greet anyone on the road. That doesn't sound like Jesus. In that culture greetings could easily take several hours. We are not to stop on the way and dilly-dally around. Jesus at this point in Luke's Gospel was focusing on the Jewish people. Night comes when no one can work. (See John 9:4.) We are to go where Jesus sends us (v.4). We don't go where we want to go or where we feel safe. Our mission is to go where he sends us.

People are motivated more by a great cause than by comfort. We want our lives to count for something. We want to make a difference. We want to know we are doing something worthwhile, be it costly or painful. This is what caused the disciples to face the wolves. Jesus called them to a vision.

Isaiah's prophecy paints a picture of God's Kingdom where the wolves and the lambs will lie down together. (See Isaiah 11:6.) Jesus sends us into the harvest field to help fulfill that fantastic prophecy.

Jesus, thank you for calling me into the harvest field. Open my eyes to see the ripe fields today. Lord, as you commanded, I pray for more workers. Use me in reaping the harvest. Thank you. Amen.

February 25

Person of Peace

Matthew 10:13 and Luke 10:5

"Whatever town...you enter, search for some worthy person there and stay at this house until you leave. As you enter the home give it your greeting. If the home is deserving, let your peace rest on it; if it is not, let your peace return to you" (Matthew 10:11-13 NIV).

When Jesus sent out the seventy disciples he said, "When you enter a home, greet the family, 'Peace.' If your greeting is received, then it's a good place to stay. But if it's not received, take it back and get out. Don't impose yourself" (Luke 10:5-6 Msg).

We need to find persons of peace, persons of respect, worthy persons. In other words God has prepared the hearts of some to receive his word before we enter an area. If we can't find them, Jesus says, "Don't stay there." Paul and Jesus found those people: Lydia (Acts 16:14-15), Cornelius (Acts 10, 11), the woman at the well (John 4), the demoniac (Mark 8:20) and others.

In my fifty years of pastoral ministry God led me to many persons of peace. One man came and over the next couple years was influential in bringing 30 others. Another man, an alcoholic for twenty-six years, brought his buddies and extended family and friends to Jesus. Another woman, a school teacher, brought her extended family and friends. Others brought their acquaintances. An international person from Cameron opened the door for many internationals to come to Christ and the church. I wonder how many churches were planted from the demoniac's witness of the work of Jesus in his life as he went through the Decapolis. The Decapolis was composed of ten cities, each it is estimated with five thousand or more. This opened the door in a dramatic way to those in the Greek culture. Let's not be surprised that the Lord uses those with a background of overt sin in a great way.

Pray that you can find persons of peace. When they open their hearts to the Lord, disciple and empower them to reach their families as well as their peers. At least four different times in the book of Acts when one person met Jesus the whole household came to our Lord. (See Acts 11:14, 16:15, 31, 18:8.) We must find these persons, mentor them and empower them for ministry.

Lord, open my eyes to see these persons of peace so your gospel can penetrate into their culture. Amen.

February 26

"Do Not Take a Purse or Bag or Sandals"

Luke 10:4

Jesus instructed the seventy as he sent them out to not take a purse, or bag or sandals (v.4). *The Message* Bible says, "Travel light. Comb and toothbrush and no extra luggage." Why no extra clothes or shoes? We are not to depend on our ingenuity, nor our money or possessions, or our training. By allowing the people to help us, the door is open for them to hear us. Why did Jesus ask the woman at the well for a drink? He could have performed a miracle to get the water for himself. Why did Jesus ask more than 150 questions? He knew the answers. Jesus humbled himself. He invited others to assist him. He reached across to them. We must do the same so people will hear us.

What do we do when we arrive at our destination? We heal their sick, (v. 9). We go to the needy. Maybe we feel more at home in the middle class. We like the country club atmosphere but Jesus calls us to the margins. There are more than 400 biblical passages demonstrating God's concern for orphans, widows, prisoners, aliens, the homeless, the poor, the hungry, the sick and the disabled. "He (God) gives justice to orphans and widows. He shows love to the foreigners living among you and gives them food and clothing. You too must show love to foreigners, for you yourselves were once foreigners in the land of Egypt" (Deuteronomy 10:18-19 NIV).

We bless people, and they bless us. We reach across, not down. They may provide our physical needs. We need to be humble enough to accept their gifts. In doing this we empower them. They are more open to hearing the Good News of God's Kingdom. People will not hear until they have been heard. Since they provide us with our basic necessities they are more open to receiving and hearing us. That's a principle we need to take seriously.

Lord Jesus, help me not to depend on my education, on my wallet, but to look to you for love, and power to meet the needs of those I meet today. Thank you. Amen.

February 27

Rejoice Because Your Name Is Written in Heaven

Luke 10:17-20

In Luke 10:17-20, the disciples returned from their mission trip full of joy with a triumphant report, but Jesus said don't rejoice just because evil spirits obey you; rejoice because your names are recorded in heaven. *The Message Bible* reads: "The great triumph is not in our authority over evil, but in God's authority over you and presence with you. Not what you do for God but what God does for you—that's the agenda for rejoicing" (Luke 10:18-19).

We rejoice over what God does for us: our names are written in the Lamb's Book of Life. We rejoice in the wonder of our salvation much more than the fact that demons are subject to us.

Why did Jesus feel it was necessary to warn the disciples about being excited over casting out demons? Might it have been because we are apt to believe that it's because of our power that we can cast out demonic forces? Remember, we are simply tools in the hands of the potter. Anything we do is only as a result of abiding in him. (See John 15:4.) The Lord told Zerubbabel: "Not by might nor by power, but by my Spirit, says the Lord Almighty" (Zechariah 4:6 NIV).

Paul was disgusted at the Corinthians for their divisions. He writes: "Who do you think Paul is, anyway? Or Apollos, for that matter? Servants, both of us—servants who waited on you as you gradually learned to entrust your lives to our mutual Master. We each carried out our servant assignment. I planted the seed. Apollos watered the plants, but God made it grow. It's not the one who plants or the one who waters who is at the center of this process but God who makes things grow. Planting and watering are menial servant jobs at minimum wages. What makes them worth doing is the God we are serving" (I Corinthians 3:5-8 Msg).

Let's remember to give God the credit for everything we do since we cannot make one hair white or black. (See Matthew 5:36).

Lord, help me to rejoice in your gift of salvation through Christ Jesus my Lord. Amen.

February 28

Let's Be Courageous

Luke 10:17-20

"When the seventy-two returned with joy and said, Lord, even the demons submit to us in your name." He replied, I saw Satan fall like lightning from heaven. I have given you authority to trample on snakes and scorpions and to overcome all the power of the enemy; nothing will harm you. However, do not rejoice that the spirits submit to you, but rejoice that your names are written in heaven" (Luke 10:17-20 NIV).

May God help us to move out in faith. We will not see Satan fall in our churches unless we are obedient in our mission. I believe Satan frequently rejoices as we spend hours trying to solve an internal squabble or form another committee to help squelch yet another internal problem. If we would put more of our energy into our mission of reaching a lost world, the internal problems will often dissipate. Satan loves to keep us in internal conflict. The "kitchen worker" issues or the "color of our carpet" issues in our churches become more important than our mission.

As long as we think we must get our petty differences settled in our churches before we can go to our peers and neighbors with the Good News, we will not see Satan fall.

The early church was far from perfect but the Good News spread because that was the priority of the apostles and early church. Satan is having a heyday in our churches because our efforts are often focused on internal problems rather than on announcing to the world that God's Kingdom is here!

Conflict in our churches is often more comfortable for us than going where Jesus wants us to go! Jesus sends each of us into our world just as the Father sent him. (See John 20:21.) On the judgment day God will ask us if we were faithful in our mission.

Father, enable me to not let Satan defeat me or my church by spending all my time on internal differences but to make the Great Commission our priority. Amen.

February 29

Suffering for our Lord

I Peter 4:1

"He who suffers in the body is done with sin" (I Peter 4:1 NIV).

For many years in China the Christians sang this song: "Martyrs for the Lord." [vii]

From the time the church was birthed on the day of Pentecost.
The followers of the Lord have willingly sacrificed themselves
Tens of thousands have died that the Gospel might prosper
As such they have obtained the crown of life

Chorus:
To be a martyr for the Lord, to be a martyr for the Lord
I am willing to die gloriously for the Lord.

Those apostles who loved the Lord to the end
Willingly followed the Lord down the path of suffering
John was exiled to the lonely isle of Patmos
Stephen was stoned to death by an angry crowd
Matthew was stabbed to death in Persia by a mob
Mark died as horses pulled his two legs apart
Doctor Luke was cruelly hanged
Peter, Philip and Simon were crucified on a cross
Bartholomew was skinned alive by the heathen
Thomas died in India as five horses pulled his body apart
The apostle James was beheaded by King Herod
Little James was cut in half by a sharp saw
James the brother of the Lord was stoned to death
Judas was tied to a pillar and shot by arrows
Matthias had his head cut off in Jerusalem
Paul was a martyr under Emperor Nero
I am willing to take up the cross and go forward
To follow the apostle down the road of sacrifice
That tens of thousands of precious souls can be saved
I am willing to leave all and be a martyr for the Lord.

March 1

Pride

I Chronicles 21

Pride is the president of hell. Pride is the root of all sin. It started in the garden. Eve was saying she knew better than God. We say and do the same thing. We are self absorbed. When you look at a group picture who is the first person you look for? If your picture is lousy you don't like the picture. "The heart is deceitful above all things and beyond cure" (Jeremiah 17:9 NIV).

In I Chronicles 21 David insisted on taking a census. Joab, with better judgment, resisted strongly but reluctantly obeyed King David. God punished Israel for David's "substituting statistics for trust" (v.7 Message). God disciplined David by giving him three choices: three years of famine, three months of being overrun by the enemy or three days encountering the sword of the Lord. David chose the latter and 70,000 died. (See v. 14.) David repented saying, "I am the one who sinned and did wrong. …O Lord my God, let your hand fall upon me and my family, but do not let this plague remain on your people" (v.17).

My Mother reminded me often that "Pride goes before destruction and a haughty spirit before a fall" (Proverbs 16:18 NIV). And "If you think you are standing firm, be careful that you don't fall" (I Corinthians 10:12 NIV).

The scriptures are full of warnings about pride. Most of my life I prayed before I preached that I would be humble. Later in my ministry as I was praying before I was to speak, the Lord seemed to be saying he is tired of me praying that prayer. Then a thought came to me, I feel sure it was from the Holy Spirit: look in Strong's Concordance how often the New Testament tells us to be humble and how often it describes Christians who are bold. The ratio is two to one on the side of boldness.

Pride is the president of hell and the root sin of our lives. We must understand we are nothing and Jesus is everything. But at the same time Jesus has redeemed us and has chosen to use us. We must speak confidently and boldly so people can leave the broad way that leads to destruction and come to Jesus.

Father, help me to always die to self and to trust your Holy Spirit to speak through me and use me to share your love with others. Amen.

March 2

You Can't Be That Fanatical Or Can You?

Mark 2:1-12

"After a few days, Jesus returned to Capernaum, and word got around that he was back home... A crowd gathered, jamming the entrance so one could not get in or out. They brought a paraplegic to him, carried by four men. When they weren't able to get in because of the crowd, they removed part of the roof and lowered the paraplegic on his stretcher. Impressed by their bold belief, Jesus said to the paraplegic, Son, I forgive your sins" (Mark 2:1-5 Msg).

Apparently the people heard about the miracles Jesus performed and came to see and hear him. The testimonies of the healed people raised the faith level of the four men who brought the paralytic to Jesus. As Jesus was preaching these men came carrying a stretcher with the paralyzed man. The house was packed. There was no way they could get through the door. Determined to bring him to Jesus they climbed the stairs to the roof. Can you imagine, they removed the tiles and lowered the paralyzed man in front of Jesus? On seeing the faith of the four men He said to the paralyzed man, "My son, your sins are forgiven."

These four men were fanatics. Maybe their roofs were easier to patch than ours, but who of us would think of going to our neighbor's house and tearing off part of the roof to bring someone into the presence of Jesus? Our neighbors would think we were crazy. We might end up in prison or a mental hospital for such a crime. We all know people in need. Are we taking risks to bring them to Jesus? How serious are we in helping others?

Our zeal needs to be according to knowledge. Paul in speaking about his Jewish brothers says, "I know what enthusiasm they have for God but it is misdirected zeal" (Romans 10:2 NLT). We need to pray for wisdom so our zeal is according to God's will.

Dear Lord Jesus, when I compare my zeal with the zeal of these four men I fall short. Forgive me. Give me greater faith. Show me what I need to do to bring people to you. Give me the courage I need to bring my friends to you. Amen.

March 3

Who are the Evangelists?

Mark 2:3-5

"Some men came, bringing to him a paralytic, carried by four of them. Since they could not get him to Jesus because of the crowd, they made an opening in the roof above Jesus and, after digging through it, lowered the mat the paralyzed man was lying on. When Jesus saw their faith, he said to the paralytic, Son, your sins are forgiven" (Mark 4:3-5 NIV).

Are all four men evangelists? Perhaps. But one had to start by saying to the others, "This paralyzed man needs to meet Jesus. Will you help me get him to Jesus?" Perhaps the other three had the gift of mercy or the gift of service, or helps, or maybe a mix of other gifts. Someone had to take the initiative to get this man to Jesus. We need people to take leadership—someone to get things moving.

Could the leader do it alone? No, he needed three others. Perhaps he also needed help to repair the roof. Maybe others beside the four repaired the room. To bring someone to Jesus often takes many gifts. God designed it so we frequently need to utilize others in the body of Christ to bring people to Jesus. Others are needed in the discipling process.

We see many gifts in operation in this encounter with Jesus. Prayer is a vital gift that released the power of God. God gifts certain persons with the gift of intercession. Faith is a key. God gifts certain persons with the gift of faith. Leadership is a key and some have the gift of leadership. Mercy, service, helps, healing are also evident in this encounter.

As I Peter 1:10 NIV states: "Each one should use whatever gift he has received to serve others, faithfully administering God's grace in its various forms." Let's always remember it's important to invite others to help us bring people to Jesus.

Lord, help me to use whatever gift(s) you have given me and to invite others to work with me so many can come to Jesus and be healed. Amen.

March 4

Power in the Cross

Mark 2:4

"They (the four men) couldn't get to Jesus through the crowd, so they dug through the clay roof above his head. Then they lowered the sick man on his mat, right down in front of Jesus" (Mark 2:4 NLT).

If the devil can't squelch our evangelistic enthusiasm he will do his best to misdirect it. He will tell us we are better than other Christians because they don't seem interested in helping us. He may have us focus on some good psychological principles that we have learned at our latest seminar or in our Sunday school class. Often God can use these principles, but these principles do not have the power to deliver a person from death to life. Only Jesus can do that. Usually the more training we have the more we are tempted to trust our training than to trust Jesus for deliverance. Too often we trust in our psychological principles when Jesus is the only source of real deliverance.

The reason the psychological principles fall short is because they usually do not deal with the root of the problem which is our sin nature. We can take people through many good and helpful psychological steps and still not deal with their sinful self-centered nature. As long as that self-centered nature is not dealt with we are spinning our wheels. We may see progress but we do not see victory over sin.

Remember to take people to Jesus. Remember to keep the cross central. Paul wrote, "I decided to concentrate only on Jesus Christ and his death on the cross" (I Corinthians 2:2 NLT). Again he writes: "Everything else is worthless when compared with the priceless gain of knowing Christ Jesus my Lord…As a result, I can really know Christ and experience the mighty power that raised him from the dead. I can learn what it means to suffer with him, sharing in his death" (I Corinthians 3:8 & 10 NLT).

Did Jesus give the men what they wanted? Yes and No. He forgave the man's sins. They wanted physical healing. Might Jesus be teaching us that forgiveness is a greater gift than physical healing?

Lord, I want to bring people to you. Give spiritual healing and grant physical healing as you deem best. Thank you. Amen.

March 5

Holy Spirit Power

John 20:21-23

After the resurrection Jesus spoke to the disciples and said, "Peace be with you." Then he breathed on them and said to them, Receive the Holy Spirit" (John 20:23 NIV).

If you feel you need more courage, boldness or power and authority in your witness for Jesus ask him to "breathe on you," ask him to fill you with his spirit. Paul admonishes us to be filled with the Spirit. The Greek New Testament indicates this is a continuous filling. (See Ephesians 5:18.) In other words we lose the fullness of God's Spirit unless we go back to the source again and again to be refilled, reenergized by his Holy Spirit.

We may enjoy a great meal today, but tomorrow we need to eat and be filled again. So we need to be filled continually with the Holy Spirit.

Jesus says: "Ask and keep on asking and it shall be given you; seek and keep on seeking, and you shall find; knock and keep on knocking and the door shall be opened to you. For everyone who asks and keeps on asking receives, and he who seeks and keeps on seeking finds and to him who knocks and keeps on knocking the door shall be opened. What father among you if his son asks for a loaf of bread, will give him a stone; or if he asks for a fish will instead of a fish give him a serpent; Or if he asks for an egg, will give him a scorpion? If you then, evil-minded as you are, know how to give good gifts—gifts that are to an advantage—to your children, how much more will your heavenly Father give the Holy Spirit to those who ask and continue to ask Him!" (Luke 11:9-13 AMP.)

Don't be afraid or hindered by the various interpretations concerning the filling of the Holy Spirit. Don't for one minute get hung up on such controversial terms as baptism of the Holy Spirit, second work of grace, or whatever. Simply cling to the Lord, asking for His power and the fullness of the Holy Spirit.

Father, I need you. I am helpless without you. You alone have the power to draw people to yourself. Lord, I beg of you to bless me with more of your Holy Spirit. Through your Son Jesus I pray. Amen.

March 6

Power to Forgive Sins

John 20:23

"If you forgive anyone's sins, they are forgiven. If you refuse to forgive them, they are unforgiven" (John 20:23 NLT).

Doesn't this give us too much authority? There is nothing, no power whatsoever intrinsic or natural ability in any person that can forgive sin. But since Jesus is in us, he gives us this right and authority to announce his forgiveness to others, if they are willing to accept this forgiveness. We do not condemn people. (See John 3:17.) We ask them if they are willing to accept the acceptance Jesus has for them.

While humility, which includes repentance, is an absolute must to enter the kingdom of heaven we are also given authority. This authority is not based on our natural self, our authority is all through Jesus. He is our brother. (See Hebrews 2:11-13.) The most insignificant person in the Kingdom of God is greater than John the Baptist who was the greatest born among women. (See Matthew 11:11.) We are seated with Christ in heavenly places. (See Ephesians 2:6.) This has nothing to do with our good works but it is only because of God's grace that we have this position and therefore this authority.

As we explain to the pre-believer our need for a Savior, because of our sin, we can expect the Holy Spirit to convict and convince them of their need for a Savior. We might say, "I need God's forgiveness all the time. I get irritated and treat my wife or my children inappropriately as a Christian. I have thoughts of envy, jealousy, pride, impatience. I need forgiveness. Jesus is there to forgive me. What joy and freedom it is to walk in God's forgiving love. God has forgiven you. Are you ready to receive the forgiveness he has for you?

Jesus added that we have the power to retain someone's sins. While this is more difficult to accept, I believe if a person is arrogantly and deliberately living in sin they cannot be forgiven in that state. They are denying the application of the cross of Christ which is the only remedy for our sins.

Lord, help me never to abuse this power you give but to humbly realize that you entrust us with your Spirit of wisdom to minister to others. So help me God. Amen.

March 7

Wounded Healers

Matthew 18:23-35

Peter asked Jesus how many times he must forgive a brother when he sins against him. To answer that question, Jesus told the parable of the unmerciful servant. In this parable a man who owed the king a million dollars begs the king to have mercy on him by giving him more time to pay. The King forgave the debt, but the man who owed the debt never "heard" the kings answer. At least he lived as if he was in debt because he didn't apply this forgiveness to a fellow servant who owed him a few dollars.

When the king heard about this man's actions we are told: "In anger, his master turned him over to the jailers to be tortured, until he should pay back all he owed. This is how my heavenly Father will treat each of you unless you forgive your brother from your hearts" (vv. 34-35 NIV).

All of us are servants who are in debt far more than we could ever pay. In fact when you consider the wages of this servant, he would have needed more than 27,000 years to pay back the million dollars. He was hopelessly in debt. We are hopelessly in debt. Do we realize our indebtedness? Until we realize our indebtedness we will never be as grateful as we should be to our Lord who paid the debt for us on the cross.

"For you know that it was not with perishable things such as silver or gold that you were redeemed from the empty way of life handed down to you from your forefathers, but with the precious blood of Christ, a lamb without blemish or defect" (I Peter. 1:18-19 NIV).

Let's thank God continually for his great sacrifice, forgiving us so we can go free. In response to this freedom, let us gladly serve him with all our heart, soul, mind and strength.

Lord, thank you for the gift of your Son, a gift too wonderful for words. I'll serve you as long as I live. Amen.

March 8

Mary and Martha

John 11:17-44

It is helpful to observe Jesus relating to Mary and Martha in their grief following the death of their brother, Lazarus. When they learned that Jesus had finally come they both said to Jesus: "If you had been here, my brother would not have died" (vv. 21 and 32 NIV). However, Jesus responded to them differently.

To Martha who was more cognitive, more left-brain than Mary, he said, "Your brother will rise again…I am the resurrection and the life. He who believes in me will live, even though he dies; and whoever lives and believes in me will never die. Do you believe this?" (vv. 23-26 NIV) To Mary who is more feeling-oriented and emotional, John reports that Jesus was deeply moved in spirit and troubled. (See v. 33.) Then Jesus wept with Mary.

In reaching people with the Good News, it is necessary that we identify with people on a deep level. As we mature in our love and understanding of people, God will give us insight into their inner soul. He will teach us to be sensitive so they feel loved. God's love will flow through us. People tell us how we are to witness to them by what they say as they share their hurts and how they act but we have to listen and observe. We have to give ourselves to them—to love others as we love ourselves. They feel loved when they know we understand them. We must pray for this deep identification. God will answer our prayer as we do our part in making every effort to understand them.

Most people I had the joy of bringing to Jesus needed emotional understanding. Often their need was acceptance because of rejection, or overcoming guilt, or overcoming feelings of insignificance. If they ask intellectual questions we need some answers. Some have spiritual needs like those caught in cults, legalistic traditions or addictions. Jesus drew the seeker to himself. Seekers need to feel your love; if they don't like you, they will have a difficult time loving your Savior. Persevere, pray, evangelize. How wonderful it is that God has chosen to use us in this great task of bringing others to a life of discipleship in Christ. Are you inviting people to our Lord?

Lord, give me a heart of wisdom to really hear people. May your Holy Spirit use me today to bring people to you. Amen.

March 9

The Priority of Relationships

Luke 10:38-42

Luke 10:38-42 NIV reports that Jesus was on his way to Jerusalem but stopped in Bethany about two miles from Jerusalem where Martha and Mary lived. Martha welcomed him. "Her sister, Mary, sat at the Lord's feet, listening to what he taught. But Martha was worrying over the big dinner she was preparing. She came to Jesus and said, 'Lord, doesn't it seem unfair to you that my sister just sits here while I do all the work? Tell her to come and help me.' But the Lord said to her, 'My dear Martha, you are so upset over all these details! There is really only one thing worth being concerned about. Mary has discovered it—and I won't take it away from her."

Jesus was headed for the cross. The last thing he wanted was a banquet meal. He desired quiet. He preferred a relaxed conversation with someone whose heart was set on learning from her master. Martha wanted to love Jesus in the way she thought best. She did not take time to think of Jesus' real need. How often do we love people or try to show love to people in the way we like to be loved, rather than show love in the way they feel loved.

Jesus saw the heart of Mary as one who was a listener and a learner. Martha's heart while she desired to give sacrificial service was self-motivated in that she wanted to do things her way. My wife wants my heart more than my service. If she has my heart she will have my service. Let's take time to think, pray and discover the approach to others that they desire, so they feel loved and can receive our love.

Jesus desires relationship more than service. He desires worship more than our efforts to please him. God seeks worshippers (see John 4:23). After Mary sat at Jesus feet, I believe she could have served Jesus very well meeting his physical needs. Let's keep our priorities in order: worship first, service follows.

Lord, help me to fellowship with you, to know you more intimately, before I seek to serve you. Amen.

March 10

Love is the Key

I Corinthians 8:1,3

Paul wrote, "You think that everyone should agree with your perfect knowledge. While knowledge may make us feel important, it is love that really builds up the church... The person who loves God is the one God knows and cares for" (I Corinthians 8:1 & 3 NLT).

Francis of Assisi said that we are to witness 24/7 and if necessary use words. While I believe the majority of Christians are far too shy about verbalizing their faith, some place more emphasis on verbal witness and forget that love is absolutely necessary.

Paul writes, "If I could speak in any language in heaven or on earth, but didn't love others, I would only be making meaningless noise like a loud gong or a clanging cymbal. If I had the gift of prophecy, and if I knew all the mysteries of the future and knew everything about everything, but didn't love others, what good would I be? And if I had the gift of faith, so that I could speak to a mountain and make it move, without love I would be no good to anybody. If I gave everything I have to the poor and even sacrificed my body, I could boast about it; but if I didn't love others, I would be of no value whatsoever" (I Corinthians 13:1-3 NLT).

Jesus' number one emotional response mentioned in the Gospels is compassion! Jesus saw people as sheep that had been bruised, beaten, and confused. Rather than being filled with disdain, he was filled with love. (See Matthew 9:36.) Jesus, of course, was spiritually mature. As spiritual maturity increases, love and approachability increases. Do we really love and accept others? They can tell if we are genuine.

How can we increase our love level? The fruit (singular) of the Holy Spirit is love. (See Galatians 5:22 NIV.) In Ephesians 5:18 we are told to be filled with the Spirit. "Being filled" is in the present tense in the Greek, which means we are to keep on being filled. It's like eating. We are filled now, but a few hours from now we are ready to be filled again. Keep abiding in Jesus and he will fill you with his love.

Lord, fill me with your love. Amen.

March 11

Sacrifice is the Price

II Corinthians 4:11-12

"We live under constant danger of death because we serve Jesus, so that the life of Jesus will be obvious in our dying bodies. So we live in the face of death, but it has resulted in eternal life for you" (II Corinthians 4:11-12 NIV).

Did you notice how our life affects others, even to the point of bringing eternal life to them? At times we are tempted to feel that our life is not an effective witness. I believe there is a principle here: the more we suffer and face difficult circumstances and rise above those circumstances, the more Jesus is lifted up. In many countries where there is persecution the church grows. Of course there are other countries where persecution seems to be so intense that the Christian church is almost wiped out, at least for a time.

Just before Jesus went to the cross he prayed: "As you sent me into the world, I have sent them into the world. For them I sanctify myself, that they too may be truly sanctified" (John 17:18-19 NIV). *The Message* Bible puts verse 19 this way: "I give them a mission in the world. I'm consecrating myself for their sake so they'll be truth-consecrated in their mission."

Jesus consecrates himself for us. Jesus not only died on the cross for us but he lived daily for us. That's how we are to live not only for him but for others.

Frequently, Paul thanks the Lord for the Christians in his churches because they are an encouragement to him. Even though there were many problems in those churches, he could see the positive side. He writes: "You and I may be mutually encouraged by each other's faith" (Romans 1:12 NIV). Peter writes: "Even if they accuse you of doing wrong, they will see your honorable behavior, and they will believe and give honor to God when he comes to judge the world" (I Peter 2:12 NLT).

Father, help me to live faithfully for you so that those around me may be encouraged to live for you as well. Through the strong and powerful name of Jesus we pray. Amen.

March 12

Sent Ones

John 17:18

"As you sent me into the world, I have sent them into the world" (John 17:18 NIV).

We are sent. Many Christians believe they are to serve others, but are not conscious of being sent. We have a mission, a charge, a mandate. We are commissioned by Jesus, God's Son! Note with what authority we are sent. Jesus says, "As the Father sent me I am sending you." Jesus didn't say we are sent differently than he was. We have the same authority that Jesus had.

The same truth is stated in the Great Commission: "All authority in heaven and on earth has been given to me. Therefore go and make disciples of all nations, baptizing…, and teaching them to obey everything I have commanded you. And surely I am with you always, to the very end of the age" (Matthew 28:18-20 NIV). As a result of Jesus authority we are sent to go and make disciples.

The question I am often faced with is, why are we not as effective as the apostles? While I do not have the complete answer, notice how the apostles became much more effective after Pentecost. Peter is a powerful example. Before Pentecost he denied the Lord, after Pentecost he boldly preached and thousands were saved. He boldly stood up to the authorities and suffered and sang in prison because of his faith. Let's be conscious of the Holy Spirit's power flowing through us.

Paul had power to do unusual miracles, "so that even when handkerchiefs or cloths that had touched his skin were placed on sick people, they were healed of their diseases, and any evil spirits within them came out" (Acts 19:11 NLT). But later, near his death, he instructs Pastor Timothy to take a little wine for the sake of his frequent illness. Paul had times when the Holy Spirit was not flowing through him in exactly the same way. Even so the Gospel was advancing and the world was being reached.

We too will be effective witnesses for our Lord as we go forth in the power of the Holy Spirit. (See Acts 1:8.)

Jesus, thank you for sending me to my world just as you came to our world. Help me to move out in your power today. Amen.

March 13

Encouragement

I Thessalonians 5:11,14

"Encourage one another and build each other up just as, you are doing" (I Thessalonians 5:11NLT). "Encourage the timid" (v.14). "May our Lord Jesus Christ himself and God our Father, who loved us and by his grace gave us eternal encouragement and good hope, encourage and strengthen you in every good deed and word" (II Thessalonians 2:16-17 NIV).

Someone has said there are three things people need: "Encouragement, encouragement, encouragement, and if that doesn't work try encouragement." Paul says to the Corinthians, "Encourage each other" (II Cor. 13:11 NLT). Again he writes: "You know that we treated each of you as a father treats his own children. We pleaded with you, encouraged you and urged you to live your lives in a way that God would consider worthy. For he called you into his kingdom to share his glory" (I Thessalonians 2:11-12 NLT). Just as a father needs to encourage his children we need to encourage each other.

"Think of ways to encourage one another to outbursts of love and good deeds. And let us not neglect our meeting together, as some people do, but encourage and warn each other, especially now that the day of his coming back again is drawing near" (Hebrews 10:24-25 NLT).

In the New Testament, according to the *NIV Complete Concordance*, "encourage" in its several forms appears 46 times. Luke depicts Paul as an apostle of encouragement: "Paul sent for the believers and encouraged them. Then he said good-bye and left for Macedonia. Along the way, he encouraged the believers in all the towns he passed through" (Acts 20:1-2 NLT).

As you relate to people, be an encourager. Be conscious of your language, your tone of voice, your faith in building others up. Some people have the gift of encouragement, but I believe as we mature we mature in the use of all the spiritual gifts. Ask God to help you grow in the gift of encouragement. Everyone needs encouragement. Encouragement will help open the door for you to share the Good News of Jesus.

Dear God, make me an encourager today, especially as I meet others who are discouraged. Give me words to say that point them to Jesus the greatest encourager of all. Thank you for your Holy Spirit who is the Spirit of encouragement. Amen.

March 14

When I am Weak Then I Am Strong

II Corinthians 12:9

The Lord said to Paul, "My gracious favor is all you need. My power works best in your weakness" (II Corinthians 12:9 NLT).

God gave Paul a thorn in the flesh to keep him from being proud. Three times he begged God to remove it. God told him, "My grace is enough; it's all you need. My strength comes into its own in your weakness" (v.9 Msg). Then Paul responds: "Once I heard that, I was glad to let it happen. I quit focusing on the handicap and began appreciating the gift. It was a case of Christ's strength moving in on my weakness. Now I take limitations in stride, with good cheer, accidents, opposition, bad breaks. I just let Christ take over! And so the weaker I get, the stronger I become" (II Corinthians 12:9-10 Msg).

All we need is God's grace! Do I believe that? Life, by its very nature, has times of discouragement and bad news. Do I take bad news in stride because Jesus was not caught off guard? He knew about it before I heard about it. Paul learned to glory in tribulation. (See Romans 5:3 KJV.) Whatever the situation is, Jesus is sufficient. When others see his sufficiency in us the light of Christ shines brighter and brighter. They are drawn to the Savior.

How do we reach this level of maturity? We must deny ourselves and take up our cross and follow Christ. (See Matthew 16:24.) We must surrender ourselves to him. No matter what he asks we have one answer: "YES Lord!" "Anyone who intends to come with me has to let me lead. You're not in the driver's seat; I am. Don't run from suffering, embrace it. Follow me and I'll show you how. Self-help is no help at all. Self-sacrifice is the way, my way, to finding yourself, your true self" (Matthew 16:24-25 Msg).

Lord, when bad news comes, when disappointment comes, I choose to trust you. In faith I thank you realizing you are in control. In my weakness you are strong. Teach me the lessons I am to learn and use me for your glory. Thank you. Amen.

March 15

Does Jesus get Disgusted with Us?

Matthew 17:17

When James and John came down the mountain after seeing Jesus transfigured before their eyes, they were immediately inundated by a huge crowd. A father had brought his demon possessed son to the other disciples, but they were unable to cast out the demon. Jesus' response is stated in Matthew 17:17 NIV, "Unbelieving and perverse generation," Jesus replied, "How long shall I stay with you? How long shall I put up with you?"

The Message Bible puts it this way: Jesus said, "What a generation! No sense of God! No focus to your lives! How many times do I have to go over these things? How much longer do I have to put up with this?" Later the disciples asked Jesus why they couldn't cast the demon from the boy. (See v. 19.) He replied, "Because you have so little faith. I tell you the truth, if you have faith as small as a mustard seed, you can say to this mountain, 'Move from here to there' and it will move. Nothing will be impossible for you" (vv. 20-21 NIV).

A few verses later in Matthew 18:4-5 NIV, the disciples were asking about rank in God's kingdom? Jesus said, "Whoever humbles himself like this child is the greatest in the kingdom of heaven. And whoever welcomes a little child like this in my name welcomes me."

Children trust their parents for food, clothing and shelter. They trust their parents for everything. Too often we worry, which displeases God.

What disturbs Jesus more than anything else? Our lack of faith. Our lack of trust. How do we get more faith? Paul writes, "Faith comes from hearing the message and the message is heard through the word of Christ" (Romans 10:17 NIV). May the Lord help us to feast on the Word so our faith can grow.

The writer of Hebrews says, "Without faith it is impossible to please God, because anyone who comes to him must believe that he exists and that he rewards those who earnestly seek him" (Hebrews 11:6 NIV). As we feast on the Word. and see God's faithfulness in our daily lives we grow in faith.

Lord help my unbelief. Help my faith to grow and mature. In Jesus' name. Amen.

March 16

Power for Witness

Acts 1:8

The final words of Jesus were: "You will receive power when the Holy Spirit comes on you; and you will be my witnesses in Jerusalem, and in all Judea and Samaria, and to the ends of the earth" (Acts 1:8 NIV).

Final words are important words. Here Jesus states our purpose for life: to be witnesses. The Greek word is "matures," which means martyrs. This implies that we are commissioned by Jesus to share the Good News even to the point of death.

This was not the first time the disciples heard this message. In Luke 10 Jesus told the seventy disciples he was sending them out as lambs among wolves. He had exclaimed more than once that if they were going to be his followers they must take up their cross.

Jesus commissions us in Matthew 28:18-20 that we are to go and make disciples of all people…and that he will be with us to the end of the age. Since Jesus is with us we need not fear. If we are going to be faithful witnesses we must trust the Lord Jesus to take care of us even if our witness leads to death.

In the early 20th century some missionaries did not pack a suitcase. They built their own caskets and used them as suitcases believing they would not return. In the Great Commission Jesus told us to go. He didn't promise we would return. He did promise he would never forsake us. As Job says, "Though he slay me yet will I put my trust in him" (Job 13:15 KJV).

It may be helpful to remind ourselves that approximately 150,000 persons give their life for the witness of the Good News each year.

Lord, help me to be faithful to the point of death. Amen.

March 17

The Priority of our Witness

Acts 1:4-8

Just before Jesus ascended to heaven he said: "Do not leave Jerusalem, but wait for the gift my Father promised, which you have heard me speak about. For John baptized with water, but in a few days you will be baptized with the Holy Spirit." So when they met together, they asked him, "Lord, are you at this time going to restore the kingdom to Israel?"

He said to them: It is not for you to know the times or dates the Father has set by his own authority. But you will receive power when the Holy Spirit comes on you; and you will be my witnesses in Jerusalem, and in all Judea and Samaria, and to the ends of the earth" (Acts 1:4-8 NIV).

Today many Christians get caught in the debate concerning the date of the Lord's return. As pastor I have had persons in my congregation who were "sure" the Lord had to return in a particular year because of their understanding of a prophecy and its "perfect" fit with today's world scene.

Bestselling "Christian" books focus on the end times. But here Jesus says there is something more important than the date of my return. We are to focus on witnessing or sharing the Good News in "Jerusalem" or across the street, then in the neighboring town and state, and finally around the world. While the return of our Lord is a central doctrine of the Christian faith the date of his return is not for us to know. It is known only by the Father. (See Mark 13:32 and Acts 1:7.) Don't get trapped into arguing over the date. Point people to Jesus and the necessity of knowing him so they can experience eternal life.

The apostles took Jesus' command seriously as they spread the Good News first in Jerusalem, Samaria, Ethiopia and then throughout the known world. Many even died because of their faithful witness.

Let's remember Jesus' directive to his disciples concerning the date of his return and apply it to our own lives.

Lord Jesus, help me to keep my focus on being a faithful witness for you today. Amen.

March 18

The Necessity of the Holy Spirit

Acts 1:8 and John 20:19-23

"You will receive power when the Holy Spirit comes on you; and you will be my witnesses in Jerusalem, and in all Judea and Samaria, and to the ends of the earth" (Acts 1:8 NIV).

After the resurrection, his disciples were gathered with the doors locked. Jesus appeared to them and said, "Peace be with you!" After he said this, he showed them his hands and side. The disciples were overjoyed when they saw the Lord. Again Jesus said, "Peace be with you! As the Father has sent me, I am sending you." And with that he breathed on them and said, "Receive the Holy Spirit. If you forgive anyone his sins, they are forgiven; if you do not forgive them, they are not forgiven" (John 20:19-23).

"I have come to understand that it is completely impossible for even a single lost person…to become a Christian unless a great miracle takes place. Lost human souls are firmly chained prisoners of Satan and his demonic forces. They cannot be argued into the kingdom of God because their problem is not an intellectual one. Nor is there any point in trying to change their outward behavior if they do not have the inward spiritual power that only Jesus can give. The Bible clearly says that every person outside of Christ is spiritually dead, and a battle needs to be waged for his or her soul. People living outside the grace of Jesus Christ are trapped by the devil,…(II Tim. 2:26).

"The demonic forces that hold souls captive are far more powerful than we are, in our own strength. There is not the slightest possibility that we can lead anyone to the foot of the cross unless Jesus himself becomes involved. Only his power can save a sinner. The good news is that we can be completely sure that Jesus will help us to reach the lost for him, for the Word of God says, 'He is patient with you, not wanting anyone to perish, but everyone to come to repentance'" (II Peter 3:9). [viii]

Lord, help me to always be conscious that unless the Holy Spirit is working in the heart of the unbeliever, my efforts are useless. Amen.

March 19

Not Either But Both: Authority and Power

Acts 1:8

Before he ascended to heaven, Jesus gave what I believe are his most important words. He commissioned us by saying: "All authority in heaven and on earth has been given to me. Therefore go and make disciples of all nations, baptizing them in the name of the Father and of the Son and of the Holy Spirit, and teaching them to obey everything I have commanded you. And surely I will be with you always, to the very end of the age" (Matthew 28:18-20 NIV).

"You will receive power when the Holy Spirit comes on you; and you will be my witnesses in Jerusalem, and in all Judea and Samaria, and to the ends of the earth" (Acts 1:8 NIV).

Jesus assures us of both authority and power. It's one thing to have authority and another to have power. In years past I was a substitute school teacher. I had the authority because of the position of a teacher but I did not always have the power. Being a young substitute school teacher in a correctional institution for boys was quite a challenge. I had the position, but I had to earn their respect. I have witnessed situations where the principal had the authority but lacked the respect of the students.

On the other hand one can have the power but lack authority. As a parent you may be bigger and stronger than your child, but it seems that often the child is in charge of the situation. The parents lacked the "power" to discipline. Parents and policemen have the position, but often do not have the power or dynamic they need to maintain respect. A neighbor may have the power to control your neighborhood but not the authority. Therefore he or she is usually resented by their neighbors.

Jesus has given us both the authority and the power to witness for him. Let's share Jesus with humbleness and with confident boldness. Follow the leading of the Holy Spirit as you witness with Jesus' authority and power.

Father, thank you for giving me both the authority and the power to be a witness for your today. Amen.

March 20

Converts or Disciples?

Matthew 28:18-20

The last words of anyone are usually words that are especially important to us. Some of Jesus last words are recorded for us in Matthew 28, usually referred to as the Great Commission.

"I have been given complete authority in heaven and on earth. Therefore go and make disciples of all the nations, baptizing them in the name of the Father and the Son and the Holy Spirit. Teach these new disciples to obey all the commands I have given you. And be sure of this: I am with you always, even to the end of the age" (Matthew 28:18-20 NLT).

One of the reasons the church in the United States is so anemic is because we have made converts rather than disciples. This, to me, is about the same as a mother who is about to give birth. She goes to the hospital and is blessed with a beautiful healthy child. After a short stay, she is dismissed from the hospital with her baby but instead of taking the baby home, she leaves it on the street in front of the hospital to take care of itself. Of course, the baby will die.

That to me is often how we treat new Christians. I believe we are doing much better than in past decades but we need to always remember Jesus commands us to make disciples, not converts. It is usually much more time consuming and much more demanding to grow mature Christians than to make converts. Jesus spent most of his time with the disciples, training them so they could reproduce.

Remember how Paul worked diligently with the churches he started so they would grow to the fullness of the stature of our Lord. Perhaps his most vigorous dedication was to the church at Ephesus. "Remember the three years I was with you—my constant watch and care over you night and day, and my many tears for you" (Acts 20:31 NLT).

While Paul was primarily an apostle and an evangelist, he also focused on making disciples, not just converts.

Lord Jesus help me to be diligent in following through with those I introduce to salvation, so they in turn become faithful disciples able to disciple others. Amen.

March 21

Jonah

Jonah 1:3

If God can use Jonah, he can use you!

The Lord told Jonah: "Get up and go to the great city of Nineveh! Announce my judgment against it, because I have seen how wicked its people are… But Jonah got up and went in the opposite direction in order to get away from the Lord. He went down to the sea coast, to the port of Joppa, where he found a ship leaving for Tarshish. He bought a ticket and went on board, hoping that by going away to the west, he could escape from the Lord" (Jonah 1:2-3 NLT).

How often has the Lord asked you to be a witness and you went in the opposite direction? Have you lived beside your neighbor for years or worked beside your peers and never took the opportunity to share your faith? Have you sat beside an unsaved friend in class for a semester and never prayed for them or shared your faith with them? Do they know you are a follower of Jesus? Since Jesus commissioned or mandated us to share the Gospel (Matthew 28:18-20 and Acts 1:8), we have a responsibility to not only live our faith but to proclaim our faith in word and deed.

John writes that if we ask anything according to his will he will hear us. (See I John 5:14.) Since we know it is his will that none perish and that all come to repentance (II Peter 3:9), we can ask in faith knowing he will help us witness to our extended family, our neighbors and our work peers.

Ask Jesus to open your eyes to see the opportunities to share your faith. Pray for courage and Holy Spirit boldness to speak with a gentle but confident word of God's grace and love. Remember he promised never to leave you. He will give you the words to say if you ask him. Be sure your life is lined up with your message.

Lord, forgive me for my timidity. Help me to share my faith. Thank you that you will enable me to be your faithful and effective witness for you today. Amen.

March 22

Always Be Ready To Give an Answer!

I Peter 3:15

"Always be prepared to give an answer to everyone who asks you to give the reason for the hope that you have. But do this with gentleness and respect, keeping a clear conscience…" (I Peter 3:15-16 NIV).

Some Christians never talk about their faith. They have the philosophy: my life speaks for Christ or my life is my witness. In one sense this is the most egotistical philosophy anyone could have. In essence they are saying my life is perfect. Just look at what I do, or how I act and you will see Jesus and who he is. This is a half-truth. (Admittedly there is no such thing as a half-truth.) It's true that we are Christians, i.e. little Christ's, modeling the life of Christ. The problem is that none of us are perfect models. John, writing to Christians, says: "If we claim to be without sin, we deceive ourselves and the truth is not in us" (I John 1:8 NIV). James writes: "We all stumble in many ways" (James 3:2 NIV).

People need more than models. They need a Savior and Lord. Our life, as imperfect as it is, must point people to Jesus, but there are times when we are ineffective as a model so we need to verbalize our faith. We need to explain that Jesus is our source of life. We must share with the pre-believer that we need daily cleansing because of our sinful nature. This means there are times when we do not model the life of Christ. He was sinless. We are not.

We need to witness both in word and deed. As James writes: "Faith without deeds is dead" (James 3:26 NIV). Peter writes, "Be ready to give an answer to those who ask about why you have a hope for the future."

Lord, help me to live faithfully for you, and to boldly and confidently share with others the Good News of salvation. Amen.

March 23

Is the Order Important?

Matthew 28:18-20

Jesus gave us the great commission: "All authority in heaven and on earth has been given to me. Therefore, go and make disciples of all nations, baptizing them in the name of the Father and of the Son and of the Holy Spirit, and teaching them to obey everything I have commanded you..." (Matthew 28:18-20 NIV).

It's clear in Jesus' commission that we are to make disciples. How do we make disciples? We make disciples by baptizing and teaching. Is the fact that Jesus placed baptizing before teaching important? On the Day of Pentecost, Peter preached and three thousand responded to his message. Peter said, "Repent and be baptized....for the forgiveness of your sins. And you will receive the gift of the Holy Spirit" (Acts 2:38 NIV). If a person is repentant and desires to be baptized, we need to let the Holy Spirit do His work in molding their life. Our responsibility is to teach. It is the Spirit that transforms us and moves us from one degree of glory to another. We put to death the sinful earthly things lurking within and clothe ourselves with Christ-like qualities. (See Colossians 3:1-17.) Growth cannot be legislated by us. That's the work of the Spirit.

We have extensive teaching in the New Testament concerning how a Christian should live. These passages were written to Christians. The early church was messy because everyone needs daily cleansing from sin.

I believe I have too often set a standard for new Christians to attain before I baptized them. This can lead to legalism rather than freedom in the Spirit. Paul writes: "Christ has set us free to live a free life. So take your stand! Never again let anyone put a harness of slavery on you. I am emphatic about this. The moment any one of you submits to circumcision or any other rule-keeping system, at that same moment Christ's hard-won gift of freedom is squandered" (Galatians 5:1-2 Msg). (See also Acts 15:19.)

Paul balances this with: "You...were called to be free. But do not use your freedom to indulge the sinful nature, rather serve one another in love. The entire law is summed up in a single command: 'Love your neighbor as yourself.'" (Galatians 5:13-14 NIV).

Lord Jesus, thank you for the work of your Holy Spirit molding us into Christlikeness. Amen.

March 24

Chosen by God

Ephesians 1:4

"He chose us in him before the creation of the world to be holy and blameless in his sight" (Ephesians 1:4 NIV).

"You didn't choose me, remember; I chose you and put you in the world to bear fruit, fruit that won't spoil. As fruit bearers, whatever you ask the Father in relation to me, he gives you" (John 15:15-16 Msg).

Are you conscious of being chosen? God chose you before the world was created. Why did he choose you—to be holy and blameless and to bear fruit that doesn't spoil, fruit that will last for eternity. What a high calling!

Who is chosen? Jesus said many are called or invited but few are chosen. (See Matthew 11:22.) The "many" includes everyone. "He (the Lord) is patient with you, not wanting anyone to perish, but everyone to come to repentance" (II Peter 3:9 NIV).

In elementary school we chose sides to play games. It felt good to be chosen. If you were a poor player you were chosen last. That did not feel good. We were chosen before the world was created. We were not some afterthought with God. We were not last or even close to the end of the line.

We were chosen to be blameless in God's eyes! That is only possible through Jesus Christ. He is our righteousness, holiness and redemption. (See I Corinthians 1:30.) We were chosen to bear eternal fruit. God could have created robots but he chose to use you and me.

There is a mystery here. God wanted to shower his love and be in relationship with humanity, so he created us with freedom to love him or reject him. As we love him with all our "heart, soul, and mind" (see Matthew 22:37), he uses us to impact the lives of countless others for eternity.

How privileged we are to be chosen by God for his wonderful work of being involved in extending his Kingdom.

Thank you Lord, for the privilege of working with you to bring many to glory. What an awesome privilege you have given to us. Amen.

March 25

Filled With the Spirit

Ephesians 5:18

"Let the Holy Spirit fill and control you" (Ephesians 5:18 NLT).

"Jesus full of the Holy Spirit, left the Jordan River. He was led by the Spirit to go out into the wilderness where the devil tempted him for forty days" (Luke 4:1-2 NLT).

"Then Jesus returned to Galilee, filled with the Holy Spirit's power" (Luke 4:14. NLT).

"The Lord's healing power was strongly with Jesus" (Luke 5:17 NLT).

"Jesus called together his twelve disciples. He gave them the power to force out evil spirits and to heal every kind of disease and sickness" (Matthew 10:1 CEV).

On the day of Pentecost, "everyone present was filled with the Holy Spirit" (Acts 2:4 NLT). Jesus breathed on them before and told them to receive the Holy Spirit but I believe this was not a filling as Pentecost had not come at that point. (See John 20:22.)

In Acts 10:44-45 the same gift was given to the Gentiles as to the Jews at Pentecost.

These seven accounts along with others indicate to me there are degrees of the Holy Spirit's power. Apparently even in Jesus life there were times when the Spirit was there to heal and other times when that was not the case. (See Matthew 13:58, Mark 6:5.)

We need the power of the Spirit to be victorious Christians. Paul lists three results of being filled with the Spirit: our hearts will be filled with music, we will have a thankful attitude and we will submit to one another. (See Ephesians 5:19-20). Ask the Spirit to fill you before you leave your house in the morning. Ask him to empower you so the pre-believers are convicted of their need to accept Jesus. (See Acts 1:8.) If you are confronted with a person who is ill and the Spirit has given you faith, pray for their healing. Ask God to fill you with his Spirit for your ministry.

Lord, fill me with your Holy Spirit so people will be aware of God's work today and respond in obedient faith. Amen.

March 26

Stench or Perfume?

II Corinthians 2:14-16

"Thanks be to God, who made us his captives and leads us along in Christ's triumphal procession. Now wherever we go he uses us to tell others about the Lord and to spread the Good News like a sweet perfume. Our lives are a fragrance presented by Christ to God. But this fragrance is perceived differently by those being saved and those perishing. To those who are perishing we are a fearful smell of death and doom. But to those who are being saved we are a life-giving perfume. And who is adequate for such a task as this?" (II Corinthians 2:14-16 NLT).

Like me I'm sure you have met people who are full of the Holy Spirit. Their joy, peace and patience radiates from them. It's great to be with them. You don't want to leave their presence. When you do need to leave their presence, your spirits have been lifted and your day is transformed. You wish every day could be like this.

Then there are others who are not receptive to anything that is pure and of good report. If you have to work beside them, you pray for God's grace to be a positive influence on them and to see God's Spirit soften their hearts so they can begin to see Jesus in you.

These people resent your presence. They joke with others about your faith and your pure life. They wish you were not there so they could live their life without being reminded and convicted of their sin.

Paul reminds us that Jesus leads us in his triumphal procession, since wherever we go, his Spirit shines through our life. The triumphal procession was the procession of victorious soldiers returning from the battle with the loot, and the captives marching in submission. Picture yourself with Jesus marching and leading this triumphal procession as your life radiates the aroma of our Lord.

Lord, may my life be a sweet perfume to those I meet today. Amen.

March 27

Are You Tired?

II Corinthians 4:14-18 and Luke 15

"We know that the same God who raised our Lord Jesus will also raise us with Jesus and present us to himself along with you. … And as God's grace brings more and more people to Christ, there will be great thanksgiving and God will receive more and more glory. That is why we never give up. Though our bodies are dying, our spirits are being renewed every day. For our present troubles are quite small and won't last very long. Yet they produce for us an immeasurable great glory that will last forever! So we don't look at the troubles we can see right now, rather we look forward to what we have not yet seen. For the troubles we see will soon be over, but the joys to come will last forever" (II Corinthians 4:14-18 NLT).

I have conducted approximately one hundred and fifty funerals in my fifty years of pastoral ministry. These fantastic words of Paul have blessed countless persons in grief. These words also bring much encouragement to each of us. Our spirits are being renewed day by day. One pastor said, "I would be grateful if some people I pastor would be renewed once a year let alone once a day."

God's mercies are new every morning so why shouldn't we be renewed every day? (See Lamentation 3:22.)

We never give up! Why not? Because God's grace brings more and more people to Jesus. Jesus says, "Heaven is happier over one lost sinner who returns to God than over ninety-nine others who are righteous and haven't strayed away" (Luke 15:7). "There is joy in the presence of God's angels when even one sinner repents" (v.10). "We had to celebrate this happy day. For your brother was dead and has come back to life! He was lost but now he is found!" (v. 32. NLT).

There is no greater joy than seeing people come to Christ.

Lord, help me to focus, not on my troubles but on the joy of seeing people come to you. Amen.

March 28

Joy in Parting

John 16:7-11

"It is actually best for you that I go away, because if I don't, the Counselor won't come. If I do go away, he will come because I will send him to you. And when he comes he will convince the world of its sin, and of God's righteousness, and of the coming judgment. The world's sin is unbelief in me. Righteousness is available because I go to the Father, and you will see me no more. Judgment will come because the prince of this world has already been judged" (John 16:7-11 NLT).

When our best friend moves away or dies there is sorrow, not joy. How could Jesus tell the disciples they should be joyful because he is leaving?

Jesus is sending the "Paraclete" which means he is sending the Comforter, or Encourager, or Advocate or Counselor. The Paraclete or Holy Spirit is all of these and more. In the body, Jesus was confined by human limitations of place and time. The Spirit has no limitations. Now the promise that Jesus would be with us always would be a reality. (See Matthew 28:19.) We can have continual fellowship with the great God of the universe. That's the reason for the joyful parting.

The Spirit will do at least three things: (1) he will convince and reprove the world of its sin. The world's sin is unbelief in Jesus. (2) The Spirit convinces us of our wrong, our sin, and he convinces us of the need for a Savior. (3) The Spirit convinces us that there is judgment to come.

Remember the Holy Spirit is with us. Our responsibility is to share the Good News of eternal life in Christ. It's the Spirit that brings conviction to the unbeliever.

Lord, thank you for sending the Holy Spirit who lives in us. Teach me to tune into his guidance. Help me to obey his voice today. Amen.

March 29

Come into Community

Revelations 22:17 and Matthew 11: 28-29

"The Spirit and the bride say, 'Come.' Let each one who hears them say, 'Come.' Let the thirsty ones come—anyone who wants to. Let them come and drink the water of life without charge" (Revelations 22:17 NLT).

The word "come" appears approximately 2,300 times in the Bible. Let's invite people to come to Jesus. One of the greatest needs of humanity is relationships and community. Misbehavior in prison is often punished by placing people in isolation. We are meant to live in relationship with others and with God. It was not good for Adam to be alone so God created a helper for him. (See Genesis 2:18.) Jesus longs for our fellowship and our worship. (See John 4:23.)

He said, "Are you tired? Worn out? Burned out on religion? Come to me. Get away with me and you'll recover your life. I'll show you how to take a real rest. Walk with me and work with me—watch how I do it. Learn the unforced rhythms of grace. I won't lay anything heavy or ill-fitting on you. Keep company with me and you'll learn to live freely and lightly" (Matthew 11:28-29 Msg).

Again Jesus said, "If anyone is thirsty, let him come to me and drink. Whoever believes in me,... streams of living water will flow from within him.' By this, he meant the Spirit, whom those who believed in him were later to receive" (John 7:37-38 NIV).

James writes: "Come near to God and he will come near to you" (James 4:8 NIV).

Isaiah says, "Come, all you who are thirsty, come to the waters; and you who have no money, come, buy and eat! Come, buy wine and milk without money and without cost. Why spend money on what is not bread, and your labor on what does not satisfy? Listen, listen to me, and eat what is good, and your soul will delight in the richest of fare" (Isaiah 55:1-2 NIV).

Jesus said, "You diligently study the Scriptures because you think that by them you possess eternal life. These are the Scriptures that testify about me, yet you refuse to come to me to have life" (John 5:39-40 NIV). Come to Jesus today. Invite others to come, too.

Jesus, thank you for the invitation to come to yourself. I accept your invitation with deep gratitude! Amen.

March 30

Keep Your Focus

John 12:32

"When I am lifted up from the earth I will draw all men to myself" (John 12:32 NIV).

"No one can come to Jesus unless the Father who sent me draws him, and I will raise him up on the last day" (John 6:44 NIV). The Greek word for "draws" can be translated "drag". The Amplified version reads: "No one is able to come to Me unless the Father Who sent Me attracts and draws him and gives him the desire to come to Me; and then I will raise him from the dead at the last day."

How does the Father draw people to Jesus? Verse 32 says he draws people to himself when we lift up Jesus. Do you and I lift up Jesus? Some wear a cross but unless we take up our cross and live as he designed for us to live, we are not lifting him up. There is no other name whereby we must be saved but there is no other name that is more offensive to the world than the name of "Jesus." Let's be bold and reverently use the name of Jesus. It is powerful, beyond any other name!

He alone is the answer to our needs. We can use our psychology, our logic, our common sense but it is only Jesus who can give us the Bread of Life. (See John 6:35.)

"All that the Father gives me will come to me, and whoever comes to me I will never drive away" (John 6:37 NIV). Let's pray for the Father to draw people to himself. Pray for his Holy Spirit to draw them. He will use you in the process of bringing people to Jesus. Remember that it is only through his Spirit that they are drawn to Jesus who is the giver of eternal life. And when they come to him he will never reject them or drive them away.

Father, help me to always keep my focus on you. You, and you alone, can bring a lost soul into abundant life. Amen.

March 31

Whose Will is Important?

John 6: 37-40

"I have come down from heaven not to do my will but to do the will of him who sent me. And this is the will of him who sent me, that I shall lose none of all that he has given me, but raise them at the last day. For the Father's will is that everyone who looks to the Son and believes in him shall have eternal life, and I will raise him up at the last day" (John 6:37-40 NIV).

Jesus came to do the will of the Father. Why were we born: not to do our will but the will of Jesus. As long as we are alive we will make the choice of our will or Jesus' will. When God reveals his will to us, we must not deliberate. We must say, "Yes, Lord." Delayed obedience is often disobedience. If we ask our children to clean their room and they say later, and we meant now, that is disobedience. We may give grace but how much more pleasing it is to the parent if obedience is immediate.

The will is key. Let's learn to surrender our will. A child who argues about a request does not make for a pleasant atmosphere in the home. If the child loves and understands the parent's request, there is no need for an argument or even questions. The child trusts and obeys the parents. As we mature in our faith we don't need to ask a lot of questions. We step out in obedience to the Lord's will in our daily walk. When the angel came to Mary informing her that she will bear the Son of God she responded, "I am the Lord's servant, and I am willing to accept whatever he wants" (Luke 1:38 NLT).

The more education we have, the more likely it is for us to be tempted to raise questions or to argue that our will is better than God's will. We must learn to put our will, our knowledge, yes even common sense aside and trust our Father. He knows best.

Lord, forgive me when I want to question your will or argue that my will is best. Help me to accept your will and act in prompt obedience. Thank you for your grace. Amen.

April 1

Where is Your Focus?

John 12:32

"When I am lifted up from the earth I will draw all men to myself" (John 12:32 NIV).

Recently I attended a celebration designed to highlight the history of a church. One person after another talked about the relationships that encouraged them through the years. I was conscious that no one mentioned Jesus. No one thanked Jesus for his faithfulness again and again through those many years. We sang about him. We did not sing directly to him but about him. To me there is a big difference in worship if I sing about him or sing to him. It's like saying to you, "My wife is wonderful," instead of saying to my wife, "Honey, you are wonderful."

Maybe Jesus doesn't mind when we talk about all the wonderful times we have when we come together at church, but wouldn't it be appropriate to thank him personally and for the congregation to express thanks directly to him? Isn't that what we are going to do in heaven? Let's get used to it now. Let's enjoy the power that flows from this kind of heart worship. Worship from our spirit to his Spirit. (See John 4:24). We can learn from a picture of worship in heaven.

"I looked and there before me was a great multitude that no one could count, from every nation, tribe, people and language, standing before the throne and in front of the Lamb. They were wearing white robes and were holding palm branches in their hands. And they cried out in a loud voice; 'Salvation belongs to our God, who sits on the throne, and to the Lamb.'

"All the angels were standing around the throne and around the elders and the four living creatures. They fell down on their faces before the throne and worshiped God, saying: 'Amen! Praise and glory and wisdom and thanks and honor and power and strength be to our God for ever and ever. Amen!'" (Revelation 7:9-12 NIV).

You will find a new power and joy in your worship when you express your worship directly to God.

Lord Jesus, you are everything to me. I will lift you up today! Amen.

April 2

Criticism Often Comes From Within the Church

Acts 11:1-3

"The apostles and the brothers throughout Judea heard that the Gentiles also had received the word of God. So when Peter went up to Jerusalem, the circumcised believers criticized him and said, 'You went into the house of uncircumcised men and ate with them'" (Acts 11:1-3 NIV).

When you love people and witness to them, the Holy Spirit will open their hearts to receive the Word of God. As you introduce them to your church family, there will likely be some who are uncomfortable because these new seekers or these new Christians will be different. They have not been trained in the church traditions, custom, liturgy and protocol. They have a different culture. Their music tastes are different. Their lifestyle is different. This will make some church people very uncomfortable.

If these new people are shy and stay in the background, not rocking the boat, all may go well. Most older traditional congregations can accept new persons as long as they sit quietly in the pew and give in the offering, but if they make suggestions or are moved into church leadership, then the tension begins to rise. One church authority reports that the crisis comes when new believers number about 15% of the congregation. At that point, the new people become a threat.

The best way to confront this evil is for the leadership to keep the Great Commission the driving force of our Christian lives and the driving force of the congregation. As long as I have a passion and the people of my church have a passion to see new people born into God's family and see them become disciples, much of the criticism will be abated. The first thing is to keep the first thing the first thing. The first thing is making disciples of all ethnic groups. (See Matthew 28:18-20.)

Lord, help me to welcome new believers even when they have different traditions, different opinions and different lifestyles. Mold me and the members of my congregation into a powerful unity to reach others for you. Amen.

April 3

Perseverance

Romans 5:3-5

"We rejoice in our sufferings, because we know that suffering produces perseverance, perseverance, character; and character, hope. And hope does not disappoint us, because God has poured out his love into our hearts by the Holy Spirit, whom he has given us" (Romans 5:3-5 NIV).

Again Paul writes, "We are pressed on every side by troubles, but we are not crushed and broken. We are perplexed, but we don't give up and quit. We are hunted down, but God never abandons us. We get knocked down, but we get up again and keep going. Through suffering, these bodies of ours constantly share in the death of Jesus so that the life of Jesus may also be seen in our bodies" (II Corinthians 4:8-10 NLT).

We so often pray for God to remove us from our trial when he wants to improve us through the trial. Abraham had to wait twenty-four years for his promise to be fulfilled. David ran from Saul for ten years. Joseph was in prison for thirteen years.

John Wesley knew what perseverance was. Here is a snap shot from John Wesley's diary... "Sunday, A.M. May 5, Preached in St. Anne's. Was asked not to come back anymore. May 5 P.M., Preached in St. Jude's. Can't go back there either. Sunday, A.M., May 19, Preached in St. Somebody Else's. Deacons called special meeting and said I couldn't return. Sunday, P.M., May 19, Preached on street, Kicked off street. Sunday, A.M., May 16, Preached in meadow. Chased out of meadow as bull was turned loose during service. Sunday, A.M., June 2, Preached out at the edge of town. Kicked off the highway. Sunday, P.M., June 2, Afternoon, preached in a pasture. Ten thousand people came out to hear me." [ix]

On several occasions, I heard or read about Christians who are imprisoned for Christ today, who do not pray to be released, but they pray that they can be faithful.

Lord, help me to be faithful in the situation I find myself. Thank you. Amen.

April 4

Grow in Grace

II Peter 3:18

Peter concludes his writing by stating: "Grow in the grace and knowledge of our Lord and Savior Jesus Christ. To him be glory both now and forever! Amen" (II Peter 3:18 NIV).

How do we grow in grace? Elam Stauffer, an outstanding missionary to Africa who is now with the Lord, said, "No need—no grace, much need—much grace." Peter's final words are for us to grow in grace and knowledge of our Lord and Savior Jesus Christ.

Paul, while in Macedonia, wrote to the Corinthians who were challenging his apostleship: "Because of the extravagance of those revelations and so I wouldn't get a big head, I was given the gift of a handicap to keep me in constant touch with my limitations. Satan's angel did his best to get me down; what he in fact did was push me to my knees. No danger then of walking around high and mighty! At first I didn't think of it as a gift, and begged God to remove it. Three times I did that, and then he told me

'My grace is enough; it's all you need. My strength comes into its own in your weakness.'

Once I heard that, I was glad to let it happen. I quit focusing on the handicap and began appreciating the gift. It was a case of Christ's strength moving in on my weakness. Now I take limitations in stride, and with good cheer, these limitations that cut me down to size—abuse, accidents, opposition, bad breaks. I just let Christ take over. And so the weaker I get, the stronger I become" (II Corinthians 12:7-10 Msg).

God's grace is all I need. Have you learned that truth? If we can't thank God for the "thorn in the flesh" or the difficulties of life, then we must grow in grace. We grow in grace as we come to his cross and tell the Lord we are helpless to help ourselves. We ask for grace to accept our situation knowing he never makes a mistake or causes us a needless tear.

Lord, I am your jewel, keep knocking the rough edges off my life. Help me to see my weakness and my needs as opportunities to grow in grace, so you can shine brightly through my situation and my adversity. Amen.

April 5

Dandelions

I Corinthians 9:21

"When I am with the Gentiles who do not have the Jewish law, I fit in with them as much as I can. In this way, I gain their confidence and bring them to Christ. But I do not discard the law of God; I obey the law of Christ... I try to find common ground with everyone so that I might bring them to Christ. I do all this to spread the Good News, and in doing so I enjoy its blessings" (I Corinthians 9:21-23 NLT).

The other day I was in the home of a pastor. He was lamenting the fact that he has tried to relate to his neighbors but they were not receptive or even hospitable. One would not even come to the door and yet he and his wife tried to take gifts to them. Before I entered his house I was very conscious of the dandelions with their tall seed heads profusely throughout his lawn. All the neighbor's lawns were basically free of weeds and very well manicured.

Chatting later in the evening, he commented that he waits to mow his grass until it is worthwhile. Why mow so often? I have little question in my mind that his unkept lawn affected his witness to his neighbors. When Paul writes that we become all things to all people so we can by all means save some, he was saying that we make every effort to not offend people. In this pastor's context, a well-kept lawn is important to gain the respect of his neighbors. They will not hear the Good News of the Gospel from him until they respect him.

Paul writes, "I'd be more than happy to empty my pockets, even mortgage my life, for your good" (II Corinthians 12:15 Msg). I am obligated to everyone I meet. (Romans 1:14 free translation.)

Lord help me to be sensitive to cultural differences that become a barrier to sharing the Good News of the Gospel to my neighbors. Amen.

April 6

Enoch Walked With God

Genesis 5:24

"When Enoch was sixty-five years old, he had Methuselah. Enoch walked steadily with God. After he had Methuselah, he lived another 300 years, having more sons and daughters. Enoch lived a total of 365 years. Enoch walked steadily with God. And then one day he was simply gone: God took him" (Genesis 5:21-24 Msg). The *Amplified Bible* reads that Enoch walked in habitual fellowship with God.

It's interesting that Enoch went to heaven at a young age. Of the deaths recorded in this chapter seven lived over 900 years, one other died at age 777. Enoch was taken by God at the young age of 365. Although I cannot be certain I believe the Lord took him because of the increasing evil in the world at that time. (See Jude 14-16.) Genesis 6:1-3 informs us that because of the evil in the earth God shortened the life span to 120 years.

Paul informs us that if we partake of the communion service, "unworthily, not honoring the body of Christ, you are eating and drinking God's judgment upon yourself. That is why many of you are weak and sick and some have even died" (I Corinthians 11:29-30 NLT).

God may choose to shorten one's life to relieve their pain because of a sinful culture as in Enoch's situation. (See also Lot's situation as described in Second Peter 2:7-8.) Or, he may shorten people's lives because of their sinful practices.

As we pray for people and work and witness to them remember the principle Paul gives in Galatians 6:7 NLT: "Don't be misled. Remember that you can't ignore God and get away with it. You will always reap what you sow!" Jude writes: "Show mercy to those whose faith is wavering. Rescue others by snatching them from the flames of judgment. There are still others to whom you need to show mercy, but be careful that you aren't contaminated by their sins" (Jude 22-23 NLT).

Lord, help me to be like Enoch who continually walked with you even though there is evil on every side. Help me to snatch others from the flames of God's judgment before it is too late. Amen.

April 7

Cracked Pots

II Corinthians 4:7

"We have this treasure in jars of clay to show that this all surpassing power is from God and not from us" (II Corinthians 4:7 NIV).

It's amazing that God uses us—clay jars or cracked pots. We are God's channels of his treasures to our world. The treasure Paul is referring to is the Good News that Christ is the true light.

"Our Message is not about ourselves; we're proclaiming Jesus Christ, the Master. All we are is messengers, errand runners from Jesus for you. It started when God said, 'Light up the darkness!' and our lives filled up with light as we saw and understood God in the face of Christ, all bright and beautiful. If you only look at us, you might well miss the brightness. We carry this precious Message around in the unadorned clay pots of our ordinary lives. That's to prevent anyone from confusing God's incomparable power with us. As it is, there's not much chance of that. You know for yourselves that we're not much to look at. We've been surrounded and battered by troubles, but we're not demoralized; we're not sure what to do, but we know that God knows what to do; we've been spiritually terrorized but God hasn't left our side; we've been thrown down, but we haven't broken. What they did to Jesus, they do to us—trial and torture, mockery and murder; what Jesus did among them, he does in us—he lives! Our lives are at constant risk for Jesus' sake, which makes Jesus' life all the more evident in us. While we're going through the worst, you're getting in on the best" (II Corinthians 4:5-12 Msg).

We are messengers, errand runners for Jesus! I love that. It's not about us. It's about him. At Capital Christian Fellowship, where I pastored, I frequently had the congregation repeat: "It's not about me, it's not about you, it's all about Jesus!"

Let's remember it's not about us, he uses us, we are only his instruments but we are his instruments. We are his beloved allowing the all surpassing power of God to flow from our lives.

Lord, use me, clay pot that I am. Make me a messenger of your grace. Amen.

April 8

Vision

Proverbs 29:18

"Without a vision the people perish" (Proverbs 29:18 KJV).

Can you imagine a ship in the ocean drifting alone without a destination? Many people are in the midst of the ocean of life but have no destination, no direction, no vision, and no goals.

Many people and many pastors are maintenance oriented. They are content year after year with a plateaued or declining congregation even though new people move into their community each month. Even though a U-Haul just unloaded its contents, they have no motivation to welcome them or invite them to church. It seems that often pastors and church members are content as long as the church bills are paid. With this lethargic and visionless attitude Christians are not the salt, the light or the leaven that Jesus said we are to be. (See Matthew 5:13-16.)

Where is our passion? Where is our vision? How do we receive a vision? As we turn to the Lord, his Holy Spirit places a desire in our hearts to know him and serve him and proclaim him. We pray, we search the Word, we seek him. We ask God for eyes to see and hearts to discover his will for us. Once discovered, it becomes our passion. The vision will line up with our gifts. Jesus gifted every one. (See Romans 12:3-6.) He expects us to develop our gifts to serve others. (See I Peter 4:10.)

The NIV renders Proverbs 29:18: "Where there is no revelation, the people cast off restraint; but blessed is he who keeps the law." *The Message* reads: "If people can't see what God is doing they stumble all over themselves. But when they attend to what he reveals, they are most blessed." God has a specific work, or ministry for everyone. We have a responsibility to discover our ministry, attend to it and walk in it. When we do this, we will be blessed and fruitful. We will walk rightly before him and be a blessing to others.

Lord, help me to see what you are doing and to work with you in fulfilling your vision for my life. Use me to bear fruit for you. Amen.

April 9

Preaching or Teaching?

Acts 8:4

"The believers who had fled Jerusalem went everywhere preaching the Good News about Jesus" (Acts 8:4 NLT).

Most church people desire for their pastor to be a preacher rather than a teacher. As Paul lists the gifts that build up the church, he doesn't list the gift of "preacher" but apostles, prophets, evangelists, pastors and teachers. (See Ephesians 4:11.) Preaching in the New Testament is for persons who have not yet responded to the Christian faith. Once we become followers of Jesus, we need teachers. Whenever the word "preach" is used in the New Testament, it implies the proclamation or presentation of the Gospel, the Good News which is mainly for pre-believers.

Could it be that one reason our churches are so anemic is that we want preachers rather than teachers? Teachers give lessons and expect accountability. If people are not growing, teachers are frustrated. They feel they are not doing their job. It's easier for Christians to listen to preaching and go home and forget about the message, because there is no accountability. This fits well with our American individual focused culture: "No one will tell me what to do." Until teaching becomes our preferred style we will have anemic Christians, not disciples.

This is why small groups, whether in small congregations or in mega churches have become so important. There is a catch phrase that we hear more and more in church life: "You can only go so far in rows—Jesus used circles." In other words, Jesus and the early church had face-to-face encounters with their house church structure where there was more accountability. We lost that by sitting in rows in our pews.

Since Jesus sent each one (See John 17:18 and 20:21), we first preach i.e. share the Good News, and then as people respond we teach, i.e. make disciples. Let's not be afraid of the term, "preach" even though it is not a politically correct term, since this is what every follower of Jesus is called to do.

Lord, help me be a good preacher—sharer of the Good News to those who do not know you. Then use me to teach and disciple those who respond to the Good News. Amen.

April 10

Resurrection Power

Ephesians 1:18-23

Paul prays that the Ephesians can know Christ better. Then he writes: "I pray also that the eyes of your heart may be enlightened in order that you may know the hope to which he has called you, the riches of his glorious inheritance in the saints, and his incomparable great power for us who believe. That power is like the working of his mighty strength, which he exerted in Christ when he raised him from the dead and seated him at his right hand in the heavenly realms, far above all the rule and authority, power and dominion, and every title that can be given, not only in the present age but also in the one to come. And God placed all things under his feet and appointed him to be head over everything for the church which is his body, the fullness of him who fills everything in every way" (Ephesians 1:18-23 NIV).

There is absolutely nothing that can defeat Christ. He is above everything else. We are seated with Christ in that position of authority. (See 2:6.) In that seat beside Jesus we have incomparable great power. Are our eyes enlightened to see where we are? Are we daily living in that experience, operating from that perspective? If we are, there is no need for despair. There is no need for worry. There is no need to be shy about sharing our faith.

Let's pray with Paul that the eyes of our heart would be open to see the position of being seated with Christ and to make his power applicable to us in our experience today. The Holy Spirit did it for Paul and he will do it for us if we believe and act upon it.

The ark in the Old Testament was a place of safety. God told Noah to enter the ark, not hang on the outside. Let's enter into the position Jesus provided for us seated beside him. What a place of victory.

Lord Jesus, you tell me that your incomparable great power is for me. Help me to believe you and operate from that position of security and confidence. Thank you. Amen.

April 11

Servants or Friends

John 15:15

Just days before Jesus went to the cross he said: "I'm no longer calling you servants because servants don't understand what their master is thinking and planning. No, I've named you friends because I've let you in on everything I've heard from the Father" (John 15:15 Msg).

We are friends of Jesus. We work with him more than for him. Working for him has the servant stance. Friends are transparent. Jesus has revealed so many "secrets" to us. So often we don't comprehend the great truths he shared with us but we are encouraged to ask for wisdom whenever we lack it. (See James 1:4.)

Abraham was the only person in the Old Testament who is referred to as the friend of God. God spoke to him and informed him that from him all the families of the earth would be blessed.

Jesus wants us to be his friend. Martha was focused on serving while Mary was concerned about intimacy and being a friend of Jesus. (See Luke10:38-41). Jesus wants our friendship before our service. We can't serve effectively until we know him. The Father seeks worshippers first then we can respond in fruitful service. (See John 4:23-24.)

Moses knew the ways of God. "He made known his ways to Moses, his deeds to the people of Israel" (Psalm 103:7 NIV). The people saw his deeds. There is a huge difference between understanding God's way and seeing his deeds. As you walk with God you will begin to understand more and more of his ways and learn to trust his character. You will have fewer questions. Just as a child asks many question in the beginning, as they mature they understand the ways of the parents. So it is with our relationship with God.

Jesus wants to be our friend. It's true we are his servants, but let's also see ourselves as his friend. Paul writes: "Become friends with God; he's already a friend with you" (II Corinthians 5:20b Msg).

Lord, I delight to serve you but I rejoice even more in our friendship. Amen.

April 12

Ambassadors

II Corinthians 5:20

"We are …Christ's ambassadors, as though God were making his appeal through us. We implore you on Christ's behalf: Be reconciled to God" (II Corinthians 5:20 NIV).

Ambassadors are privileged people. The position is prestigious. The greater the dignitary you represent, the more prestigious the position. We are ambassadors of the King of Kings, who is "far above any ruler or authority or power or leader or anything else in this world or in the world to come" (Ephesians 1:21 NLT). What an honor!

Do we see our privileged position as an honor, a privilege? Too often Christians see it as a burden. As someone quibbled: Many Christians would rather have a root canal than share their faith. Why is that? Is it because we feel we are invading someone's private realm. Is it because we do not really believe we are ambassadors? Is it because we are not excited about what Jesus has done for us? How can we not be excited when we read the next verse: "God made him (Jesus) who had no sin to be sin for us, so that in him we might become the righteousness of God" (I Corinthians 5:21).

When I invited Jesus into my life I made an exchange—my sin for his righteousness and his righteousness for my sin. He takes my worthless evil and gives me something of indescribable worth. How grateful I am for his exchange. Let's be enthusiastic to share this Good News.

Think again about the prestigious position he gives you. You are an instrument he uses to change the eternal destiny of your friends and the people around you. He has no other plan. When he left he commissioned you to be his disciple maker.

It's a joy to set aside our own desires and walk in the desires of the one we represent. He promises us great rewards. (See Matthew 10:41-42.) "When I am with those who are oppressed, I share their oppression so that I might bring them to Christ. Yes I try to find common ground with everyone so that I might bring them to Christ. I do all this to spread the Good News, and in doing so I enjoy its blessings" (I Corinthians 9:22-23 NLT). "The Lord will reward each one of us for the good we do" (Ephesians 5:8 NLT).

Lord, help me to be your faithful ambassador. Amen.

April 13

For Such a Time as This

Esther 4:14

"Who can say but that you have been elevated to the palace for just such a time as this?" (Esther 4:14b).

Do you believe in God's providence? God knows exactly what he is doing. According to Psalm 139 he knows my thoughts, where I am, what I do, what I am going to say even before I say it. (See vv. 1-4). God will use you in the place where you are if you let him control your life. I'm sure Esther did not want to be where she was—a Jew in the palace of a Gentile King. Her life was in danger, grave danger. But God used her to save her people.

God wants to use you. "You are a chosen people. You are a kingdom of priests, God's holy nation, his very own possession. This is so you can show others the goodness of God, for he called you out of the darkness into his wonderful light" (I Peter 2:9 NLT).

The Message Bible clearly states: "You are the ones chosen by God chosen for the high calling of priestly work, chosen to be a holy people, God's instruments to do his work and speak out for him, to tell others of the night-and-day difference he made for you—from nothing to something, from rejected to accepted."

Is Jesus making a change in your life? If so, share your story. If you pray in the morning for him to guide you and cultivate the habit of a holy conversation throughout the day you will find God opening the door to share his love. The Holy Spirit will use you as his tool of blessing both in your words and in your actions. You'll find yourself often serving others by going the second mile. Out of you will flow rivers of living water to the thirsty souls you meet. Claim his presence and his power each morning. His mercies are new each day and they never run dry. Hallelujah!

Lord, make me an instrument of your love and peace today. Amen.

April 14

Set Your Heart on Things Above

Colossians 3:1-3

Sometimes Christians are accused of being so heavenly minded they are no earthly good. Do you know anyone like that?

Paul writes: "Since you have been raised with Christ, set your hearts on things above, where Christ is seated at the right hand of God. Set your minds on things above, not on earthly things. For you died, and your life is now hidden with Christ in God" (Colossians 3:1-3 NIV).

Perhaps *The Message* Bible which takes some interpretation liberties is easier to understand: "So if you're serious about living this new resurrection life with Christ, act like it. Pursue the things over which Christ presides. Don't shuffle along, eyes to the ground, absorbed with the things right in front of you. Look up, and be alert to what is going on around Christ—that's where the action is. See things from his perspective. Your old life is dead. Your new life, which is your real life - even though invisible to spectators - is with Christ in God. He is your life" (Colossians 3:1-4 Msg).

As Christians our mind and heart needs to be controlled by Christ. When we set our hearts and minds on Christ we have no self-centered goals, it is his life lived through us. Galatians 2:20 NIV, "I am crucified with Christ and I no longer live, but Christ lives in me." Christ's life, lived through us is the most exciting life one can have. No more worries—he's in charge, no more shame over our sins—he's taken care of them, no more uncertainties since he takes care of the sparrows he will certainly take care of us. (See Matthew 6:25-34.)

I grew up with a motto on my wall: "Your life will soon be past, only what's done for Christ will last." Let's set our hearts on things above—on Christ and allow him to give you life abundant. (See John 10:10).

Lord, help me to seek those things that are eternal, those things that honor and please you. Enable me to live in this perspective with every thought and action today. Amen.

April 15

Priority of Home Witness

Acts 1:8

Jesus' final instructions to his disciples were: "You will receive power when the Holy Spirit comes on you; and you will be my witnesses in Jerusalem, and in all Judea and Samaria, and to the ends of the earth" (Acts 1:8 NIV).

Where do we begin to share Jesus? In Jerusalem, which means across the street. The disciples had denied him in Jerusalem just a few weeks before. Jesus is saying go back to where you made your biggest mistake, go back to where you blew it. Go back to where they know you.

If you yelled at your spouse when you're expecting people for a backyard cookout and the neighbor heard you, ask God to give you courage to go to them and say, "I think you heard me yell at my wife/husband. I blew it. I asked her/him to forgive me and things are OK again. I want you to forgive me too. God can use your confession. The neighbor will think these people are for real. Transparency and vulnerability are materials the Holy Spirit will use to bring conviction.

Many churches have reached large numbers abroad, but are not bringing their next door neighbors to Christ. Remember how Jesus empowered the woman at the well. She went back home and the whole village responded. The man among the tombs met Jesus and wanted to go with him but Jesus said, "Go home to your family and tell them how much the Lord has done for you" (Mark 5:19b-20 NIV). They knew him in the surrounding town. That's where he was most effective.

Levi invited his peers to a banquet when he met Jesus. They knew his past life as a tax collector. He risked ridicule from those who knew him but God used him in a mighty way. People connect with people. They need to connect with you before you can bring them to Jesus. Jesus said, "Anyone who welcomes you is welcoming me. (See Matthew 10:40 NLT.) "He who listens to you listens to me: he who rejects you rejects me" (Luke 10:16 NIV).

He will use you and me when we blow it. We model God's forgiveness to our family and others by our willingness to admit our mistakes and ask for forgiveness.

Lord, help me to be vulnerable and transparent so others see Jesus in me. Amen.

April 16

Share Your "Bread" With the Hungry

II Kings 7:3-10

King Benhadad of Aram mobilized his army and surrounded Samaria. There was a great famine in the city. "Now there were four men with leprosy sitting at the entrance of the city gates. 'Why should we sit here waiting to die?' they asked each other. We will starve if we stay here, and we will starve if we go back into the city. So we might as well go out and surrender to the Aramean army. If they let us live, so much the better. But if they kill us, we would have died anyway'" (II Kings 7:3-4 NLT).

"When the lepers arrived at the edge of the camp, they went into one tent after another, eating, drinking wine, and carrying out silver and gold and clothing and hiding it. Finally, they said to each other, 'This is not right. This is wonderful news, and we aren't sharing it with anyone! If we wait until morning, some terrible calamity will certainly fall upon us. Come on, let's go back and tell the people at the palace. So they went back to the city and told the gatekeeper what had happened...'" (II Kings 7:8-10a. NLT).

They shared the good news! We have the Bread of Life. People are starving. Are we willing to share it? Does it take "leprosy" and/or "starvation" to humble us to risk our all for Jesus?

Years ago I often sang the chorus of Ira D. Sankey:

> "Lord lay some soul upon my heart,
> And love that soul through me;
> And may I nobly do my part
> To win that soul for Thee." [x]

This chorus had a tremendous effect on my life. Let's ask ourselves if the Lord has to humble us like he did the lepers before we are willing to risk our lives to share the Good News.

Father, give me a passion to share the Good News today. Amen.

April 17

Come Near to God

James 4:8

"Submit yourselves ... to God. Resist the devil, and he will flee from you. Come near to God and he will come near to you" (James 4:7-8a NIV). *The Message* Bibles reads: "So let God work his will in you. Yell a loud "no" to the devil and watch him scamper. Say a quiet "yes" to God and he will be there in no time."

Coming near to God is another key for effective witness. When we are close to Jesus, his light will shine through us. "You are to live clean, innocent lives as children of God in a dark world full of people who are crooked and stubborn. Shine out among them like beacon lights" (Philippians 2:15 LB).

Paul helps us put this in experiential terms: "Our hearts ache, but we always have joy. We are poor, but we give spiritual riches to others. We own nothing, and yet we have everything" (II Corinthians 6:10 NLT). "In thy presence is fullness of joy; at your right hand there are pleasures for evermore" (Psalm 16:11 KJV). "You will show me the way to life, granting me the joy of your presence and the pleasures of living with you forever" (NLT).

This position of abiding in Jesus provides pleasures that the unchurched know nothing about—peace with God, divine guidance, the daily company of his presence in this life, and a secure future in the next.

The writer of Hebrews sums it up best: "Let us cling to him (Jesus) and never stop trusting him.... for he faced all of the same temptations we do, yet he did not sin. So let us come boldly to the throne of our gracious God. There we will receive his mercy and we will find grace to help us when we need it" (Hebrews 4:14-16 NLT).

Father, thank you for the joy of your presence. May others see you at work in my life. I know you will supply all I need for today. Amen.

April 18

Getting God's Perspective

II Kings 6

The King of Aram was constantly frustrated because everywhere he planned to attack, Israel was already armed for battle. The King thought there were traitors in his ranks, never realizing the God of Israel was giving Elisha inside information. The King sent a great army to capture Elisha. When Elisha's servant got up early the next morning he saw this huge army. "Ah, my Lord, what will we do now?" he cried out to Elisha. "Don't be afraid!" Elisha told him, "For there are more on our side than on theirs!" Then Elisha prayed, "O Lord, open his eyes and let him see!" The Lord opened his servant's eyes, and when he looked up, he saw that the hillside around Elisha was filled with horses and chariots of fire" (II Kings 6:15-17 NLT).

Billy Graham has stated that this is one of the most encouraging stories of the Bible. When it feels like everyone is against you, look to the Lord. As God's children, he provides a special insight and knowledge into life's dilemmas. He wants to give us a new perspective. Pray a prayer of faith asking God to open your spiritual eyes to see what he sees. Seeing from God's perspective will make all the difference.

We are often like the two disciples on the seven mile walk to Emmaus after Jesus had arisen from the grave. They were in grief. Jesus came and walked with them but they did not recognize him. He explained to them from the writing of Moses and all the prophets how it was clearly stated that the Messiah would suffer all these things before he entered into his glory. "They begged him to stay the night with them, since it was getting late. So he went home with them. As they sat down to eat, he took a small loaf of bread, asked God's blessing on it, broke it, and gave it to them. Suddenly, their eyes were opened, and they recognized him" (Luke 24:29-31 NLT).

Lord, open my eyes to see things from your perspective. Amen.

April 19

Let it Shine, Not Make it Shine

Matthew 5:14-16

Jesus didn't say, "Make it shine," he said, "Let it shine." "Let your light shine before men, that they may see your good deeds and praise your Father in heaven" (Matthew 5:16 NIV).

The Message Bible reads: "You're here to be light, bringing out the God-colors in the world. God is not a secret to be kept. We're going public with this, as public as a city on a hill. If I make you light-bearers, you don't think I'm going to hide you under a bucket, do you? I'm putting you on a light stand. Now that I've put you there on a hilltop on a light stand—shine! Keep open house; be generous with your lives. By opening up to others, you'll prompt people to open up with God, this generous Father in heaven" (Matthew 5:14-16 Msg).

Jesus said, "Let it shine." He is in us. All we need to do is be channels of the Good News. A light from a city on the top of a hill cannot be hidden. If we live for Jesus his light will shine through us. The NIV Study Bible says: "We hide our light by (1) being quiet when we should speak, (2) going along with the crowd, (3) denying the light, (4) letting sin dim our light, (5) not explaining our light to others, or (6) ignoring the needs of others. Be a beacon of truth—don't shut your light off from the rest of the world." [xi]

Paul writes: "Put into action God's saving work in your lives, obeying God with deep reverence and fear. For God is working in you, giving you the desire to obey him and the power to do what pleases him" (Philippians 2:12-13 NLT).

Note again that it is God's saving work in you. It is he who gives you the desire to obey him and the power to do what pleases him. The key is to submit to God's Spirit in you.

Lord, help me to submit to your Spirit. Thanks for providing both the desire and power to please you. Enable me to be a channel of light and life to others today. Amen.

April 20

I Can't Speak

Exodus 3:11

Jesus reminds us that we are all called. "Many are invited, but few are chosen"(Matthew 22:14 NIV). God loved the world, that is, the people of the world to the extent that he gave his son. (See John 3:16.) He calls everyone. He calls and he sends you and me. (See John 17:18 and 20:21.)

God appeared to Moses in the burning bush, informing him that he is sending him to Pharaoh to bring Israel out of slavery in Egypt.

"But Moses said to God, 'Who am I that I should go to Pharaoh and bring the Israelites out of Egypt?'" (Exodus 3:11 NIV.) God's response was that he would be with Moses and give him the ability to perform signs so Pharaoh would be convinced. "Moses said to the LORD, 'Pardon your servant, Lord. I have never been eloquent neither in the past nor since you have spoken to your servant. I am slow of speech and tongue… Please send somebody else" (Exodus 4:10 & 13 NIV). (See also 6:12.)

Moses was not the only one to be reluctant when God called. Elijah had experienced a mighty victory over Baal, Queen Jezebel's god. In a frenzy of rage Jezebel retaliated with a death sentence to be carried out within twenty-four hours. In despair Elijah says in essence, "I have had enough, Lord, let me die." (See I Kings 19:4 & 10.)

As a youth I stuttered. How could I preach with stammering speech? Yet God seemed to be saying, "I want you to prepare to become a pastor." While my deliverance from stuttering coupled with a poor self-image took many years to overcome, God was faithful. As in the Biblical examples of Moses and Elijah there were many times I was tested and still am tested. But the God who calls, also promises to equip us for the task. If it seems best he will remove the physical obstacles. But one thing is sure, he will never forsake us. Say, "Yes Lord, I am willing to do whatever you say."

Lord, I thank you for calling me. Help me to be a faithful witness for you today. Amen.

April 21

Enthusiasm

Romans 12:11-12

"Never be lacking in zeal, but keep your spiritual fervor, serving the Lord. Be joyful in hope" (Romans 12:11-12a NIV). "Don't burn out; keep yourselves fueled and aflame. Be alert servants of the Master, cheerfully expectant" (Msg).

Timothy was a shy young pastor who needed encouragement. Paul writes: "I remind you to fan into flame the gift of God which is in you through the laying on of my hands. For God did not give us a spirit of timidity, but a spirit of power, of love, and of self-discipline" (II Timothy 1:6-7 NIV). *The Message* reads: "The gift of ministry you received when I laid hands on you and prayed—keep that ablaze! God doesn't want us to be shy with his gifts, but bold and loving and sensible."

As Christians grow older, many seem to lose their enthusiasm and zeal. John writes to the Christians at Ephesus, a church with thirty or more years of history, "You have lost your first love" (Revelation 2:4 NIV). Jesus says, "Because of the increase of wickedness, the love of most will grow cold" (Matthew 24:12 NIV).

How do we move from cold to hot? We come back to the cross. Jesus is the source of life. We drink of him, we eat of him—remember the communion elements? We confess our sins. He forgives and heals us. (See I John 1:9.) The lukewarm, indifferent, and discouraged persons will be transformed into his likeness. (See Romans 8:29.)

We fight the good fight of faith. (See I Timothy 6:12.) We bring every thought into obedience to Christ. (See II Corinthians 10:5.) We come to Jesus and drink. He said, "If anyone thirsts, let him come to me and drink. Rivers of living water will brim and spill out of the depths of anyone who believes in me this way" (John 7:37-38 Msg).

Father, I come to you, thirsty. I drink of you, knowing you give living water that transforms me from indifference to an enthusiastic servant. Thank you Jesus! Amen.

April 22

Learning to Hear Revelation

Revelation 3:20

"Here I am! I stand at the door and knock. If anyone hears my voice and opens the door, I will come in and eat with him, and he with me" (Revelation 3:20 NIV).

Jesus says the sheep follow the shepherd because they recognize his voice. (See John 10:4.) Have we learned to hear his voice?

The church at Laodicea has become lukewarm. They said, "'I have acquired wealth and do not need a thing. But you do not realize that you are wretched, pitiful, poor, blind and naked" (Revelation 17 NIV). They need to hear from the Lord but their spiritual ears are deaf. Several times Jesus said: "He who has ears, let him hear." (NIV.) The *Message Bible* reads: "Are you listening to me? Really listening?" (Matthew 13:9 NIV.)

I will not hear until I pay attention. Am I paying attention? It takes time, concentration and devotion to hear—not a mere rushing into God's presence and exiting quickly. Focus on God's agenda not just your own. Our hearts need to say, "Whatever you say I will do. I'll go where you want me to go. I'll do what you want me to do. I'll be what you want me to be. I'll lay everything on the altar."

One recent survey indicated that only ten percent of Christians were willing to move to help plant a church. Another survey indicated that only thirteen percent were inviting others to Jesus and his church. Another survey question revealed that we give more than three hours a day to viewing TV and/or the internet. If we fill our minds with trivia, we will miss God's divine appointment. We will not hear his still small voice.

Jesus' message in Revelations 3:20 is primarily directed to Christians, to church members. You will hear his knock only when you give your heart in full dedication to him. "He who has ears to hear, let him hear." Are you listening? Really listening?

Father, I will wait in your presence with a surrendered heart. I will listen. Amen.

April 23

Tears are Liquid Prayers

Acts 20:31

"Remember that for three years I never stopped warning each of you night and day with tears" (Acts 20:31 NIV). The NLT reads: "Remember the three years I was with you—my constant watch and care over you night and day, and my many tears for you."

"I have done the Lord's work humbly—yes, and with tears" (Acts 20:19 NLT). Again Paul writes: "My heart is filled with bitter sorrow and unending grief, for my people, my Jewish brothers and sisters. I would be willing to be forever cursed—cut off from Christ!—if that would save them" (Romans 9:2-3 NLT).

"While Jesus was here on earth, he offered prayers and pleadings, with a loud cry and tears, to the one who could deliver him out of death. And God heard his prayers because of his reverence for God" (Hebrews 5:7 NLT).

"Those who sow in tears will reap with songs of joy. He who goes out weeping carrying seed to sow, will return with songs of joy, carrying sheaves with him" (Psalm 126:5-6 NIV).

These verses show strong feeling and passion. Have we wept before the Lord for our lost friends? "For I wrote to you out of great distress and anguish of heart and with many tears, not to grieve you but to let you know the depth of my love for you" (II Corinthians 2:4 NIV).

Eighty percent of intercessors are women. What about us men? It's interesting the verses I just quoted are mainly referring to men. Have we men lost our passion? Are we so western that we have buried our emotions?

Perhaps we say, "We love God with our mind and our will." Let's loosen up and tell God we love him with our heart and soul. God is moved by our tears: "You've kept track of my every toss and turn through the sleepless nights. Each tear entered in your ledger, each ache written in your book" (Psalm 56:8 Msg).

Thank you Lord for your love and passion in giving us LIFE through your Son, Jesus. Forgive me for my lack of passion for others. I give my all to you. Amen.

April 24

Continual Prayer

I Thessalonians 5:17

I Thessalonians 5:17 has always been a challenge to me: "Pray continually" (NIV). "Keep on praying" (NLT). "Pray at all times" (Msg). "Pray without ceasing" (KJV).

Other Biblical writers encourage the same: "Look to the Lord and his strength; seek his face always" (I Chronicles 16:11 NIV).

"Jesus told his disciples a parable to show them that they should always pray and not give up" (Luke 18:1 NIV). "Devote yourselves to prayer, being watchful and thankful" (Colossians 4:2 NIV).

The early church: devoted or committed themselves to the teaching of the apostles, to sharing life together, the common meal and the prayers. (See Acts 2:42.) The early church was a praying church. Jesus said, "My house shall be a house of prayer" (Mark 11:19 NIV). Is your church known as a house of prayer? Do I spend more time praying for physical needs, or for my lost friends and neighbors? Which is more important?

In 1953 Frank Lauback wrote a very popular pamphlet: "The Game with Minutes, in which he challenged the reader to think of Jesus every minute of the day. He was passionate about keeping Jesus in our minds and encouraged multitudes to:

"1. Read and reread the life of Jesus…thoughtfully and prayerfully at least an hour a day. Find fresh ways and new translations, so that this reading is never dull…Thus we walk with Jesus through Galilee by walking with him through the pages of his earthly history.

2. We make him our inseparable chum. We try to call him to mind at least one second of each minute. We do not need to forget other things nor stop our work, but we invite Him to share everything we do or say or think… In fact it is no harder to learn this new habit then to learn the touch system in typing…

Not spiritual chills and fevers, but an abiding faith which presses the will toward Christ all day, is a sign of a healthy religion." [xii]

Lord, center my thoughts on you. Amen.

April 25

Trials Have a Purpose

I Peter 4:12-13

"Do not be surprised at the fiery trials you are going through, as if something strange were happening to you. Be glad about trials because trials will make you partners with Christ in his suffering, and afterwards you will have the wonderful joy of sharing his glory when it is displayed to all the world" (I Peter 4:12-13 NLT).

Trials will make you partners with Christ in his suffering. Paul's desire was that he might know Christ and the power of the resurrection and the fellowship of his suffering becoming like him in his death. (See Philippians 3:10.)

Again Paul writes: "We continue to shout our praise even when we're hemmed in with troubles, because we know how troubles can develop passionate patience in us, and how that patience in turn forges the tempered steel of virtue, keeping us alert for whatever God will do next. In alert expectancy such as this, we're never left feeling shortchanged. Quite the contrary—we can't round up enough containers to hold everything God generously pours into our lives through the Holy Spirit" (Romans 5:3-5 Msg).

In working with people there are times when we need to let them suffer. God did not run after the prodigal son. He did go after the lost sheep. The prodigal was rebellious; the lost sheep was not mature enough to understand the consequences of wondering off. The shepherd at times breaks the leg of a sheep that is rebellious and keeps wondering off so they learn to depend on him. Sometimes God allows us to suffer to teach us to trust him.

"Although he (Jesus) was God's Son, he learned trusting obedience by what he suffered, just as we do." (Hebrews 5:8 Msg.)

"In this all-out match against sin, others have suffered far worse than you, to say nothing of what Jesus went through—all the bloodshed! So don't feel sorry for yourselves. Or have you forgotten how good parents treat children, and that God regards you as his children? My dear child, don't shrug off God's discipline, but don't be crushed by it either. It's the child he loves that he disciplines, the child he embraces, he also corrects" (Hebrews 12:4-6 Msg).

Lord, help me to remember that each trial is meant to help me mature. Amen.

April 26

Name is Very Important

Matthew 1:21

Before Jesus was born he was named Jesus, meaning 'God saves' (Matthew 1:21).

Our name gives us an identity. God named the trillions of stars. He knows us by name. He had Adam name the animals. When someone calls us by name we know they have made an effort to remember us. One particular chain of restaurants makes it a point to call its customers by name. The waiter or waitress says, "My name is…. and he or she writes their name so the customer can see it. Then they turn the paper and ask your name and write it so you can see it. Throughout the meal they call you by name. I was impressed. How much more important for us to call people by name. Thus indicating we care.

Jesus called the disciples by name. He didn't say, "Hey you, come follow me." He used their names. He calls us by name. He knew us before we were born (Psalm 139:13).

A family whose roots were in Africa came to church regularly for more than a year, but I could not persuade them to become members although they had a definite faith in Jesus. Finally in the privacy of their home they revealed to me what was their holdup. They informed me that they can't agree on their names. "What do you mean?" Well when you are baptized you must have a new name and we can't decide on our names. In their culture you gave yourself a new name at baptism.

A new name means you have a new identity. Your name affects the way you see yourself—the way you act and live. Those who are faithful followers of Jesus have their names written in the book of life (Revelation 3:5).

One practice that will help you remember someone's name is to repeat his/her name as soon as it is said. Repeat it again throughout the conversation. This will seem awkward at first, but you will be surprised at how this helps you remember them. It also helps to let them know you are respecting them.

Lord, help me to love people and express that love by remembering their name. Amen.

April 27

Positive People

I Corinthians 13:7

"Love never gives up, never loses faith, is always hopeful, and endures through every circumstance" (I Corinthians 13:7 NLT).

This week I met an old friend. I left with a spring in my step and a smile on my face. He put a positive twist on everything. What a blessing!

God is a positive God. Think of all the trees in the Garden. Only one was forbidden. Even the Ten Commandments in the Hebrew Scriptures began with the positive affirmation: "I am the LORD your God, who rescued you from slavery in Egypt" (Exodus 20:1 NLT). This positive word of grace was the first "commandment" for the Hebrew people. We number the commandments differently beginning with verse three which begins with statements that are negative, i.e. "You shall not..."

Then in the New Testament Jesus states that the Old Testament can be summed up: "'You must love the Lord your God with all your heart, all your soul, and all your mind.... A second is equally important: 'Love your neighbor as yourself.' All the other commandments and all the demands of the prophets are based on these two commandments'" (Matthew 22:37-40 NLT). Jesus begins the Sermon on the Mount with nine ways to be blessed of God. (Matthew 5:3-12.)

Paul was very positive. He began all his letters with the exception of Galatians by complimenting the Christians. The Christian message is very positive. The Gospel is Good News. Contrast this with the daily news on the TV or local newspaper. The early church message, especially in the book of Acts, focuses more on the resurrection than on the cross of Christ. Of course there couldn't have been a resurrection without the cross. Without the cross there is no forgiveness of our sins.

Let's encourage people by our positive attitude and demeanor. From his prison cell Paul encourages us to think of things that are: "true and honorable, and right... pure and lovely, and admirable, excellent and worthy of praise. (Philippians 4:8 NLT).

Lord, give me a positive attitude. Help me to think about your goodness and grace to me, as well as your grace for others. Amen.

April 28

Questions

Matthew 16:15-18

Jesus asked the disciples: "Who do you say I am?" (Matthew 16:15 NLT.)

Jesus asked more than 150 questions. Is it because he did not know the answer? Of course not! Questions are usually an indication that we respect the other's opinion. We value them as people. People will not hear us until they have been heard. People don't care how much we know until they know how much we care.

Each person has needs. If we can discover their needs, we have a door through which we can reach them. We usually discover those needs through observation and questions. Jesus knows our needs and ministers to us by meeting our needs. We must do the same for others.

We, like Jesus, must learn to ask sincere questions. This, of course, means you will need to listen and really hear what they are saying. There is very little difference between careful listening and loving. We show love by listening. Someone has wisely said, we are as sick as our secrets. Jesus knows our secret thoughts and hurts. With the Holy Spirit's guidance and his gift of wisdom, we too can often discover those secrets by asking questions.

It's best not to ask "why" questions. "Why" questions usually make people defensive. Ask clarifying questions such as how did that make you feel, or please tell me more. Hopefully you can uncover their needs and minister to them through their needs. What you are doing is reaching across not placing yourself above them.

Most people I work with have emotional needs. They may struggle with rejection and insecurity or live with a lack of significance. Others worry over their finances, the direction of their children, their health, or concerns of losing their job. Some have legitimate questions that cause them to stumble in their search for God. If so, we need to provide some reasonable answers and at the same time freely admit we do not have all the answers.

Lord, give me your love and wisdom so I can ask the right questions as I relate to others today. Thank you. Amen.

April 29

Hunger and Thirst for Righteousness

Matthew 5:6

"Blessed are those who hunger and thirst for righteousness, for they shall be filled" (Matthew 5:6 NIV). "God blesses those who are hungry and thirsty for justice, for they will receive it in full" (NLT).

The Greek word "dikaiosune" is usually translated "righteous" but it can also be translated "justice." We usually think of righteousness as primarily a vertical relationship, i.e. our relationship with God, while justice is often thought of as horizontal, i.e. our relationship with others. Jesus is saying we are to both hunger and thirst for a right relationship with God and with others.

The hunger and thirst described here is the hunger of one starving for food and of one who will die unless he/she has water. Therefore Jesus is asking: "How much do you want righteousness or justice? Do we want it as much as one wants it if they are starving or dying of thirst? Can you imagine what our world would be like if we desired righteousness and justice to that degree? There is so much injustice in our world. Think of the poverty, the multitudes born in repressive governments, the millions born who are unwanted. Think of the nearly two billion who have never heard the name of "Jesus" and have no secure future.

If we long for righteousness and justice as Jesus desires, we will work to bring injustice to an end in our world. There are 430-some scriptures encouraging us to not neglect the widow, the orphan, the immigrant or foreigner and the less fortunate. Think of Jesus' example as he identified with the lepers, the hated tax collectors, the Samaritans, the Pharisees, the prostitutes, and those who were ill and oppressed.

In our own strength we can never attain righteousness. Jesus gives us a righteous status: "It is because of him (God) that you are in Christ Jesus, who has become for us wisdom from God—that is, our righteousness, holiness and redemption" (I Corinthians 1:30 NIV). (See Isaiah 61:10.)

Father, thank you for Jesus who places us in this position of righteousness. Father, I long with all my heart to practice righteousness and justice to my fellowman. Work through me to that end. Amen.

April 30

Anointing for Preaching

Luke 4:18-19

After Jesus was tempted in the wilderness he returned to Galilee, filled with the Holy Spirit's power (v. 14). Arriving in Nazareth, his boyhood town, he went to the synagogue where he read from Isaiah (61:1-2): "The Spirit of the Lord is upon me, for he has appointed me to preach Good News to the poor. He has sent me to proclaim that captives will be released, that the blind will see, that the downtrodden will be freed from their oppressors, and that the time of the Lord's favor has come" (Luke 4:18-19 NLT).

Luke reports in 4:14 that Jesus was filled with the Spirit. Jesus read from Isaiah stating that the Spirit of the Lord was upon him. Before we can minister as Jesus did we too need the fullness of the Holy Spirit. We need to spend extended periods of time with the Father as he did. (See verses. 1-13.)

We have the same Holy Spirit Jesus had. Romans 8:9 states that if we do not have the Holy Spirit we are not Christians. Ephesians 5:18 informs us that we are to be filled with his Holy Spirit. This means that just as Jesus was anointed for this ministry we are anointed for our ministry.

Our job then is to be like Jesus: (1) preach the Good News to the poor, (2) proclaim release to the captives, (3) give sight to the blind, (4) free the downtrodden from their oppressors, and (5) state clearly that the time for the Lord to act is now. When God does not act as we desire, we need to accept the fact that our Father knows best. Many times in the New Testament the anointing on Paul and the other apostles did not cover physical healing, e.g. Timothy was frequently ill, I Timothy 5:23; Paul left Trophimus sick in Miletus, II Timothy 4:20; Epaphroditus almost died, Philippians 2:17; Paul's eyes were bad, Galatians 4:13. Paul writes in Romans 8:23 NLT, "we groan to be released from pain and suffering. Jesus said in Matthew 25:36 we are to visit the sick while at other times he said heal the sick.

With the Holy Spirit's empowerment move out in faith ministering to others.

Father, as you anointed Jesus to preach and to set people free, enable me by your Holy Spirit to be an instrument of healing and hope today. Amen.

May 1

Jesus Chose the Disciples to be with Him

Mark 9:30-31

"Jesus tried to avoid all publicity in order to spend more time with his disciples and teach them" (Mark 9:30-31 NLT).

A pastor who had served a congregation for years died. At the memorial service many people shared how they appreciated his ministry and how he had helped them. But I noticed that not one person mentioned his good messages. He impacted people by the quality of relationship they had with him. Sometimes pastors and all of us are more concerned about imparting facts and being sure our "sermons" are perfect, than we are about the quality of our relationship with others.

Jesus chose the disciples to be with him and to teach them. Let's be conscious that people read our lives and are influenced more by our demeanor than by what we say.

Think about the people who influenced you. Was it because they were so brilliant or was it their relationship with you? Relationships are supreme. Jesus spent time with his disciples. He could have sent a manuscript from heaven. That's what God did before he sent Jesus. Angels gave the law to Moses who was the mediator between God and the people. (See Galatians 3:19.) That was not satisfactory. We need a priest who understands us. (See Hebrews 4:14-16.)

Jesus understands us because he was tempted in all points as we are. Our experiences are not wasted. God will use your trials to mature you and make you more like Jesus. Others will be comforted as we relate to them from our experience. "He comforts us in all our troubles so that we can comfort others. When others are troubled, we will be able to give them the same comfort God has given us. You can be sure that the more we suffer for Christ, the more God will shower us with his comfort through Christ" (II Corinthians 1:4-5 NLT).

There is no substitute for relationships—relationships with Jesus and relationship with others. The love relationship sums up all the law and the prophets—loving God and loving others. (See Matthew 22:37-39.)

Lord, help me to keep relationships supreme in my schedule today. Amen.

May 2

Jesus' Passion

Matthew 23:37

"O Jerusalem, Jerusalem, the city that kills the prophets and stones God's messengers! How often I have wanted to gather your children together as a hen protects her chicks beneath her wings, but you wouldn't let me" (Matthew 23:37 NLT).

Notice the word "often." Jesus longed to reach the people of Jerusalem. The title in my NIV is; "Jesus grieves over Jerusalem again." Notice the persistence of Jesus. How many times is often? Paul said he had a great sorrow and unceasing anguish in his heart for his people. (See Romans 9:1-2.) For both Jesus and Paul there was a continual burden for the lost.

How many times do we pray for and make serious efforts to reach our loved ones for Christ? Jesus in Luke 14:23 tells us to compel, to make them come, or urge, or force them to come to the banquet.

While Jesus expresses this strong emotion for his people, it's appropriate to ask: "Was Jesus a driven person?" He held a perfect balance between passion for the lost and at the same time he was not overwhelmed. He was able to enjoy life and at the same time carry this deep concern. Jesus was driven to go through Samaria (John 4:4), to cleanse the temple (Luke 19:45), to confront the Pharisees (Matthew 23). He got up before sunrise to pray and prayed all night (Luke 6:12), he was driven with compassion for the multitudes, denying himself food and rest (Mark 3:20) and most importantly, he was driven to give his life on the cruel cross for sinful persons like myself. Seventeen times the Gospel records that Jesus must do this or that, yet at the same time his life was characterized by calmness and gentleness. (See Matthew 11:29, II Corinthians 10:1, and Philippians 1:8.)

As we rest in his love, as we draw close to him in prayer, we will be sensitive to the Holy Spirit. His Spirit will move us, even cause a fire to burn in our heart when he wants us to show love by helping or verbally sharing God's love.

Lord Jesus, I want to have a passion like you and Paul had for people. Give me that passion today. Amen.

May 3

Don't be Distracted

I Corinthians 9:26

"I run straight to the goal with purpose in every step" I Corinthians 9:26 NLT.

"In a race everyone runs, but only one person gets the prize. You also must run in such a way that you will win. All athletes practice strict self-control. They do it to win a prize that will fade away, but we do it for an eternal prize. So I run straight to the goal with purpose in every step. I am not like a boxer who misses his punches. I discipline my body like an athlete, training it to do what it should. Otherwise, I fear that after preaching to others I myself might be disqualified" (I Corinthians 9:24-27 NLT).

Paul had a goal. That goal was to "become a servant of everyone so that I can bring them to Christ" (I Corinthians 9:19 NLT). Jesus had a similar goal, i.e. "to seek and save the lost" (Luke 19:10). He says, "I have come to call sinners to turn from their sins, not to spend my time with those who think they are already good enough" (Luke 6:32 NLT). Many Christians have lost that focus.

Pray for your neighbors, your work peers, your school peers by name. Ask God to give you eyes to see how you can build a bridge of relationship to them so you can share Christ. Paul says he became a servant of everyone. Do you and I see ourselves as servants to our neighbors?

Ask yourself what you can cut out of your busy schedule so you have time to be a servant to them. It is often the good things that remove us from doing what is best. Do we need to read the newspaper every day? What about TV and Internet time? Are our hobbies recreating us? Can we use them to build bridges to share Jesus?

Lord, help me to run straight to the goal with purpose in every step. And help me to become a servant to everyone so that I can bring them to Christ. Amen.

May 4

God is Sorry He Made Man?

Genesis 6:6

"The LORD observed the extent of the people's wickedness, and he saw that all their thoughts were consistently and totally evil. So the LORD was sorry he had ever made them. It broke his heart" (Genesis 6:6 NLT).

Since the Lord is omniscient, why did he create people? If he knew we were going to fail him why did he create us? He was sorrowful because of what we did to ourselves as a parent expresses regret and sorrow over a rebellious child. He was sorry that we chose sin and death instead of a relationship with him. God could see down through time and knew that he could redeem us. The redemption would cost him indescribable pain and suffering, but he thought we were worth the cost. Can we imagine our worth? Do we dare question our value when we see the price tag God places on us!

God gave his only Son to redeem us. Peter writes: "The ransom he (God) paid was not mere gold or silver. He paid for you with the precious life blood of Christ, the sinless, spotless Lamb of God. God chose him for this purpose long before the world began, but now in these final days, he was sent to the earth for all to see. And he did this for you" (I Peter 1:18-20 NLT). Paul says, "Thank God for his Son—a gift too wonderful for words!" (II Corinthians 9:15 NLT.)

No wonder the hymn writer states: "Such love demands my soul, my life, my all." Horatius Bonar wrote: "Toil on, faint not, keep watch, and pray; Be wise the erring soul to win; Go forth into the world's highway, Compel the wanderer to come in." [xiii] Knowing the value God places on us should give us a passion to win people for our Lord. Along with Jesus we say, "I give myself entirely to you so they also might be entirely yours" (John 17:19 NLT).

Father, I thank you for giving your very best, your only son Jesus. I give you my life, my soul, my all. Amen.

May 5

Complete Joy

John 15:11

"I have told you this so that my joy may be in you and that your joy may be complete" (John 15:11 NIV).

"Those who remain in me, and I in them, will produce much fruit" (v.5 NIV). Jesus told us this so our joy would be complete.

Lyn got a job over Christmas vacation. Her boss was the nastiest, meanest human being who loved to come up to her sales people and criticize and royally chew them out in front of the customers. Lyn said, "Nothing I did pleased her... I cried myself to sleep at night. 'Lord,' I prayed... 'I can't go back.'"

God seemed to be saying to Lyn: "You will go back tomorrow morning, and you will stay there... you will love Miss Alma."

"Impossible," cried Lyn. "I cannot love that woman."

"You're right, you can't love her," the Lord plainly said. "But, I can. In fact I already love her. I died for her."

Lyn went back. "At first I thought that would be impossible, but it wasn't," she says. "Because I now saw Miss Alma in such a different light. I saw her as someone who needed the Lord. I began to learn what it meant to turn the situation over to Jesus and let him work through me. The woman was just as nasty, but I had changed. Now when she corrected me, I smiled and thanked her for straightening me out. I never tried to excuse my behavior."

The other employees couldn't understand how Lyn could take all the guff. When they asked, she had the opportunity to witness to every woman in that department. As the account ends, Miss Alma's attitude changed. She invited Lyn to come back and work for her.

"In my own strength I couldn't have done it. Even the stock boy was amazed, and I got a chance to witness to him. ...Just love people for the sake of loving them because Jesus commanded us to. [xiv]

Father, help me to remain in you today. Like Lyn, I can't love them but you can love them through me. Thank you. Amen.

May 6

Servants to Friends

John 15:14-15

"You are my friends if you obey me. I no longer call you servants because a master doesn't confide in his servants. Now you are my friends, since I have told you everything the Father told me" (John 15:14-15 NLT).

Most Christians are aware that they need to serve others. Jesus came not to be served but to serve. (See Matthew 20:28.) Paul writes: "Serve one another in love" (Galatians 5:13 NIV). The Greek word we translate "servant" can just as well be translated "slave." Service is a definite aspect of our Christian lifestyle.

Jesus moves us from servants to friends. This does not remove our responsibility to serve but it makes service easier.

There is the story that in the days of slavery the bidding at the slave auction kept going higher and higher. The slave greatly feared meeting his new owner because he felt he could not possibly be worth that much. The new owner approached him and said, "I have bought you to set you free. You are a free man!" The slave fell on his knees and said, "I will serve you as long as I live." That needs to be our response to Jesus. Jesus bought us to set us free. He is our friend and we are his friends and children (I Peter 1:15). He paid for us with the life of his only Son. (See I Peter 1:18-19.) Our response is to fall down and say, "Jesus, you are Lord. I will serve you as long as I live!" That's what we commit to at baptism.

Jesus delights in us. He loves us. We come boldly to his throne. (See Hebrews 10:19-20.) The Hymn writer, Joseph Scriven, expresses it well: "What a friend we have in Jesus, all our sins and griefs to bear! What a privilege to carry everything to God in prayer! O what peace we often forfeit, O what needless pain we bear, all because we do not carry everything to God in prayer!" [xv]

Jesus, I thank you for not only being my master but my friend. I can never pay you back for the high cost you paid for me but I promise I will serve you until the day I die. Thank you. Amen

May 7

WWJD

Romans 8:29

"For God knew his people in advance, and he chose them to become like his Son, so that his Son would be the firstborn, with many brothers and sisters. And having chosen them, he called them to come to him. And he gave them right standing with himself, and he promised them his glory" (Romans 8:29-30 NLT).

A few years ago there was a fad among many Christian groups to wear a wrist band or tie pin that had the letters: WWJD, which stood for: "What would Jesus do?" Maybe a better slogan is WIJD = "What is Jesus doing?" That is a great way to remind ourselves that Jesus is our model and guide for all our actions. We are to become like him since we are his brothers and sisters. He is not ashamed to call us his siblings: "Jesus and the ones he makes holy have the same Father. That is why Jesus is not ashamed to call them his brothers and sisters. For he said to God, 'I will declare the wonder of your name to my brothers and sisters. I will praise you among all your people.' He also said, 'I will put my trust in him.' And in the same context he said, 'here I am—together with the children God has given me" (Hebrews 2:11-13 NLT).

God doesn't preach to us or at us. He is our model Father. "Follow God's example in everything you do, because you are his dear children" (Ephesians 5:1 NLT). Jesus is our older brother! Modeling is miles ahead of an instruction manual. We "watch," "observe," "question," and "imitate." I pray often before I meet someone or before I answer the phone: "Lord, what would you have me share with this person. Help me to be a good listener so I can see their heart." God loves to answer these prayers.

The Holy Spirit is creative. He will give us words to say as we witness to people. Jesus used a different approach for everyone he met. When we have a passion to see people come to Jesus, we will be creative because the Holy Spirit is creative. As we say and do what the Spirit prompts us to do, we will find a joy in sharing the Good News.

Father, help me to be continually aware that I am your child. Jesus, help me remember I am your brother or sister. Remind me to ask WWJD. Amen.

May 8

Jacob's Approach

Genesis 32

After being away from Esau for many years, Jacob returned. He sent messengers ahead to inform Esau he was coming. The messengers returned informing Jacob that Esau was on his way to meet him with an army of 400 men. Jacob prayed, "O Lord, you told me to return to my land and to my relatives, and you promised to treat me kindly. I am not worthy of all the faithfulness and unfailing love you have shown to me, your servant… O Lord, please rescue me from my brother, Esau. I am afraid that he is coming to kill me" (Genesis 32:9-11 NLT).

He sent hundreds of animals on ahead as gifts to appease Esau. That night Jacob sought time alone. A man came and wrestled with him until dawn. The man told him he had struggled with both God and men and had won (v.28). The man blessed Jacob. Jacob named the place Peniel—"face of God"—for he said, "I have seen God face to face, yet my life has been spared" (v.30).

God sends us to be his witnesses: "As the Father has sent me, so I send you" (John 20:21 NLT). Like Jacob, we are often fearful. Jacob had to come to the end of himself. He feared for his life. As we give our fears to God,—admit we are helpless to give a positive witness, and wrestle with Him, he will bless us. His Holy Spirit will empower us.

Jesus said, the first step into the Kingdom is to be poor in spirit. (See Matthew 5:3). *The Message* Bible reads: "You're blessed when you're at the end of your rope." Unless we take up our cross, denying ourselves we cannot be his disciples. (See Luke 9:23.) The NLT reads: "If any of you wants to be my follower, you must put aside your selfish ambition, shoulder your cross daily, and follow me."

Lord, break me. You send me to be a witness. Often I fail you. Forgive me. I will, with your help, put aside selfish ambitions, take up my cross and witness for you. So help me God. Amen.

May 9

Teamwork

Ezra 3

When the children of Israel returned from captivity and settled in their towns, the first thing they did, even though they were afraid of the local people, was to build an altar to the Lord. They had learned to put first things first. Normally, they would first build a wall to keep the enemies out. They were learning to give God his rightful place. They offered sacrifices on the altar every day, morning and evening, as Moses had commanded.

Next they bought materials for the building of the temple. Everyone got involved. They appointed leaders, age twenty and older, from the tribe of Levi to direct the rebuilding of the Temple. When the foundation was laid, the priests and Levites with their trumpets and cymbals praised God in the tradition of King David.

They sang and praised the Lord. "All the people boomed out hurrahs, praising God as the foundation of the Temple of God was laid. As many were noisily shouting with joy, many of the older priests, Levites, and family heads who had seen the first Temple,..wept loudly for joy. People couldn't distinguish the shouting from the weeping. The sound of their voices reverberated for miles around" (Ezra 3:11-13 Msg).

What do you think the people thought when they heard their shouts of praise to God? Might they begin to think these people really love their God as they saw the beautiful temple being built?

In the New Testament, God's people are the temple of God. Do the unchurched know we enjoy our worship services? Do we tell them how excited we are to worship and praise the Lord? Emotion is not the primary criteria to prove we love the Lord but showing some emotion is certainly one aspect of loving our Lord from our heart. We are not afraid of getting excited at a ball game. Let's not be afraid of worshipping our Lord with some excitement in private and in our public worship services. After all, the world just might catch on to the reality that we love Jesus.

Lord, deliver me from seeing my worship with God's people as routine. Help me to be free to express my praise to you and to share my joy with others. Amen.

May 10

Open Your Eyes

John 4:34-38

"As you look around right now, wouldn't you say that in about four months it will be time to harvest? Well, I'm telling you to open your eyes and take a good look at what's right in front of you. These Samaritan fields are ripe. It's harvest time! The Harvester isn't waiting. He's taking his pay, gathering in his grain that's ripe for eternal life. Now the Sower is arm in arm with the Harvester, triumphant. That's the truth of the saying, 'This one sows, that one harvests.' I sent you to harvest a field you never worked. Without lifting a finger, you have walked in on a field worked long and hard by others" (John 4:35-38 Msg).

The disciples were blind to the harvest around them. They were blind because they did not have a passion to see the Samaritans come to eternal life. Their mind was on physical food but Jesus had food that really nourished (v.34). They had to learn to overcome cultural barriers. They had to overcome their prejudice. They had to learn that there were somethings far more important than physical food.

Are we any different? We go past houses in all directions from our home, day after day and don't think to pray for the people, or invite them to meet Jesus. There are fields all about us, and all around our churches that are ripe but we are blind. We need eyes to see like Jesus saw. And when we see as he saw, and show love and acceptance as he did, we too can reap a huge harvest.

"Many of the Samaritans from that village committed themselves to him because of the woman's witness" (v 39). What was the woman's witness? "He knew all about the things I did. He knows me inside and out!" (Msg).

Perhaps one of the most effective witnesses we can give to our neighbors is that Jesus knows me inside and out and still chooses to love and forgive me. That is freedom.

Jesus, thank you for crossing the cultural barriers and accepting this sinful woman. I too am sinful. Thank you for accepting me. Help me to share, just like this woman, what you did for me. By your grace I will. Amen.

May 11

Politically Correct?

Jude 22-23

"Be merciful to those who doubt; snatch others from the fire and save them; to others show mercy, mixed with fear—hating even the clothing stained by corrupted flesh" (Jude 22-23 NIV). The NLT reads: "Show mercy to those whose faith is wavering. Rescue others by snatching them from the flames of judgment. There are still others to whom you need to show mercy, but be careful that you aren't contaminated by their sins."

"Snatch others from the fire and save them, or rescue others by snatching them from the flames of judgment." We live in a time when judgment and eternal hell is pooh-poohed. Many Christians don't believe in eternal hell, however, most Christians believe in eternal heaven. While hell was not made for humans, but for the devil and his angels, it is clear that Jesus believed in hell. (See Matthew 25:41).

The objection is that a loving God would not send anyone to hell. They send themselves by the choices they make. Seven times Jesus speaks of "outer darkness where there is weeping and gnashing of teeth." (Matthew 8:12, 13:42, 50 etc.) Jesus speaks more about eternal separation, punishment and judgment than any of the New Testament writers. While Christians do not agree on the precise meaning and implication of these terms, it is clear there are very serious consequences to our rejection of our Lord Jesus.

Knowing this, Jesus' brother Jude says we are to rescue others by snatching them from the flames of judgment. Paul writes: "For we must all appear before the judgment seat of Christ, that each one may receive what is due him for the things done while in the body, whether good or bad. Since then, we know what it is to fear the Lord, we try to persuade men" (II Corinthians 5:10-11 NIV).

When we come to the judgment day, will our unchurched neighbors say to us: "We talked with you many, many times but you never warned us about our need to come to Christ." What will we say?

Lord, forgive me for my lack of urgency to snatch people from the flames. Give me a passion and the power of your Holy Spirit to speak with love, gentleness and urgency to those that don't know you, inviting them to your eternal Kingdom. Amen.

May 12

The Power of One

Daniel

"Run up and down every street in Jerusalem, says the Lord, 'Look high and low, search throughout the city! If you can find even one person who is just and honest, I will not destroy the city. Even when they are under oath, saying, 'As surely as the Lord lives, they all tell lies!'" (Jeremiah 5:1-2 NLT).

"I looked for someone who might rebuild the wall of righteousness that guards the land. I searched for someone to stand in the gap in the wall so I wouldn't have to destroy the land, but I found no one" (Ezekiel 22:30 NLT).

"God looks down from heaven on the entire human race; he looks to see if there is even one with real understanding, one who seeks for God. But no, all have turned away from God; all have become corrupt. No one does good, not even one!" (Psalm 53:2-3 NLT).

"The Godly people have all disappeared; not one fair-minded person is left on the earth…" (Micah 7:2 NLT).

Noah alone was found righteous in the eyes of the Lord. (See Genesis 6:9). God used him to save humanity from destruction.

Daniel would not bow down to the King. The whole nation was affected by his powerful witness. (See Daniel 6).

You and I are called to stand in the gap! We can make a difference in our school, in our workplace, yes in our town, in our city! I am close friends of a man who chose to bowl on a team of unchurched men so he could be a witness to them. He is making a difference. Another friend served on the school board and made a definite impact on the school system. I know Ron who sits with the gang whose language becomes decent when he gives his noon hour to them. One person makes a difference. This is what it means to be the salt, the light, and leaven of our communities.

Father, help me to be an effective witness for you even if I must stand alone. Thank you. Amen.

May 13

Let Your Light Shine

Matthew 5: 14-16

"You're here to be light, bringing out the God-colors in the world. God is not a secret to be kept. We're going public with this, as public as a city on a hill. If I make you light-bearers, you don't think I'm going to hide you under a bucket do you? I'm putting you on a light stand. Now that I've put you there on a hilltop, on a light stand—shine! Keep open house, be generous with your lives. By opening up to others, you'll prompt people to open up with God, this generous Father in heaven" (Matthew 5:14-16 Msg).

Helen, my wife, spends time with our neighbors showing love and sharing the difference Jesus makes in her life. However, she felt checked by the Holy Spirit that now was not the time to confront one neighbor concerning her relationship with God. My wife found out later that a person knocked on her door and asked if she was a Christian. She said, "No." He told her she was going to hell. She said, "When I heard that a preacher was moving across the street I was angry. You are different. No matter what I say you just accept me." Over the next weeks she and her family came to our church and became new creations in Christ Jesus.

Francis of Assisi said to the effect . . . witness 24/7, if necessary use words. There are times when the witness of our actions and good works are most effective. However, there are other times when we do need to use words. Jesus came and lived a perfect life but if he would not have explained salvation to us we would still be lost. Someone suggested that we take Assisi's words and say, "Wash, if necessary use water." We need both deeds and words.

As Paul wrote: "How can they hear without someone preaching to them? And how can they preach unless they are sent" (Romans 10:14-15 NIV)? People need to know why we live as we do. The Holy Spirit will prompt you to share how Jesus is making a difference in your life.

Father, help me to both live and speak for you today. Amen.

May 14

Pathways to God

John 14:6

Jesus said, "I am the way, the truth and the life. No man can come to the Father except through me" (John 14:6 NLT). Paul writes: "There is only one God and one Mediator who can reconcile God and people. He is the man, Christ Jesus" (I Timothy 2:5 NLT).

When I talk of pathways to God, I'm not talking about a pathway to other gods. I am talking about the Creator God whose Son is Jesus Christ. We come through Jesus to our Heavenly Father. Also we all come through the blood of Jesus Christ the new life-giving way. (See Ephesians 2:13.)

However, since God made us all different, with different spiritual temperaments we find closeness to God in different ways. Gary Thomas, in his book, *Sacred Pathways*, lists nine common ways that people take to draw near to Jesus. [xvi] "Abraham had a religious bent, building altars everywhere he went. Moses and Elijah revealed an activist's streak in their various confrontations with forces of evil and in their conversations with God. David celebrated God with an enthusiastic style of worship, while Solomon, expressed his love for God by offering generous sacrifices. Ezekiel and John described loud and colorful images of God, stunning in sensuous brilliance." [xvii]

Which of the nine sacred pathways seem to be more helpful to your approach in walking with Jesus: (1) Naturalists: Loving God in the out of doors, (2) Sensates: Loving God with the senses, (3) Traditionalists: loving God through ritual and symbol, (4) Ascetics: Loving God in solitude and simplicity, (5) Activists: Loving God through confrontation, (6) Caregivers: Loving God by loving others, (7) Enthusiasts: Loving God with mystery and celebration, (8) Contemplatives: Loving God through adoration, and (9) Intellectuals: Loving God with the mind.

When we share Jesus with people we need to allow them to approach Jesus through their spiritual temperament. Let's not force people to come to Jesus through our spiritual pathway. Give them the freedom to follow the refreshing pathway of the Holy Spirit in their lives.

Father, I thank you that you have made us all different. Help me to celebrate the difference and learn from others as they share their close and life-invigorating walk with you. Amen.

May 15

Talking Too Much?

Proverbs 21:23

"Watch your words and hold your tongue; you'll save yourself a lot of grief" (Proverbs 21:23 Msg).

In coaching different church leadership teams, I come across persons whose tongue has not been tamed. They have to be the first to answer everything. Pretty soon the others don't talk much. There is little discussion and progress is stymied. The whole church is affected by one person's tongue.

Jesus asked more than one hundred fifty questions? He wanted his listeners to think. He made us with one mouth and two ears—perhaps we need to listen at least twice as much as we talk. It's hard to learn while we are talking.

James paints some startling pictures concerning the tongue: "The tongue is a fire, a world of evil… It corrupts the whole person, sets the whole course of life on fire and is itself set on fire by hell" (James 1:6 NIV). Verse 8, "No man can tame the tongue. It is a restless evil, full of deadly poison."

It's true none of us can tame our tongues, only God's Holy Spirit can do that. One of the most common sins among God's people is defensiveness. Why do we need to defend ourselves, and justify ourselves? This is a sign of self not being broken. We need to take our desire to defend ourselves and justify ourselves to the foot of the cross and confess it as sin—the sin of pride. Are we afraid others will not think well of us? Are we so insecure that we can't really listen to their ideas? If we do listen, too often we come up with negative responses.

Our churches will not grow unless we grow out of our self-centered pride into God-centered action. It's not about me. It's not about you. It's all about Him!

Lord Jesus, I come to the cross and confess my defensiveness. Help me Jesus to love others, to listen and really hear what others are saying and then respond with understanding. Amen.

May 16

Love at Home

I Corinthians 13

What do we mean by love? Paul's standard will open our eyes to our need to come to Jesus for his cleansing and power to live a life of love described in verses 4-8 in *The Message* Bible.

Love never gives up. Love cares more for others than for self.
Love doesn't want what it doesn't have. Love doesn't strut,
Doesn't have a swelled head, Doesn't force itself on others.
Isn't always "me first," Doesn't fly off the handle,
Doesn't keep score of the sins of others, Doesn't revel when others grovel,
Takes pleasure in the flowering of truth, Puts up with anything,
Trust God always, Always looks for the best,
Never looks back, But keeps going to the end.

How are we measuring up? Are we often impatient or unkind in the way we answer back? Do you envy your spouse? Do the children have envy between them? Are we courteous or do we answer curtly? How is our tone of voice? Are we proud or conceited? Do we have to have our own way? Do we think we know best? How is our attitude? Do we blame others? Do you keep track of the sins of others? Do we forgive their sins or do we hold grudges, reminding our spouse of their mistakes? Does our love put up with anything or do we constantly complain about their habits that we despise?

We all fall short. What do we do? Live in guilt? No, we confess our sins. We come to the cross and ask for his forgiveness. He forgives us of all our sins. (See I John 1:9.) How often do we need to do this? Perhaps many times a day. But we will grow stronger so that there can be more space between our confession times. We are learning to walk in the light. (See I John 1:7.) And when we walk in the light we have fellowship with each other. Love flows!

Lord Jesus, only you can give me this selfless perfect love. Please forgive me for my lack of love. Cleanse me and enable your love to freely flow through me. Amen.

May 17

A Great Contrast

John 15:1-17

Six times we are told by Jesus in John 14-16 that if we ask anything in his name he will do it. We are also told that apart from him we can do nothing.

"The Father will give you whatever you ask in my name" (John 15:16 NIV). "I am the vine; you are the branches. If a man remains in me and I in him, he will bear much fruit; apart from me you can do nothing" (John 15:5 NIV).

Here we get our cues from Jesus. He says: "For I did not speak of my own accord, but the Father who sent me commanded me what to say and how to say it. I know that his command leads to eternal life. So whatever I say is just what the Father has told me to say" (John 12:49-50 NIV). "The Son can do nothing by himself; he can do only what he sees his Father doing because whatever the Father does the Son also does" (John 5:19 NIV).

Jesus has such an intimate relationship with the Father that he does and says only what the Father tells him to say and do. Not only that, but the Father tells him how to say it. We can have the same relationship with the Father as Jesus had. He says: "You (the Father) are in me and I am in you. May they (you and me) also be in us (in God and Jesus)" (John 17:21 NIV). I believe this is what Jesus desires for us. If we draw close to him he will draw close to us. (See James 4:8.) We know his voice. (See John 10:3-4.) Our steps are ordered by the Lord. (See Psalm 37:23.)

When we abide in Christ we will begin to experience the joy of prayers that line up with the Father and we will have whatever we ask. Apart from him we cannot do or say anything that has eternal value. This wonderful relationship with the great God of the Cosmos is beyond our imagination. It results in complete joy. (See v. 11.)

Jesus, as you give me your Holy Spirit I will remain in you. Help me to hear your voice and be obedient to your every command. Thank you for the fantastic promise that whatever I ask in your name you will do. Amen.

May 18

"We Heard This Before"

Hebrews 5:11-14

"I have a lot more to say about this, but it is hard to get it across to you since you've picked up this bad habit of not listening. By this time you ought to be teachers yourselves, yet here I find you need someone to sit down with you and go over the basics on God again, starting from square one—baby's milk, when you should have been on solid food long ago! Milk is for beginners, inexperienced in God's ways, solid food is for the mature, who have some practice in telling right from wrong" (Hebrews 5:11-14 Msg).

After speaking to a group of Christians in an older declining congregation it came to my ears that the attitude was, we heard this before. Jesus said, He who has ears, let him hear—pay attention and apply what is said. James says, "Do not merely listen to the word, and so deceive yourselves. Do what it says" (James 1:22 NIV). John writes: "Let us not love with words or tongue but with actions and in truth" (I John 3:18 NIV).

One of the great weaknesses of many American churches is that our members hear hundreds of sermons but are like the Dead Sea. They continually take but give out very little. They think that coming to church regularly they are doing God and others a favor. This is especially true in the area of evangelism. When you're active in evangelism you will be "forced" to grow because you will find yourself in situations where you will be challenged to answer questions. The answers you give will not hold water if your life does not model your answer. "I pray that you may be active in sharing your faith so that you will have a full understanding of every good thing we have in Christ" (Philemon 6 NIV). Paul is saying, as you share your faith your understanding of the Good News will grow!

Growing churches reach out to their friends and neighbors. Declining churches may be doctrinally sound, but are sterile and empty of spiritual vitality.

Lord Jesus, help me to move from the milk stage to maturity. Whatever it takes Lord I will serve you. Lead me today to someone I can help. Thank you Jesus. Amen.

May 19

Happiness or Joy

John 15:11

What is the source of our joy? Notice that it is Jesus' joy in us. Jesus said as he prayed to his Father, "I'm returning to you. I'm saying these things in the world's hearing so my people can experience my joy completed in them" (John 17:11 Msg). "I have told you this so that my joy may be in you and that your joy may be complete" (John 15:11 NIV). "Your joy will be a river overflowing its banks!" (John 16:24 Msg).

Do you experience this joy? Is joy an off again, on again, experience? Church planter Paul writes: "Be joyful always," or "Be cheerful no matter what" (I Thessalonians 5:16 NIV and Msg).

Happiness comes and goes with the circumstances. If we win we are happy. If our team loses we are sad. Joy is different. It transcends the circumstances. Paul writes that he is immersed in tears, yet always filled with deep joy. (See II Corinthians 6:10 Msg.) In Romans 9:2 the *Message Bible* reads: "I carry with me at all times a huge sorrow. It's an enormous pain deep within me, and I am never free of it." Paul learned to carry the deep pain as well as the joy of Jesus all at the same time. If we are filled with the spirit, we are filled with joy. (See Ephesians 5:18 and Galatians 5:22.)

There is a paradox here that we can only understand through experience.

Jesus' joy is a deep satisfying peace. Jesus' joy is a feeling of continual contentment that transcends words. It goes much, much deeper than the laughs we might experience from a good joke. It is healing. It is satisfying. It includes feelings of peace and contentment. If you want more joy, ask Jesus to fill you with his Spirit. Walk in obedience and in complete abandonment to his every command. "In his presence is fullness of joy. At thy right hand are pleasures evermore" (Psalm 16:11 KJV).

David informs us that joy and praise are the result of living in God's presence: "Surely the godly are praising your name, for they will live in your presence" (Psalm 140: 13 NLT).

Thank you Lord, for your abiding joy that meets my deepest need. May your joy overflow in praise so others are drawn to you. Amen.

May 20

Preaching or Teaching/ Rows or Circles

I Corinthians 3:1-3

"Brothers, I could not address you as spiritual but as worldly—mere infants in Christ. I gave you milk, not solid food, for you were not yet ready for it. Indeed, you are still not ready. You are still worldly" (I Corinthians 3:1-3 NIV).

Jesus gathered his disciples around him and taught them. Jesus was primarily a teacher. A teacher gives a lesson and expects a report. If you are in class with a good teacher you will be expected to learn. A good teacher will ask you what you learned and how you are applying it. A teacher is not satisfied unless he or she sees some fruit. Do you remember what you heard last Sunday? It's easy to attend church, sit in our pews, listen to the sermon, go home, and forget about it. Someone has suggested that we only develop so far sitting in rows. We grow more in circles like Jesus taught his disciples.

When you witness to those who are pre-believers make every effort to get them involved in a group where there is some accountability so they can see that Christians take their Christian life seriously. Jesus trained his disciples from day one. He modeled as he taught.

We teach discipleship to pre-believers by our example. They feel more and more part of the group as the group walks with them and relates closely to them. It took four men to bring the paralytic to Jesus. (See Mark 2:1-12.) It usually takes more than our personal witness to bring people to Jesus. It takes a team. Get others involved.

One of the reasons the early church was able to turn the world upside down was because their structure was primarily the house church rather than the larger assembly. The larger assembly lends itself to preaching whereas the small group—circles lend themselves to teaching and forming disciples. Whether you are in a mega-church or a house church ask yourself: Am I part of a small group of disciples who are involved in faithful ministry? If not, consider making that a high priority.

Father, help me to make my small group a group that disciples prebeleivers and new believers. Amen.

May 21

For Whom do you Consecrate Yourself?

John 17:18-19

Jesus said, "For them I sanctify myself that they too may be truly sanctified" (John 17:19 NIV). Who is the "them" Jesus is referring to?" Jesus is referring to his disciples as he sends them into the world. The New Living Translation helps clarify this: "As you sent me into the world, I am sending them into the world. And I give myself entirely to you so they also might be entirely yours" (John 17:18-19 NLT).

Ask yourself: For whom do I sanctify (purify, or consecrate) myself? Just as Jesus lived a pure life for his disciples we live a pure life for others. They see our lives and as a result are encouraged to move on in their Christian walk.

Jesus lived a pure life for us. Therefore we are motivated to live a pure life for others. Jesus promised blessings to those who live pure lives: "God blesses those whose hearts are pure" (Matthew 5:8 NLT).

To be pure in heart means that we are focused. We are not double-minded. We are doubled minded in almost everything we do. When John Bunyan was told that he preached a good sermon, he responded saying that the devil told him that when he came down the steps from the pulpit.

Do we work to please Jesus, or work to receive praise from our employers? When we read our Bible, pray or attend worship, is it to draw closer to God or because it gives us a pleasant feeling that we have done what is best and fulfilled our duty? There are few things that even the most dedicated Christian does with unmixed motives. This is why Paul writes to the Church: "He made you holy by means of Christ Jesus, just as he did all Christians everywhere—whoever calls upon the name of Jesus Christ, our Lord and theirs" (I Corinthians 1:2 NLT).

We always need grace. Peter reminds us with his final words: "Grow in grace" (II Peter 3:18 Msg.) We need his grace continually to live in joyful freedom. The neat thing is that Jesus is there to give us his grace.

Jesus, purify my motives so others can see you in me and be drawn to you. Amen.

May 22

Fruit Bearers

John 15:1-17

We emphasize faithfulness. But God desires fruitfulness as well as faithfulness. Jesus gives us the secret of how to be fruitful i.e. to dwell or remain in him. Eleven times the word "remain" appears in John 15:1-10. If we remain in him we will bear fruit.

He cuts off branches that do not produce fruit. He prunes branches that do bear fruit so they will produce more fruit, (v.2); His "word" prunes us so we will be more fruitful, (v.3); We can't produce fruit if we are separated from the vine—separated from Jesus, (v.4); If Jesus remains in us and we remain in him we will bear much fruit, (v.5); True disciples bear much fruit, (v.7); He chose us to produce much fruit, (v.16).

Fruit comes as a result of remaining in Jesus. Bearing fruit is no option. We can't produce fruit by working up a sweat. Branches don't groan and complain. They don't push or shove. They abide and receive life from the vine. As we receive our life from Jesus we bring forth fruit, much fruit.

What is this fruit? It is Christlikeness. It is the fruit of the Holy Spirit—love, joy, peace, patience, kindness, goodness, faithfulness, gentleness, and self-control. But fruit is also people. Paul wanted to come to Rome so that "I might have some fruit—some results of my labor—among you, as I have among the rest of the Gentiles" (Romans 1:13 AMP). "You know that the household of Stephanas were the first converts and our first fruits in Achaia..." (I Corinthians 16:15 AMP). The fruit of the believer is another believer.

When Jesus gave his final words in Matthew 28:18-20 and Acts 1:8 he was commissioning us to bring in a harvest of people in order to disciple them, i.e. make them followers of Jesus, fishers of men. (See Matthew 4:19.)

"You didn't choose me, remember, I chose you, and put you in the world to bear fruit, fruit that won't spoil. As fruit bearers, whatever you ask the Father in relation to me, he gives you" (John 15:16 Msg).

Lord, I chose to remain in you. Enable me to bear fruit that lasts for eternity. Thank you. Amen.

May 23

Catch the Wave

I Corinthians 3:6-11

"I planted the seed, Apollos watered it, but God made it grow. So neither he who plants nor he who waters is anything, but only God, who makes things grow. The man who plants and the man who waters have one purpose, and each will be rewarded according to his own labor. For we are God's fellow workers; you are God's field, God's building. By the grace God has given to me, I laid a foundation as an expert builder, and someone else is building on it. But each one should be careful how he builds. For no one can lay any foundation other than the one already laid, which is Jesus Christ" (I Corinthians 3:6-11 NIV).

It is God who makes things grow. The wonder is that he chooses to use you and me as his instruments to bring in the harvest. Without him we are nothing. As we are faithful instruments we will be rewarded appropriately. Jesus had more to say about rewards than anyone. He says, "Anyone who receives a prophet because he is a prophet will receive a prophet's reward, and anyone who receives a righteous man because he is a righteous man will receive a righteous man's reward. And if anyone gives even a cup of cold water to one of these little ones because he is my disciple, I tell you the truth, he will certainly not lose his reward" (Matthew 10:40-42 NIV).

God chooses to use us and to reward us. We need to pray for eyes to see where he is working. We can't create a wave—that's God's work. However, he takes into account our prayers in creating waves. He places a burden on the heart of those who are sensitive to him, they pray and God begins to move. We discern God's movement; we discern God's wave and do our part, whether it is planting or watering. This is the most exciting time in history as more people are coming to Christ now than ever before.

Father, I thank you for creating one wave after another, extending your kingdom around the world. May the more than 100,000 who are born into your kingdom each day become faithful disciples bringing your light into this dark world. Amen.

May 24

I Love the Church

Matthew 16:15-19

"Who do you say I am?"

Simon Peter said, "You're the Christ, the Messiah, the Son of the living God."

Jesus came back, "God bless you, Simon,…! You did not get that answer out of books or from teachers. My Father in heaven, God himself, let you in on this secret of who I really am. And now I'm going to tell you who you are, really are. You are Peter, a rock. This is the rock on which I will put together my church, a church so expansive with energy that not even the gates of hell will be able to keep it out… You will have complete and free access to God's kingdom, keys to open any and every door; no more barriers between heaven and earth, earth and heaven. A *yes* on earth is *yes* in heaven. A *no* on earth is *no* in heaven" (Matthew 16:15-19 Msg).

No organization, except the church can bring lasting peace to our troubled communities. The local community service clubs and sports organizations can provide some helpful structure to promote cooperation and assist humanity. The military can help bring order. The Red Cross helps in disasters. But there is only one organization that God has chosen that can change the heart of humanity. That is his body—the church.

Despite all the faults of the church due to our sinfulness, it is by far the best concept this world has ever experienced. As Rick Warren writes, "It has been God's chosen instrument of blessing for two thousand years. It has survived persistent abuse, horrifying persecution, and widespread neglect. Parachurch organizations and other Christian groups come and go, but the church will last for eternity. It is worth giving our lives for and it deserves our best." [xviii]

"He is the head of the church, which is his body" (Colossians 1:18 NLT). This explains the endurance and effectiveness of the church in spite of all its shortcomings.

Father, forgive us for the sin, the divisions, the carnality within your body. Have mercy upon us and heal us. Amen.

May 25

Here Am I, Send Me

Isaiah 6

"I heard the Lord saying, 'Whom should I send as a messenger to my people? Who will go for us?' And I said, "Lord I'll go! Send me" (Isaiah 6:8 NLT).

I had always thought this was a special call directed to Isaiah because he was God's prophet. Oswald Chambers says, "God did not direct His call to Isaiah—Isaiah overheard God saying, "..who will go for Us?" [xix]

His point is that God calls all of us. Isaiah was tuned into God's call. We too will hear God's call if our hearts are open to his call. It's a matter of attitude. Jeremiah writes, "If you look for me in earnest, you will find me when you seek me. I will be found by you" (Jeremiah 29:13-14 NLT). Jesus says, "Many are called, but few are chosen" (Matthew 22:14 NLT). When the New Testament speaks of the "many" it usually includes everyone. Adam brought death to many through his sin. (See Romans 5:15.) John the Baptist says: "The one who is the true light, who gives light to everyone, was going to come into the world" (John 1:9 NLT). God's call comes to everyone.

Paul writes: "The truth about God is known to them instinctively. God put this knowledge in their hearts. They can clearly see his invisible qualities—his eternal power and divine nature. So they have no excuse whatsoever for not knowing God" (Romans 1:19-20 NLT). God is no respecter of persons. He is not willing that any perish. (See II Peter 3:9.)

When you are sharing the Good News, know that the Holy Spirit has already planted a desire in everyone's heart to know Jesus Christ, our Lord and Savior. This is true even for those millions who have never heard the name of Jesus.

Lord, I thank you that beginning in the Garden of Eden you sought us out. I thank you that you are still calling us to yourself. I pray for others to hear your voice and respond to your call. Amen.

May 26

Perfect Conditions?

Ecclesiastes 11:4

"If you wait for perfect conditions, you will never get anything done" (Ecclesiastes 11:4 NLT).

Because of sin it is highly unlikely you will ever have perfect conditions. When we sense the Holy Spirit is nudging us to begin building a relationship with another person, there will always be some obstacles. He or she will be too busy. You will be too busy. Unless you are tuned into the Spirit you will come up with a dozen or more reasons why you cannot relate to this person. You are not perfect and the conditions are never perfect.

When you sense God nudging you to do something you need to act in faith. Pray for God's guidance and the courage to act. Ask him to give you words to say and how to say them. Ask Jesus for faith to overcome your doubts and fears. Claim the promise, "I will trust in him and not be afraid" (Isaiah 12:2 NLT). Or you may claim the verse, "When I am afraid, I put my trust in you" (Psalm 56:3 NLT). There are times when we will move out in fear knowing God is calling us. He will help us overcome our fear or will work in spite of our fear. Perfect love drives out fear. (See I John 4:18.)

If we wait for perfect conditions we will never witness. We will never plant a church. The early church was far from perfect. The New Testament letters were written to help correct sins in the church, yet God used the early church to spread the Good News throughout the world. God works in spite of us. God uses our imperfections when we come to him in humility and repentance. He works in "impossible" circumstances.

When he nudges we must say, "Lord I will go."

Thank you Lord for working through me. Help me to obediently step out in faith at your command, even though I feel so inadequate and the situation looks impossible. Turn my fears into childlike trust in you. Amen.

May 27

Miracles Alone are Not Adequate

John 6:30

"They asked him, 'What miraculous sign …will you give that we may see it and believe you? What will you do?"(John 6:30 NIV).

People naturally want to see the miraculous. In my fifty years of ministry I have experienced many miraculous answers to prayer as well as manifestations of the Holy Spirit's power visibly moving upon people. I have observed in some cases that these supernatural manifestations have little lasting impact on their lives. Jesus said, "Do not rejoice that the spirits submit to you, but rejoice that your names are written in heaven" (Luke 10:20 NIV). Emotions and feelings come and go. Being committed to Jesus is primarily a matter of our will—loving him with all our heart, soul, mind and strength and loving our neighbor as ourselves. (See Matthew 22:37-39.)

In another account Jesus tells of a rich man who died and, "In hell and in torment, he looked up and saw Abraham in the distance and Lazarus in his lap. He called out, 'Father Abraham, have mercy! Have mercy! Send Lazarus to dip his finger in water to cool my tongue. I'm in agony in this fire" (Luke 16:22-24 Msg).

After Abraham informed him that was not possible, the rich man requested Abraham to send Lazarus to the house of his father to warn his five brothers to not come to this place of torment. "Abraham answered. 'They have Moses and the Prophets to tell them the score. Let them listen to them" (v. 29). The rich man responded, "They're not listening. If someone came back to them from the dead, they would change their ways" (v. 30). And Abraham replied, "If they won't listen to Moses and the Prophets, they're not going to be convinced by someone who rises from the dead" (vv. 31).

While the miraculous is always encouraging and has brought multitudes to Christ, let's focus on Jesus and the Holy Spirit who enlivens our heart. Paul writes to Timothy: "From infancy you have known the holy Scriptures, which are able to make you wise for salvation through faith in Christ Jesus" (II Timothy 3:15 NIV).

Father, thank you for the miraculous way you provided salvation for us through your word. Amen.

May 28

Moving Mountains / Faith or Presumption

Mark 11:22-25

"Jesus said to the disciples, 'Have faith in God. I assure you that you can say to this mountain; 'May God lift you up and throw you into the sea,' and your command will be obeyed. All that's required is that you really believe and do not doubt in your heart. Listen to me! You can pray for anything, and if you believe you will have it. But when you are praying, first forgive anyone you are holding a grudge against, so that your Father in heaven will forgive your sins, too" (Mark 11:22-25 NLT).

"If you stay joined to me and my words remain in you, you may ask any request you like, and it will be granted" (John 15:7 NLT).

What a fantastic promise. There are some conditions that we must meet: we must forgive others, have genuine faith, and his words must remain in us. There are other conditions: timing is one of them. Only God sees all the circumstances. He may choose to move the mountain over time rather than instantly. This is illustrated in John 17 where he prays for his followers to be one. Persistence and earnestness is frequently necessary. (See Luke 18:1-8 and James 5:17.)

While I cannot explain the times when it seems God does not answer, as we forgive everyone, grow in faith and trust, and abide in him our understanding and appreciation of these seemingly broad promises become more and more real to us. Mountain after mountain is moved.

When my wife, Helen, was talking with someone who was crying because she knew her husband, who very seldom came to church would never come since we just decided to move the congregation ten miles from his house. Helen said to her, "I don't know your husband but I know God, and he will see that your husband comes." He came and became a committed disciple. God is in the mountain moving business. As we learn to abide in the vine and learn to discern his voice we will find ourselves making bold statements since the Holy Spirit is speaking through us.

Father, I thank you for the joy of seeing mountains move. Help me to trust you more. Amen.

May 29

Love Myself?

Galatians 5:13-14

"For you, dear friends, have been called to live in freedom—not freedom to satisfy your sinful nature, but freedom to serve one another in love. For the whole law can be summed up in this one command: 'Love your neighbor as yourself'" (Galatians 5:13-14 NLT).

Jesus says, "You must love the Lord your God will all your heart, all your soul, and all your mind. This is the first and greatest commandment. A second is equally important: 'Love your neighbor as yourself.' All the other commandments and all the demands of the prophets are based on these two commandments" (Matthew 22:37-39 NLT).

Sometimes we hear it is wrong to love oneself. Such verses as Psalm 22:6 NIV, "But I am a worm, and not a man," and "Do nothing out of selfish ambition or vain conceit, but in humility consider others better than yourselves" Philippians 2:3-4 NIV, are quoted to remind us we are nothing. In Psalm 22 the people of God are in the midst of terrible agony and God seems to be silent. They are feeling totally abandoned. This feeling, and it is a feeling—not a fact since we're created in God's image, is expressed in poetic language. Philippians does not tell us it is wrong to love ourselves but rather to love others and put them first.

It is right to love ourselves. Have you accepted yourself concerning things you cannot change. Ninety percent of Hollywood stars wish they were more handsome or more beautiful. Have you accepted your looks, your physical attributes, your intelligence, and your personality. Can you thank God for making you the person you are? You need to thank God for making you, you!

That does not mean that you should not work with God in improving yourself: developing your gifts and talents, letting him knock off the rough edges that rub people the wrong way. If we don't love ourselves we block God's love flowing through us. This negatively affects our witness. Remember we are God's masterpiece. (See Ephesians 2:10 NLT.)

Lord, forgive me for complaining how you made me. Enable me to accept myself as your special creation. Amen.

May 30

Everyone You Meet

Colossians 1:28-29

"Everywhere we go, we tell everyone about Christ. We warn them and teach them with all the wisdom God has given us, for we want to present them to God, perfect (mature), in their relationship to Christ. I work very hard at this, as I depend on Christ's mighty power that works within me" (Colossians 1:28-29 NLT).

"What matters most to me is to finish what God started: the job the Master Jesus gave me of letting everyone I meet know all about this incredibly extravagant generosity of God" (Acts 20:24 Msg).

These verses could make some feel guilty. Paul says that everywhere he goes he tells everyone about Christ. I don't do that. Does the Holy Spirit want us to confront everyone? Jesus did not confront everyone he met.

I believe it is helpful to think in terms of heart's desire. All Christians should have a passion to see people come to Jesus and become his disciples. Paul was an extrovert. Sixty percent of people are introverts. Introverts usually need to have a relationship with people before it's natural for them to share Jesus with the unsaved. In fact, in our North American society few people will be open to listening to a presentation of the Gospel unless they have a relationship with the presenter. I understand in some countries where the Holy Spirit is moving in a powerful way people come to Christ in great numbers as evangelists lead people to Jesus on their first encounter.

Here in the United States it usually takes many encounters. It is also helpful if these encounters come from more than one individual. Don't be discouraged when people do not respond as quickly as we like. Pray to be faithful. Loving perseverance is usually the way the Holy Spirit works in our context. Some studies say it takes on the average of nine contacts before people respond to the Good News. Let's be faithful so we can be fruitful.

Lord Jesus, I want to be a faithful witness. Help me to be persistent and to depend on your Holy Spirit to work mightily through me to bring people to you and see them become disciples. Amen.

May 31

Target Your Mission or Go to Everyone?

Mark 2:17

"Healthy people don't need a doctor—sick people do. I have come to call sinners, not those who think they are already good enough" (Mark 2:17 NLT).

As you carry out your ministry, especially your evangelistic calling, it's appropriate to ask, is it right to target a particular group of people or just relate to those that may come across your path? It is certainly true that the Holy Spirit must lead us in our witness or we are totally ineffective. But let's ask if there are some likely paths the Spirit may direct us to follow where we are more fruitful. I think the answer is yes.

Jesus and Paul were conscious of their target. Jesus said he must go through Samaria. (See John 4:4.) Jesus sent the 70 to the towns where he was about to enter. He knew where he planned to go. (See Luke 10:1.) He instructed the disciples to find persons of peace. (See Matt.10:11.) Both he and Paul went to the Jews first (Romans 1:16), while Peter went to the Gentiles. Paul planned his missionary journeys strategically. He picked key cities and branched out from there. (See Acts 8:26-40.)

We are most effective in reaching people similar to ourselves, i.e. persons of our culture, economic status, age, gender, occupation and race. Most of us will naturally focus on this group. Those with the missionary gift are primarily called to minister cross-culturally.

Jesus presented the parable of the sower (Mark 4), in which he described the different conditions of the human heart. It's appropriate to pray for the Lord to open our eyes and to lead us to those with hearts of good soil that bring forth a crop, some thirty, sixty or even a hundred times what was sown. This, of course, does not mean that the Holy Spirit will never call a person to work in very hard soil, perhaps even for years before the first person responds to the Good News.

Lord, since you want me to bring forth much fruit and bring glory to the Father, lead me to those persons today with hearts of good soil who can bring forth a bountiful harvest. Thank you. Amen.

June 1

Mountain Top or Valley

Habakkuk 3:17-19

> Though the cherry trees don't blossom
>   and the strawberries don't ripen,
> Though the apples are worm-eaten
>   and the wheat fields stunned,
> Though the sheep pens are sheepless
>   and the cattle barns empty,
> I'm singing joyful praise to God.
>   I'm turning cartwheels of joy to my Savior God.
> Counting on God's Rule to prevail,
>   I take heart and gain strength.
> I run like a deer.
>   I feel like I'm king of the mountain! (Habakkuk 3:17-19 Msg).

What powerful words! My friend who recently died with cancer at age 66 had chosen these verses many years ago as his life verses. While he was going through the valley of the shadow of death he rested in these verses.

While I have never experienced the devastation described by Habakkuk I have had some very difficult experiences in my fifty years of pastoral ministry. There were at least two that involved organized rejection. In these situations I did not turn cartwheels of joy or feel like I was king on the mountain. I have some growing to do. However, looking back these two experiences were two of the most meaningful of my life. They changed my life's direction. They enriched me immensely. In fact I would not be writing this book or have written any book without those experiences.

While I have a long way to go in my growth, I am learning to not only trust God but to rejoice knowing God will prevail.

I have found great joy in seeing God work in my life. His peace and joy are beyond description. I rejoice in God my Savior.

Father, I thank you that you do not waste the experiences as we give them to you. Thank you for being patient with me as I slowly grow. I want to be a lump of clay in your hand. Mold me. Make me more and more like yourself. Thank you. Amen.

June 2

Lift Up Jesus

John 12:32

"But I, when I am lifted up from the earth, will draw all men to myself" (John 12:32 NIV).

When we lift up Jesus Christ, his Spirit often creates an awareness of need in people who do not know him. Jesus said, "The Spirit gives life; the flesh counts for nothing. The words I have spoken to you are spirit and they are life" (John 6:63 NIV). The sharing of my personal testimony must always point directly to Jesus so the listeners see Jesus more than me.

Lost people may see your passion, your love, your sympathy but this will never save them. It is only Jesus. No matter how much human love or elegance of speech, we can save no one. When we focus on our disappointments and trials we often detract from Jesus and his redemptive work.

Paul writes: "My message and my preaching were not with wise and persuasive words, but with a demonstration of the Spirit's power. So that your faith might not rest on men's wisdom, but on God's power" (I Corinthians 2:4-5 NIV). "We are…Christ's ambassadors, as though God were making his appeal through us" (II Corinthians 5:20 NIV). Anything that draws attention to myself makes me a conspirator to Jesus' work. When others see me instead of Jesus they see what I can do but too often do not grasp what Jesus can do.

When Jesus is lifted up, the Holy Spirit creates a need in the person for Jesus. Lift Jesus higher. "He must increase and I must decrease" (John 3:30 KJV).

People don't need our sympathy or even the sympathy of Jesus. If sympathy would save us, Jesus would not have had to go to the cross. That's why Paul says: "I resolved to know nothing while I was with you except Jesus Christ and him crucified" (I Corinthians 2:2 NIV). "In him (Christ) we have redemption through his blood, the forgiveness of sins, in accordance with the riches of God's grace that he lavished on us with all wisdom and understanding" (Ephesians 1:7-8 NIV).

Lord Jesus, I choose to lift you up in all I do and say. All my accomplishments are only because of you. Help me to always point to you for apart from you I am nothing. Amen.

June 3

Eighty-five Percent of Churches are not Growing

Acts 2:47

"The Lord added to their numbers daily those who were being saved" (Acts 2:47 NIV).

Can you imagine the Lord adding to your congregation every day? In Acts 2, the birthday of the church they experienced the dynamic working of the Holy Spirit. As Peter preached they cried out, "What shall we do?" (v.37). "Peter replied, 'repent and be baptized,…in the name of Jesus Christ for the forgiveness of your sins. And you will receive the gift of the Holy Spirit'" (v. 38). "They devoted themselves to the apostles' teaching and to the fellowship, to the breaking of bread and to prayers" (v.42).

Have you received the gift of the Holy Spirit? Jesus promised that when he is glorified he would send the Holy Spirit. Jesus was glorified in Acts 1:9. Oswald Chambers writes:

"Our waiting is not dependent on the providence of God, but on our own spiritual fitness… Once the Lord was glorified in His ascension, the Holy Spirit came.…We have to receive the revealed truth that he is here. When we receive the Holy Spirit, we receive reviving life from our ascended Lord."

It is not the baptism of the Holy Spirit that changes people, but the power of the ascended Christ coming into their lives through the Holy Spirit. We all too often separate things that the New Testament never separates. The baptism of the Holy Spirit is not an experience apart from Jesus Christ—it is the evidence of the ascended Christ. [xx]

The baptism of the Holy Spirit is Christ's life in us. Oh that we would be so broken that he could fill us with his Spirit. Then we too would devote ourselves to the apostles teaching, to fellowship, breaking of bread and prayers. Needs would be met, God's miracles would occur and the Lord would add to his Church those who were being saved. (See Acts 2:38-47).

Lord Jesus, break me and heal me. Fill me with your precious Holy Spirit so rivers of living water will flow to the thirsty souls about me. Amen.

June 4

Irrelevance is Irreverence

Acts 2:47

"The church grew in strength and numbers. The believers were walking in the fear of the Lord and in the comfort of the Holy Spirit" (Acts 9:31 NLT).

Today many people are positive on Jesus Christ but down on the church. To them the church seems irrelevant. There are certain things a church needs to offer if people are going to be committed to the body of Christ. Yesterday's reading presented a vibrant church using Biblical and theological terminology. Today's reading is focused on our contemporary situation.

We affirm the absolute necessity of the work of the Holy Spirit, the apostles teaching, fellowship, breaking of bread and prayers, for they are foundational. But these need to be expressed or lived out in our context and culture. (See I Corinthians 9:20-23.)

(1) The teaching and preaching must be positive, life-changing Good News of our resurrected Lord Jesus. The key here is "life-changing." This is only possible with the anointing of the Holy Spirit.

(2) The church must have a discipleship training process which includes a strong emphasis on both local and foreign mission. This includes the members being involved in ministry outside the four walls of the church in their community.

(3) Members of the church are excited about what God is doing in their midst and love to invite their unsaved friends to Christ and his church.

If these are in place there will be no problem about being relevant to your context because lives are being transformed, broken families are being made whole, economic needs are being met, the sick and imprisoned are ministered to.

In one community if the police have a problem they frequently call the pastor, when the school superintendent or principal has a problem they often call the pastor. Oh may the day come when the church is known for its relevance in the community and not for its divisions. (See John 17:21.)

The older a church gets the more ingrown it tends to become. Too often it becomes a rest home for saints instead of a hospital for the unchurched. Ask yourself: What am I doing to reach the unchurched in my community?

Lord Jesus, help me to reach out to those who need your love today. Amen.

June 5

"The Kingdom of God is . . . Righteousness . . ."

Romans 14:17

"The kingdom of God is not a matter of eating and drinking, but of righteousness, peace and joy in the Holy Spirit" (Romans 14:17 NIV). The word "righteous" can also be translated justice as the New English Bible translates it. Justice is very rare in this world. We will have disappointments unending if we expect to find justice in this world. If you expect justice you will end up indulging yourself with self-pity. However you are called to act justly, to live justly.

Justice is something we as God's children try our best to give even though we do not receive it. Too often when we don't receive justice we blame God. God didn't promise justice in this life. "In the world you will have trouble. But take heart! I have overcome the world" (John 16:33 NIV). When we are treated less than just, instead of asking, "Why me?" Let's learn to ask, "Why shouldn't it be me?" When will we be mature to the point where our faith accepts what comes our way without blaming God?

Jesus said, "Blessed are those who hunger and thirst for righteousness (or justice) because they will be filled" (Matthew 5:6 NIV). The NLT says "they will receive it in the full. The fulfillment comes to those who may not completely achieve justice or righteousness but long for it as a man longs for food when he is starving and for water when he is dying of thirst. The promise is that he will be satisfied.

Jesus said, "Unless your righteousness (justice) surpasses that of the Pharisees and the teachers of the law, you will certainly not enter the kingdom of heaven" (Matthew 5:20 NIV). Paul writes to Timothy: "Pursue righteousness (justice), godliness, faith, love, endurance and gentleness" (I Timothy 6:11 NIV). In ourselves we cannot attain righteousness. It is not in our nature. Jesus gives us this gift. He is our righteousness. (See I Corinthians 1:31.) We must have a new nature—God's nature. That is exactly what he gives us. (See II Peter 1:4.) He "arrayed me in a robe of righteousness" (Isaiah 61:10 NIV). Hallelujah!

Father, we long for justice in our world. Use us as instruments of your righteousness and justice today. Amen.

June 6

"The Kingdom of God is... Peace..."

Romans 14:17

"The kingdom of God is not a matter of what we eat or drink, but of living a life of goodness and peace and joy in the Holy Spirit" (Romans 14:17 NLT).

Jesus in the upper room tells his disciples: "Peace I leave with you; my peace I give you. I do not give to you as the world gives. Do not let your hearts be troubled and do not be afraid" (John 14:27 NIV).

In the same discourse he states that he needs to go away but will be coming back: "I have told you all this so that in me you may have peace. In this world you will have trouble. But take heart! I have overcome the world" (John 16:33 NIV).

"My peace I give you," and "in me you may have peace." Peace is a gift from Jesus. He is the source of our peace. It is his peace he gives us. I must receive it as his gift. I can't work it up from within me. That means I must humbly accept it; acknowledging the giver. As a gift it is not something I earn or deserve. This makes it all the more precious.

When I receive a gift it makes a difference who it is from. If I receive an autographed baseball from the most valuable player of the major leagues it is valuable to those who love baseball. If I receive an autographed baseball from someone unknown to me the gift is not as meaningful. Jesus, the King of kings gives me this wonderful gift of peace. He triumphed victorious over death guaranteeing him the authority to give us peace. If we accept his peace there is no need to worry. In fact, if we worry we are rejecting his gift.

Jesus' gift is supernatural. As long as you live in his presence you will not lose it. It abides in you and gives you a boldness and confidence that flows from your life. It's just part of the living water that Jesus promised will flow from our inmost being to the thirsty souls of others around us.

Teach me Lord to live in your peace. May your peace flow through me 24/7 so others are drawn to you. Amen.

June 7

"The Kingdom of God is . . . Joy"

Romans 14:17

"The kingdom of God is not a matter of what we eat or drink, but of living a life of goodness and peace and joy in the Holy Spirit" (Romans 14:17 NLT). *The Message* reads: God's kingdom, "is what God does with your life as he sets it right, puts it together, and completes it with joy." Then the next verse reads: "Your task is to single-mindedly serve Christ."

It is fascinating that the apostle who suffered most spoke more about joy than any of the other apostles. It is also interesting that the closer Jesus came to the end of his earthly life the more he spoke of joy.

As you relate to older people have you experienced their murmuring and complaining or their joyful attitude? Unless you are experiencing joy now you will not likely be experiencing joy in your older years.

Where does our joy come from? Joy is rarely mentioned in the Gospels. Mark never uses the word. The absence of joy in the Gospels is because the Holy Spirit had not yet come. Joy comes from Jesus and Jesus is made real to us through the work of the Holy Spirit. John's Gospel informs us that Jesus gives us his joy. Joy comes from Jesus through the ministry of the Holy Spirit. In the context of Jesus teaching about our need to abide in the vine, he says, "I have told you this so that you will be filled with my joy. Yes, your joy will overflow!" (John 15:11 NLT).

He explains, "You have sorrow now, but I will see you again; then you will rejoice, and no one can rob you of that joy. At that time you won't need to ask me for anything. The truth is, you can go directly to the Father and ask him and he will grant your request because you use my name... Ask, using my name, and you will receive, and you will have abundant joy" (John 16:22-24 NLT).

Lord Jesus, thank you for sending your Holy Spirit. Fill me today with your joy so it can overflow to those who have no hope. Amen.

June 8

"The Kingdom is Living... in the Holy Spirit"

Romans 14:17

"The kingdom of God is not a matter of what we eat or drink, but of living a life of goodness and peace and joy in the Holy Spirit" (Romans 14:17 NLT).

Most Christians feel more comfortable speaking about God and Jesus then they do speaking about the Holy Spirit. God is one. (See Deuteronomy 6:4.) God is a Spirit. (See John 4:24.) God, Jesus and the Holy Spirit are one.

The Spirit makes real to me what Jesus did for me. We are born of the Spirit (See John 3:5), indwelt by the Spirit (See I Corinthians 6:19), sealed by the Spirit (See Ephesians 1:13-14), filled with the Spirit (See Ephesians 5:18), empowered for witness by the Spirit (See Acts 1:8), and anointed for service by the Spirit (See Luke 4:18, Acts 10:38). The Spirit produces fruit in us (See Galatians 5:22-23). He guides us (See Romans 8:14). He interprets the Scriptures for us. (See I Corinthians 2:9-14.)

"The Spirit of God, who raised Jesus from the dead, lives in you. And just as he raised Christ from the dead, he will give life to your mortal body by this same Spirit living within you" (Romans 8:11 NLT).

"The Holy Spirit helps us in our distress. For we don't even know what we should pray for, nor how we should pray. But the Holy Spirit prays for us with groanings that cannot be expressed in words. And the Father who knows all hearts knows what the Spirit is saying, for the Spirit pleads for all believers in harmony with God's own will" (Romans 8:26-27 NLT).

"The Holy Spirit speaks to us deep in our hearts and tells us that we are God's children. And since we are his children, he will share his treasures—for everything God gives to his Son, Christ, is ours, too" (Romans 8:16-17 NLT).

When we see how Jesus depended on the Spirit, it should make us realize how we need to depend on the spirit. He was conceived and born of the Spirit, led by the Spirit, anointed by the Spirit, crucified in the power of the Spirit, raised by the Spirit, gave his teaching through the Spirit, and is the giver of the Spirit.

Jesus, I thank you for sending the precious Holy Spirit to us. Fill me with your Spirit so rivers of living water will overflow to others. Amen.

June 9

In Debt

Romans 1:14

"I have a great sense of obligation to people in our culture and to people in other cultures, to the educated and uneducated alike. So I am eager to come to you in Rome, too, to preach God's Good News. For I am not ashamed of this Good News about Christ. It is the power of God at work, saving everyone who believes…" (Romans 1:14-16 NLT).

When someone does something for us we want to repay them. We feel it is our duty. The Son of God got us out of the pit we were in, got rid of the sins we were doomed to keep repeating. (See Colossians 1:14.) Paul in prison started thinking about God's blessings (See Ephesians 1), and couldn't get stopped. No wonder he says he is under obligation to share these blessings with everyone. The more we realize what Jesus has done for us the more we want to share these unearned blessings with others.

Our world is full of needs. Every day we see people in poverty, multitudes living in repressive governments and suffering from violence. We are warned concerning possible pandemics and natural disasters. We become overwhelmed with the needs. If we approach these needs with our human sympathy and energy we will eventually experience burnout. Our human resources become depleted.

We need divine resources and motivation. Our motivation is not from human sympathy but from our King who commissioned us to go and make disciples, to do the works that he did. "Jesus arrived from Nazareth anointed by God with the Holy Spirit, ready for action. He went through the country helping people and healing everyone who was beaten down by the devil. He was able to do all this because God was with him" (Acts 10:38 Msg). He is our model. Since he came to serve and give his life for others we must do the same. (See Matthew 20:28.) We are in debt, we are under obligation. "I have an obligation to discharge and a duty to perform and a debt to pay" (Romans 1:14 AMP).

Lord, I need your Holy Spirit today to fulfill my obligation. Make me a faithful witness and servant for you today. Amen.

June 10

Quality or Quantity

John 3:16

"God so loved the world that he gave his only Son, so that everyone who believes in him will not perish but have eternal life. God did not send his Son into the world to condemn it, but to save it" (John 3:16-17 NLT).

God loved the world—that is the people of the world. That includes everyone ever born or will be born. If you or your church are saying we are not interested in increasing our numbers we are saying, "You can go to hell." If you have two children and they get lost you search day and night for them until they are found. If you find one and not the other imagine a neighbor saying to you: "You found the quality child, just forget about the other one." That's what we are saying when we are not making efforts to reach people for Jesus and make disciples.

We count people because numbers represent people. Numbers are not our goal, transformed individuals are our goal. As Rick Warren writes: "Anytime someone says, 'You can't measure success by numbers,' my response is, 'It all depends on what you're counting!' If you're counting marriages saved, lives transformed, broken people healed, unbelievers becoming worshipers of Jesus and members being mobilized for ministry and missions, numbers are extremely important. They have eternal significance."

The book of Acts is permeated with numbers. The Gospels frequently inform us that multitudes followed Jesus or that the house was so full that others could not enter. The Shepherd left the 99 and sought the one lost sheep. Every person is important! Don't let people deceive you with the idea that numbers are not important.

Those who don't like to talk about numbers frequently state appreciation for their little church that does little to reach their community. They need to pray:

Father, give me passion like you had in giving your only Son for my salvation. Jesus, give me passion like that which took you to the cruel cross so I could have life. Holy Spirit, give me passion like that which enabled you to leave heaven in all its splendor to come and live in my sinful heart, now made holy by your work. Father, help me to be passionate about people today. Amen.

June 11

People Want and Need Significance

Luke 14:33

American Christianity has been described as a mile wide and an inch deep. In too many churches, people make no commitment other than to attend regularly, which means they attend when it is convenient. For many there is no instruction or entry point class before being received into membership. Community clubs have higher standards for membership than many churches. Christianity is too often just an add-on to your already full schedule.

Churches that grow and make disciples have high standards. They start where people are and move them towards maturity. They usually have a membership covenant, whereby the candidates for membership promise in writing that they will participate in the worship service, pray for their church, invite and welcome new persons to the church, protect the unity of the church by not gossiping and by cooperating with the leadership. They promise to serve the Lord and to give regularly to the church's vision and mission. They are urged to participate in a small group that not only meets for their needs but serves in the mission of the church.

Jesus raised the bar very high: "Any of you who does not give up everything he has cannot be my disciple" (Luke 14:33 NIV). "If anyone would come after me, he must deny himself and take up his cross and follow me" (Matthew 16:24 NIV). Paul writes: "Those who belong to Christ Jesus have crucified the sinful nature with its passions and desires" (Galatians 5:24 NIV). *The Message* says: "Among those who belong to Christ, everything connected with getting our own way and mindlessly responding to what everyone else calls necessities is killed off for good—crucified" (Galatians 5:24).

Challenging people to a serious commitment attracts people because they want to be part of something that makes a difference in their community or world. We all need something significant to give our lives to.

When we are witnessing to our unsaved friends we don't say: "Come to church, it only takes an hour of your time." We say, "Jesus makes life worthwhile, you'll find new meaning. It'll open up a new world for you."

Father, thank you that your call is life-changing. Help me to challenge people to become radical disciples. Amen.

June 12

The Lord Must be the Builder

Psalm 127:1

"Unless the Lord builds the house, its builders labor in vain" (Psalm 127:1 NIV).

The church is more than a community club. It's more than a business. It is God's house, and the body of Christ, who is its head. (See Colossians 1:18.)

While the church is far more than a business, there are certain principles it can learn from a business. If businesses were managed as poorly as many churches, they would be closed long ago. Churches often have a handful of people who will not give up their opinions and outdated traditions. They are determined to keep things the same. Someone said, "People are open to new things as long as they are exactly like the old ones."

If we keep doing the same thing and expect different results, we need to wake up. I received the Keystone Farmer Degree but that was 50 plus years ago. What do I know about farming?—Nothing! Farming has changed. Churches must change. The message never changes but the method of delivering the message and the organizational patterns change. A small church operates drastically different from a large church.

Will dedication cause a church to grow? Not necessarily. Many churches are dedicated to traditions, programs, or buildings. Some are even dedicated to prayer and Bible study. The Holy Spirit must enliven the people. Prayer must be a two-way communion. If we're convinced we are right, we can't hear from God as to what needs to change for the church to be both faithful and fruitful.

It is God's church but he chooses to use human instruments to grow and mature his church. Paul was an expert builder. (See I Corinthians 3:10.) He struggled and labored day and night for the Lord as he planted churches and made disciples. "We proclaim him (Christ), admonishing and teaching everyone with all wisdom, so that we may present everyone perfect in Christ. To this end I labor, struggling with all his energy, which so powerfully works in me" (Colossians 1:28-29 NIV). "For three years I never stopped warning each of you night and day with tears" (Acts. 20:31 NIV).

Lord, help me to hear your voice. Give me the courage to change whatever is hindering my church from being faithful and fruitful. Amen.

June 13

Living Gets Better and Better

John 14:12

It doesn't matter how long you have been a Christian or how mature you are in your walk with Jesus, there is a higher plane ahead. Growth is exponential. You never reach your potential.

Consider the following:
- "The truth is anyone who believes in me will do the same works I have done, and even greater works, because I am going to be with the Father" (John 14:12 NLT).

- "You can ask for anything in my name, and I will do it, because the work of the Son brings glory to the Father. Yes, ask anything in my name, and I will do it" (John 14:13-14 NLT).

- "Don't worry about everyday life—whether you have enough food, drink, and clothes....Look at the birds. They don't need to plant or harvest or put food in barns because your heavenly Father feeds them... Why worry about your clothes? Look at the lilies and how they grow. They don't work or make their clothing, yet Solomon in all his glory was not dressed as beautiful as they are.... Your heavenly Father already knows all your needs, and he will give you all you need from day to day if you live for him and make the Kingdom of God your primary concern" (Matthew 6:25-33 NLT).

- "I have learned how to get along happily whether I have much or little. I know how to live on almost nothing or with everything. I have learned the secret of living in every situation, whether it is with a full stomach or empty, with plenty or little. For I can do everything with the help of Christ who gives me the strength I need" (Philippians 4:11-13 NLT).

- "God who takes care of me will supply all your needs from his glorious riches, which have been given to us in Christ Jesus" (Philippians 4:19 NLT).

- "The Lord is my Shepherd; I have everything I need" (Psalm 23:1 NLT).

After being a Christian for 60 years, it's exciting to know I can grow and grow and grow. What a wonderful future we have in Christ.

Lord Jesus, thank you for all the resources we have yet to experience. Thank you for this exciting future. Amen.

June 14

God's Creation

Psalm 24:1

"The earth is the Lord's, and everything in it. The world, and all who live in it" (Psalm 24:1 NIV).

The other day I went to a church ministry meeting. The ten of us sat at picnic tables. The birds provided a symphony of beautiful background music, although at times it was so loud their songs demanded our attention.

The view was absolutely spectacular. The trees and the fields were lush green; the corn straight as a plumb line—eight feet tall, not a weed in sight. In the distance a farmer was in the field sowing seed with a huge tractor and drill. The sky was blue. There was not an insect in the pure air. A man walked his dog through the grass a short distance away. The scene was a foretaste of heaven.

When humankind and God cooperate, we experience a bit of the fulfillment of the prayer Jesus taught us: "Your kingdom come, your will be done on earth as it is in heaven" (Matthew 6:10 NIV).

Paul wrote, "Since you have been raised to new life with Christ, set your sights on the realities of heaven, where Christ sits at God's right hand in the place of honor and power. Let heaven fill your thoughts. Do not think only about things down here on earth. For you died when Christ died, and your real life is hidden with Christ in God. And when Christ, who is our real life, is revealed to the whole world, you will share in all his glory" (Colossians 3:1-4 NLT).

We will share in all God's glory! Heaven is indescribable. Paul was forbidden to tell us what he saw. (See II Corinthians 12:4) Why? If we had just a glimpse of heaven perhaps we would be so enamored or captivated by it we would be ineffective here. Nevertheless heaven should be one of our primary motivators for sharing the Good News. Jesus said, "Do not let your hearts be troubled. Trust in God.... In my Father's house are many rooms; ... and I am going to prepare a place for you" (John 14:1-2 NIV).

Lord, thank you for the hope of heaven. Help me to share the Good News so others can know this wonderful hope as well. Amen.

June 15

Make the Most of Every Opportunity

Ephesians 5:16

"Be very careful...how you live—not as unwise but as wise, making the most of every opportunity, because the days are evil" (Ephesians 5:15-16 NIV).

"Be wise in the way you act toward outsiders; make the most of every opportunity" (Colossians 4:5 NIV).

"I consider my life worth nothing to me, if only I may finish the race and complete the task the Lord Jesus has given me—the task of testifying to the Gospel of God's grace" (Acts 20:14 NIV).

"Teach us to number our days aright, that we may gain a heart of wisdom" (Psalm 90:12 NIV).

"Show me, O Lord, my life's end and the number of my days; let me know how fleeting is my life. You have made my days a mere handbreadth; the span of my years is as nothing before you. Each man's life is but a breath" (Psalm 39:5 NIV).

Life is so very short. Time is a precious gift from God. I pray daily for the Lord to help me not to waste time. Each day brings us one day closer home. Paul mentions the days are evil implying that is the reason we need to take advantage of the opportunities. In evil days the opportunities are not as frequent. People may not be as open to hearing the Good News. Noah preached for 120 years with no response. In Revelation the people who did not die in the plagues still refused to turn from their evil deeds. (See Revelation 9:20.)

Opportunities are often not repeated. When we miss an opportunity to witness for Jesus we feel badly. We feel guilty and rightly so. Tell Jesus you blew it. Ask him to forgive you. He will. Ask him to give you another opportunity. He will. When that opportunity comes allow him to speak through you in a gentle but confident manner. He will. You will be surprised and exceedingly grateful. You are growing!

Lord, help me to make the most of every opportunity. Amen.

June 16

Be Filled with the Spirit

Ephesians 5:18

"Do not get drunk on wine, which leads to debauchery. Instead, be filled with the Spirit. Speak to one another with psalms, hymns, and spiritual songs. Sing and make music in your hearts to the Lord, always giving thanks to God the Father for everything, in the name of our Lord Jesus Christ. Submit to one another out of reverence for Christ" (Ephesians 5:18-21 NIV).

The pagan culture in that day and in our day tends to find happiness in wine and sex and worldly pleasures. The Christian finds happiness when he or she is filled with the Holy Spirit.

Paul lists three results of being filled with the Holy Spirit:

(1) The heart is changed. The Holy Spirit fills it with music—psalms, hymns and spiritual songs. It's wonderful to have a heart filled with praise to the Lord. Most mornings I awake to music of praise in my heart to God. That's when it is easy to say: "Good morning God" instead of "Good God, morning!" My dad was a whistler. He would whistle hymns in praise to God throughout the day. What a blessing to have those memories.

(2) We give thanks to God our Father for everything, in the name of Jesus our Messiah. How can this be possible? It's possible because we have come to trust him. We know he never makes a mistake or causes us a needless tear. Even when we receive discouraging news we claim the promise that all things will work together for our good. (See Romans 8:28.) In other words, in everything God works it out for good. We are astonished with the wonder of God's great love in providing salvation or deliverance for us.

(3) We respect, honor and submit to each other because we reverence Christ. (See Ephesians 5:21.) Jesus died not only for me but for everyone, therefore if Jesus loved them that much, how can I not love and respect them?

Since the Greek text states this command to be filled with the Holy Spirit in the present tense, that means we need to be continually filled. Why, because we leak. So come to Jesus continually requesting his filling. We come, ask, and he fills us again and again. Praise his name!

Father, thank you for your Holy Spirit. Fill me until your love overflows into the lives of all I meet. Amen.

June 17

We are Fountains Not Wells

John 4:14

"The water I give them takes away thirst altogether. It becomes a perpetual spring within them, giving them eternal life" (John 4:14 NIV).

Jesus uses the imagery of a fountain rather than a well. There is a huge difference. Jesus said the water is a perpetual spring within. Well water is of value only if you take the effort to bring it to the surface. Fountain water takes no effort. It is free flowing and it is fresh.

Where is the source of this fountain water? It's from within us. How is that possible? Many times we read that Jesus is in us, e.g., "Remain in me and I will remain in you" (John 15:4 NLT).

Jesus is the source of this living water. It flows without effort. Jesus said in John 7:38 NLT, "Rivers of living water will flow out from within." Move from a well of water which we work to bring to the surface to a fountain which turns into rivers of water gushing from within!

Is this your experience? Jesus wants his life to flow out from within you. If it is not flowing, something is obstructing the flow. Something is blocking what Jesus wants to come out. Jesus presents the same principles in John 15:5 NLT, "Those who remain in me and I in them, will produce much fruit." Note it says they will produce much fruit, not they can or might produce much fruit.

Sin blocks the flow of the fountain within. Remaining in Jesus is the key. He is the source. Sin separates you from God. Whenever the fountain is not flowing, whenever we are not producing fruit; ask, have I removed myself from Jesus? Have I grieved his Spirit? As you wait in his presence and listen to his voice you will find what is blocking the flow.

If nothing comes to mind thank him for loving you and blessing you. The rivers of water will begin to flow. Praise him from your innermost being. This attitude of praise will bubble up and overflow through you to others.

Jesus, I thank you for the fountain you put within me. Make me a fountain of blessing to others today. Amen.

June 18

Climb a Tree

Luke 19:1-10

"He ran ahead and climbed a sycamore tree beside the road, so he could watch from there" (Luke 19:4 NLT).

"Zacchaeus was one of the most influential Jews in the Roman tax-collecting business, and he had become very rich" (v.2 NLT). He was short of stature. Zacchaeus was so determined to see Jesus that he put aside his pride and climbed a tree to catch a glimpse of Jesus among the crowd. Jesus noticing tree-climbing Zacchaeus, calls him by name. Jesus said, "Zacchaeus, come down immediately. I must stay at your house today" (v.5 NIV). Like Jesus, we too should call people by name. Jesus could read his heart. We need to pray for the gift of knowledge to read people's hearts. Jesus knew Zaccheaus longed to visit with him so he invited himself.

Zaccheaus was very excited and full of joy. Among the "crowd" of people you meet, pray to find those who are ready to hear the Good News. In Matthew 10:11 Jesus calls these people, people of peace or worthy people. Pray to find them.

"The crowds were displeased. 'He has gone to be the guest of a notorious sinner,' they grumbled'" (v. 7 NLT). The person of peace may not be appreciated by others. You will need to take the risk of being misunderstood when you are obeying Jesus' command to be a witness for him. Many people at church will not appreciate your efforts because you are inviting the wrong kind of people to your church. How sad but you need to remember that's how they treated Jesus.

Zaccheaus' response is clear and concise. He confesses any dishonesty he may have committed. Jesus response is just as clear and concise: "Salvation has come to this home today, for this man has shown himself to be a son of Abraham. And I, the Son of Man, have come to seek and save those like him who are lost" (vv. 9-10 NLT).

Lord, give me eyes to see those who are open to receive the Good News. Help me to share it with persons like Zaccheaus even though others may not appreciate their character. Thank you. Amen.

June 19

The Hearts of Fathers Is for the Children

Malachi 4:5-6

"Look, I will send you the prophet Elijah before that great and dreadful day of the Lord comes. He will turn the hearts of the fathers to their children, and the hearts of the children to their fathers; or else I will come and strike the land with a curse" (Malachi 4:5-6 NIV).

One of the great tragedies of our time is that multitudes of children grow up without a father. Even in homes where he is present physically, he often is not involved emotionally or spiritually with the family. A prison chaplain, asked the prisoners if they wanted cards to send to their mother for Mother's Day. Everyone wanted one. When the same question was asked concerning Father's Day no one desired a card for their father. Only a small percentage of children grow up living with the same father their first eighteen years.

When Paul writes to the Thessalonians he gives a good description of a father: "You know that we treated each of you as a father treats his own children. We pleaded with you, encouraged you, and urged you to live your lives in a way that God would consider worthy. For he called you into his Kingdom to share his glory" (I Thessalonians 2:11-12 NLT).

One of the more effective ways we witness to the power of the Good News is through our families. Are our hearts, as parents, centered on work, recreation, getting ahead or do we have a heart for our family?

One of the qualifications of church leaders is that, "He must manage his own family well with children who respect and obey him. For if a man cannot manage his own household, how can he take care of God's church?" (I Timothy 3:4-5 NLT). The world takes notice when they see a godly family. Paul admonished us to submit to one another because of our reverence of Christ: wives to husbands and husbands to wives. (See Ephesians 5:21.)

Lord, help me to be a goodly parent today. Help me show love to my spouse and children. Give me wisdom to guide, nurture and set an example for them in the ways of the Lord. Thank you. Amen.

June 20

Running the Race

I Corinthians 9:24-27

"You've all been to the stadium and seen the athletes race. Everyone runs; one wins. Run to win. All good athletes train hard. They do it for a gold medal that tarnishes and fades. You're after one that's gold eternally. I don't know about you, but I'm running hard for the finish line. I'm giving it everything I've got. No sloppy living for me! I'm staying alert and in top condition. I'm not going to get caught napping, telling everyone else all about it and then missing out myself" (I Corinthians 9:23-27 Msg).

The NIV states: "I do not run like a man running aimlessly; I do not fight like a man beating the air. No, I beat my body and make it my slave so that after I have preached to others, I myself will not be disqualified for the prize" (vv. 16-27).

Paul uses Olympic imagery here. The runners train for years to win the race. They deny themselves many pleasures for the pleasure of running the race to hear the affirmation of the fans and receive a medal. They deny themselves certain enjoyable foods; they discipline themselves to exercise even when they don't feel like it. They follow the strict rules of their coach. How serious are you in living for Jesus? Are you conscious that you are in training? Are you seeing progress or are you just beating the air? How serious are you in pressing toward the goal?

Paul writes to the Philippians: "I press toward the goal to win the prize for which God has called me heavenward in Christ Jesus" (3:14 NIV). And when he sees the end coming he writes: "I have fought a good fight, I have finished the race, I have kept the faith. Now there is in store for me the crown of righteousness, which the Lord, the righteous Judge, will award to me on that day—and not only to me, but also to all who have longed for his appearing" (II Timothy 4:7-8 NIV).

Jesus, help me to run with discipline, with determination, my eyes fixed on you. Help me keep the faith and receive the crown of righteousness. Amen.

June 21

All I Have

II Corinthians 12:15

"I will very gladly spend for you everything I have and expend myself as well" (II Corinthians 12:15 NIV).

Once we enter God's Kingdom our eyes our opened to an entirely new world. He is King! Our own interests and desires change. Jesus' goals become our goals.

Are we committed like Paul? What things come between you and Jesus? Are you willing to move if he calls you to help plant a church in the next town or half way around the globe?

I have a close friend who had a high position in a large institution but he gave it up because Jesus wanted him to be a teacher. He sacrificed not only salary but prestige and years of training to be a witness for Jesus in the classroom. Jesus has multiplied his joy and provided ample for his financial needs. He has no regrets!

Another friend gave up a medical practice here in the states to serve as a doctor in a very poor culture. He has the joy of touching many lives for Jesus.

Perhaps God will ask you to make some sacrifices or he may ask you to remain right where you are and be a witness for him. Do you have reservations in following through in what you know God is asking you to do? To refuse to follow where you know what God is asking you to do will block the free flowing rivers of living water from within you. Your life will become stagnant.

The real test of the Christian is not our willingness to preach the Gospel, but our willingness to do whatever Jesus wants us to do no matter how lowly or seemingly unimportant. On the other hand, Jesus is able to do abundantly above what you can imagine.

"Let us throw off everything that hinders and the sin that so easily entangles, and let us run with perseverance the race marked out for us" (Hebrews 12:2 NIV).

Lord Jesus, search my heart and see if there is any sin that entangles my feet. Take complete control of my life. Amen.

June 22

Work Out Your Salvation

Philippians 2:12-13

"Continue to work out your salvation with fear and trembling, for it is God who works in you to will and to act according to his good purpose" (Philippians 2:12-13 NIV). The NLT reads: "Put into action God's saving work in your lives, obeying God with deep reverence and fear. For God is working in you giving you the desire to obey him and the power to do what pleases him."

Salvation is a gift to all who will receive it. (See Ephesians 2:8-9). But we must put our salvation into action. It's God who works in us giving us this desire to obey and the power to perform his purpose for us. Why is it so difficult if God's power is performing his will in us? It's difficult because we are not willing to die to self and trust Jesus to lead us. David wrote: "The Lord says, 'I will guide you along the best pathway for your life. I will advise you and watch over you'" (Psalm 32:8 NLT). What a blessed promise!

However, we must yield to his discipline. We must work hard: "Work hard at living at peace with others" (I Peter 3:11 NLT). "Make every effort to apply the benefits of these promises to your life. Then your faith will produce a life of moral excellence" (II Peter 1:5 NLT). "Work hard to prove that you really are among those God has called and chosen. Doing this, you will never stumble or fall away" (II Peter 1:10 NLT). "Make every effort to live a pure and blameless life" (II Peter 3:14 NLT). Many times we are reminded to work hard.

We are absolutely helpless to earn salvation but once we are born into God's family we need to give ourselves wholeheartedly to our Lord and Savior. After all he died for us. We can never repay him for his wonderful gift of eternal life.

Father, I thank you for providing both the will and the power to live the Christian life. I promise by your grace to give my every effort to cooperate with your will in my everyday living to please you in all things. Amen.

June 23

A Home For Jesus

John 14:2,23

Paul prays that: "Out of his (God's) glorious riches he may strengthen you with power through his Spirit…, so that Christ may dwell in our hearts through faith" (Ephesians 3:16-17 NIV). How is it possible for Jesus to dwell in us?

Jesus said, "I am going to prepare a place (home) for you" (John 14: 2 NIV). In verse 23 NIV, we have the same word used when he says: "My Father will love him and we will come… and make our home with him." Just as Jesus was going to heaven to prepare a home for us we can prepare a home for him in our hearts.

How can I make a home for Jesus? Pentecost came; God came in the form of his Spirit. Through the miracle of the Holy Spirit, God lives in our hearts. He knocks on our heart's door.

Holman Hunt painted a picture of Jesus knocking on the door. If you check, there is no handle on the outside. You must open the door. "Here I stand at the door and knock. If anyone hears my voice and opens the door, I will come in and eat with him, and he with me." (Revelations 3:20 NIV).

My body is the temple of the Holy Spirit. (See I Corinthians 3:16.) Jesus lives there. "The one who is in you is greater than the one who is in the world" (I John 4:4 NIV). If we submit to him we will overcome all sin. "The tools of our trade… are for demolishing that entire massively corrupt culture. We use our powerful God-tools for smashing warped philosophies, tearing down barriers erected against the truth of God, fitting every loose thought and emotion and impulse into the structure of life shaped by Christ" (II Corinthians 10:4-5 Msg).

Jesus can purify every thought, emotion and impulse into the likeness of himself. That is victory.

Lord Jesus, since you live in my heart, I give you every emotion, every desire, every thought. My heart and mind are yours, my desires are your desires. Search me and know my heart and see if there is anything displeasing to you. Wash me and make me pure. Thank you. Amen.

June 24

Everyone Preaching

Acts 8:4

"Those who had been scattered preached the word wherever they went" (Acts 8:4 NIV). "Wherever they were scattered they preached the message about Jesus" (Acts 8:4 Msg).

Ideally the Great Commission should scatter us, but the church seems to gravitate toward staying in the salt shaker. Perhaps it will take persecution, as it did here in Acts 8, to scatter us. In our salt shakers we do not make people thirsty for the water of life. Too often we hide our light under a bushel rather than allow it to brighten the darkness.

Why is that? Like the church at Ephesus which was at least thirty years of age, we lose our first love. "You have forsaken your first love. Remember the height from which you have fallen! Repent and do the things you did at first. If you do not repent, I will come to you and remove your lampstand from its place" (Revelation 2:4-5 NIV). As a general rule the longer we are Christians the less zeal we have. Perhaps the axiom, familiarity breeds contempt is too often true even with Christians.

Another church the same age had a similar problem: "I know you inside and out, and find little to my liking. You're not cold, you're not hot—far better to be either cold or hot! You're stale. You're stagnant. You make me want to vomit. You brag, 'I'm rich, I've got it made, I need nothing from anyone,' oblivious that in fact you're a pitiful blind beggar, threadbare and homeless" (Revelation 3:15-17 Msg).

According to church history there is one sin that will weaken the church every time, i.e. riches. Often when we become Christians, God blesses us and then we get our eyes on the blessings and off of the blesser—Jesus.

Paul admonished the Roman church to serve the Lord enthusiastically. "Never be lacking in zeal" (12:11 NIV). "Don't burn out; keep yourselves fueled and aflame" Msg).

Lord Jesus, I confess my zeal is lacking. Empower me with enthusiasm by your Holy Spirit as I feed on your word. Use me to witness for you today! Amen.

June 25

Find Your Style: Serving

Ephesians 4:7,11

We all are made differently. "Everything you are and think and do is permeated with Oneness. But that doesn't mean you should all look and speak and act the same" (Ephesians 4:11 Msg).

It's helpful to realize that while we are all witnesses we go about sharing our faith in different ways, using different styles. Bill Hybles lists six different styles of evangelism. Each of us has one or more of these styles that we will find comfortable. Today we focus on serving.

Serving—How Can I Help? Most Christians believe they are called to serve. We should enjoy serving others. However, too often we have not shared the Good News with those we serve. Dorcas was serving the Lord by helping the poor. (See Acts 9:36.) Dorcas died. Her friends sent for Peter. When he came they showed him the clothing she made. Her deeds of serving impacted many lives.

John and Rhoda continually serve the Lord by helping people move, by lending one of their vehicles to someone when their car lets them sit, by taking food to those in need or fixing a broken pipe under the kitchen sink or providing grocery money. Their sacrificial acts of service impact many lives for Christ both inside the church as well as those who are unchurched.

Some Christians feel like second-class citizens because "all they can do" is serve others. Serving with joy from a heart of compassion frequently leads people to thank you for your acts of kindness. Respond by saying, "God has been good to me, I can't help passing on this goodness to others." You can add, "He changed me and made my life wonderfully different. I enjoy helping others. I want you to know you matter to God too."

You will plant seeds that others can water and the Holy Spirit can bring to fruition. Many unbelievers need someone like you to soften their hearts through your acts of service. Be that person for them.

Jesus, help me to be your joyful servant today. Open my eyes to those who need help. Enable me to share your love both in word and deed. Amen.

June 26

Find Your Style: Relational or Friendship Evangelism

Luke 5:28-29

"Jesus saw a tax collector by the name of Levi sitting at his tax booth. 'Follow Me,' Jesus said to him, and Levi got up, left everything and followed him. Then Levi held a great banquet for Jesus at his house, and a large crowd of tax collectors and others were eating with them. But the Pharisees and teachers of the law who belonged to their sect complained to his disciples, 'Why do you eat and drink with tax collectors and 'sinners'?" (Luke 5:28-30 NIV).

A relational style is often referred to as friendship evangelism. When Jesus called Levi, Levi left his lucrative business and followed Jesus. Levi wasted no time in hosting a large crowd of his peers at a banquet to feature Jesus as the guest of honor. The Pharisees were turned off with Jesus associating with tax-collector Levi. They were concerned about keeping the church pure. They did everything to give the impression that they were sinless. Jesus spent time not with these self-righteous leaders, but with people who sensed their need for God.

We need to identify with society and even those in church we may not appreciate. Let's not neglect those with a poor reputation. They might be the very ones who are open to hearing the invitation of God's love.

If you're an impatient extrovert you will need to exercise patience because relationship building usually happens over a period of time. You don't make a friendship in one encounter. It's easy to be friendly but being a friend demands sacrifice. It will affect your schedule, your priorities, and your finances. There is a million miles between being friendly and being a friend. How many new friends have you made this past year?

Audrey, a beauty salon stylist, shares with her clients how Jesus is transforming her life. She has invited many to church and some have come. Audrey is a relational evangelist.

Angie related to her neighbor for several months to build a friendship. Over the course of time her neighbor came to church and brought others with her. New people bring new people and the Kingdom of God grows.

Lord Jesus, help me to love those who need a friend and to lead them to yourself. Amen.

June 27

Find Your Style: Testimonial

John 9

"I know this, I was blind, and now I can see!" (John 9:25 NLT).

In John 9 Jesus healed a blind beggar. The Pharisees were upset that Jesus would heal on the Sabbath. They asked the beggar what he thought of the man who healed him. His answer was straight forward: "I was blind, now I see!" This experience applies not only to physical blindness but to spiritual blindness. All of us were blind spiritually until Jesus gave us sight. We too can say, "I was blind but now I see! Messiah Jesus changed my life. He can change yours too."

Testimonial evangelists usually are not people who became Christians as children and followed a steady path to spiritual maturity. Often they will say they thought they were Christians. They say, "I went to church and tried to live a good moral life. Then I turned control of my life over to Jesus and began to trust Jesus as my personal Savior. That decision made all the difference in the world. It was the best decision I ever made. If you are interested I would love to tell you more."

A testimony is not preaching; it is basically giving facts about how Jesus has impacted your life. Paul used this approach in Acts 22 and 26 before the multitude in Jerusalem and before King Agrippa. You will find the following questions Paul asked in Acts 26 helpful as you think through your own testimony: Where were you spiritually before receiving Jesus? How did that affect you in your relationships? What caused you to consider Jesus as the solution to your needs? Specifically, how did you receive Christ? How did your life begin to change after you trusted Jesus? What other benefits have you experienced since becoming a Christian? Most of these questions can be answered in a sentence or two.

You have a testimony. Most seekers don't need to hear a sermon: they need a Christian like yourself to share with them how Jesus made a difference in your life. Your testimony will be one more step the Holy Spirit uses to bring them closer to Kingdom citizenship.

Lord, loosen my tongue. I will share what you are doing for me. Amen.

June 28

Find Your Style: Confrontational

Acts 2:23

"You followed God's prearranged plan. With the help of lawless Gentiles, you nailed him to the cross and murdered him… So let it be clearly known by everyone in Israel that God has made this Jesus whom you crucified to be both Lord and Messiah! Peter's word convicted them deeply, and they said to him and to the other apostles, 'Brothers, what should we do?'" "Peter replied, 'Each of you must turn from your sins and turn to God, and be baptized in the name of Jesus Christ for the forgiveness of your sins. Then you will receive the gift of the Holy Spirit'" (Acts 2:23, 36-38 NLT).

Peter laid it on the line and three thousand responded. (v.41) Some people must be confronted directly for the Holy Spirit to get through to them. Maybe you have the personality, temperament and the ability to confront under the guidance of the Holy Spirit so people are faced with their sin and their need of the Savior.

Billy Graham often used the phrase: "You must be born again!" Charles Stanley repeatedly says in his message: "Listen! Listen!"

Joe used the confrontational approach. There were times when I was embarrassed as we walked into a home and he abruptly asked, "Is your dog saved yet?" He then shared what Jesus did for him and asked them if they wanted to receive Jesus into their life? When Joe suddenly died because of a heart attack, I had his funeral and gave opportunity for persons to share how Joe touched their life. For more than an hour, one person after another spoke of Joe's boldness and how they appreciated his witness. One person flew from another state to attend the funeral and thanked Joe's family for his witness.

Acts 4:13, 19-20 NLT, "The members of the council were amazed when they saw the boldness of Peter and John, for they could see that they were ordinary men who had had no special training….Peter and John replied, 'Do you think God wants us to obey you rather than him? We cannot stop telling about the wonderful things we have seen and heard.'" "The righteous are as bold as a lion" (Proverbs 28:1 NIV).

Lord Jesus, help me to be a bold witness for you today. Amen.

June 29

Find Your Style: Intellectual

Acts 17:3

"He (Paul) was explaining and proving the prophecies about the sufferings of the Messiah and his rising from the dead. He said, 'This Jesus I'm telling you about is the Messiah'" (Acts 17:3 NLT).

If you like to wrestle with intellectual questions, you may find it natural to use this style to witness. In this approach you refer seekers to books and other resources. You spend time studying with them.

Invite people to follow Jesus in spite of their doubts and questions. All of us have questions. Questions are good, not questions that are asked in defiance about God, but seeking questions. This is evidence of our humanity and humility both necessary attributes for us to discover God. We must recognize we never have all the answers. We need to make a commitment to Christ before we have everything figured out.

Acts 19:9 records that Paul went to the lecture hall of Tyranus and debated daily for two years. He conversed with the intelligentsia and debated with the philosophers of Athens. In his sermon on Mars Hill, he ingeniously used the Athenians' altar to an unknown god as an introduction to his presentation of the true God.

Don't let persons with a high intellect intimidate you. Often their questions are a smoke screen to hide a guilty conscience. They intuitively know they need salvation. Only the Holy Spirit can break their wall of resistance. On the other hand we need to discern that honest questions need honest answers.

Lee Strobel, once a skeptical journalist, freely recognizes the difficult questions and exposed them, revealing that faith in Christ is an answer very much worth considering. Josh McDowell, known worldwide for his ministry to university students uses this approach very effectively. My friend Mike relates to Jehovah Witnesses and goes on the Internet and debates with those of other faiths. He uses his gift of intellect to invite people to encounter Jesus. In using this approach, always remember that we are not called to win an argument but to show God's love with gentleness and respect.

Lord, help me to diligently study and present the best answers to those who have sincere questions concerning Christianity. Amen.

June 30

Find Your Style: Invitational

John 1:41

"Andrew, Simon Peter's brother, was one of the two who heard what John had said and who had followed Jesus. The first thing Andrew did was to find his brother Simon and tell him, 'We have found the Messiah' (that is, the Christ). And he brought him to Jesus" (John 1:40-41 NIV).

George Barna says, "One out of four" will come to church if a friend would invite them." I believe the key word here is "friend." If you first have a relationship with the unchurched people and invite them, perhaps Barna's findings are true.

Some studies conclude that more than half the people who come to Jesus in the United States come through this style. This has certainly been true in my ministry. Jesus built a relationship with people. They heard about him and observed him.

Our friends know us and accept us. Jesus said, "Anyone who accepts your message is also accepting me. And anyone who rejects you is rejecting me" (Luke 10:16 NLT). This teaching indicates that we need to win people to ourselves so they receive Jesus' message of Good News. That is not being proud; it is being expedient. If we are always conscious of Jesus living in us, I believe most people will like us and be drawn to him who lives his life through us. (See Galatians 2:20.)

For the invitational approach to be effective, churches need to have services at which the unchurched feel comfortable and the gospel is presented in a way they can understand. Unchurched friends should not sense that they will be put on the spot or in some way embarrassed.

Gentle persistence in a loving manner communicates to the unchurched that we care. When Elwood, a new believer, went to a church conference, someone asked him why he started coming to church. He said, "Pastor Dave kept inviting me, he wouldn't give up." I had gone to his home and visited with him and his family many times. I called occasionally and prompted others in the church to do the same. This is how we "compel" them to come. (See Luke 14:23.)

Lord Jesus, give me eyes to see those people today who are open to an invitation to come to you. Give me gentle boldness to extend that invitation. Amen.

July 1

Vision

Isaiah 35:7

"Then will the eyes of the blind be opened and the ears of the deaf unstopped. Then will the lame leap like a deer and the mute tongue shout for joy. Water will gush forth in the wilderness and streams in the desert. The burning sand will become a pool, the thirsty ground bubbling springs" (Isaiah 35:5-7 NIV).

Has God given you a vision? What do you long for? David wrote: "Delight yourself in the Lord and he will give you the desires of your heart. Commit your ways to the Lord; trust in him and he will do this; He will make your righteousness shine like the dawn, the justice of your cause like the noonday sun" (Psalm 37:4-6 NIV).

Christians are people with vision. On the birthday of the church Peter quoted the prophecy of Joel, "Your sons and daughters will prophesy, your young men will see visions, your old men will dream dreams" (Acts 2:17 NIV).

I am working with some churches that are dying. One miracle to me is that not all the committed youth have left the church. I suggested they bring these youth to the leadership meetings and hear from them. I marvel, and rejoice greatly at their vision. Joel's prophecy is true today. Empower the youth in your congregation. Spot their gifts and encourage them. It's absolutely amazing what God will do through them. Remember the disciples were young, very young. Jesus could have picked mature people—he wanted vision people.

If you have lost your vision, cry out to God for a fresh vision. We need people with sanctified imagination, which is another way of defining vision. We need to sing a new song that the world will hear.

Let the fire of God's presence consume you, give you a passion that opens your eyes to the reality that it's Jesus living through you fulfilling the vision. It won't be fulfilled overnight. In fact, he will likely take you through some deep valleys to burn away the selfish motives. This refining process will likely be repeated many times but you will come forth as gold bearing much fruit for God's glory.

Lord, thank you for vision, refine it, make it your vision and heal me so you can trust me in fulfilling your vision through me. Amen.

July 2
Follow Me
Luke 5:27

"Jesus went out and saw a tax collector by the name of Levi sitting at his tax booth. 'Follow me,' Jesus said to him, and Levi got up, left everything and followed him" (Luke 5:27 NIV).

A church was making serious efforts in reaching people for Jesus. They spent hours planning and preparing for a community evening at the park providing food and drink, games, a movie, welcoming material but no one mentioned anything about follow up. The welcoming people never thought about getting people's names or how they might keep in touch. When I mentioned this, it was clear they did not want to offend anyone by being that assertive.

Did you notice that Jesus was assertive? He said to Levi, "Follow me." Have you become so concerned about offending people that you never ask anything of them? Ask them to go with you to a ball game or some other activity in order to build a relationship if you feel it's inappropriate to invite them to church which may be a bit more threatening. After you have a relationship ask them to come with you to church. Do you ask people to consider Jesus? Remember what Paul wrote to Timothy, "God doesn't want us to be shy with his gifts, but bold, and loving and sensible" (I Timothy 1:7 Msg).

Jesus asked 150 questions in the Gospels. He asked the Woman at the Well for a drink of water. He frequently asked the sick, blind, and those who were physically challenged if they wanted to be healed. Here Jesus did more than ask. He gave a command, "Follow me," and Levi followed.

Often we are too shy, or fearful of offending people. We say, "It is not politically correct to invade another's territory." Coming to Jesus is a life and death issue. At the judgment our neighbors may look at us and say, "I talked with you many, many times. You never told me I needed to follow Jesus. Why didn't you tell me I would need to give an account to him? I never knew I would need to give an account of my life to Jesus."

Lord, help me to be sensitive to your Holy Spirit. Help me to be bold, loving and sensible. Amen.

July 3

Fishing For People

Matthew 4:19

"As Jesus was walking beside the Sea of Galilee, he saw two brothers, Simon called Peter and his brother Andrew. They were casting a net into the lake, for they were fishermen. ' Come, follow me,' Jesus said, 'and I will make you fishers of men.' At once they left their nets and followed him. Going on from there, he saw two other brothers, James son of Zebedee and his brother John. They were in a boat with their father Zebedee, preparing their nets. Jesus called them, and immediately they left the boat and their father and followed him" (Matthew 4:18-22 NIV).

There are many today who make the point that we are to love people not for the sake of getting them into the Kingdom of God but love them because they are God's creation. Love them for who they are. That takes the pressure off witnessing. I can see their point. We don't want to manipulate people or make them our project. This sounds spiritual and difficult to oppose. However, I think Jesus in this account gives us the OK to have a clear motive of relating to and loving people, i.e. Jesus makes it clear we are called to fish for people. That is our motive. God is not willing that any perish. His Spirit is the only pressure they should encounter. As the Spirit flows through you to persons who are prebelievers you don't need to pressure them. It is God's Spirit that draws them to himself. You are simply the tool he has chosen to use.

We love our children unconditionally. Whatever they do they will always be our child and we will go on loving them. However we make it clear that we want them to follow the path that leads to life and godliness in Christ Jesus. John writes: "I have no greater joy than to hear that my children are walking in the truth" (III John 4 NIV). Jude writes that we are to snatch people from the fire (v.23), while Jesus said we are to compel them to come to the banquet (Luke 14:23).

Father, search me and know my heart and see if there are any impure motives. Help me to love people as you love them with all your heart. Help me to be an instrument in your hands to bring them to Jesus. Amen.

July 4

Urgency

Mark 2:15-16

"As he was walking along, he saw Levi...sitting at the tax collector's booth. 'Follow me,' Jesus told him, and Levi got up and followed him. While Jesus was having dinner at Levi's house, many tax collectors and 'sinners' were eating with him and his disciples for there were many who followed him" (Mark 2:15-16 NIV).

Most Bible commentators assume the same day Jesus came to Levi's house, Levi prepared a banquet so he could honor Jesus and have Jesus introduced to his peers and friends. Levi didn't waste any time starting to witness! The Woman at the Well went immediately to tell her village about Jesus (John 4). The demoniac wanted to go with Jesus immediately after he was made whole but Jesus told him to go to the Decapolis. I feel sure he didn't wait to learn more about Jesus. New believers can share their faith immediately with whatever knowledge or experience they have.

I have seen it dozens of time in my ministry: new people bring new people. They want to share the Good News with their friends. Let's encourage them. They already have the relationship with networks of people that we don't know. As they witness, and as we mentor these new believers they will mature and become disciples who disciple others.

In working with new believers the Lord will give you a vision of their future. Inform them that you can see them being used mightily for the Lord as they invite their friends to meet Jesus. Tell them you can see them growing and enjoying their new life in the Lord to the point where this joy will overflow to others. You paint faith pictures in their mind as, "I can see you being baptized, giving your testimony with your friends watching and listening to you. Some of your friends will come to Jesus. You will be his instrument and discover a joy you never knew was possible."

Lord, help me to grow in my faith to reach a prebeliever for you and equip them in faith to reach their family and unsaved friends. Amen.

July 5

A New Wardrobe

Colossians 3:5-17

In moving from the old life to a new life Paul describes it as changing our wardrobe.

He begins by informing us to kill everything connected with the way of death: "sexual promiscuity, impurity, lust, doing whatever you feel like whenever you feel like it, and grabbing whatever attracts your fancy. That's a life shaped by things and feelings instead of by God. It's because of that kind of thing that God is about to explode in anger. It wasn't long ago that you were doing all that stuff and not knowing any better. But you know better now, so make sure it's all gone for good; bad temper, irritability, meanness, profanity, dirty talk.

"Don't lie to one another. You're done with that old life. It's like a filthy set of ill-fitting clothes you've stripped off and put in the fire. Now you're dressed in a new wardrobe. Every item of your new way of life is custom-made by the Creator, with his label on it. All the old fashions are obsolete. Words like Jewish and non-Jewish, religious and irreligious, insider and outsider, uncivilized and uncouth, slave and free, mean nothing. From now on everyone is defined by Christ, everyone is included in Christ.

"So chosen by God for this new life of love, dress in the wardrobe God picked out for you; compassion, kindness, humility, quiet strength, discipline. Be even-tempered, content with second place, quick to forgive an offense. Forgive as quickly and completely as the Master forgave you. And regardless of what else you put on, wear love. It's your basic, all-purpose garment. Never be without it.

"Let the peace of Christ keep you in tune with each other, in step with each other. None of this going off and doing your own things. And cultivate thankfulness. Let the Word of Christ—the Message—have the run of the house. Give it plenty of room in your lives. Instruct and direct one another using good common sense. And sing, sing your hearts out to God! Let every detail in your lives—words, actions, whatever—be done in the name of the Master, Jesus, thanking God the Father every step of the way" (Colossians 3:5-17 Msg).

Father, by your grace I will wear my new wardrobe. Amen.

July 6

Can We Answer Jesus' Prayer?

John 17:21-22

Jesus prayed: "The goal is for all of them to become one heart and mind—Just as you, Father, are in me and I in you, So they might be one heart and mind with us. Then the world might believe that you, in fact, sent me. The same glory you gave me, I gave them, so they'll be as unified and together as we are—I in them and you in me" (John 17:21-22 Msg).

Jesus also says: "A new command I give you; Love one another. As I have loved you so you must love one another. By this all men will know that you are my disciples, if you love one another" (John 13:34-35 NIV).

There are well over 300 denominations in the United States. With the rise of independent churches there seems to be more divisions than ever.

Our unity is found in Jesus. Paul's words in I Corinthians 15:1-6 NIV give us what I believe to be the core absolutes on which we can base our unity. "I want to remind you of the Gospel I preached to you, which you received and on which you have taken your stand. By this Gospel you are saved, if you hold firmly to the word I preached to you. Otherwise, you have believed in vain. For what I receive I passed on to you as of first importance: that Christ died for our sins according to the Scriptures, that he was buried, that he was raised on the third day according to the Scriptures, and that he appeared to Peter, and then to the Twelve. After that, he appeared to more than five hundred of the brothers at the same time."

I find these verses foundational for our unity. Let's be open to listening to others who differ with us on interpretations and deductions realizing that we may not agree with their interpretation. Hopefully we can work together and fellowship together setting aside our personal preferences, subjective opinions and feelings. I believe it is possible to do this without compromising our convictions.

Lord, forgive us for our disunity with all our divisions. Help me to focus on the supreme values of Jesus who is the way, the truth and the life. Bring us together. Amen.

July 7

Compassion

Matthew 9:36

"When he (Jesus) looked out over the crowds, his heart broke. So confused and aimless they were, like sheep with no shepherd. 'What a huge harvest!' he said to his disciples. 'How few workers! On your knees and pray for harvest hands'" (Matthew 9:36-38 Msg).

Jesus loved people deeply. When you consider that he was sinless but constantly surrounded by sin and sinful people we are amazed at his love. There was injustice, envy and hate on every side. He had every right to condemn the sinner, to take a moral stand, form protests and attack individuals. Yet when he saw the crowds he had compassion on them because they had no hope, wandering like lost sheep without a shepherd.

Rather than being filled with disdain, he was filled with love. He laid down his life for these lost sheep. We need new eyes to see people as Jesus saw them. The more we grow in our walk with Jesus the more we need to have Jesus attitude for the lost sheep we meet each day. Jesus' love showed through him so that sinners were drawn to him. His life set forth the clear statement that the more spiritually mature I am, the more approachable I should be to people who are hurting and who are outside God's Kingdom. Our approachability needs to increase as we become more like Christ.

Let's ask ourselves: "Are those outside the faith drawn to us?" It's heart breaking to see that the religious people of Jesus' day were put off and even hated Jesus. They were self-righteous and judgmental. Are any of those elements in your heart? Are they in your church? Or are sinners drawn to you and to your church? Do you spend more time praying for the lost or for physical needs? Are you praying for more workers to enter the harvest? God give us the passion of Jesus.

Lord, I am a sinner. Cleanse me and make me clean. Forgive my lethargy. Give me passion for the lost to love as you loved and pray as you prayed. Amen.

July 8

What is Success?

Matthew 28:18-20

Jesus has made it clear what he came to do, what we are to do and what the church is to do. Jesus came to seek the lost. (See Luke 19:10.) We are sent into the world just as the Father sent Jesus. (John 17:18) The church is to go and make disciples. (See Matthew 28:18-20.)

Persons who were very close to death were asked, "What regrets do you have as you look back over your life?" Eighty-four percent of the people said they wish they would have done…and then named the direction they would have chosen while sixteen percent said they regret doing something they did. We need to be risk takers for the Lord.

In Matthew 25:14-30 Jesus gives the parable of the man who went off on a journey and called three of his servants and gave one $5,000, another $2,000 and another $1,000 according to their ability. When the owner returned they reported to him. The ones with $5,000 and $2,000 doubled their investment. The owner was very complimentary: "Well done, good and faithful servant! You have been faithful with a few things, I will put you in charge of many things. Come and share your master's happiness!" (v.23 NIV).

The servant given the one talent reported: "I knew that you are a hard man, harvesting where you have not sown and gathering where you have not scattered seed. So I was afraid and went out and hid your talent in the ground. See, here is what belongs to you. His master replied: 'You wicked, lazy servant! So you knew that I harvested where I have not sown… Well then, you should have put my money on deposit with the bankers, so that when I return I would have received it back with interest. Take the talent from him and give it to the one who has the ten talents. For everyone who has will be given more, and he will have an abundance. Whoever does not have, even what he has will be taken from him. And throw that worthless servant outside, into the darkness, where there will be weeping and gnashing of teeth" (vv.24-30 NIV).

Lord Jesus, forgive me for not taking risks for you. Help me to seek your will and not be afraid to move out in obedient service for you. Amen.

July 9

Jesus and the Holy Spirit

John 5:19

Jesus told the disciples that he said only what the Father told him to say and he did nothing except what he saw the Father doing. (See John 5:19, 12:49-50.) How is that possible? It was possible because Jesus was tuned into the Holy Spirit.

We have the same Holy Spirit. Are we conscious of the Holy Spirit? Pray continually for the Holy Spirit to fill you. Was Jesus always full of the Holy Spirit? Luke records, "Jesus, full of the Holy Spirit, returned from the Jordan and was led by the Spirit in the desert" (4:1 NIV). After the temptation "Jesus returned to Galilee in the power of the Spirit" (Luke 4:14 NIV).

I believe even in Jesus' life there were times when the power of the Holy Spirit was more intense than other times. For example, "The power of the Lord was present for him to heal the sick" (Luke 5:17 NIV). Several times the Gospels report that there was power to heal. This implies that the fullness of the Spirit was present with Jesus in various degrees. If Jesus needed to be filled with the Spirit, so do we.

Do you pray frequently for the fullness of the Spirit? We need to be more conscious of God's Holy Spirit. We need his spirit for everything, especially for witnessing (Acts 1:8).

The Father cut off every branch in Jesus that did not bear fruit and pruned those branches that were bearing fruit so they would bear more fruit. (See John 15:2.) If Jesus had to be cut and pruned how much more do we need to be cut and pruned so we can bear more fruit? Jesus also had to learn obedience: "Although he was a son, he learned obedience from what he suffered" (Hebrews 5:8 NIV). If Jesus needed to learn obedience how much more do we need to learn to be obedient?

Lord Jesus, thank you for your example for us. Help me today to learn obedience through the things I suffer. Help me not to complain when you remove the parts of my life that are not bearing fruit and prune the parts that are bearing fruit so it will be more fruitful. Amen.

July 10

Methods That No Longer Work

Matthew 23:5

"Everything they (the Pharisees) do is done for men to see" (Matthew 23:5 NIV).

A church continuing to use methods that no longer work is being unfaithful to Christ. If your employer trains you to complete a task using a new approach and yet you insist on continuing using the traditional method you are unfaithful. You will lose your job to someone who is willing to use the method prescribed by the employer.

Are we willing to experiment with new forms of worship or are we stuck in our traditions and rituals? Which is more important, our comfort or our love for the lost? Which is more important, our traditions, our likes, our preference or the salvation of our youth who are going to other churches or not going anywhere?

In Matthew 23 Jesus is straight forward to those who hang onto their traditions that are not effective in changing lives. Jesus addresses these religious hypocrites repeatedly in Matthew 23: "You're hopeless! What arrogant stupidity!" (See the *Message Bible*).

Let's check our attitudes toward our youth who are committed to Jesus but want to change things. What are our attitudes towards other congregations that are making disciples and reaching many lives for Jesus? Are we willing to visit them to learn from them? Do we raise questions about their approach or methods in a condemnatory spirit or do we rejoice with them and learn from them?

Be humble enough to learn from others. Let's cry out to Jesus to open our eyes to new ways that can reach our youth. Paul says, he becomes all things to all people to win them to Christ. (See I Corinthians 9:22.) If we are not taking any risks for Jesus, it means we don't have faith. Without faith you cannot please God. (See Hebrews 11:6.)

Lord Jesus, help me to be more flexible. Help me to be humble so I can learn from others who seem to be more effective in making disciples. Teach me Lord to follow your Holy Spirit through all these changes. Amen.

July 11

The Holy Spirit

Acts 2

Why was the early church so effective in sharing the Gospel? I believe it was because they depended on the Holy Spirit. The Holy Spirit is mentioned more than forty times in the book of Acts. Are we depending on the Holy Spirit's power to make our witness effective to today's world? If not, why not? Too often we have neglected to talk about the Holy Spirit because Christians have different interpretations concerning manifestations of the Spirit today.

Jesus said to the disciples after the resurrection: "'Peace be with you! As the Father has sent me, I am sending you.' And with that he breathed on them and said, Receive the Holy Spirit. If you forgive anyone his sins, they are forgiven; if you do not forgive them, they are not forgiven" (John 20:21-23 NIV).

Are we aware that we are sent under the anointing of the Holy Spirit? We are sent with the spirit of peace, Jesus' peace. (John 14:27). Jesus knew there would be controversy surrounding the Holy Spirit so he gave them a spirit of unity and peace. Have we lost that Spirit?

In his longest prayer recorded in the Gospels (John 17) just before the cross, Jesus prays for unity of the believers so the world will be drawn to the Christian Gospel. It's this unity among Christians that is a power-drawing card for the work of God's Kingdom. How often have we divided over the very power that should unite us.

Jesus simply said, "Receive the Holy Spirit." We don't need to argue or split hairs over such terms as the baptism of the Holy Spirit, the anointing of the Holy Spirit, the second work of grace or whatever: Just ask Jesus to make your heart and spirit open to receiving more of his Holy Spirit. And when you receive the Spirit you will walk in newness of life, (Romans 8:1-4) you will have power for witnessing (Acts 1:8), you will forgive or withhold forgiveness (John 20:23).

Father, I need your Holy Spirit. I receive your Holy Spirit so Jesus can live his life through me. I am helpless without your Spirit. Flow through my heart, my mind and my being. Make me wholly yours. Amen.

July 12

We are as Sick as our Secrets

Psalm 139:23-24

"Nothing in all creation is hidden from God's sight. Everything is uncovered and laid bare before the eyes of him to whom we must give account" (Hebrews 4:13 NIV).

Everyone has hidden secrets. Psychologists tell us we spend enormous amounts of emotional energy guarding those secrets. We think: "If people really knew me they would reject me."

David was a man after God's own heart. (See Acts 13:22). He prayed: "Search me, O God, and know my heart; test me and know my anxious thoughts. See if there is any offensive way in me, and lead me in the way everlasting"(Psalm 139:23-24 NIV). Pray David's prayer. Take those sins that come to your mind and confess them to God. "If we claim to be without sin, we deceive ourselves and the truth is not in us. If we confess our sins, he is faithful and just and will forgive us our sins and purify us from all unrighteousness. If we claim we have not sinned, we make him out to be a liar and his word has no place in our lives" (I John 1:8-10 NIV).

It's important for your psychological and emotional well-being to name your sins. Picture Jesus taking each sin and forgiving it. See him giving his life's blood to wash you clean and make you pure. See yourself participating in his divine nature (II Peter 1:4 NIV).

If you still do not feel forgiven, go to a mature Christian whom you can trust to keep confidences. "Confess your sins to each other and pray for each other so that you may be healed" (James 5:16 NIV). The mature Christian will assure you that you are forgiven. Their forgiveness will assist you in accepting your forgiveness from God.

Don't hide your sin. Take it to the cross. Carrying sin is a slap in the face of our Lord because we are saying that his work on the cross was not sufficient for us. Let Jesus set you free!

Jesus, I confess all my sins to you including my sinful nature. Wash me and make me clean. Thank you. Amen.

July 13

Opposition From Home

Luke 4:24-29

Jesus said, "No prophet is accepted in his hometown. I assure you that there were many widows in Israel in Elijah's time, when the sky was shut for three and a half-years and there was a severe famine throughout the land. Yet, Elijah was not sent to any of them, but to a widow in Zarephath in the region of Sidon. And there were many in Israel with leprosy in the time of Elisha the prophet, yet not one of them was cleansed—only Naaman the Syrian. All the people in the synagogue were furious when they heard this. They got up, drove him out of the town, and took him to the brow of the hill on which the town was built, in order to throw him down the cliff" (Luke 4:24-29 NIV).

Why were the hometown people so furious at Jesus? They were all speaking well of him (v.22), but immediately things changed 180 degrees from praise to fury. Why? They could not imagine that God would love the people who were not like them. The people from Zarephath and Syria were not Jewish. When you witness to people and bring them to Jesus and to your church, the church may not always give you a warm welcome.

Evangelists are often the least appreciated persons in our older traditional congregations. They bring the "wrong" people to church. Jesus said, "Count yourself blessed every time people put you down or throw you out or speak lies about you to discredit me. What it means is that the truth is too close for comfort and they are uncomfortable. You can be glad when that happens—give a cheer, even!—For though they don't like it, I do! And all heaven applauds. And know that you are in good company. My prophets and witnesses have always gotten into this kind of trouble" (Matthew 5:10-12 Msg).

Father, help me to be faithful in witnessing for you even though others may not understand. Amen.

July 14

Foolishness of Preaching the Cross

I Corinthians 1:21

"Since the world in all its fancy wisdom never had a clue when it came to knowing God, God in his wisdom took delight in using what the world considered dumb—preaching, of all things!—to bring those who trust him into the way of salvation" (I Corinthians 1:21 Msg). The NIV reads: "Since in the wisdom of God the world through its wisdom did not know him, God was pleased through the foolishness of what was preached to save those who believe."

Remember that preaching in the New Testament was used to describe the Christians' communication to non-Christians. Preaching is proclaiming the Good News! Teaching is the term used for communicating with other Christians. This means every Christian is called to preach or proclaim the Good News. God uses the method of preaching, or presenting the Good News, to bring your friends to salvation. Unless the Holy Spirit has softened their hearts and is drawing the unsaved to Jesus through the prayers of God's people they will look at your sharing the Good News as foolishness or as stupidity. (See verses 22-25.)

"God chose the foolish things of the world to shame the wise; God chose the weak things of the world to shame the strong. He chose the lowly things of this world and the despised things—and the things that are not—to nullify the things that are, so that no one may boast before him" (verses 27-28 NIV).

While it may be difficult for you to consider yourself a preacher when you share the Good News with the prebeliever, that is what you are in the New Testament sense. Accept your New Testament title and make your boast in Jesus Christ (v.31). To the world, the cross is just another story. To the Christian, the cross is central. It's the only plus sign that makes things add up. It is more important than all the empires of history. Our preaching may be interesting but it will not transform or translate lives from the kingdom of darkness to the kingdom of Jesus Christ unless it includes an awareness of the work of Jesus as he paid for our sins. (See Colossians 1:14.) When we share Christ Jesus be sure to take people to the cross.

Jesus, thank you for the cross. Help me to keep the cross foundational and central in all my sharing of the Good News. Amen.

July 15

Global Positioning System (GPS)

Romans 8:14

Global Positioning Systems (GPS) have become popular. No more getting lost. Parents can now track their children as long as the GPS is in their car. When you don't follow instructions the GPS recalculates. If you think you know better than the GPS and take a different turn it recalculates. One fellow commented "I got so tired of hearing it recalculating that I turned it off."

Someone likened the GPS to the Holy Spirit. The Holy Spirit is our guide. "Those who are led by the Spirit of God are sons of God" (Romans 8:14 NIV). "Live by the Spirit, and you will not gratify the desires of the sinful nature." "Since you live by the Spirit, let us keep in step with the Spirit" (Galatians 5:16 and 25 NIV).

The Spirit led the apostles. "Paul and his companions traveled throughout the region of Phrygia and Galatia, having been kept by the Holy Spirit from preaching the word in the province of Asia. When they came to the border of Mysia, they tried to enter Bithynia, but the Spirit of Jesus would not allow them to" (Acts 16:6-7 NIV).

When we do not follow the Spirit's leading we grieve the Spirit (Ephesians 4:30). The Spirit, like the GPS, recalculates. The Spirit calls us to return to the proper path (repent). When we insult and ignore the Spirit he recalculates calling us back to our senses. (See Hebrews 10:29.) When we lie, the Spirit is there to discipline us. (See Acts 5:3.)

Let the Holy Spirit be your GPS 24/7. He is our victory over sin. (See Galatians 5:16 and Romans 8:2.) He is our comforter. (See John 14:16.) He lives in us. (See I Corinthians 6:19.) He gives us spiritual gifts. (See I Corinthians 12:4). He is our power for witness. (See Acts 1:8.) He is the Spirit of truth. (See John 14:17.)

Lord Jesus, as the GPS guides the driver of the car, may your Holy Spirit guide me. Help me to be obedient to you. You know every detour. You know every hill and valley, every curve in my path. Thank you for your guidance. Amen.

July 16

A Heart Issue

Matthew 15:18-20

"The things that come out of the mouth come from the heart, and these make a man 'unclean.' For out of the heart comes evil thoughts, murder, adultery, sexual immorality, theft, false testimony, slander. These are what make a man 'unclean' but eating with unwashed hands does not make him 'unclean'" (Matthew 15:18-20 NIV).

Jesus warned the Pharisees: "You clean the outside of the cup and dish, but inside they are full of greed and self-indulgence" (Matthew 23:25 NIV).

"See to it that none of you has a sinful, unbelieving heart that turns away from the living God" (See Hebrews 3:12 NIV.)

"The heart is deceitful above all things and beyond cure. Who can understand it?" (See Jeremiah 17:9. NIV.)

On the other hand Jesus says we are to have a pure heart: "Blessed are the pure in heart, for they will see God" (Matthew 5:8 NIV). The *Message Bible* reads: "You're blessed when you get your inside world—your mind and heart—put right. Then you can see God in the outside world."

How is your inside world? Can you clean it up? That is impossible. We are born in sin, with a sin nature. David writes: "Surely I was sinful at birth, sinful from the time my mother conceived me" (Psalm 51:5 NIV). When I am open and honest before God, I know that Jesus is right in His diagnosis of me. But the good news is that Jesus can cleanse my heart.

Jesus was perfect, sinless. Jesus is a high priest who, "meets our need—one who is holy, blameless, pure, set apart from sinners, exalted above the heavens" (Hebrews 7:26 NIV). "If we confess our sins, he is faithful and just to forgive us our sins and purify us from all unrighteousness" (I John 1:9 NIV). We are free from condemnation! (See Romans 8:1).

Father, I thank you that even though my heart is wicked you sent Jesus the perfect, sinless high priest to take away my sin and give me a new heart, one that is seeking to follow you. Amen.

July 17

Efficient or Effective?

II Corinthians 13:5-6

"Test yourselves to make sure you are solid in the faith. Don't drift along taking everything for granted. Give yourselves regular checkups. You need firsthand evidence, not mere hearsay, that Jesus Christ is in you. Test it out. If you fail the test, do something about it" (II Corinthians 13:5-6 Msg). (See also Psalm 139:23-24 & I John 1:7.)

Let's examine our hearts but also let's examine our effectiveness. Jesus said, "When you are joined with me and I with you, the relation is intimate and organic, the harvest is sure to be abundant" (John 15:5 Msg). "This is to my Father's glory, that you bear much fruit" (John 15:8 NIV).

We want to be effective Christians. Peter Drucker says, "Efficiency is doing things right. Effectiveness is doing the right things." So often our lives are full of activities but our productivity is low. The same is true for many churches. God also wants our lives and our churches to be effective and productive.

In John 15, Jesus links effectiveness and productiveness with prayer. "If you remain in me and my words remain in you, ask whatever you wish, and it will be given you" (John 15:7 NIV). This verse removes much of the mystery of how Jesus remains in us. He says if my words remain in you, your prayers will be answered and you will produce a large harvest (v.8).

Let's not skirt around this or try to make excuses for a poor crop. Let's cry out to Jesus in prayer claiming this wonderful promise. If his word is not remaining in you, than you need to ask him for a love for his word as David states: "I meditate on your name all night, God, treasuring your revelation, O God." "My soul is starved and hungry, ravenous!—insatiable for your nourishing commands" (Psalm 119:55 & 20 Msg). (See also Colossians 3:16-17.)

Lord Jesus, I want my roots to go down deep into your word. I will feast on your word. I will, by your power, produce a large harvest for your glory. So help me Father. Amen.

July 18

No Grumbling or Arguing

Philippians 2: 14-16

"Do everything without complaining or arguing. So that you may become blameless and pure, children of God without fault in a crooked and depraved generation, in which you shine like stars in the universe as you hold out the word of life — in order that I may boast on the day of Christ that I did not run or labor for nothing" (Philippians 2:14-16 NIV).

How is your grumbling or complaining gauge? One study indicates that five percent of people were born dissenters. In one church I coached, nearly every meeting someone was complaining. No matter what you do they oppose the direction you are going.

Paul writes: "Do not let any unwholesome talk come out of your mouths, but only what is helpful for building others up according to their needs, that it may benefit those who listen. And do not grieve the Holy Spirit of God.... Get rid of all bitterness, rage, and anger, brawling and slander, along with every form of malice. Be kind and compassionate to one another, forgiving each other, just as in Christ, God forgave you" (Ephesians 4:28-32 NIV).

James writes: "If anyone considers himself religious and yet does not keep a tight rein on his tongue, he deceives himself and his religion is worthless" (1:26 NIV). When we allow complaining, bitterness, anger, and slander to come out of our mouths or out of our heart, we grieve the Holy Spirit. We allow the darkness of the world to enter the church. Claim the Holy Spirit's power to give you a clean heart and mouth. Confess that you can't control your thoughts or your tongue. He will change your "ought to" to "want to." Victory will be yours. Learn to walk in the Spirit, live by the Spirit and stay in step with the Spirit.

Jesus Christ in you, is the secret you need to live with a clean mind, heart and mouth. Ask him to cleanse your inner being so you speak only what is wholesome for the building up of others.

Jesus, forgive me for my complaining. Cleanse my heart, my mind and my mouth. Put a guard over my mouth so I speak only what you want me to speak. Amen.

July 19

Sailors Perspective

Jonah 1:5

"All the sailors were afraid and each cried out to his own god. And they threw the cargo into the sea to lighten the ship. But Jonah had gone below deck, where he lay down and fell into a deep sleep" (Jonah 1:5 NIV).

The sailors facing danger in desperation cried out to their god(s). They go to great lengths to avoid disaster, even throwing their cargo into the sea. People today frantically chase after their gods. They demand the latest model cars, large houses, or the next fix or a party lifestyle. Many live with a shipload of fear that their gods won't come through.

Don't dwell on people's wickedness, but rather try to understand their desperate search for peace and satisfaction. Are we like Jonah, indifferent to people who are facing danger or death? Have we fallen asleep? We know God is not willing that any should perish. We know that God loves the people of the world. We know we are sent. But are we willing to do what we need to do to bring them to Jesus?

Why was Jonah so adverse to seeing the Ninevites coming to God? Nineveh was a wicked city. The Ninevites were the enemy. Jonah was sucked into the religious self-righteous culture of his time. Why are Christians often reluctant to welcome the unchurched into their church family? Are we afraid our children will adopt their lifestyle? Whenever those thoughts enter our minds we are saying, "Our God is anemic. He is not adequate to keep us." In the Jonah account the people of Nineveh repented. They changed. The Holy Spirit is in the business of changing people's lives today.

Jonah knew they might change. That's why he became depressed when they changed. We too know intuitively people will change when they meet Jesus. Is that why we are so slow to share the Good News with them?

Lord, give me courage to share your love to the unchurched around me. Give me a heart of compassion like Jesus who didn't exclude anyone but gave his life freely for everyone. Amen.

July 20

I Would Rather be a Sailor than a Jonah

Jonah 1:12-14

"They (the sailors) asked him (Jonah), "Tell us, who is responsible for making all this trouble for us? What do you do? Where do you come from? What is your country? From what people are you?" (1:8 NIV).

After Jonah informed them who he was and who his God was, the sailors cried out to the Lord. They even tried to keep from throwing Jonah overboard. "Pick me up and throw me into the sea,' he replied, 'and it will become calm. I know that it is my fault that this great storm has come upon you.'... "Instead, the men did their best to row back to land..."" "Then they (the sailors) cried to the LORD, 'O Lord', please do not let us die for taking this man's life. Do not hold us accountable for killing an innocent man, for you, O Lord, have done as you pleased" (1:12 -14 NIV).

Jonah in his stubbornness was willing to die rather than say "yes" to God's call to go to Nineveh. Does this remind you of the Pharisees in Jesus' day? Jesus said, "Woe to you, teachers of the law and Pharisees, you hypocrites! You shut the kingdom of heaven in men's faces. You yourselves do not enter nor will you let those enter who are trying to" (Matthew 23:13-14 NIV). These sailors had a greater fear of God than Jonah did. Some people in our society have a fear of God even though they may deny it. They know they will be accountable to God some day.

I'd rather be a sailor, open to God's will, than a Jonah who knew God's will but rejected it. Many parents and many churches know they are called to be a witness to their community. But like Jonah they have become self-absorbed and have put a wall around God's love. Often we lose our youth because we are unwilling to allow changes in our worship style or we condemn them for their cultural practices that are different from ours.

Lord, help me to see my preChristian friends as persons who respect the power of God and are willing to be taught once I share the Good News with them. Lead me to them today. Amen

July 21

What Do I Do to Insure that I Do Not Become Like Jonah?

Jonah 1:1 and 4:1-2

Jonah knew God. "The word of the Lord came to Jonah" (Jonah 1:1 NIV). Too often like Jonah, "the more we know about God," the more we become self-righteous. Many Christians know a lot about God but do not know the heart of God (Matthew 22:37-39). What do I do to insure that I do not become like Jonah?

When he shared God's message and they obeyed, "Jonah was furious, he lost his temper. He yelled at God, 'God! I knew it—when I was back home, I knew this was going to happen! That's why I ran off to Tarshish! I knew you were sheer grace and mercy, not easily angered, rich in love, and ready at the drop of a hat to turn your plans of punishment into a program of forgiveness!'" (Jonah 4:1-2 Msg).

In Luke 4 when Jesus announced in his home town synagogue in Nazareth that the good news was for everyone, even to the Gentiles, the Jewish people were ready to kill him.

We may not be ready to kill the evangelist who brings "Gentiles" into our church, but our "anger" shows by our lack of acceptance. How do I insure that I do not become like Jonah or the Pharisees?

Go back to the cross and see again the love that drove Jesus. See the Father giving his only Son. See the Holy Spirit leaving heaven, coming to live in sinful humanity. See the great cloud of witnesses who have been faithful, many of them giving their lives for the cause of the Good News.

Hear again the great commission of our Lord. Thank him for the power to be a witness (martyr) for the Gospel. Experience the joy of being faithful. Know that all heaven rejoices over one sinner who repents. Experience the peace of Christ, which is not like the peace of the world. Finally, pray over your Jerusalem as Jesus prayed and wept over those who were lost.

Father, forgive my indifferent attitude, forgive my anger when people come to you who are different from my culture, traditions, opinions and preferences. Remove the "Jonah spirit" from me. Give me your heart of compassion. Amen.

July 22

Grace, the Core of the Christian's Life

I Corinthians 15:9-10

Grace is at the very core of Christ's Kingdom. It is a clear characteristic of Christ. I Corinthians 16:23 NIV, "The grace of the Lord Jesus be with you." The *Message Bible* reads: "Our Master Jesus has his arms wide open for you."

When I think of grace I think of the simple but profound fact that God loves me. How could God love me? I don't deserve his love. As Paul says, "I am less than the least of all God's people, this grace was given me; to preach to the Gentiles the unsearchable riches of Christ" (Ephesians 3:8 NIV). And again he writes: "For I am the least of the apostles and do not even deserve to be called an apostle, because I persecuted the church of God. But by the grace of God I am what I am, and his grace to me was not without effect" (I Corinthians 15:9-10 NIV).

Grace was expressed daily in the life of our Lord. He chose to relate to ostracized women (John 4 & 8), he touched those with leprosy (Luke 5:13), he ate with sinners like Levi (Luke 5:29) and Zacchaeus (Luke 19:7), he welcomed the defiant, (Luke 15:20), he highly praised the generosity of the stranger, the good Samaritan (Luke 10:33), he showed concern for the children and invites us to love our enemies and pray for our persecutors (Matthew 5:44). Jesus is a grace person.

We are called to grow in grace. (See II Peter 3:18). As Paul says, "I'm not about to let his grace go to waste. Haven't I worked hard trying to do more than any of the others? Even then, my work didn't amount to all that much. It was God giving me the work to do, God giving me the energy to do it" (I Corinthians 15:9-10 Msg). (See Zechariah 12:10.)

Life for the Christian begins with grace and ends with grace. The more we mature the more we understand it is all about grace. Don't let his grace be without effect in you.

Lord Jesus, all that I am, and all that I have is a gift from you. Your grace is the center of my life. My desire is to allow your grace to motive me 24/7. With your help I will serve you and love you with all my heart. Amen.

July 23

We Need Each Other

Romans 1:11-12

We need each other. "I long to see you so that I may impart to you some spiritual gift to make you strong—that is that you and I may be mutually encouraged by each other's faith" (Romans 1:11-12 NIV). I'm tempted to think that Paul was so advanced in the Lord that he did not need others. Listen to the following scriptures from his pen.

"When he (Timothy) comes back, he can cheer me up by telling me how you are getting along" (Philippians 2:19 NLT).

"I was glad when Stephanas, Fortunatus and Achaicus arrived, because they have supplied what was lacking from you. For they refreshed my spirit and yours also. Such men deserve recognition" (I Corinthians 16:17-18 NIV).

"May the Lord show mercy to the household of Onesiphorus, because he often refreshed me and was not ashamed of my chains" (II Timothy 1:16 NIV).

The writer of Hebrews adds: "Let's see how inventive we can be in encouraging love and helping out, not avoiding worshiping together as some do but spurring each other on, especially as we see the big Day approaching" (Hebrews 10:24-25 Msg).

From the opening chapters of the Bible, God made it clear that it was not good for us to be alone (Genesis 2:18). There is no such thing as a Christian choosing to live in isolation. Christianity must be expressed in community. Every time the Lord's supper is mentioned in scripture it is always in the context of community. In participating in the communion service we promise not only to be faithful to our Lord but we promise to be in a loving relationship with each other. We need each other. A Christian who chooses to isolate him or herself will develop a warped faith. We need to not only hear from the Holy Spirit ourselves but we need to hear what the Spirit is saying to our brothers and sisters. In Acts 2:17 NIV, Peter records that God says, "I will pour out my Spirit on all people."

Lord, our culture has taught us to be independent. Enable me to love and encourage others and to be encouraged by them. Amen.

July 24

Pure Eyes

Job 31:1

Job made a covenant with his eyes not to look lustfully on a girl (Job. 31:1 NIV). "I promised myself never to stare with desire at a young woman" (CEV).

Surveys show that 40 million Americans regularly view Internet pornography, which accounts for $2.5 billion of the $12 billion U.S. porn industry. Twenty percent of men and thirteen percent of women admit accessing porn at work.

Douglas Weiss says, "Wherever I am...and no matter what the denomination, at least half of the men in the church admit to being sexually addicted. The clergy doesn't differ that much from the general population—between a third and half." (Jane Lampman—staff writer of the *Christian Science Monitor*.)

Paul prays that the eyes of our heart would be enlightened. Ask God to let your spiritual eyes bring light into your body. Jesus said, "The eyes are windows into your body. If you open your eyes wide in wonder and belief, your body fills up with light. If you live squinty-eyed in greed and distrust, your body is a dank cellar. If you pull the blinds on your windows, what a dark life you will have!" (Matthew 6:22-23 Msg). Jesus also said, "If your eye causes you to sin pluck it out" (Matthew 18:9 NLT). Jesus is saying nothing less than a radical commitment to him will deliver you from this sin. Do whatever you need to do for victory including humbling yourself before God and before an accountability group of other mature men or women.

Remember there is no victory apart from Jesus. Only he can give you the power to live above this sin or any other sin. Start out by claiming Matthew 5:3, "Blessed are the poor in spirit or blessed are those who realize their need for him. You're blessed when you are at the end of your rope" (Msg). Then Jesus can move in and bring deliverance moment by moment.

Lord Jesus, put a guard over my physical eyes and over the eyes of my mind and heart. Help me to have a pure heart. Amen.

July 25

Check Your Motives?

I John 4:18

"There is no room in love for fear. Well-formed love banishes fear. Since fear is crippling, a fearful life—fear of death, fear of judgment—is one not yet fully formed in love" (I John 4:18 Msg).

Do you serve the Lord out of fear or out of love? When I was a kid I invited Jesus into my life primarily because I was afraid of going to hell when I died. I did not comprehend the great love of God in providing Jesus, his only Son as the atoning sacrifice for the covering of my sin. The prodigal son returned to the father (Luke 15:17-20), because he realized that his father's servants had it so much better than he did. He did not return home because he fully understood the Father's heart of love.

As we grow in our understanding of the great love of the Father for us our motive for service becomes more mature. "We love him because he first loved us (I John 4:19 KJV). We respond to his love from a heart of love. But it's important to remember that our heart of love came to us only because the Father loved us first. We owe everything to our Father.

How often do you thank God for his love? Paul described it, "Thank God for this gift, his gift. No language can praise it enough!" (II Corinthians 9:15 Msg).

No wonder Paul prayed for the Christians in Ephesis, "I pray that out of his glorious riches he may strengthen you with power through his Spirit in your inner being, so that Christ may dwell in your hearts through faith. And I pray that you, being rooted and established in love, may have power, together with all the saints to grasp how wide and long and high and deep is the love of Christ and to know this love that surpasses knowledge—that you may be filled to the measure of all the fullness of God" (Ephesians 3:16-19 NIV).

Lord, I want to grow in my love for you so my motives are pure. I desire to love you with all my heart, soul, mind and strength. Amen.

July 26

Everything I Have is Yours

Luke 15:25-32

The three parables of Luke 15: The Lost Sheep, the Lost Coin, and the Lost Son show Jesus' desire to seek what is lost. The parable of the lost son was given by Jesus for the purpose of turning the spotlight on the older brother. The Father said to the older brother, "'My son,' you are always with me, and everything I have is yours. But we had to celebrate and be glad, because this brother of yours was dead and is alive again; he was lost and is found'" (Luke 15:31-32 NIV).

The older brother's resentment of his rebellious younger brother is like the attitude repeated again and again throughout the scriptures: Jonah's attitude concerning the people of Nineveh, the disciples' attitude toward the woman at the well, or the Pharisees' attitude toward the Gentiles. Not surprising, it is the same attitude we too often find among God's people today.

It is the opposite of the Father's attitude when the arrogant and rebellious son returns saying, "Father, I have sinned against heaven and against you. I am no longer worthy to be called your son" (v. 21 NIV). "But the father said to his servants, 'Quick! Bring the best robe and put it on him. Put a ring on his finger and sandals on his feet. Bring the fatted calf and kill it. Let's have a feast and celebrate. For this son of mine was dead and is alive again, he was lost and is found.' So they began to celebrate" (vv.22-24 NIV).

The Father's love included both brothers. Examine your heart to see if you love the rebels in your community. If they come to your church does your church welcome them with open arms? Those who come to Jesus after leading notoriously sinful lives are often held in suspicion. Let's rejoice like the angels in heaven when they repent and turn to God. Like our Father we need to accept repentant sinners wholeheartedly and give them the support and encouragement they need to grow in Christ. "Accept each other just as Christ has accepted you so that God will be given glory" (Romans 15:7 NIV).

Jesus, give me the heart of the Father to accept others just as Christ Jesus has accepted me. Amen.

July 27

How Do You See Yourself?

Romans 12:3

"For by the grace given to me I say to every one of you: Do not think of yourself more highly than you ought, but rather think of yourself with sober judgment, in accordance with the measure of faith God has given you" (Romans 12:3 NIV). *The Message* Bible reads: "I'm speaking to you out of deep gratitude for all that God has given me, and especially as I have responsibilities in relation to you. Living then, as every one of you does, in pure grace, it's important that you not misinterpret yourselves as people who are bringing this goodness to God. No, God brings it all to you. The only accurate way to understand ourselves is by what God is and by what he does for us, not by what we are and what we do for him."

How do you see yourself? Notice again how *The Message* Bible reads. "The only accurate way to understand ourselves is by what God is and by what he does for us, not by what we are and what we do for him." Who God is and what he does for you is the key to how you need to understand yourself.

God is our creator, we are his creation. Like our first parents, Adam and Eve, we chose to go our own way and cut ourselves off from God. But in his grace and indescribable love he came seeking for us, even while we were running and hiding from him. He even gave his only Son as the sacrifice for our rebellion against him. Through the sacrifice of his Son we are offered forgiveness and new life, his life lived through us.

See yourself as a channel of God's love flowing through you to others, especially to those who do not yet know God's love expressed through Jesus Christ his Son. You are God's ambassadors to those still in darkness (I Corinthians 5:20).

Father, I thank you for who you are and for what you have done for me. Help me to give my life for others, even as you gave your Son for me, so they too might have eternal life. Amen.

July 28

Front Line Engagement

II Timothy 2:3-4

"Endure hardship with us like a good soldier of Christ Jesus. No one serving as a soldier gets involved in civilian affairs—he wants to please his commanding officer" (II Timothy 2:3-4 NIV).

A soldier on the front lines is engaged in offense. His buddies are side by side with him. They have vowed to risk and even give their lives for each other and for the cause of their country. There is no room for disunity on the front lines. Friction or arguing often happens while they are on rest and recreation, but not when they are carrying out the commanding officer's orders and engaging the enemy.

If churches focused on the Great Commission of our Lord and engaged the enemy, we would not have all the friction and infighting that is too common in our churches today. The Great Commission must be the focus, the vision, and the driving force of our lives and of our churches.

The author of Hebrews writes: "Since we are surrounded by such a great cloud of witnesses, let us throw off everything that hinders and the sin that so easily entangles, and let us run with perseverance the race marked out for us. Let us fix our eyes on Jesus, the author and perfecter of our faith, who for the joy set before him endured the cross, scorning its shame, and sat down at the right hand of the throne of God. Consider him who endured such opposition from sinful men, so that you will not grow weary and lose heart. In your struggle against sin, you have not yet resisted to the point of shedding your blood" (Hebrews 12:1-4 NIV).

Let us keep our eyes on Jesus! The good news is that Jesus not only commands us to go and make disciples, he gives us the power to carry out the commission (Acts 1:8).

Lord Jesus, forgive me for too often focusing on my preferences and not on engaging the enemy. Thank you for the power of the Holy Spirit to guide and lead me as I engage in front line offensive battles today. Amen.

July 29

Discipline is Critical

II Timothy 2:5

"If anyone competes as an athlete, he does not receive the victor's crown unless he competes according to the rules" (II Timothy 2:5 NIV). "Train yourself for spiritual fitness" (I Timothy 4:7 NLT).

Athletes exercise long hours, forcing their bodies to endure pain. They practice, practice, practice. They watch their diet. They get adequate sleep. Their social life is often cut to a minimum. Some travel, living away from family and friends in order to compete to win a victor's crown. They memorize the rules so they know them without thinking twice.

Beginning in chapter three of the Bible, we already decided we will not follow God's rules. There is something about our old nature that resists being told what is best for us. Galatians 5:7-8 NIV reminds us, "A man reaps what he sows. The one who sows to please his sinful nature, from that nature will reap destruction; the one who sows to please the Spirit, from the Spirit will reap eternal life."

Jesus gave us guidelines. If we break them they will break us. The basic guideline is to love God with all our heart, soul, mind and strength and to love our neighbor like we love ourselves (Matthew 22:37-39). Jesus said, "If you hold to my teaching you are really my disciples. Then you will know the truth, and the truth will set you free" (John 8:32 NIV). "The Lord is the Spirit, and where the Spirit of the Lord is, there is freedom" (II Corinthians 3:17 NIV). "Exercise your freedom by serving God, not by breaking the rules" (I Peter 2:16 Msg).

God's rules are not burdensome. (I John 5:3) They are liberating. Paul writes, "Through Christ Jesus the law of the Spirit of life set me free from the law of sin and death" (Romans 8:2 NIV). "So I say, live by the Spirit, and you will not gratify the desires of the sinful nature" (Galatians 5:16 NIV).

Lord Jesus, I discipline my body by the power of your Spirit. By your grace I will say no to the desires of the flesh and yes to the law of life in Christ Jesus. So help me God. Amen.

July 30

Work Hard

II Timothy 3:6

"The hardworking farmer should be the first to receive a share of the crops" (II Timothy 3:6 NIV).

This is the third example we need to follow. The first is a soldier who does his best to please his commander, the second is the athlete who competes according to the rules of the game, and the third is a farmer who works hard.

Farmers get up early and work to sunset. I grew up on a farm. The cows have to be milked at least twice a day usually 5:30 AM and 5:30 PM. This means getting up early and staying up late. There is field work which until these last couple decades was strenuous. Weeds and pests are a constant battle. The risk is great. If there is no rain or too much rain often the crops are lost. Just as a farmer must work hard and take risks, the same is true in our Christian life.

Many times we are admonished to "work hard": "Make every effort to apply the benefits of these promises to your life" (II Peter 1:5 NLT). "Work hard to prove that you really are among those God has called and chosen. Doing this, you will never stumble or fall away. And God will open wide the gates of heaven for you to enter into the eternal Kingdom of our Lord and Savior Jesus Christ" (vv. 10-11). A few verses later Peter says, "I will work hard to make these things clear to you. I want you to remember them long after I am gone" (v. 15). Again he writes: "Make every effort to live a pure and blameless life" (3:14). "Work hard at living in peace with others" (I Peter 3:15 NLT). We are to train ourselves for spiritual fitness. (I Timothy 4:7).

While salvation is a gift, we are to prove our love for Jesus by serving him 24/7. "He has created us anew in Christ Jesus, so that we can do the good things he planned for us long ago" (Ephesians 2:10 NLT).

Lord Jesus, forgive my laziness and lethargy. Fill me with your Spirit of enthusiasm and zeal. I will serve you with my whole heart today. Amen.

July 31

Is There Time to Retire?

Revelation 2:2-5

"I know all the things you do. I have seen your hard work and your patient endurance. I know you don't tolerate evil people… You have patiently suffered for me without quitting. But I have this complaint against you. You don't love me or each other as you did at first. Look how far you have fallen from your first love! Turn back to me again and work as you did at first. If you don't, I will come and remove your lampstand from its place among the churches" (Revelation 2:2-5 NLT).

A retired pastor participated in a retreat with 100 other retired pastors. The subject came up concerning the lack of growth in our American churches. It seemed the general consensus was that they did their part, now let's let others step up to the plate and carry the ball. Where do we read in Scripture that there is retirement time for the Christian?

Where is our zeal, our enthusiasm? Have you lost your first love? "Never be lazy in your work, but serve the Lord enthusiastically" (Romans 12:11 NLT). Can you imagine Paul retiring? While it is appropriate to turn the leadership over to younger Christians we never retire from being a faithful witness for our Lord.

Jesus heard that John the Baptist was killed. He tried to get alone but the crowds came. He healed their sick. Then he fed the multitude. Now he finally gets alone but what does he do? He prays and then teaches the disciples a dramatic lesson at 5:00 in the morning. What a model! (See Matthew 14:25).

Paul writes, "Be strong and steady, always enthusiastic about the Lord's work, for you know that nothing you do for the Lord is ever useless" (I Corinthians 5:58 NLT). "So don't get tired of doing what is good. Don't get discouraged and give up, for we will reap a harvest of blessing at the appropriate time. Whenever we have the opportunity, we should do good to everyone" (Galatians 6:9-10 NLT). "Never get tired of doing good" (II Thessalonians 3:13 NLT).

Lord Jesus, help my Spiritual temperature to stay red hot until the day you call me home. Amen.

August 1

A Brand New Life

II Corinthians 5:17-20

"Anyone united with the Messiah gets a fresh start, is created new. The old life is gone; a new life burgeons! Look at it! All this comes from the God who settled the relationship between us and him, and then called us to settle our relationships with each other. God put the world square with himself through the Messiah, giving the world a fresh start by offering forgiveness of sins. God has given us the task of telling everyone what he is doing. We're Christ's representatives, God uses us to persuade men and women to drop their differences and enter into God's work of making things right between them" (II Corinthians 5:17-20 Msg).

Can you imagine a greater message than this? We are guaranteed a fresh start! The old life of sin is gone, we think differently. We see things from God's perspective. What a difference that makes. We have new desires. The things of the world have lost their attraction and their power over us.

Has God changed the things that really matter to you? If you still desire and long for the old ways you need to go to the cross and lay the old ways on the altar. You know deep down you had nothing to do with this change except give yourself to God. He did the changing for you. Your desires changed, your love for him became predominate. It's impossible to describe other than to say, it is God's life in me, it is no longer me who lives but Jesus lives his life through me. (See Galatians 2:20).

If you haven't experienced this change—throw yourself once again at the foot of the cross and say, Lord, all that I am, all that I have I give to you. Use me to extend your Kingdom.

Thank you Lord Jesus, for translating me from the kingdom of darkness to the Kingdom of your beloved Son. Use me to persuade men and women to drop their differences and enter into God's work of making things right between them. Amen.

August 2

Come and See

John 1:45-46

"Nathaniel said, 'Nazareth? You've got to be kidding.' But Philip said, 'Come and see for yourself'" (John 1:45 Msg).

Jesus called people to himself. Do people see Jesus shining through you? One church has a large sign, "Come and See! John 1:46." Is anything happening in my church that compels me to invite my unchurched neighbors to "come and see?"

Many Christians are embarrassed to invite their friends to church because they know their friends would not feel comfortable. Our uneasiness about their level of comfort often comes not from a confrontation of sin in their life but from not being able to relate to a ritual of traditional worship that is second nature to us.

While the message of the Gospel never changes, the methods we use to bridge the message to the people must change with every generation. I have the Pennsylvania State Farmers Degree but in the last fifty years farming has changed so drastically that I know nothing about farming. What vocation hasn't changed? Yet our churches resist change more than any other organization. We want to preserve the past.

Jesus said, "No one sews a patch of unshrunk cloth, on an old garment, for the patch will pull away from the garment, making the tear worse. Neither do men pour new wine into old wineskins. If they do, the skins will burst, the wine will run out and the wineskins will be ruined. No, they pour new wine into new wineskins, and both are preserved" (Matthew 9:16-17 NIV). We need to drop the love for the old wine skins and love the new wine that Jesus has for us.

When we keep doing the same things we have always done and there are no baptisms of adults we need to ask, "Is it time to change wine skins?"

Lord, give us wisdom to understand our church culture and the courage to make the changes we need to make so our unchurched neighbors can be brought to Christ and become his disciples. Amen.

August 3

Miracles

Acts 4:13-16

"'When they saw the courage of Peter and John and realized that they were unschooled ordinary men, they were astonished and they took note that these men had been with Jesus. But since they could see the man who had been healed standing there with them, there was nothing they could say. So they ordered them to withdraw from the Sanhedrin and then conferred together. 'What are we going to do with these men?' They asked. 'Everyone living in Jerusalem knows they have done an outstanding miracle and we cannot deny it'" (Acts 4:13-16 NIV).

Throughout the Bible, miracles were usually signs that God was breaking through to meet human needs. Today miracles occur for the same reason and have the same effect. People have to either accept them or reject them. The Sanhedrin rejected this miracle while others were drawn to the Savior.

Often it is the church people who reject the miracles of God especially if the miracles are a result of the Holy Spirit using the "unschooled" or ordinary persons as the channel to bring about the miracle. In this account there was irrefutable evidence of God's power and grace but the Jewish leaders rejected it. Don't be surprised if some reject your witness. When minds are closed, even the clearest evidence of Christ's power will not open their minds.

Perhaps the greatest miracle is a changed life. Do people see your supernatural life of love, joy, peace, patience, etc. (See Galatians 5:22-23). Others will see your exemplary attitude and be drawn to Jesus. We must never give up. Pray for those who refuse to accept the truth and go on spreading the light of Christ.

After the authorities warned Peter and John to not speak or teach in the name of Jesus they responded: "Judge for yourselves whether it is right in God's sight to obey you rather than God. For we cannot help speaking about what we have seen and heard" (Acts 4:18-20 NIV). Their faith was so strong they could not keep quiet. May the Lord help you to be bold for him even in the face of persecution.

Lord, give me the same boldness today that Peter and John had. Amen.

August 4

Not a False Bone

John 1:47-49

"When Jesus saw him (Nathanael) he said, 'There's a real Israelite, not a false bone in his body. Nathanael said, 'Where did you get that idea? You don't know me.' Jesus answered, 'One day, long before Philip called you here, I saw you under the fig tree.' Nathanael explained, 'Rabbi! You are the Son of God, the King of Israel!'" (John 1:47-49 Msg).

Jesus is always encouraged to find integrity. We all have a streak of hypocrisy in us. Like Adam and Eve we try to hide our sin. "The heart is deceitful above all things and beyond cure. Who can understand it?" (Jeremiah 17:9 NIV). *The Message* Bible reads, "The heart is hopelessly dark and deceitful, a puzzle that no one can figure out."

David was a man after God's heart. Why? Not because he was sinless. He was guilty of a multitude of sins: adultery, deceit, pride and lies. But whenever he sinned and became aware of his sin he came running to God in sincere repentance, confessed his sin and was forgiven. He asked God for direction in his life. Relationship with God was restored. This did not mean that he did not suffer the consequences of his sin. When he committed adultery with Bathsheba, he prayed and fasted for seven days but the child died. (See II Samuel 12:19).

The Lord says, "'These are the things you are to do. Speak the truth to each other, and render true and sound judgment in your courts; do not plot evil against your neighbor, and do not love to swear falsely. I hate all this;' declares the Lord'" (Zechariah 8:16-17 NIV). Paul reminds the Christians in Ephesus, "Put off falsehood and speak truthfully to your neighbor, for we are all members of one body" (Ephesians 4:25 NIV).

Honesty is a foundation principle necessary for mutual relationships.

Pray with David, "Investigate my life, O God, find out everything about me; Cross-examine and test me, get a clear picture of what I'm about; See for yourself whether I've done anything wrong—then guide me on the road to eternal life" (Psalm 139:23-24 Msg).

August 5

Where Did Faith Go?

Hebrews 11:6

"It's impossible to please God apart from faith. And why? Because anyone who wants to approach God must believe both that he exists and that he cares enough to respond to those who seek him" (Hebrews 11:6 Msg).

Faith is more than the mental assent you give to Biblical truths you hear over and over. Many Christians scorn a faith that prays for a parking place or lost car keys or for help on a test. We as Christians must have heart-faith and childlike trust in the risen Christ—a faith that affects every aspect of our life.

Perhaps you once had that level of faith when you were a young Christian. Did the devil steal it from you? Are you like the Christians described in II Timothy 3:5, who have a form of godliness but deny its power? Believing—prayer is the life-line to God's power. Too often I have mechanically gone through the ritual of prayer while experiencing nothing of God's moving.

God can revive our faith if we ask him. He will bring faith alive in us through his Word. "Faith comes from hearing the message, and the message is heard through the word of Christ" (Romans 10:17 NIV).

Paul planted the church in Thessalonica in only three weeks, then he was forced to leave. He writes to the church and is concerned about their faith. Note these phrases in chapter 3 of his first letter to them: v.2 Paul and his companions sent Timothy to strengthen and encourage them in their faith, v. 5, Paul sent to find out about their faith, v. 6, Timothy brought good news about their faith, v. 7, Paul and his companions were encouraged because of their faith, and v. 10, Paul prayed that they would see them again and supply what is lacking in their faith.

"The fundamental fact of existence is that this trust in God, this faith, is the firm foundation under everything that makes life worth living. It's our handle on what we can't see" (Hebrews 11:1 Msg).

Jesus, help me to feed on your word so that my faith will grow and my walk with you will be strengthened. Amen.

August 6

Can You Amaze Jesus?

Luke 7:9 and Matthew 9:29

"When Jesus heard this, he was amazed at him, (the Roman officer) and turning to the crowd following him, he said, 'I tell you, I have not found such great faith even in Israel'" (Luke 7:9 NIV).

"Jesus said to them, 'Only in his hometown among his relatives and in his own house is a prophet without honor.' He could not do any miracles there, except lay his hands on a few sick people and heal them. And he was amazed at their lack of faith" (Mark 6:4-7 NIV).

Jesus was amazed at two opposites: great faith and lack of faith. When Jesus told the Roman centurion he would go to his house to heal his servant, and the centurion said not to come, but simply speak the word of healing, Jesus was amazed at his great faith. When the home town people did not believe in him he likewise was amazed at their lack of faith.

When our faith slides into an indifferent attitude, it is because we have grown cold. Paul admonishes Timothy to fan into flame the gift he was given. (See II Timothy 1:6). We need to fan into flame our gift of faith. Why do we meet together? "Let us not give up meeting together….but let us encourage one another…" (Hebrews 10:25 NIV). Is our church an encouraging church? Paul told the Corinthian Christians their gatherings do more harm than good. (See I Corinthians 11:17). We are to build each other up in the most holy faith. (See Jude 20). Jesus gave gifts to the church to build up the body. (See Ephesians 4:12).

Our faith is built up as we hear the word presented as it is the very words of God. (See I Peter 4:10). Faith is built up as people give up-to-date testimonies of God working in their lives. It is built up as we worship in songs of praise with thankful hearts. (See Ephesians 5:19-20). Faith must be exercised. It grows best in cloudy days. Spiritual gifts are all given for service. "Each one should use whatever gift he has received to serve others, faithfully administering God's grace in its various forms" (I Peter 4:10 NIV).

Lord, thank you for the gift of faith. Give me faith to see people drawn to you as you work through me in witnessing to them. Amen.

August 7
Faith is Not a Formula

Isaiah 29:13

"The Lord says: 'These people come near to me with their mouth and honor me with their lips, but their hearts are far from me. Their worship of me is made up of rules taught by men'" (Isaiah 29:13 NIV).

Some Christians teach that you cannot admit that you are sick, poor or have problems because that is a negative confession. Some are on their death bed but claim they are getting better physically. Others naively claim prosperity while over-extending themselves in charge card debts. Faith is not repeating a certain magic formula. A Christian does not deny reality or play mind games. God wants hearts of integrity and authenticity.

When we are battling anger, envy, pride, jealousy, pornography, etc. we need to be honest. We face reality, confess our sin, our lack of faith, ask God's forgiveness and take steps to refresh our faith. True faith comes from an honest heart. We need to confess: "Lord, I am helpless in myself. Purify my heart. You alone can give me the victory over this sin. You can guide me through financial crisis. You can sustain and bring healing to my body in your time and way. I submit to your schedule knowing you will never leave me nor forsake me. Thank you Jesus." Now you can rest in perfect peace.

We are to fight the good fight of faith. We no longer struggle in our own strength. The fight of faith is claiming the promises of Christ's sufficiency. With Christ we can go through every situation victoriously. (See Philippians 4:13) God will supply our every need. (See Philippians 4:19.) Since the Lord is our Shepherd we will not lack anything! (See Psalm 23:1).

Apart from God's grace and his power flowing through me I am nothing. I've been a Christian for sixty years but the old nature is still there. I don't try harder to overcome sin, I run to the cross for his cleansing blood and his resurrection power! Hallelujah!

Lord, I thank you for your cleansing blood and resurrection power! They are as powerful today as the day God raised Jesus from the tomb. Praise your name. Amen.

August 8

Removing Walls

John 17:21

Jesus prayed: "The goal is for all of them to become one heart and mind—Just as you, Father, are in me and I in you, so they might be one heart and mind with us. Then the world might believe that you, in fact sent me. The same glory you gave me, I gave them, so they'll be as united and together as we are—I in them and you in me" (John 17:21-22 Msg).

No matter what happens in our life, what difficult experiences we have, God is using these experiences, to answer Jesus' prayer that we may be one just as He was one with the Father. Such oneness is only possible in Christ.

In John 13 just after instituting the last supper Jesus said, "A new command I give you; Love one another. As I have loved you, so you must love one another. By this all men will know that you are my disciples, if you love one another" (John 13:34-35 NIV).

There are well over 300 denominations and thousands of independent churches throughout the U.S. In many communities there are more and more opportunities for churches to work together rather than compete with each other. It is good when persons come from other churches to welcome them and encourage them to take greetings back to their home congregation. This is one small step in breaking down the barriers that spring up between congregations and Christians.

More and more Christians from many groups are engaging in service projects together. It seems we can work together easier than worship together. Sunday morning is still the most segregated hour of the week.

Jesus taught us to pray that his kingdom come on earth as it is in heaven. Revelation 7:9 NIV, informs us there was a "great multitude that no one could count, from every nation, tribe, people and language, standing before the throne and in front of the Lamb."

Lord Jesus help me to work along with other Christians so that the world may know that we are your disciples and come to believe that you are the Messiah. Amen.

August 9

What Rights Do I Have?

Matthew 16:24-25

Jesus said, "Anyone who intends to come with me has to let me lead. You're not in the driver's seat, I am. Don't run from suffering; embrace it. Follow me and I'll show you how. Self-help is no help at all. Self-sacrifice is the way, my way, to finding yourself, your true self" (Matthew 16:24-25 Msg).

The NLT reads: "If any of you wants to be my follower you must put aside your selfish ambition, shoulder your cross, and follow me. If you try to keep your life for yourself, you will lose it. But if you give up your life for me, you will find true life."

Jesus calls me to abandon my rights, my independence and self-will. He's in charge! He is LORD! We are his servants—really the Greek word is slaves. A slave has no rights. His master is in charge of him 24/7.

That doesn't sound fair. Did you earn any rights? What have you that God has not given you? (See I Corinthians 4:7). We say, "But Lord, some things I do are helpful to your Kingdom — they are good things." It is often the good things that are not the best things. Have you given your ministry to the Lord? Suppose the Lord removes that ministry from you. Could you still rejoice in him? Our ministry may become just that—our ministry and not His ministry. We may receive satisfaction and joy from our ministry rather than from his presence.

We must lay everything on the altar otherwise we can't say with Paul: "I have learned how to get along happily whether I have much or little. I know how to live on almost nothing or with everything. I have learned the secret of living in every situation whether it is with a full stomach or empty, with plenty or little. For I can do everything with the help of Christ who gives me the strength I need" (Philippians 4:11-13 NLT).

Lord, I give you all my "rights." You are Lord. You are my leader, I am your servant. Whatever you say, I will do. So help me. Amen.

August 10

Do Not Grieve the Spirit

Ephesians 4:30-32

"Do not grieve the Holy Spirit of God, with whom you were sealed for the day of redemption. Get rid of all bitterness, rage, and anger, brawling and slander, along with every form of malice. Be kind and compassionate to one another, forgiving each other, just as in Christ God forgave you" (Ephesians 4:30-32 NLT).

The Message reads: "Don't grieve God. Don't break his heart. His Holy Spirit, moving and breathing in you, is the most intimate part of your life, making you fit for himself. Don't take such a gift for granted" (v. 30). Intimacy for the Christian should be defined as: into-him-you-see!

Paul gives a similar admonition to the Thessalonians: "Do not stifle the Holy Spirit" (I Thessalonians 5:19 NLT). How do we stifle or grieve the Spirit? We can grieve the Spirit by our speech and conduct. In the Ephesian context he warns us concerning unwholesome speech: bitterness, anger, brawling, slander, and poor attitudes. Instead we need to forgive each other just like Jesus forgives us.

The voice of the Spirit is very gentle. (See I Kings 19:12). We will very seldom hear His voice in our rush of living.

We need to keep an up-to-date intimacy with Jesus to hear his voice. Just as the Father told him what to say and how to say it, we too can hear the Spirit's voice telling us what to say and how to say it. (See John 12:49). To hear his voice we need to walk in the light as he is in the light. (See I John 1:7). This is an everyday walk, not just a Sunday church walk.

"Since we live by the Spirit, let us keep in step with the Spirit" (Galatians 5:24 NIV). Let's keep up to date with the Spirit. Welcome him, and invite him into your life every moment of the day.

Lord Jesus I thank you for your Spirit who makes real all you have done for me. Help me to keep in step with your Spirit today. Amen.

August 11

Make the Most of Every Opportunity

Ephesians 5:15-17

"Watch your step. Use your head. Make the most of every chance you get. These are desperate times! Don't live carelessly, unthinkingly. Make sure you understand what the Master wants" (Ephesians 5:15-17 Msg).

"Be wise in the way you act toward outsiders; make the most of every opportunity. Let your conversation be always full of grace, seasoned with salt, so that you may know how to answer everyone" (Colossians 4:5-6 NIV).

"If you are asked about your Christian hope, always be ready to explain it. But you must do this in a gentle and respectful way. Keep your conscience clear. Then if people speak evil against you they will be ashamed when they see what a good life you live because you belong to Christ" (I Peter 3:15-16 NLT).

Peter and Paul were focused. Every encounter with those both inside and outside God's Kingdom was an opportunity to share Jesus. Are you consciously asking the Holy Spirit to prompt you to speak for the Lord? The time is short; therefore we need to make the most of every opportunity. We never know when our last opportunity will be to share the Good News.

Peter reminds us that we must be gracious. We lose our effectiveness if we are not polite. What we say should be salty or tasty. Hopefully it will arouse curiosity. Use the "AA" approach, i.e. arouse curiosity and answer questions. When we are walking in the Spirit many doors will open. We will sense when people have a need. Their need is an open door to reaching them. Usually it is appropriate to mention that we will be praying for them. Then check back to see how things are developing letting them know we have been praying for them. This is showing love and hopefully building a positive relationship to continue your witness for Jesus.

If we are excited and enthusiastic about what Jesus has done for us and praying for the Holy Spirit to draw others to the Savior we can be sure we will reap a harvest.

Lord Jesus, help me to be tuned into your Sprit so I can use every opportunity to share the Good News with others today. Amen.

August 12

The Isaac Factor

Genesis 22

"God tested Abraham, He said to him, 'Abraham!' 'Here I am,' he replied. Then God said, 'Take your son, your only son, Isaac, whom you love, and go to the region of Moriah. Sacrifice him there as a burnt offering on one of the mountains I will tell you about.' Early the next morning Abraham got up and saddled his donkey. He took with him two of his servants and his son Isaac…" (Genesis 22:1-3 NIV).

God was testing Abraham. Isaac was Abraham's heart and soul! He had waited 13 years for God to miraculously give him the son of promise.

Abraham passed the test in flying colors. Abraham told the servants, "Stay here with the donkey while I and the boy go over there. We will worship and then we will come back to you" (v. 5 NIV). WE will come back. Abraham believed God would provide another sacrifice or raise Isaac from death.

Have you faced your Isaac factor? Has God asked you to take your most precious "idol" and place it on the altar? What is the "idol" you are hanging onto? Is he asking you to move so you can serve him in another location, perhaps help plant a church or serve in foreign missions? Is he asking you to move to help care for your aging parents? Is he asking you to give up your more than adequate salary with great benefits? Is he asking you to stay in your marriage even though you want out? For some of you the greatest test you will face is to either stay with your church or to move to another congregation. For others God may be asking you to give up your present ministry and move to a less appealing situation.

In my 50 years of ministry, the two most difficult situations I encountered resulted in the best experiences of my life. God had better things than I could envision.

Whatever God is asking you to give up, respond like Abraham: "Early the next morning Abraham got up and saddled his donkey…" No rebuttal, no argument, no asking 'why.'

Lord, I lay everything on the altar. Whatever you say or wherever you ask me to go, I will obey. Amen.

August 13

False Hope

Matthew 7:21-23

"Not everyone who says to me, 'Lord Lord,' will enter the kingdom of heaven, but only he who does the will of my Father who is in heaven. Many will say to me on that day, 'Lord, Lord, did we not prophesy in your name, and in your name, drive out demons and perform many miracles?' Then I will tell them plainly, 'I never knew you. Away from me, you evildoers!'" (Matthew 7:21-23 NIV).

The Message Bible reads: "Knowing the correct password—saying 'Master, Master,' for instance—isn't going to get you anywhere with me. What is required is serious obedience—doing what my Father wills. I can see it now—at the Final Judgment thousands strutting up to me and saying, 'Master, we preached the Message, we bashed the demons, our God—sponsored projects had everyone talking.' And do you know what I am going to say? 'You missed the boat. All you did was use me to make yourselves important. You don't impress me one bit. You're out of here.'"

Jesus said, "False Christs and false prophets will appear and perform great signs and miracles to deceive even the elect—if that were possible" (Matthew 24:24 NIV).

Paul writes: "The coming of the lawless one will be in accordance with the work of Satan displayed in all kinds of counterfeit miracles, signs and wonders" (II Thessalonians 2:9 NIV). (See also Revelations 13:13; 16:14; 19:20 and Exodus 7 and 8).

Not everyone who claims to know Jesus knows him. There are satanic and demonic powers that can do amazing miracles but they do not obey our Lord. At the judgment they will be greatly disappointed as Jesus says, "Depart, I never knew you." We must search the word of the Lord to see if teachers are teaching the truth and bearing fruit that lasts for eternity. Don't be fooled by the false claims even when they are backed up with miracles. Check to see if the fruit remains faithful to the teaching of our Lord.

Lord, help me to be discerning when I become aware of people performing various signs and miracles. Help me to walk my talk, to be obedient to you in all things. Amen.

August 14

Angels

Hebrews 1:14

"Are not all angels ministering spirits sent to serve those who will inherit salvation?" (Hebrews 1:14 NIV).

How conscious are you of angels? How blessed we are that God would not only provide his Holy Spirit to dwell in us but he also sends his angels to minister to us. They are created beings to serve us. (See Hebrews 1:14). They proclaim God's message. (See Revelation 14:6-12). They execute God's judgment. (See Acts 12 and Revelation 20). They brought the law to Moses. (See Galatians 3:19 and Hebrews 2:2). However, they are created beings and we are not to worship them. (See Colossians 2:18).

"See that you do not look down on one of these little ones. For I tell you that their angels in heaven always see the face of my Father in heaven" (Matthew 18:10 NIV). Apparently certain angels are assigned to watch over the children. While many are not delivered or spared from accidents nevertheless angels are with them to comfort them.

Peter was sleeping in prison facing a trial the next morning. An angel came and delivered him. (See Acts 12:7-10). How often have we been spared from accidents or evil and been unaware of the angel's deliverance?

"He ordered his angels to guard you wherever you go. If you stumble, they'll catch you; their job is to keep you from falling" (Psalm 91:11-12 Msg). These were the words the devil used to tempt Jesus. He refused to yield to the devil's trap. The angel of the Lord shut the mouths of the lions so that Daniel was not harmed. (See Daniel 6:22). An angel stood by Paul and informed him that he and all the people on the ship would be spared. (See Acts 27:23). "The angel of the Lord encamps around those who fear him, and he delivers them" (Psalm 34:7 NIV).

Peter informs us that the angels long to understand salvation but they were not able to comprehend that Jesus would come and provide this great redemption. (See I Peter 1:12).

Lord Jesus, while there is much I don't understand about angels I thank you for their ministry. Thank you for delivering me from harm many times. You are so wonderful. Amen.

August 15

The Mature Christian

Romans 8:29 and Psalm 34

"Those God foreknew he also predestined to be conformed to the likeness of his Son" (Romans 8:29 NIV). The goal is clear: be like Jesus.

Two of the most mature saints, David and Paul were honest. Listen to their words: In Psalm 34, David's faith is very high. He says that God will deliver us from fear (v.4), save us out of our troubles (v.6), guard and deliver us (v.7), show us goodness (v.8), supply our needs (v.9), listen when we talk to him (v. 15), and redeem us (v.22). Wow! What promises!

David reminds us in the same Psalm we must seek him, vv. 4 & 10, cry out to him. vv. 6 & 17, trust him, v.8, fear him, vv. 7 & 9 refrain from lying, v. 13, turn from evil, do good and seek peace, v.14, be humble v. 18 and serve him. v. 22.

Other times in David's life he writes: "O Lord, heal me, for my bones are in agony. My soul is in anguish. How long, O Lord, how long?" (Psalm 6:2-3 NIV). I am worn out from groaning; all night long I flood my bed with weeping and drench my couch with tears. My eyes grow weak with sorrow; they fail because of all my foes" (Psalm 6:6-7 NIV).

Paul's emotional stability was similar to David's. He writes in I Corinthians 1:8—10 NLT: "We were crushed and completely overwhelmed, and we thought we would never live through it. In fact, we expected to die. But as a result, we learned not to rely on ourselves, but on God who can raise the dead. And he did deliver us from mortal danger." In chapter 6:10 NIV he writes: We are "dying and yet we live on; beaten, and yet not killed; sorrowful, yet always rejoicing; poor, yet making many rich; having nothing, and yet possessing everything." Again he writes: "Be joyful always; pray continually; give thanks in all circumstances" (I Thessalonians 5:16-18 NIV).

Mature Christians can go through the valleys or ride on the mountain tops and still rejoice in the sufficiency of Jesus.

Jesus, I thank you for your grace that reaches out to us when we do not fully attain or live up to your will for us. With your help I pledge again to walk as you walked.

August 16

Boundaries or Center Focus

John 12:32

"When I am lifted up from the earth, I will draw all men to myself" (John 12:32 NIV).

How do you view Christ and Christianity? Many view the Christian faith with Christ at the center, but then see all kinds of fences or boundaries in relationship to Christ. An example of boundaries might be the implication that a person couldn't be a Christian if they live a materialistic lifestyle or if they are covered with tattoos, etc. Rather than set up those artificial boundaries, let's think of Jesus as the center and see people coming to him from every arena of life and lifestyles. He said, "But I, when I am lifted up from the earth, I will draw all men to myself" (John 12:32 NIV). Notice the word "all" men.

Setting up boundaries inevitably leads to legalism and a religion of the Pharisees. Jesus is in the business of tearing down walls. (See Ephesians 2:11-22). Legalistic attitudes rob us of our joy. The Holy Spirit is grieved when we become legalistic.

Paul gives us a helpful word on this theme: "You, my brothers, were called to be free. But do not use your freedom to indulge the sinful nature; rather, serve one another in love. The entire law is summed up in a single command: 'Love your neighbor as yourself.' If you keep on biting and devouring each other, watch out or you will be destroyed by each other.

"So I say, live by the Spirit, and you will not gratify the desires of the sinful nature. For the sinful nature desires what is contrary to the Spirit, and the Spirit what is contrary to the sinful nature. They are in conflict with each other, so that you do not do what you want. But if you are led by the Spirit, you are not under law.

"The acts of the sinful nature are obvious: sexual immorality, impurity and debauchery, idolatry and witchcraft; hatred, discord, jealousy, fits of rage, selfish ambition, dissensions, factions and envy, drunkenness, orgies, and the like. I warn you, as I did before, that those who live like this will not inherit the kingdom of God" (Galatians 5:13-21 NIV).

Lord Jesus, help me to live by the Spirit and never to use my freedom to gratify my sinful nature. Amen.

August 17

Worthless Fasting

Isaiah 58

"Shout with the voice of a trumpet blast. Tell my people Israel of their sins! Yet they act so pious! They come to the Temple every day and seem delighted to hear my laws. You would almost think this was a righteous nation that would never abandon its God.... 'We have fasted before you!' they say. "Why aren't you impressed? We have done much penance, and you don't even notice it!'" (Isaiah 58:1-3 NLT).

This is not a nice, pious, gentle reminder. This is no light slap on the hand. Isaiah shouts to get their attention. He is talking with "nice" church people who love to gather to worship. They sing all the right words, hear all the good sermons and come back next Sunday for worship.

"I will tell you why! It's because you are living for yourselves even while you are fasting. You keep right on oppressing your workers. What good is fasting when you keep on fighting and quarreling? This kind of fasting will never get you anywhere with me. 'You humble yourselves by going through the motions of penance, bowing your heads like a blade of grass in the wind...Do you really think this will please the Lord?'" (vv. 3-5 NLT).

How many of us know the primary calling of a Christian is to be a witness, (See Acts 1:8, Matthew 28:18-20), to let our light shine, (See Matthew 5:14-16), to love and serve others (See I Peter 4:10-11, Matthew 25:31-46)? Too often our theology is not matched with our sociology: our worship doesn't translate into life, and our Sunday doesn't carry over into Monday. We must repent from dead works. (See Hebrews 6:1).

"'No the kind of fasting I want calls you to free those who are wrongly imprisoned and to stop oppressing those who work for you. Treat them fairly and give them what they earn. I want you to share your food with the hungry and to welcome poor wanderers into your homes. Give clothes to those who need them, and do not hide from relatives who need your help. If you do these things, your salvation will come like the dawn. Yes, your healing will come quickly...Then when you call, the Lord will answer...'" (vv.6-9).

Jesus, help me to do what I promise as I sing to you and as I hear your word. Amen.

August 18

Joy For Today

John 15:11

"I have told you this so that my joy may be in you and that your joy may be complete" (John 15:11 NIV).

Sometimes I think Christians are the least joyful people around. What a poor advertisement! The joy of the Lord does not radiate from them. A smile would greatly help their countenance. Is it because they have deep hurts that were never healed? Is it because they are carrying heavy burdens? Is it because they believe God doesn't want us to enjoy life?

Review again the many Scriptures that point to joy: "The Kingdom of God is....righteousness, peace and joy in the Holy Spirit" (Romans 14:17 NIV). "In your presence is fullness of joy" (Psalm 16:11 KJV). That's straight forward. We live in his presence. (See James 4:8, John 14:23) "Our hearts ache but we always have joy" (II Corinthians 6:10 NLT). "The joy of the Lord is your strength" (Nehemiah 8:10 NIV). "Ask and you will receive, and your joy will be complete" (John 16:23 NIV). "Always be full of joy in the Lord. I say it again—rejoice!" "Philippians 4:4 NLT). Joy or joyful is mentioned hundreds of times in the Bible.

Do you want more joy in your life? The source is Jesus. If you obey his commands your joy will be full! (See John 15:9-11). His command is to make disciples. When he sent them out the first time (see Luke 10:1ff), they returned with joy because they were successful. Jesus tells them in essence that they are not to rejoice in successful service but to rejoice because of their relationship with him.

Joy comes when we know the risen Christ. Do I trust him to work through me? Do I trust him to use me to bring people to Jesus? All authority has been given to me....Go therefore and make disciples.

Lord Jesus by your powerful Holy Spirit in me I will obey you. I trust you to use me to bring people to yourself and disciple them. May the joy of the Lord always be my strength. Amen.

August 19

Grow in Knowledge

II Peter 3:18

"Grow in the.... knowledge of our Lord and Savior Jesus Christ" (II Peter 3:18 NLT).

The word "knowledge" is experiential knowledge. There is a different Greek word for factual or head knowledge. God's truth is hidden to those who will not obey him. Jesus prays: "O Father, Lord of heaven and earth thank you for hiding the truth from those who think themselves so wise and clever, and for revealing it to the childlike. Yes, Father, it pleased you to do it this way!" (Matthew 22:25-26 NLT).

Obedience is the key to opening God's truth. We don't come to understand God in the abstract or through philosophy but through relationship. Relationship comes through obedience. It comes through walking in the light of God's truth. "If we walk in the light, as he is in the light, we have fellowship with one another, and the blood of Jesus, his Son, purifies us from all sin" (I John 1:7 NIV). When we are cleansed from sin we are born into his Kingdom. That means God is our Father. Jesus is our brother and friend. We can experience a vital, dynamic and intimate relationship with Jesus.

Studying about God with no intention or desire to know him personally is little more than an intellectual exercise. It is dead works. (See Hebrews 6:1.) Obedience brings understanding. Peter admonished us to grow in our love, friendship and obedience. No study or academic pursuit alone will bring this kind of knowledge. It will have no bearing on our life or our destiny. We must be willing to do the will of the Father, then we will know the truth and the truth will set us free.

As we walk in obedience the truth opens up to us. We feel closeness to our Lord. Paul writes in Philemon v. 6, NIV, "I pray you may be active in sharing your faith, so that you will have a full understanding of every good thing we have in Christ." As we are obedient in sharing our faith, both in word and deed our understanding of Christ will grow.

Lord, help me to walk in obedience to you so I can grow in experiencing more and more of your love and grace. Amen.

August 20

"But I'm Not So Bad!"

Matthew 22:10 and 7:1-5

"The servants went out into the streets and gathered all the people they could find, both good and bad, and the wedding hall was filled with guests" (Matthew 22:10 NIV).

Too often church people think of themselves as being good and the people of the world as bad. This can be dangerous. The Greek word "bad" is often translated "evil" or "wicked". As Christians we must not make distinctions that suggest there are "good people" and bad people", rather, let's remember that we all have sinned and come short of God's glory. We all inherited the same nature from Adam and Eve. Some people have suffered more and experienced less of the love of God than others. This makes it more difficult for them to understand and receive God's love and to accept the forgiveness Jesus has provided for them.

Hurt people tend to hurt others. We all need God's mercy. No matter how offensive one's actions, we all need God's mercy. I have experienced more of God's love than many who were not raised in a Christian family. Therefore I have more responsibility to show God's love and mercy to those who have not experienced his love as I have. This helps me see myself as on the same level as those whose actions and motives seem more obviously evil than mine.

By God's grace I have been forgiven, but I have the same sin issues as everyone else, no matter how repulsive their action and sin is to me. Let's not judge. When we judge it points to a lack of understanding our sin nature. We lack faith in the marvelous transformation God's Spirit can and will provide.

There is freedom in letting the judging to God and simply holding up the grace of Jesus. The key for Christians is to remember John 3:16, God loved the world, that is the people of the world, so much that he gave his only Son that they will not perish but have eternal life.

Jesus, thank you for saving me from my sin. Help me to share your forgiveness with others. Amen.

August 21

Both Mission and Ministry

John 17:18

"In the same way that you gave me a mission in the world, I gave them a mission in the world" (John 17:18 (Msg). This is our mission.

"Serve one another in love" (Galatians 5:13 NIV). This is our ministry. You have a mission and a ministry. It's helpful to think in terms of mission as our service outside the congregation in the world while our ministry is within the congregation.

We, like Jesus, are sent into the world. (See John 17:18 and 20:21.) Jesus understood his mission. At age 12 he said: "I must be about my Father's business." Since we are the body of Christ, his mission is our mission. He came to seek and save the lost. We must do the same.

In ministry we serve one another. (See Galatians 5:13 NIV.) We are devoted to one another, honor one another (Romans 12:10 NIV), accept one another (Rom. 15:7 NIV), instruct one another (Romans 15:14 NIV), carry each other's burdens (Galatians 6:2 NIV), bear with one another (Ephesians 4:2 NIV), submit to one another (Ephesians 5:12), encourage one another (I Thessalonians 5:11 NIV) and finally love one another (John 13:34 NIV).

Many Christians who have been in church all their lives, even in small groups for years, still do not have a vibrant, contagious faith. In order to have a vibrant faith it is helpful to not only have a ministry but also to have a mission. Unless our biological families give birth we will die. Unless our churches have an outward focus we will die even though we have an inward ministry. We need a balance. Every member needs to have a vital part in not only a ministry but also a mission in the world. Some may be physically unable to serve in mission but they can pray and witness. If they understand their inside church ministry is directly helping the mission of the church this hurdle can be overcome. Jesus calls us to be involved both in ministry and mission.

Lord Jesus, thank you for the wonderful opportunity of serving you in both ministry and mission. Enable me to follow you faithfully in ministry and mission. Amen.

August 22

From Enemies To Friends

II Corinthians 5:18

"Christ changed us from enemies into his friends and gave us the task of making others his friends also" (II Corinthians 5:18 TEV).

An apocrypha story has Jesus talking with an angel. The angel asked him how things were going on earth. He said, "Many people are coming to new life. The Kingdom of God is expanding but we have a long way to go." Looking concerned the angel questioned, "What is your strategy for reaching the others?" Jesus said, "It's for each Christian to invite others to enter my Kingdom." The angel asked, "What if that plan doesn't work?" Jesus said, "I have no plan B."

"We are sent to speak for Jesus. "God put the world square with himself through the Messiah, giving the world a fresh start by offering forgiveness of sins. God has given us the task of telling everyone what he is doing. We're Christ's representatives. God uses us to persuade men and women to drop their differences and enter into God's work of making things right between them. We're speaking for Christ himself now: Become friends with God; he's already a friend with you" (I Corinthians 5:18-20 Msg).

How do we turn enemies into friends? The King of Aram was at war with Israel. He was frustrated because Elisha would tell the people exactly where the enemy army would attack next. The King discovered it was Elisha who was causing his defeat so he sent an army to capture him. When Elisha's servant got up he saw this huge army. Elisha said, "Don't be afraid!...For there are more on our side than on theirs!" (II Kings 6:16 NLT). Elisha prayed and the servant's eyes were opened and he saw the hillside filled with horse and chariots of fire. (v. 17).

Elisha prayed for the enemy army to be blind. He led them to Samaria and after their eyes were opened he prepared a huge feast and sent them home. They were no longer enemies. "If your enemies are hungry, feed them. If they are thirsty, give them something to drink, and they will be ashamed of what they have done to you....Conquer evil by doing good" (Romans 12:20-21 NLT). That's how Elijah turned enemies into friends.

Lord, help me to do good to my enemies today. Amen.

August 23

Pray Specifically

Luke 11:9-13

"Ask and it will be given to you; seek and you will find; knock and the door will be opened to you. For everyone who asks receives; he who seeks finds; and to him who knocks, the door will be opened. Which of you fathers, if your son asks for a fish will give him a snake instead? Or if he asks for an egg, will give him a scorpion? If you then, though you are evil, know how to give good gifts to your children, how much more will your Father in heaven give the Holy Spirit to those who ask him!" (Luke 11:9-13 NIV).

Praying in generalities is much easier than praying specifically. Praying specifically takes faith. Prayers without faith are nothing more than dead ritual. General prayers are not wrong such as, "Lord bless our nation, our President, our church." There are times when God places a burden on you for a nation, or a church when you only have a general idea of the needs of that nation or church.

Specific prayers take more faith. You are expressing your desire, your burden for a person so name that person. When people are in small groups instead of praying for specific people their prayers are often in generalities or in categories such as praying for the lost or for the teachers in our schools.

I believe it is helpful to pray for persons by name. If we know the situation, mention specific needs, e.g. their marriage, their health, their finances. The more specifically you pray the more obvious it is when the answer comes. Answered prayer builds faith and is an encouragement to everyone.

Don't pray unless you are willing to do what God may want you to do to answer your prayer. Prayer is like putting your car in gear. Don't pray unless you are willing to take action.

Lord Jesus, help me to sincerely ask in faith knowing that you are more willing to answer us than earthly fathers are to answer the requests from their children. Amen.

August 24

The Priority of Prayer

Psalm 2:8

"Ask of me, and I will make the nations your inheritance, the ends of the earth your possession" (Psalm 2:8 NIV).

The first and most important action we can do as Christians is pray. People can reject our kindness, but they cannot reject our prayers. We can reach both our next-door neighbor or those half-way around the world through prayer.

We must pray for:
1. Workers: Jesus said, "The harvest is plentiful, but the workers are few. Ask the Lord of harvest to send out workers into his harvest field" (Luke 10:2 NIV).

2. Favorable circumstances to witness: "Pray for us that God may open a door for our message, so that we may proclaim the mystery of Christ, for which I am in chains" (Colossians 4:3 NIV).

" In my prayers at all times; I pray that now at last by God's will the way may be opened for me to come to you. I long to see you so that I may impart to you some spiritual gift... and have a harvest among you" (Romans 1:10-13 NIV).

3. Courage to speak up: "For our struggle is not against flesh and blood, but against the rulers, against the authorities, against the power of this dark world and against the spiritual forces of evil in the heavenly realms" (Ephesians 6:12 Msg).

4. Those who will believe: "My prayer is not for them alone. I pray also for those who will believe in me through their message, that all of them may be one, Father, just as you are in me and I am in you. May they also be in us so that the world may believe that you have sent me" (John 17:20-21 NIV).

5. The rapid spread of the message: "Pray for us. Pray that the Master's Word will simply take off and race through the country to a groundswell of response, just as it did among you. And pray that we'll be rescued from these scoundrels who are trying to do us in. I'm finding that not all 'believers' are believers. But the Master never lets us down. He'll stick by you and protect you from evil" (II Thessalonians 3:1-3 Msg).

Lord, help me to be faithful in prayer. Amen.

August 25

The Life-Giving Way

Hebrews 10

Can you imagine going to worship with your animals, the very best of the herd, then seeing your animal killed with the blood being sprinkled over the altar and sprinkled over you?

Notice the tremendous contrast in the New Testament. The blood of Jesus Christ cleanses us from all sin. (See I John 1:7). What a precious gift of life Jesus gives us! Hebrews says we come to God by the new life-giving way, not with the blood of animals but with the perfect blood of Jesus. (Hebrews 10:4)

"By one sacrifice, he (Jesus) has made perfect forever those who are being made holy. The Holy Spirit also testifies to us about this. First he says: 'This is the covenant I will make with them after that time, says the Lord. I will put my laws in their hearts and I will write them on their minds.' Then he adds: 'Their sins and lawless acts I will remember no more'" (Hebrews 10:14-17 NIV).

"So, friends, we can now—without hesitation—walk right up to God, into 'the Holy Place.' Jesus has cleared the way by the blood of his sacrifice acting as our priest before God.... So let's do it—full of belief, confident that we're presentable inside and out. Let's keep a firm grip on the promises that keep us going. He always keeps his word. Let's see how inventive we can be in encouraging love and helping out not avoiding worshiping together as some do but spurring each other on, especially as we see the big Day approaching" (Hebrews 10:19-25 Msg).

Begging God to give us salvation and deliverance from sin is useless apart from the cross. It's in him alone that we have redemption through his blood. (See Ephesians 1:7.) We can read self-help books, apply the latest psychology, we can use every ounce of will power all to no avail. When we come to the cross and receive his cleansing he gives us a new heart and a new mind. We are new creatures in Christ. Come to Jesus the life-giving way today and let him live his life through you. (See Galatians 2:20.)

Father, I come through Jesus the life-giving way. Thank you for his life lived through me today. Amen.

August 26

Insiders and Outsiders

Romans 15:7-11

"So reach out and welcome one another to God's glory. Jesus did it; now you do it! Jesus, staying true to God's purpose, reached out in a special way to the Jewish insiders so that the old ancestral promises would come true for them. As a result the non-Jewish outsiders have been able to experience mercy and to show appreciation to God. Just think of the Scriptures that will come true in what we do! ... Outsiders and insiders, rejoice together! And again: People of all nations, celebrate God! All colors and races, give hearty praise!" (Romans 15:7-11 Msg).

Our communities have become mini-worlds. People from many backgrounds live near us. We work with them and go to school with them. We eat with them in restaurants and yet Sunday morning is the most segregated hour of the week. When will we worship together? When will we answer Jesus' teaching in John 13 concerning loving one another and his prayer in John 17 concerning living in unity so the world will see Jesus in us?

In heaven we will be one from every nation, tribe, people and language." (See Revelations 7:9). Let's answer Jesus prayer by inviting these "outsiders" into our church families. Let's become inclusive. Let's cross cultural lines, economic status barriers, color or racial walls—let's just learn to see people as people for whom Jesus died.

We must build bridges to them. This will take intentional effort and time. It will have implications for our personal and church budgets. We must learn to understand and respect their language, their customs, their music, their family values. They do not care how much we know unless they know how much we care.

Have you learned to know a person of different culture in your neighborhood? Could you invite them to your home or to your church to explain their faith? People like to feel needed. They like to contribute. Give them opportunities to share so we can learn about them. We become all things to all people so we can win them to Jesus. (See I Corinthians 9:22.)

Lord Jesus, help me to reach outside my comfort zone and learn to know the people of different cultures in my community. Amen.

August 27

Privilege or Responsibility

Ezkiel 3:17-20

"Son of man, I've made you a watchman for the family of Israel. Whenever you hear me say something, warn them for me. If I say to the wicked, 'You are going to die,' and you don't sound the alarm warning them that it's a matter of life or death, they will die, and it will be your fault. I'll hold you responsible. But if you warn the wicked and they keep right on sinning anyway, they'll most certainly die for their sin, but you won't die. You'll have saved your life" (Ezekiel 3:17-20 Msg).

You are the only Christian some people know. Your mission is to share Jesus with these people. It is a privilege to share Jesus with them: "God has given us the privilege of urging everyone to come into his favor and be reconciled to him" (II Corinthians 5:18 LB).

If your neighbor had a deadly disease and you knew the cure it would be inexcusable to withhold that information. But it is worse to keep secret the way to forgiveness and eternal life. We have the greatest news in the world, and sharing it is the greatest kindness you can show to anyone.

Persons who have been Christians for a long time often forget how hopeless it felt to be without Christ. No matter how contented or successful people appear to be, without Christ they are hopelessly lost and headed for eternal separation from God. Jesus is the only One who can save people. (See Acts 4:12.) Everybody needs Jesus.

Why did God let us here after we accepted him? In heaven we can worship, fellowship, sing, pray and hear God's Word, but we won't be able to win people for Jesus and make disciples. Nothing you do will matter as much as helping people find Jesus. Why is that? Because this is a matter of life and death. Your work and your finances will all be gone in a few years. The consequences of your mission will last forever.

It's urgent. Jesus said: "As long as it is day, we must do the work of him who sent me. Night is coming, when no one can work" (John 9:4 NIV).

Jesus, thank you for the privilege of sharing the Good News with those who don't know you. Amen.

August 28

Neighbors

John 17:15 and I Corinthians 6:17

"I'm not asking that you take them out of the world but that you guard them from the Evil One" (John 17:15 Msg).

"Leave the corruption and compromise; leave it for good, says God. Don't link up with those who will pollute you. I want you all for myself" (I Corinthians 6:17 Msg).

Here we have contrasting scriptures. When it comes to neighbors, do you desire Christian neighbors or do you want nonbelievers to move close to you so you can win them to Jesus? Christians naturally desire for other Christians to move beside them because their values are similar to theirs. Maybe we think if they take care of their property it helps to keep the value of our property at a higher level. It's also usually easier to have believers which often provides a more congenial and friendly neighborhood.

Might there be a better approach when it comes to neighbors? My wife, Helen, prays for the new family who will be moving into an empty house. If they are Christians, she prays that they will be active in reaching others for Jesus and extending his Kingdom. If they are not Christians, she prays that she will be able to faithfully share Jesus with them.

Helen expressed her delight in meeting a new neighbor and mentioned she had been praying for them. The lady said, "How could you pray for us when you didn't know who was moving in? I'm a Christian, but I never thought about praying for new neighbors." Helen has had many meaningful conversations with neighbors moving them closer to Jesus. Paul writes in Ephesians 4:15 that we are to make the most of every opportunity. Let's not separate ourselves from the world by isolating ourselves with those who believe as we do. Let's be the salt, the light and the leaven that Jesus desires for us to be. (See Matthew 5:13-16).

Lord, forgive me for too often being exclusive and desiring to live where others already are Christians. Help me to get out of the salt shaker and into the world bringing the life of your salvation to my neighbors. Amen.

August 29

Use Your Gift

I Corinthians 12:1,7,11

"I write about the special abilities the Holy Spirit gives to each of us..." (I Corinthians 12:1 NLT). "A spiritual gift is given to each of us as a means of helping the entire church" (I Corinthians 12:7 NLT). "It is the one and only Holy Spirit who distributes these gifts. He alone decides which gift each person should have" (I Corinthians 12:11 NLT). "God has given gifts to each of you from his great variety of spiritual gifts" (I Peter 4:10 NLT).

These verses make it clear that you have a gift or more likely several gifts. Each gift can be used to extend God's Kingdom in the world. I am going to take the next several readings to highlight how each gift can be utilized by the Holy Spirit to draw people to Jesus and to his family of believers.

Ignorance of spiritual gifts may be at the root of much of the frustrations and guilt that plagues many Christians and stymies their ministry and mission. Too often we try to do things that we do not enjoy: we try to teach because the church needs a teacher, we sing in the choir because the director needs more tenors even though we don't enjoy singing.

When we function in areas where we are not gifted, we often become frustrated and burned out. Others will eventually see that we are serving out of obligation. This does not build up the body of Christ.

If we are to bear fruit that remains, it is helpful to find our gift(s) and use them for God's glory. One way I have found to discover our gift(s) is ask: "As a committed Christian; you love the Lord and are endeavoring to serve him. If time, energy, finances, were no hindrance what would you really like to do with your life? What makes you fulfilled? What brings you deep joy and satisfaction? What would you like to hear at your memorial service?"

These questions get at the heart of our gift(s). Pray and search your heart to discover what brings you deep joy and closer to Jesus. This is where your gifts lie.

Lord Jesus open my eyes to the gifts your have given me and I will joyfully serve you. Amen.

August 30

Gifts or Roles

Philippians 4:13

"I can do everything through him who gives me strength" (Philippians 4:13 NIV).

There are times when you will be in a situation where people need help but you feel you are not gifted to help them. In these situations God gives grace so that even though we are uncomfortable, God provides the ability to minister effectively.

This is exercising your role as a Christian rather than operating from your gift mix. Perhaps the Priest and Levite who passed up the man that was robbed felt they did not have the gift of mercy. However, even though they may not have had the gift of mercy they were responsible to help. (See Luke 10:31.) Another illustration is the rich young ruler who needed to learn to give to others even if he did not possess the gift of giving. (See Luke 18:22.)

What were Jesus primary gift(s)? I believe Jesus had all the gifts. In one sense I believe we have all the gifts too. As we mature in our Christian life we will find ourselves being called to sometimes serve in areas other than our giftedness. We can develop in those areas. However, I believe our primary focus should be in areas where we are gifted. At the same time when there is a need in the body of Christ for certain gifts we pray for the Lord to send people with those gifts. If the answer does not come he will provide grace for us in order to fulfill those needs.

It is very important to remember that the fruit of the Spirit takes priority over the gifts of the Spirit. The primary characteristic of the Christian is love. We are told fifty-five times in the New Testament to love one another. Spiritual fruit deals with relationships and the quality of our living. Spiritual gifts relate to our function and our calling. Gifts are task-oriented and fruit is character-oriented. A fruit is eternal while gifts are temporal.

Lord Jesus, help me to develop all my gifts but most importantly help me to grow in love for you and for others. Amen.

August 31

Discovering God's Will

Romans 12:1-6

"I urge you …to offer your bodies as living sacrifices, holy and pleasing to God—this is your spiritual act of worship. Do not conform any longer to the patterns of this world, but be transformed by the renewing of your mind. Then you will be able to test and approve what God's will is—his good, pleasing and perfect will. For by the grace given me I say to every one of you: Do not think of yourself more highly then you ought, but rather think of yourself with sober judgment, in accordance with the measure of faith God has given you. Just as each of us has one body with many members, and these members do not all have the same function, so in Christ we who are many form one body, and each member belongs to all the others. We have different gifts, according to the grace given us" (Romans 12:1-6 NIV).

It's clear we are to consecrate or commit ourselves to God. Often Christians commit themselves to God and expect to know God's will through their commitment. I believe this passage informs us that "gift theology" is often more helpful for knowing God's will than "consecration theology." Consecration theology means consecrating or committing ourselves to the Lord: to do the "good and pleasing and perfect will of God." You must think soberly of yourself—be realistic about the faith God has given you then discern which of the gifts described in vv.3-8 God has given you. Discover how these gifts fit your personality and passion.

We will be held accountable to God to develop each of our gifts to the peak of their potential. We tend to burn out quickly when we are not serving within our giftedness. Let's discern where we best fit. Is it through prophesying, serving, teaching, encouraging, contributing, leading or showing mercy? (See vv. 6-8.);

In the following readings we will focus on these and other gifts. Ask the Lord to open your eyes to see how you can best use your gift to bear fruit that lasts for eternity.

Lord Jesus, help me to understand my gifts to help build up the body of Christ. Amen.

September 1

Importance of Cooperation

I Corinthians 12:14-17

"The body has many different parts, not just one part. If the foot says, 'I am not a part of the body because I am not a hand,' that does not make it any less a part of the body. And if the ear says, 'I am not part of the body because I am only an ear and not an eye,' would that make it any less a part of the body? Suppose the whole body were an eye—then how would you hear? Or if your whole body were just one big ear, how would you smell anything?" (I Corinthians 12-14-17 NLT).

What a blessing our differences are. Imagine a church in which everyone wanted to be the worship leader and no one wanted to be led. Suppose no one had the gift of teaching, would you enjoy going to class? Suppose there was no one with the gift of mercy or service or administration?

Give each person a different piece of baseball equipment and tell them to play alone. What a frustrating experience. The pitcher would have no catcher, the batter would have no pitcher, etc. It takes all nine players plus another team to play. Inferiority has no place in the body of Christ; neither is there a place for superiority. We need each other.

Ultimately the gifts are not given to the individual they are given to the church. I Peter 4:10-11 NLT, "Each one should use whatever gift he has received to serve others, faithfully administering God's grace in its various forms."

Too often in our churches we develop programs and then try to find people to work in those programs. I believe a better approach is to discover the gifts of the people in the church. Develop ministry groups to serve others both within the church and in the community. We need to empower these persons to use their gifts within the vision of the church. This energizes the group and makes for an effective ministry.

Father, thank you for giving me gifts. Help me to use them most effectively for your glory. Amen.

September 2

The Teaching Gift

Luke 1:1-4

Teaching is the gift of acquiring and imparting spiritual truth so that others learn and profit by the instruction.

Luke was as excellent teacher. Notice how he begins his Gospel. Luke 1:1-4 NIV, "Many have undertaken to draw up an account of the things that have been fulfilled among us, just as they were handed down to us by those who from the first were eyewitnesses and servants of the word. Therefore, since I myself have carefully investigated everything from the beginning, it seemed good also to me to write an orderly account for you, most excellent Theophius, so that you may know the certainty of the things you have been taught."

Teaching is the most universal gift in the New Testament. The Greek word, *didasko*, to teach, appears more than 200 times. Teaching is far more predominant than preaching. Most churches want preachers, not teachers. This is one reason the American church is anemic. Teachers give lessons and expect results. We listen to preachers and tell them we enjoyed their message, but too often there is no accountability.

Teachers are curious persons: Luke "carefully investigated everything." Teachers go into detailed explanations. They desire to present truth in a systematic sequence. Luke wrote an "orderly account." Teachers tend to believe their gift is most important: "If people are just taught the truth, everything will be fine." Teachers like to know the source of the materials that are presented. Word meanings are important to them. They are word-oriented. They move from the word to the people. They prefer Biblical illustrations as compared to contemporary illustrations.

To further identify this gift ask, "Do I enjoy Bible study? Can I put together a Bible outline? Am I asked to teach? Do my students ever tell me how I have helped them? Can I sum up the important points or principles of a Bible study? Do I enjoy teaching? Am I a curious person?"

Some of the most important people in my life have been teachers? Even if you don't have the gift of teaching, you need to exercise your role as a teacher to your children, to those who work with you, and to others who ask you questions.

Lord, help me to use and develop my gift of teaching. Amen.

September 3

The Gift of Knowledge

John 4:16-19

"He told her, 'Go, call your husband and come back.' 'I have no husband,' she replied. Jesus said to her, 'you are right when you say you have no husband. The fact is, you have had five husbands, and the man you now have is not your husband. What you have just said is quite true.' 'Sir,' the woman said, 'I can see that you are a prophet'" (John 4:16-19 NIV).

The person with the gift of knowledge has the ability to receive divine revelation that builds up the body of Christ. These persons are confident concerning things the Holy Spirit has revealed to them.

The person with this gift does not need a high IQ. The gift has nothing to do with great intelligence. The gift is frequently exercised in a counseling situation. This is illustrated in the above scripture as Jesus encountered the woman at the well. It was true when Jesus told Nathaniel, "I saw you while you were still under the fig tree before Philip called you." (See John 1:48). Nathaniel was so impressed that he declared: "Rabbi, you are the Son of God; you are the King of Israel" (John 1:49 NIV).

While praying for others, the Holy Spirit frequently imparts "secrets" to the intercessor so they find themselves praying for specific things.

"Previous to President Kennedy's trip to Dallas, Billy Graham called the White House and told them he felt that something dreadful was going to happen to the President. Mr. Graham asked that President Kennedy postpone his trip. The White House thanked the evangelist for his concern, but the trip was not cancelled." [i] The President was killed.

Do you find yourself coming up with insights before others or when others seem to have no idea what direction to go? Are your insights accurate? Is it evident to you that the only explanation for your insight is the Holy Spirit? Do people come to you with questions expecting you to have the answer?

Lord Jesus, help me to use the gift of knowledge. Amen.

September 4

The Gift of Wisdom

Acts 15:2, and 12-21

After a sharp dispute between the apostles and the Pharisees, James said, "Listen to me" (v. 12) "It is my judgment...that we should not make it difficult for the Gentiles who are turning to God. Instead we should write to them, telling them to abstain from food polluted by idols, from sexual immorality, from the meat of strangled animals and from blood" (Acts 15:19-20 NIV). They all agreed.

The person with the gift of wisdom has the ability to receive divine revelation that speaks to a specific need in the body of Christ. Knowledge is truth about the situation. Wisdom is the application of knowledge for a particular situation.

This person has the ability to listen to diverse points of view and come up with a solution that satisfies everyone. Have you been in a group where there were several sides to an issue? You wondered how the group could possibly be united after this. Then God spoke through a word of wisdom. You think: "That was so simple. Why didn't I think of that?"

As with the gift of knowledge, there is no direct relationship with one's IQ. The word of wisdom is what we might often call common sense. It is a practical, almost "simple" solution. Solomon had a simple solution to a complex situation. (See I Kings 3:16-28.) People with this gift do not see problems as much as opportunities.

Do people who need advice come to you? Do members of a committee look your way before the final vote? Do you foresee the results of a particular course of action? Can you share insights so they are acceptable to others?

James writes: "If any of you lacks wisdom, he should ask God who gives generously to all without finding fault, and it will be given to him. But when he asks, he must believe and not doubt, because he who doubts is like a wave of the sea, blown and tossed by the wind. That man should not think he will receive anything from the Lord; he is a double-minded man, unstable in all he does" (James 1:5-8 NIV).

Lord, help me to see others with this gift and also help me to listen to your voice so I can receive your wisdom. Amen.

September 5

The Gift of Exhortation

Colossians 1:28-29

"We proclaim him, admonishing and teaching everyone with all wisdom, so that we may present everyone perfect in Christ. To this end I labor, struggling with all his energy, which so powerfully works in me" (Colossians 1:28-29 NIV).

The exhorter is one who can speak words of comfort, admonition, and encouragement to motivate Christians toward maturity in Christ. So intense is Paul that he struggles with all his energy to bring this about. The word for "struggle" here is the same word used to describe Jesus' experience in Gethsemane when he sweat, as it were, drops of blood in prayerful agony for our redemption.

The exhorter is motivated to discover where you are so they can help you move to maturity. Questions like: "What is God teaching you in your prayer life? What did you learn in your devotions today? Or, where do you want to be a month from now?" are examples of questions he or she will ask.

Present-day counselors are usually more passive than the exhorter. Paul was constantly urging, warning, and pleading with persons to grow in Christ.

The exhorter has the ability to visualize spiritual progress in the life of others and then use that vision to motivate them to take step-by-step action. The exhorter, or encourager as we may identify them, can see the potential God has given you. They eagerly desire for you to move to a new level of maturity.

"I want you to know how much I am struggling for you and for those in Laodicea, for all who have not met me personally. My purpose is that they may be encouraged in heart and united in love, so that they may have the full riches of complete understanding, in order that they may know the mystery of God, namely, Christ, in whom are hidden all the treasures of wisdom and knowledge" (Colossians 2:1-3 NIV).

The exhorter is comfortable ministering to strangers. The exhorter likes to work one-on-one. This gift can operate with groups, but it is more difficult to present step-by-step solutions since individuals are at different places in their understanding and maturity.

Lord, help me to be an encourager to others, moving them to new levels of maturity in Christ. Amen.

September 6

The Gift of Exhortation, Part II

I Thessalonians 5:11

"Encourage each other and build each other up, just as you are already doing" (I Thessalonians 5:11 NLT). Verse 14 adds, "Encourage those who are timid."

Three things people need: encouragement, encouragement, and encouragement. If that doesn't work, try encouragement. Someone else said there are three things people need: significance, community, and transcendence. The church can provide all three. The gift of exhortation and encouragement helps the person experience community and belonging. Encouragement also helps persons feel significant. If someone cares about me enough to encourage me or admonish me in love, that is a tremendous boost to my emotional wellbeing.

The exhorter and encourager is also motivated to bring harmony in the Body of Christ. He or she will not be afraid to move into the middle of a squabble because they see the potential for healing. The person with the gift of mercy sees and feels the problem. The prophet is vocal and direct but often is not heard because they have no action plan for solving the problem. Paul in Galatians and Corinthians speaks into the situation and is able to correct many of their problems.

The exhorter watches people and then makes applications from the Word of God to the life of the individual(s). The teacher begins with the Word and then goes to the people. The exhorter knows that learning and spiritual growth are often painful. They are not afraid to let you suffer pain in order to see you move to a deeper level of faith. (See Hebrews 12:5-6.) We may think they over simplify because they often present simple steps of action to a longstanding problem. The exhorter listens to a problem you lived with for years and then says: "Now here's what you need to do: first… second, and finally.

Do you follow specific steps of action to solve personal problems? Do you feel comfortable sharing insights with others in order to move them to maturity in Christ? Do you like to mediate in a group when there are differences of opinion? Do you call people on the phone or seek them out to encourage them?

Lord, help me to be an encourager to others today. Amen.

September 7

The Gift of Service

Hebrews 6:10-12

"God is not unjust; he will not forget our work and the love you have shown him as you have helped his people and continue to help them. We want each of you to show this same diligence to the very end, in order to make our hope sure. We do not want you to become lazy, but to imitate those who through faith and patience inherit what has been promised" (Hebrews 6:10-12 NIV).

"The Son of Man did not come to be served, but to serve" (Mark 10:45 NIV).

The person with the gift of service has the ability to sense community needs and utilize community resources for the advancement of the Kingdom. They notice what others overlook; e.g. a broken book shelf, the lack of coat hangers, the lawn mower not cutting cleanly, or the dripping faucet. If you are setting up and taking down chairs, they cannot resist offering to help.

Wherever the need, these persons step up to the plate. Even if they are not especially gifted in music, they will try to help out. Do you need a teacher or an administrator? The server will often be the first to fill in until others more gifted come on the scene.

Servants tend to feel unqualified for spiritual leadership. Others need to empower those with the gift of service so they do not feel like second-class citizens. When other people thank them, help them respond with statements like: "God has been so good to me; I just want to pass some of his love along to others." They are often turned off with long-range goals. Visionaries need to break down the three-to-five-year goals into smaller short-range projects, and as a result those with the gift of service will work night and day to complete the task.

Do you usually sense what needs to be done before others? Do you often go ahead and do it. Is it easier for you to accept a work assignment than to lead out in directing others? Does red tape frustrate you? Do you find it easy to neglect your personal needs and the needs of your family to work for the church or others? If so, you likely have the gift of service.

Lord, help me to be a faithful servant today. Amen.

September 8

The Gift of Helps

Acts 13:5

"When they (Barnabas and Saul) arrived at Salamis, they proclaimed the word of God in the Jewish synagogues. John Mark was with them as their helper" (Acts 13:5 NIV).

The person with the gift of helps has the ability to help other members of the Body of Christ so they can more effectively utilize their gift in serving Christ. They receive a sense of fulfillment in helping others so they can minister more effectively. They are not as focused on completing the project as they are on freeing others to do ministry.

Persons with the gift of helps often remember the little idiosyncrasies or likes and dislikes of the person they are serving. They express God's love by being sensitive to others' needs and pleasing them. They, along with those with the gift of service, tend to neglect or disregard their own needs or their families' needs to help others. One church secretary was so dedicated she took work home with her. I was often concerned that she might neglect her family.

Onesiphorus was a helper who exercised much effort and was likely ridiculed until he finally found Paul in prison. (See II Timothy 1:16-17.)

This gift is probably given to more Christians than any other gift and may be illustrated in I Cor. 12:22-23 NIV: "Those parts of the body that seem to be weaker are indispensable, and the parts that we think are less honorable we treat with special honor." These people are glad to work behind the scenes, and are insulted if you offer to pay them. They like to volunteer.

Do you find fulfillment in helping others so they are free to minister more effectively? Do you exercise initiative in approaching others, asking them if you can do something specifically for them? The person with this gift usually has a specific project in mind when they offer to help, rather than asking, "Can I be of help to you?" These people usually enjoy helping indefinitely as long as they know their service is needed and others are not taking advantage of them.

Lord, I thank you for the many people who have helped me. Enable me to help others as well. Amen.

September 9

The Gift of Hospitality

Matthew 25:23,35

"Do not forget to entertain strangers, for by so doing some people have entertained angels without knowing it" (Hebrews 13:2 NIV).

The person with the gift of hospitality has the ability to entertain others, including strangers, so they feel at ease. The idea of loving strangers is foreign to most Christians. Church leaders must have this gift. (See Titus 1:8; I Timothy 3:2). Until our practices and attitudes change whereby church people learn to include new persons into their circle of friends, we will not reach the unchurched in our communities.

The most frequent questions asked by visitors is: "Do I fit here? Do they want me here?" We must take the initiative to talk with them the moment they drive in the parking lot. Smile and introduce yourself to them. Ask them their name and say, "It's great to have you here today. May I show you around?"

Hospitality overcomes the walls that separate "insiders" and "outsiders." The longer a congregation has been in existence, the higher the walls are that keep outsiders from becoming insiders. We must learn to recognize the presence of Jesus in others who are not yet Christians. Matthew 25:31-46 informs us that when we reach out to those who are poor, thirsty, hungry, sick, homeless or imprisoned we are reaching out to Jesus.

Hospitality-gifted people serve others in a way they feel accepted. If they are hosting persons overnight, they are free to give their guests the freedom to get up when they want and leave the house when they like. The guests feel they are not imposing and are free to return at a later time.

Groups have a window of about six months to gain new members. We must show hospitality or form new groups to provide acceptance for new people.

One in every four persons in the U.S. admits to having no close friends. What an opportunity to extend friendship! Do you invite first time visitors to the restaurant or bring them to your home for a meal after church? Do you enjoy visiting people who just moved to your community?

Lord, help me to show your love to new people in my church and community. Amen.

September 10

The Gift of Giving

Acts 9:36

"In Joppa there was a disciple named...Dorcas, who was always doing good and helping the poor" (Acts 9:36 NIV).

The persons with the gift of giving have the special ability to share sacrificially, cheerfully, and consistently of their material blessings to advance the cause of Christ. They like to give anonymously and do not appreciate pressure appeals. They want facts not pressure. They do not appreciate the pastor saying, "We need $10,000. Who will give me $1,000?" They want to give "in secret." They are tuned into what God wants them to give.

The gift of giving is not tied to how much wealth one possesses. The poor widow who gave her two pennies had the gift of giving. (See Mark 12:43-44). The Corinthian Church gave sacrificially out of their poverty. (See II Corinthians 8:2-7.) Joseph gave from his abundance. (See Luke 23:50-53). They all seemed to possess this gift.

True givers know that nothing they possess is their own. They find fulfillment in giving generously, sacrificially, and cheerfully. (See II Corinthians 9:7.) Givers are good stewards of their finances and resources in order to give to the Lord's work. They are careful to give high quality gifts and are interested in knowing how their gifts are being used.

Joyful givers have a clear belief in the principle of reciprocity however this belief is never their primary motivation for giving. They give not to receive but to advance the Kingdom of God. Those with the gift of giving are free to give to unglamorous projects. A church discovered that a drainage pipe had to be replaced costing thousands of dollars. The person with the gift of giving is glad to give major monies to this unglamorous project. Those with the gift of giving have a desire to use their gift to motivate others to give. Acts 20:35 NIV, "I showed you that by this kind of hard work we must help the weak, remembering the words the Lord Jesus himself said, 'It is more blessed to give than to receive.'"

Would you rather meet another's need than your own need? Do you give consistently and systematically to causes that you know you can trust? Do you have great joy in giving?

Lord, help me to be a cheerful giver. Amen.

September 11

The Gift of Voluntary Poverty

Mark 14:3-9 and Acts 2:44-45

"Some of those present were saying indignantly to one another, 'Why this waste of perfume? It could have been sold for more than a years' wages and the money given to the poor.' And they rebuked her harshly'" (Mark 14:4-5 NIV).

The person with the gift of voluntary poverty gives most of his/her material possessions for the cause of Christ. Generally speaking, the characteristics of the person with the gift of giving apply to the person with the gift of voluntary poverty. In addition, we can add the following.

The person with the gift of voluntary poverty gives sacrificially. They often neglect their own needs in order to meet the needs of others. They live frugally and appear to have little of this world's goods. Perhaps they drive an older car, live in a house that does not have the latest conveniences, or dress in clothes that are not up-to-date.

These persons give a high percentage of their income to the work of the Kingdom of God. Most people would complain if they had to live on the level of their lifestyle. John Wesley left a well-worn coat and two silver teaspoons in his estate; but during his lifetime he gave $150,000 to the Lord's work. (See *Your Spiritual Gifts Can Help Your Church Grow* by Peter Wagner, 1979, p. 97.) George Muller was poor all his life, yet he gave $180,000 to the Lord's work. Orie Miller, founder of Mennonite Central Committee, a relief agency, gave 90% of his income to the Lord.

Persons with the gift of voluntary poverty are tempted with the sin of gift projection. Gift projection is taking a gift that we have and projecting it on others, expecting them to operate the way we do.

Do you enjoy giving most of your income to helping the poor and contributing to other Christian causes? Do you say, "People tell me that I give sacrificially but I don't see it that way at all. I enjoy giving. I have enough to meet my basic needs and that's all I care to have. I'll never be a rich person."

Lord, help me to give myself fully to you and to give for your work at the level you want me to give. Amen.

September 12

The Gift of Leadership

Titus 1:5

"The reason I left you at Crete was that you might straighten out what was left unfinished and appoint elders in every town, as I directed you" (Titus 1:5 NIV).

The gift of leadership is the God-given ability to direct others in such a way that they want to voluntarily participate in a particular project and are blessed in their participation.

Leaders are people of vision and faith. They can anticipate the progression of events and how best to meet the challenge and move the project or process forward. Leaders are self-starters who can perceive and utilize resources to accomplish the task. They can visualize the final result.

Leaders do not sweep obstacles under the rug, but instead find resources to overcome the hurdles. They are able to remove themselves from the details of the project in order to give needed attention to the whole and move to fulfill the goal. The leader lets others focus on details while the leader focuses on the goal. Leaders have a strong desire to finish the task before them. They have a sense of urgency.

Leaders must endure criticism. They need to be God pleasers more than men pleasers. If they are in a group and no one seems to be leading, they are frustrated. They will likely either leave the group or assume leadership themselves. Leaders usually want a new challenge as soon as the present goals are reached.

Unless the leader leads, the gifts of others are often buried. People want to be led if they sense the leader is God's man with God's vision.

Do you have a strong desire to lead? Do you think ahead and know what steps to take in leading a group? Do you see the end result? Do others get behind you and implement your ideas? Can you take criticism without losing much sleep? While others are discussing a project, do you start planning how to accomplish the task?

Lord, help me to discern the gift of leadership. In areas where you want me to lead help me to be a faithful leader. Amen.

September 13

The Gift of Administrator

Exodus 18:17-27

Moses exercised the gift of leadership. The job of leading two million people soon became too great for one man. Then he became an administrator appointing judges over thousands, hundreds, fifties, and tens of persons. (See Exodus 18:17-27.)

Joseph was a leader before he was placed in charge of Egypt, but when he became prime minister he exercised his gift of administration. (See Genesis 41:41ff.)

When Paul mentored Titus he was leading, but when he instructed Titus to appoint elders, he exercised the gift of administration. "The reason I left you at Crete was that you might straighten out what was left unfinished and appoint elders in every town, as I directed you" (Titus 1:5 NIV).

The gift of administrator is the God-given ability to delegate responsibility to others in such a way that the goal is accomplished and the Body of Christ is built up. Moses and Joseph were leaders but their responsibilities grew so large that they had to become administrators. The leader is usually more person-centered. The administrator is more goal-oriented. The person with the gift of administration has the ability to delegate responsibility. The leader can usually work directly with all the people in accomplishing the task, while the administrator will find this impossible because of the size and complexity of the task.

The person with the gift of administration will draw up detailed organizational charts and exact time schedules. He or she will assign persons to work with every aspect of the task so the job is completed on schedule.

Sometime administrators being goal-focused are criticized for being insensitive because of their focus on the goal to complete the task. Jesus as leader and administrator was able to exercise patience as well as firmness. Just before he ascended into heaven he said, "OK team your goal is to go into all the world and make disciples but wait until the Holy Spirit comes who will provide all the power you need to be witnesses here at home and then continue in going to the ends of the earth. Remember I will be with you every day until I return." (See Matthew 28:18-20 Free translation.)

Lord, help me to appreciate the gift of administration. When the need arises help me to delegate responsibility. Amen.

September 14

The Gift of Pastoring/Shepherding

John 10:11-14

"I am the good shepherd. The good shepherd lays down his life for the sheep. The hired hand is not the shepherd who owns the sheep. So when he sees the wolf coming, he abandons the sheep and runs away. Then the wolf attacks the flock and scatters it… I am the good shepherd; I know my sheep and my sheep know me" (John 10:11-14 NIV).

The person with the gift of pastoring has the God-given ability to assume responsibility for the spiritual welfare of a group of believers over a long period of time. Since the shepherd knows his sheep intimately, he cannot care for a large number of people. When the church grows to more than 200, the pastor needs to change roles and have his elders, ministry team leaders, or small group leaders serve as pastors to the people. He moves from shepherd to administrator or vision-caster. The church needs many unofficial pastors, persons who care for others over a long period of time. They will spend long hours with those who are hurting whether physically, emotionally, mentally, or spiritually.

The exhorter will move people to Christ by outlining a plan of action. The prophet will speak words of admonition. The giver will give a gift to help. The server will perform a service. The teacher will state the truth. The administrator will organize a plan to help. The pastor will be there over the long term for the maturing of the sheep. The pastor is a true friend. He or she will lay down their life for the sheep. There is a definite intimacy that exists between the shepherd and the sheep.

The shepherd is patient but must correct the sheep. For some this will not be easy. Shepherds usually have a compassionate heart making it difficult to administer discipline. They need to learn to speak the truth in love.

Do you have the ability to develop friendships that last? Have you been used of the Lord to move people to maturity in their walk with Jesus?

Lord, I want to be a shepherd of people. Give me the heart of love for those to whom I relate. Amen.

September 15

The Gift of Mercy

Matthew 5:7 and Luke 10:25-37

"Blessed are the merciful, for they will be shown mercy" (Matthew 5:7 NIV).

"The Samaritan, as he traveled, came where the man was; and when he saw him, he took pity on him. He went to him and bandaged his wounds, pouring on oil and wine. Then he put the man on his own donkey, took him to an inn and took care of him" (Luke 10:33-34 NIV).

The person with the gift of mercy feels compassion especially towards those with emotional, mental, or physical needs and ministers to these needs with ease, so the recipient feels God's love.

Those with the gift of mercy often have difficulty ministering discipline. They don't want to see others hurt. After disciplining their children, they often feel they need to apologize because they were too harsh. If another disciplines they may come to the disciplined persons and say, "John didn't really mean that. John is a kind person." The truth may be that John really did mean what he said. The person with the gift of mercy must learn that God lets people go through hurting times to teach them lessons they need to learn. (See Hebrews 12:7-10.)

If your gift is mercy, Paul says, "Let him do it cheerfully" (Romans 12:8 NIV). The word for cheerfully only occurs twice in the New Testament: the Lord loves a cheerful giver (II Corinthians 9:7) and here. The Greek word means with hilarity or with joy. *The Message* Bible says, "Keep a smile on your face."

The merciful person can read people's feelings. They can detect the friction in a group. They have great difficulty coping with our violent culture. They feel with those who are hurting.

If your gift is mercy, be on your guard if someone corrects you or offers constructive criticism. You may feel discouraged and even become depressed. Be especially careful with your tone of voice when you correct a person with the gift of mercy because they tend to be over sensitive.

Lord Jesus, thank you for giving me the gift of mercy. Forgive me when I take correction or criticism too seriously so that I feel depressed. Thank you for helping me see that you love me even when I am not perfect. Amen.

September 16

The Gift of Evangelism

II Timothy 4:5 and Acts 21:8

"Do the work of an evangelist" (II Timothy 4:5 NIV).

Many Christians would rather have a root canal than share Jesus with their neighbor. Why are we so hesitant to share the Good News? Is it because we forget it really is Good News? Maybe we are turned off because others have used a wrong approach and embarrassed us? Is it because we believe faith is too personal? Is it because we don't know how to share our faith? Might it be that we feel we are not knowledgeable enough to share our faith, or believe the non-Christian would not feel at home in our church?

Jesus did not give the great commission as a possible option or suggestion. He gave the command for **every** Christian to obey: "You will receive power when the Holy Spirit comes on you; and you will be my witnesses (martyrs) in Jerusalem, (at home)… to the ends of the earth" (Acts 1:8 NIV).

The evangelist enjoys meeting new people. He or she is able to share Jesus with unbelievers in such a way that many become disciples of Christ and active members in the local body of believers. Every new person they meet brings another possible opportunity to share Jesus. (See Acts 8:35.)

The evangelist moves the conversation toward spiritual truths, presents Jesus, and expects a decision in the foreseeable future. To the evangelist, sharing the Good News and not asking for a decision is like a car salesman telling you all about his car but not asking for a sale. The evangelist has a holy boldness. Paul asked the Christians to pray for him to be fearless in presenting the Gospel. (See Ephesians 6:19-20.)

The person with the evangelism gift is often a loner in a congregation that is nurture-oriented. If the congregation has little concern for the lost, and new people are simply tolerated rather than loved and accepted, the evangelist will either become discouraged and bury his gift or move to another church.

Lord, help me to be obedient to your command to share with others the Good News of Jesus. Amen.

September 17

The Gift of Prophecy

Romans 12:6

"If a man's gift is prophesying, let him use it in proportion to his faith" (Romans 12:6 NIV).

The gift of prophecy is the ability God gives to some to speak an authorative word concerning a particular situation. These people have an inner compulsion to speak the truth when confronted with sin. The prophet's motivation is to warn of the consequences of sin. They think: "That's what happens when you don't follow God's instruction." Their motto is: "The truth will set you free" (John 8:32). Fathers with the gift of prophecy need to heed the instruction: "Fathers, do not exasperate your children…" (Ephesians 6:4 NIV).

Prophets tend to be blunt and therefore are often misunderstood. They usually see issues as either "white or black"—"right or wrong." They are especially turned off by hypocrisy and dishonesty or when people take advantage of the underdog. Prophets are willing to suffer for the truth. Jeremiah risked his life and was misunderstood and persecuted. The prophet often uses his own sin as an example to teach others. Prophecies, especially in the New Testament, are to be tested by the congregation. (See I Corinthians 14:29 and I Thessalonians 5:20-21.) In the New Testament the claim to be infallible is not permissible, but the claim to inspiration is permissible.

Some have the mistaken notion that prophets cannot control what is said when the Holy Spirit speaks through them. This is not the case: "The spirit of the prophets is subject to the control of prophets. For God is not a God of disorder but of peace" (I Corinthians 14:32-33 NIV). Prophets expect immediate results. They often have trouble fitting into institutional structures. Since prophets receive a word from the Lord, bureaucracy is frustrating.

Ask yourself these question to see if you have the gift of prophecy? Is it easy for you to be straightforward in a group on an issue even though you know others do not agree? Can you stand alone and feel comfortable? Do people come to you later and thank you for your admonitions even though it was difficult for them to hear you at the time?

Lord, thank you for the gift of prophecy. Help me to be bold for you when people are clearly walking away from you. Amen.

September 18

The Gift of Faith

Hebrews 11

"Faith is being sure of what we hope for and certain of what we do not see" (Hebrews 11:1 NIV).

The person with the gift of faith can discern with confidence the will of God and accomplish great things. All Christians must have faith to be saved. (See Ephesians 2:8). "Without faith it is impossible to please God, because anyone who comes to him must believe that he exists and that he rewards those who earnestly seek him" (Hebrews 11:6 NIV).

The gift of faith is the ability to "dream" God's "dreams" and move forward amidst great obstacles. People of faith can take ridicule and criticism. Elijah had to stand alone in faith on Mt. Carmel surrounded by hundreds of false prophets. There is a relationship between faith and prayer. George Muller is referred to as a person with the gift of faith. He prayed to God in faith and fed over 2,000 orphans without asking for money. Those with this gift tend to tackle big things. Jesus said in Mark 11:23 if we have faith and do not doubt we can move mountains.

The late Bill Bright was a man of faith. He writes: "It is my strong conviction that it is impossible to ask God for too much if our hearts and motives are pure and if we pray according to the Word and will of God. Remember, it is a basic spiritual principle that whatever we vividly envision, ardently desire, sincerely believe. and enthusiastically act upon will come to pass assuming, of course, that there is spiritual authority for it. It is this principle that is the foundation of praying supernaturally." (Jim Montgomery, "I'm Gonna Let It Shine" p.147.)

Has God given you any specific goals of what you might accomplish for Him? Are you frustrated when your ideas are slowed by bureaucracy? Can you rally support for such an idea to which you've made a personal commitment? Are you ready to step out in faith and put everything you have on the line to see a dream for God become reality?

Lord, I thank you for the gift of faith. Help me to grow in mountain-moving faith. Amen.

September 19

The Gift of Intercession

Luke 6:12

"Jesus went to the mountains to pray, and spent the night praying to God" (Luke 6:12 NIV).

The gift of intercession is the special ability the Holy Spirit gives to certain individuals to pray for extended periods of time for others resulting in God's moving in obvious ways.

The person with the gift of intercession knows that the effectiveness of another's ministry depends on his/her prayers. Daniel was convinced of this as he interceded for the people of God (See Daniel 9). Note the length of his prayer (vv.4-19). Samuel knew that if he did not pray for Israel he would be sinning. "As for me, far be it from me that I should sin against the Lord by failing to pray for you" (I Samuel 12:23 NIV). The intercessor's focus is for others not for themselves. Jesus taught us to pray for others by using the plural pronouns in what we call the "Lord's prayer." (See Matthew 6:9-14.) We cannot pray the Lord's prayer without praying for others.

Jesus got up early in the morning to pray. (See Luke 4:42.) He withdrew from the people to pray (See 5:16.) Luther spent a couple hours each day in prayer. It is obvious by the poor attendance in prayer meetings, that we need more people with this gift.

Intercessors pray with passion and take prayer needs seriously. The Greek word which we translate agonize, anguish, or struggle, describes this person well. Paul writes, "I want you to know how much I am struggling for you and for those at Laodicea and for all who have not met me personally" (Colossians 2:1 NIV). Paul was praying fervently for people he had never met.

Do you find it easy to spend extended periods of time in prayer? Do you enjoy praying even though it is physically exhausting? Do you have a prayer list? Do you experience regular and specific answers to your prayers? Do others come to you requesting you to pray for them? Do you find it relatively easy to "pray continually?" (I Thessalonians 5:16 NIV).

Lord, forgive me for too often treating prayer as a ritual. Teach me how to pray. Give me a greater love for you and a passion for praying for people. Amen.

September 20

The Missionary Gift

Romans 10:15

"How can they preach unless they are sent? As it is written, 'How beautiful are the feet of those who bring good news!'" (Romans 10:15 NIV).

"This man is my chosen instrument to carry my name before the Gentiles and their kings and before the people of Israel" (Acts 9:15 NIV).

The person with the missionary gift is one who has the special ability to share the Gospel and minister effectively to those in a different culture. They enjoy the challenge of working with different cultures. Language study, new food, new climate, new customs, do not intimidate them; in fact, it energizes them.

Missionaries don't mind moving from one place to another. They are home away from home and are willing to die and be buried in their new home. They don't talk about going back home in the sense they long to return to their childhood culture. Missionaries miss their families but find it relatively easy to cope with separation from loved ones. They replace the need for family by finding new "brothers" and "sisters." They love to make new friends.

This is perhaps the greatest time in the history of the world to be alive. Why? There are more than 100,000 persons being baptized into the Christian faith every day. Twenty-five thousand are baptized in China daily. While this is encouraging, we are not keeping up with the population explosion. Nearly two billion persons in the world have never heard of Jesus.

What has happened to our missionary zeal? Are you encouraging your children to serve as missionaries? Did you know that there are more missionaries coming to the United States than we are sending? Jesus said that the harvest is ripe and plentiful. He reminds us to pray for workers. Are you praying for workers in the harvest? (See Luke 10:2.)

Do you enjoy meeting and working with people from other cultures? Do you have a burden for lost souls in other countries or for persons who come to your community from other cultures?

Lord, help me to pray, to love and to witness to the international persons in my community. Amen.

September 21

The Gift of Martyrdom

Acts 5:41-42

"The apostles went out of the High Council overjoyed because they had been given the honor of being dishonored on account of the Name. Every day they were in the Temple and homes, teaching and preaching Christ Jesus, not letting up for a minute" (Acts 5:41-42 Msg).

"About midnight Paul and Silas were praying and singing hymns to God, and the other prisoners were listening to them" (Acts16:25 NIV).

The gift of martyrdom is a special ability God gives to members of the body of Christ to suffer victorious even unto death. The Greek word *martupes* appears 173 times in the New Testament and is usually translated "witness" or "testimony." A "martyr" or a "witness" in the New Testament sense is one who is willing to testify about Christ even to the point of being persecuted unto death.

There are times when foreign workers are encouraged to flee the country because it is unsafe. Those with this gift will want to remain. That does not mean they are any more spiritual or committed to the cause of Christ than those who leave.

The person with the gift of martyrdom is victorious and joyful while being persecuted. Paul and Stephen were not filled with self-pity during their sufferings. Instead they were able to rejoice and pray for those who were persecuting them. (See Acts 7:60). Peter knowing that James was just martyred fell asleep even though he knew he was next in line. (See Acts 12:6). Those with this gift have a special holy boldness. Multitudes of Christians who live in countries where they suffer persecution find this gift necessary every day. Reports estimate that more than 150,000 Christians die for their faith each year.

Do you find yourself identifying with persecuted Christians who do not recant to avoid imprisonment or death? Do you believe you can face criticism and physical torture with confidence? Can you risk your reputation in your loyalty to Christ without feelings of self-pity? Do you consistently pray for Christians who are persecuted?

Lord, give grace and strength to those who are imprisoned and suffering for you. Help me to be faithful to pray for those suffering persecution. Enable me to be faithful in my witness for you. Amen.

September 22

The Gift of Discernment of Spirits

Acts 5:1-11

"Peter said, 'Ananias, how is it that Satan has so filled your heart that you have lied to the Holy Spirit and have kept for yourself some of the money you received for the land? Didn't it belong to you before it was sold? And after it was sold, wasn't the money at your disposal? What made you think of doing such a thing? You have not lied to men but to God.' When Ananias heard this, he fell down and died'" (Acts 5:3-5 NIV).

Jesus said, "Stop judging by mere appearances, and make a right judgment" (John 7:24 NIV).

The false cults and the use of modern media at our fingertips make it necessary to practice discernment every day. All Christians are admonished to discern good and evil (Hebrews 5:14). However, we need the help of those with the gift to discern intuitively between truth and error.

For every charismatic gift, there is a counterpart. It looks real but is not. The innocent and gullible will often be deceived by these unscrupulous religious wolves in sheep's clothing that infiltrate our churches and attract many to their group. We need the gift of discernment to counteract these counterfeits. Paul in his farewell address to the Ephesian Church says, "I know that after I leave, savage wolves will come in among you and will not spare the flock. Even from your own number men will arise and distort the truth in order to draw away disciples after them" (Acts 10:29-31 NIV).

Satan often appears as an angel of light. (II Corinthians 11:14-15). We need gifted persons to discern his presence. Those with the gift of discernment can discern the motives of those who are teaching or those who are making appeals for money. There are some who make appeals for funds to feed the hungry and minister to the poor but at the same time live extravagant lifestyles.

Do people consult with you about matters involving interpersonal relationships? Do you find it easy to determine the motives of others? Does your track record indicate that the persons you spotted as phonies are truly phonies?

Lord, I need your Holy Spirit to help me to make right judgments. Amen.

September 23

The Gift of Celibacy

I Corinthians 7:7

"Since there is so much immorality, each man should have his own wife, and each woman her own husband. The husband should fulfill his marital duty to his wife, and likewise the wife to her husband.... I wish that all men were as I am. But each man has his own gift from God; one has this gift, another has that" (I Corinthians 7:2-7 NIV).

The person with the gift of celibacy has the ability to enjoy singleness without suffering undue sexual temptations. These persons do not have strong sexual drives.

Celibacy is another spiritual gift that clearly illustrates the difference between a role and a gift. All of us must exercise the role of celibacy at various times. Those who are not married and widows and widowers all must exercise the role of celibacy. Those who are married need to exercise the role of celibacy when they are separated from their spouse.

God has promised, "No test or temptation that comes our way is beyond the course of what others have had to face. All you need to remember is that God will never let you down; he'll never let you be pushed past your limit; he'll always be there to help you come through it" (I Corinthians 10:13 Msg). Again he says: "My grace is sufficient for you, for my power is made perfect in weakness" (II Corinthians 12:9 NIV).

One of the purposes of celibacy for the Christian is that you have more time to serve the Lord. "I would like you to be free from concern. An unmarried man is concerned about the Lord's affairs—how he can please the Lord. But a married man is concerned about the affairs of this world—how he can please his wife—and his interests are divided. An unmarried woman or virgin is concerned about the Lord's affairs: Her aim is to be devoted to the Lord in both body and spirit. But a married woman is concerned about the affairs of this world—how she can please her husband" (I Corinthians 7:32-34 NIV).

Lord, help me, whether single or married, to always love you and serve you with all my heart. Amen.

September 24

The Gift of Craftsmanship

Exodus 31:1-11

"The Lord said to Moses, 'See, I have chosen Bezalel… and I have filled him with the Spirit of God, with skill, ability and knowledge in all kinds of crafts—to make artistic designs for work in gold, silver and bronze, to cut and set stones, to work in wood, and to engage in all kinds of craftsmanship… and also the woven garments…'" (Exodus 31:1-11 NIV).

God gave Oholiah the ability to teach others all kinds of work as craftsmen, designers, embroiders in blue, purple and scarlet yarn and fine linen, and weavers. (See Exodus 35:30-35).

The person with the gift of craftsmanship has the ability to use their skills to advance God's Kingdom. These scriptures help us see that God's spirit is equipping people for all crafts and trades. God gifts people with skills in technology to operate our audio and visual aids department. Others blog or use facebook and media of all kinds to advance the Good News of Jesus.

Paul writes in Colossians 3:17 NIV, "Whatever you do, whether in word or deed, do it all in the name of the Lord Jesus, giving thanks to God the Father through him." Remember Jesus was a carpenter until he launched his public ministry at age 30. (See Mark 6:3 and Luke 3:23.)

If you have the gift of craftsmanship, don't ever walk around with inferior feelings and think: "I'm just a carpenter; I'm just a factory worker." Use your gifts to develop relationships between yourself and your peers. You don't need the gift of evangelism to witness for Jesus Christ—you can open the door and build close friendship with the gift of craftsmanship.

Father, thank you that Jesus graced the wood shop with his presence and skills. Thank you for gifting people in all kinds of craftsmanship today. Help me to develop my gifts in these areas and to use them for your glory in advancing the Good News. Amen.

September 25

The Gifts of Music and Writing

I Kings 4:32

"He (Solomon) spoke three thousand proverbs and his songs numbered a thousand and five" (I Kings 4:32 NIV).

Musicians and writers have a special ability God gives to certain members of the body of Christ to sing, compose, write, or play music well. The Old Testament records several expressions of these gifts: (1) The instrumentalists—"skilled in playing musical instruments" (II Chronicles 34:12 NIV). (2) The singers, Heman, Asaph and Ethan. (See I Chronicles15:19.) (3) David and Asaph are listed as lyricists or composers of music. (See II Chronicles 29:30. (4) Choir directors or conductors. (See Nehemiah 12:46). (5) Instructors. (See I Chronicles 15:22) and (6) those who made instruments. (See II Chronicles 7:6; and 29:26-27.)

The Hebrews concentrated on music and writing since painting was basically prohibited with the second commandment. (See Exodus 20:4.)

Paul in Ephesians 5:19 and Colossians 3:16 admonishes us to speak to one another in psalms, hymns, and spiritual songs. Some scholars believe the terms, "psalms, hymns, and spiritual songs were used interchangeably. According to I Corinthians 14:26, those who came to worship came having composed a hymn or having received a word or revelation or an instruction.

The person with the gift of music or writing is in touch with his/her emotions. This is one reason the book of Psalms is one of the most appreciated books of the Bible. David expresses a wide range of feelings in Psalm 119: e.g. "my soul is consumed with longing for your laws (20 NIV); "See how hungry I am for your counsel" (v. 40 Msg). "My soul faints with longing for your salvation" (v. 81 NIV).

The person with these gifts is one who is endowed with great imagination and emotion as e.g. "weeping day and night" (Psalm 42:3), as well as "extolling the Lord continuously" (34:1). Do words flow from your pen? Are you a creative person often dressing in bright colors? Do you usually appreciate the new rather than the traditional? Do form letters, assembly lines, or stereotype models turn you off?

Lord, I thank you for the gift of music and writing. Help me to develop more in these areas. Amen.

September 26

The Gifts of Music, Part II

Philippians 2:3

"In humility consider others better than yourself" (Philippians 2:3 NIV).

Since there are more "wars" fought over music styles and since music is more influential in reaching unbelievers than even the sermon, I am allotting a second reading to the subject of music.

Music speaks to our hearts more easily than the spoken word. In *Breaking the Missional Code*, Ed Stetzer and David Putman write:

"Scripture teaches that we are to 'consider others better than yourselves' (Phil. 2:3). This includes the truth that our preferences should never become more important than what our church needs to be and do missionally. For that matter, the church's focus should not be the preferences of other church members either. A truly biblical church will ask, 'What will it take to transform this community by the power of the Gospel?' not 'How many hymns do we have to sing to make everybody happy.'" [ii]

If our focus is on transforming the community by the power of the gospel, we will have solved the music issue and many others as well. God loves all kinds of music when sung from a pure heart. The question is whether it connects people with God. Does it usher them into the very presence of God?

We can broaden our appreciation for various styles of music, but it isn't easy. Here are four options: (1) Maintain the status quo if you are reaching the unchurched and lives are being transformed for Christ. (2) Offer two services: one with contemporary music and one with traditional music. (3) A transitional model: No one wants to be told they have to adjust to another style of music. (4) A blended model: Many congregations are using this approach of traditional hymns accompanied with a worship band and contemporary praise music. The blended model may be the best solution for most traditional churches. Whatever approach that appeals to the unchurched is the one the church must follow since the purpose of the church is to fulfill the great commission of our Lord.

Lord, help me to remember it is not my preferences that are important but to accept and appreciate the model that brings people to new life in Christ. Amen.

September 27

The Gifts of Healing

I Corinthians 12:9, 28, 30

"Now to each one the manifestation of the Spirit is given for the common good... to another gifts of healings by that one Spirit... (I Corinthians 12:7-9, also in verses 28 and 30 NIV).

Persons with the gifts of healing have the ability by God's Holy Spirit to cause another person to be healed apart from natural means.

In the Greek New Testament, we have the plural term, "gifts of healing" in I Corinthians 12:9, 28, 30. This may indicate that a separate enabling of the Holy Spirit is given for each individual affliction. Another possible explanation is that the Spirit uses different approaches for different situations: Sometimes Jesus laid hands on the sick, sometimes he spoke, sometimes he spat and made clay; and sometimes he sent them to wash. (See Mark 6:5; John 4:50; Mark 7:33; John 9:7.)

As you read of Jesus' suffering, it is clear that he was in charge even though they beat, scourged, jeered, tortured, and crucified him. God's grace was sufficient for Jesus. His grace will be sufficient for us in our pain and suffering if we, like him, submit to the Father's will. Both Paul and Peter instruct us to have this same attitude that Jesus had during his trial. (See Philippians 2:5-8 and I Peter 2:21-3:1.) It is clear that Paul and Peter who had special gifts of healing were at other times not given this gift. (See II Timothy 4;20; 5:23; Galatians 4:13-16; Philippians 2:26-27.) I often wonder why Jesus told the Christians to visit the sick in Matthew 25:36 and at other times to heal the sick as in Luke 10:9.

In James 5:13-20, we are instructed to have elders anoint the sick with oil in the name of the Lord and they will be healed. If there is sin involved, it needs to be confessed and forgiven for healing to take place. (See also I Cor. 11:30.)

Visit the sick, anoint them with oil, and pray for their healing. The prayers of a righteous person are powerful and effective. (See James 5:16.)

Father, I thank you for healing me many times. I thank you for answering my prayers for healing others. Pour out your Spirit of healing on those who are ill and suffering today. Amen.

September 28

The Gift of Miracles

John 14:12

"I tell you the truth, anyone who has faith in me will do what I have been doing. He will do even greater things than these, because I am going to the father" (John 14:12 NIV).

The gift of miracles is the special ability God gives to certain members of the Body of Christ to perform works that alter the course of natural law.

Some teach that the day of miracles is past. Jeremiah writes in 32:20 NIV, "You performed miracles, signs and wonders in Egypt and have continued them to this day, both in Israel and among all mankind, and have gained the renown that is still yours." The time from deliverance in Egypt to Jeremiah's time was 850 years. Many times God has spared my life. I am a walking miracle.

A fire was sweeping across the land in Illinois getting closer to a church. Two young men on their knees cried out to God and the winds changed immediately.

My father-in-law was flying in a small plane in Honduras. When they took off it was clear, but the clouds soon engulfed them. The gas tank was almost empty and the runway located in the mountain village was nowhere to be seen. There were no electronic instruments. He prayed, "God open the clouds just like you parted the Red Sea." A small opening appeared and they saw a small patch of earth—the runway. No one was around the small airport because they knew a plane could not land because of the heavy cloud cover.

Watchman Nee in his book, *Sit, Walk, Stand* preached for days in China with little effect. A new Christian who was with Nee's group asked the people why they didn't respond. They informed him that their god was adequate because he kept the rain away on their holy day for 286 years. The young Christian said to the crowd, "It will rain on that day." It flooded! The Chinese set another date. The Christians said it will rain on that day. It poured! The God of Elijah was again manifesting his mighty power and many turned to Christ.

Lord, thank you for giving the gift of miracles. May my faith grow as I trust you for miracles. Amen.

September 29

The Gifts of Tongues and Interpretation of Tongues

I Corinthians 14

"I am grateful to God for the gift of praying in tongues that he gives us for praising him, which leads to wonderful intimacies we enjoy with him. I enter into this as much or more than any of you" (I Corinthians 14:18 Msg).

"If prayers are offered in tongues, two or three's the limit, and then only if someone is present who can interpret what you're saying. Otherwise, keep it between God and yourself. And no more than two or three speakers at a meeting... Take your turn... Then each speaker gets a change to say something special from God, and you all learn from each other. If you choose to speak, you're also responsible for how and when you speak" (I Corinthians 14:27-32 Msg).

The gift of tongues and interpretation of tongues is the special ability that God gives to members of the body of Christ to speak in a language that they have never learned or to interpret the utterances of unknown languages.

The speaking in tongues is in operation today in millions of Christians worldwide. This gift was operative at Pentecost and on several occasions in the book of Acts: (1) The Day of Pentecost. (See Acts 2:1-21). "All of them (120 disciples) were filled with the Holy Spirit and began to speak in other tongues as the Spirit enabled them"(Acts 2:4 NIV). (2) In Samaria. (Acts 8:4-17). When Peter and John placed their hands on the Samaritans they received the Holy Spirit. Simon wanted to buy the ability to impart the gift. (See v.18). (3) At Paul's Conversion. (See Acts 9:1-19). Ananias baptized Saul and scales fell from his eyes. (See v. 18). Either at this time or later Paul received the gift of tongues. He says in First Corinthians 14:18 NIV, "I thank God I speak in tongues more than you all." (4) The House of Cornelius. (See Acts 10:1-46) and (5) The Ephesian Pentecost. (See Acts 19:1-6).

Speaking in tongues is one of the gifts of the Spirit. (See I Corinthians 12:10). Paul orders that speaking with tongues should not be forbidden. (See I Corinthians 14:39). It is a means of building up the believer. (See I Corinthians 14:4).

Lord, I thank you for the gift of tongues that enables us to worship with greater adoration and appreciation of your glory and for all you have done for us. Amen.

September 30

Work Is Not a Curse

Genesis 2:15

"The Lord God took the man and put him in the Garden of Eden to work it and take care of it" (Genesis 2:15 NIV).

Do you know that work is not a curse but a blessing? God worked: "By the seventh day God had finished the work he had been doing; so on the seventh day he rested from all his work. And God blessed the seventh day and made it holy, because on it he rested from all the work of creating that he had done" (Genesis 2:2-3 NIV).

Jesus is at work. "I am going to prepare a place for you" (John 14:2 NIV).

Work is not a curse. Work is a blessing. Adam and Eve were given the privilege of working in the Garden of Eden before the fall. Imagine how boring life would be if we had no work. Someone said find something you like and you will not have to work another day in your life. I like that. Perhaps it helps to think of it this way: find your purpose and you will never have to work again. In heaven we will not have to work but we will have meaningful activity so let heaven come to earth. Meaningful activity is not really work.

Perhaps a more realistic way to look at work is described in Colossians 3:22 NLT, "Slaves, obey your earthly masters in everything you do. Try to please them all the time not just when they are watching you. Serve them sincerely because of your reverent fear of Lord. Work willingly at whatever you do as though you were working for the Lord rather than for people. Remember that the Lord will give you an inheritance as your reward, and that the Master you are serving is Christ."

Do you dread going to your present job/work? Ask God to change your attitude. If you really believe you need to change jobs to be fulfilled, ask God to open the door and then make efforts to explore other options. If the door stays closed, ask God to give you grace so you can begin to enjoy your work.

Lord Jesus, thank you for my job. Help me to remember I am really working for you more than my employer. Thank you Jesus. Amen.

October 1

Faithful Minority

Deuteronomy 1:22

Moses said, "You all came to me and said, 'First, let's send out scouts to explore the land for us. They will advise us on the best route to take and which towns we should enter'" (Deuteronomy 1:22 NLT).

The scouts were not sent to determine whether they should enter the land. They were to decide the best place and gain wisdom for a strategy to enter. God had made it clear they were to enter and that he would give their enemies into their hands. However, when the scouts went, only two of the twelve courageously believed they should enter the land. The others were intimidated by the walled cities and the giants.

God calls us to move ahead sharing the Good News with our friends and neighbors. He promises to be with us. Yes, we will be in the minority. Too often, like the ten spies, we are fearful and decide not to share Jesus. When we look at our own resources we are like the ten spies, pulling back saying we can't go. The spies regretted their actions. We too pay the price for not being obedient to the Great Commission. The price is stale Christianity, dead churches and many regrets.

The family line dies out when babies are not born into our biological families. That's what is happening to thousands of churches in the U.S. More than half of our churches have not baptized a born again Christian this past year. Young people are leaving the organized churches in droves.

Lord, wake me up before it is too late. Give me the passion like you had when you sent Jesus, your only son, into the world to live and die for us. Give me the passion you demonstrated as you left your Father and worked as a carpenter, despised and rejected by your people and finally crucified. And Holy Spirit give me your passion for the lost that you demonstrated as you left heaven and came to dwell in my sinful heart, now made holy by your transforming grace. Thank you. Amen.

October 2

Come Alive!

John 14:19

Jesus said, "I will not leave you orphaned. I'm coming back. In just a little while the world will no longer see me, but you're going to see me because I am alive and you're about to come alive" (John 14:19 Msg).

"You're about to come alive." Most Christians have days when we don't feel very much alive. The vibrancy of life is nowhere to be found. We are not a good advertisement. We are not contagious. On those days we still believe the Scriptures—at least intellectually but we are not living them. Do we own God's promises or are we just periodically renting them? Jesus says, when the Spirit comes you will come alive!

Paul owned the Scriptures, he owned God's promises. "If you only look at us, you might well miss the brightness. We carry his precious Message around in the unadorned clay pots of our ordinary lives. That's to prevent anyone from confusing God's incomparable power with us. As it is, there's not much chance of that. You know for yourselves that we're not much to look at. We've been surrounded and battered by troubles, but we're not demoralized, we're not sure what to do, but we know that God knows what to do, we've been spiritually terrorized, but God hasn't left our side, we've been thrown down, but we haven't been broken. What they did to Jesus, they do to us—trial and torture, mockery and murder, what Jesus did among them, he does in us—he lives!... while we are going through the worst we're getting in on the best" (II Corinthians 4:7-12 Msg).

Paul came alive even in his worst days. Only as Jesus is in you can you come alive on those days. Claim David's promise: "The Lord delights in a man's way, he makes his steps firm: though he stumbles, he will not fall, for the Lord upholds him with his hand" (Psalm 37:23-24 NIV). Remember Jesus' words, "Because I am alive you are about to come alive."

Lord Jesus, I need you. Some days I'm sinking. Help me, especially on those days to own the Scriptures and not only to rent them. Come alive in me. Amen.

October 3

"Be still and know that I am God"

Psalm 46:10

"Step out of the traffic! Take a long, loving look at me, your High God, above politics, above everything" (Psalm 46:10 Msg).

This is a difficult admonition for me and for many in our time-conscious, action packed U.S. culture. I am an activist. I come to God with my agenda and my schedule. His agenda may not be what I think is important.

Saint Francis of Assisi prayed so appropriately:

> Lord, make me an instrument of your peace. Where there is hatred, let me sow love; where there is injury, pardon; where there is doubt, faith; where there is despair, hope; where there is darkness, light; and where there is sadness, joy. O Divine Master, grant that I may not so much seek to be consoled as to console; to be understood as to understand; to be loved as to love. For it is in giving that we receive; it is in pardoning that we are pardoned; and it is in dying that we are born to eternal life. Amen

In learning to communicate with God we need to understand that God chooses the time and the topic! His desires must trump ours. He is God, not me! Let him set the agenda. God may not always want to discuss the same topic as I want to discuss. I may want to talk about my occupation. He may want to check my attitude about my occupation. I may want to discuss my future. He may want to strengthen my faith and talk future later. I may want a WHY and he may just want me to TRUST! I may want OUT of what he wants me IN!

There are times when you want to talk, while he just wants you to be quiet.

Remember, God always reserves the right to remain silent. He may just want you to sit and wait in quietness. He may just want you to BE! [iii]

Lord, help me to "Be still and know that you are God." Amen.

October 4

You Shall Be My Witnesses

Acts 1:8 and I Peter 2:9

"When the Holy Spirit comes on you, you will be able to be my witnesses in Jerusalem, all over Judea and Samaria, even to the ends of the world" (Acts 1:8 Msg).

Peter tells us we are chosen by God "to do his work and speak out for him to tell others of the night and day difference he made for you" (I Peter 2:9 Msg).

This is what witnessing is all about—sharing the difference Jesus makes in your life. You are not to argue your case or try to prove you are right. You're not an attorney. You're a witness. You report what happens in your life and how things are changing.

Share your story. Stories attract attention. Your story is unique. You have no exact duplicate. Only you can share it. If you don't, it will be lost forever. Your testimony often has more authority than a sermon. The unchurched may see pastors as professional salesmen, but the unchurched see you as one who has voluntarily chosen to follow Jesus. This gives you credibility.

Your story is exactly that—your story. People have to accept it or write you off. If your character is consistent they cannot write you off that easily. We remember people longer than principles or doctrines. The Holy Spirit will take your testimony and use it to convict others of their need for Jesus. There will be times in the unbelievers' life when the Spirit brings you and your story to their remembrance.

Many people today don't accept the authority of the Bible but they will listen to your God moments. Paul told his experiences frequently. (See Acts 22-26.) Luke reports in Acts 8:4 the believers went everywhere sharing Jesus. I'm sure they shared how Jesus changed their lives.

Share what life was like before you met Jesus, then how you met him, and what happened when you met him. Share what difference he is making in your life today. God will use your story to bring others to himself.

Lord, help me to follow the Holy Spirit so I don't miss the opportunities to share my story. Amen.

October 5

See Others as God Sees Them

Matthew 9:36

"When he (Jesus) looked over the crowds, his heart broke. So confused and aimless they were, like sheep with no Shepherd" (Matthew 9:36 Msg). Jesus saw people, looked into their souls, and grieved over their condition. He saw them through the eyes of eternity.

We need eyes to see as Jesus sees. Do we see our work peers, school friends, neighbors, the bank teller, the checkout woman, the barber, the postman, and others—without ever wondering about their spiritual condition? Do we have compassion for them as Jesus does?

If we are to connect with the unchurched we must change the way we view the unchurched. Everyone we see is created in God's image and in need of redemption. Everyone is a "sheep without a shepherd" apart from Jesus. We are commanded to love the unchurched, but we also need to be concerned about their personal relationship with Jesus. (See Acts 4:12.)

Where in my schedule can I find the time to love the unchurched? Could the church clear the calendar at least one night a week? Let's intentionally set aside at least one block of time each week to relate to our unchurched peers. Over my nearly fifty years of pastoral ministry I usually reserved Saturday afternoon for visiting non-members. It was one of the best decisions I ever made. It affected the Sunday worship. After visiting three or four families I could often tell that I would have at least one new family present. I knew their specific need. Their presence had a direct impact on the morning worship service.

The people you meet in church are going to heaven—at least I hope so! When will you leave the 99 and help the lost one. Be a model to your congregation. Find the evangelists in your church and train them. After all Jesus said, "I will make you fishers of men" (Matthew 4:19 NIV).

Lord, help me to see the people I meet each day as you see them—sheep without a shepherd. Help me to believe you can use me to change their eternal destiny. Amen.

October 6

Today—Better Than Yesterday—Tomorrow Better Than Today

II Corinthians 3:18 and 4:16

Each day gets better! The veil separating us from God has been lifted. "Whenever anyone turns to the Lord, the veil is taken away. Now the Lord is the Spirit, and where the Spirit of the Lord is, there is freedom. And we, who with unveiled faces all reflect the Lord's glory, are being transformed into his likeness with ever-increasing glory, which comes from the Lord, who is the Spirit" (II Corinthians 3:18 NIV).

The Message Bible reads: "When God is personally present, a living Spirit, that old, constricting legislation is recognized as obsolete. We're free of it! All of us! Nothing between us and God, our faces shining with the brightness of his face. And so we are transfigured much like the Messiah, our lives gradually becoming brighter and more beautiful as God enters our lives and we become like him."

We reflect the Lord's glory—shining brighter and brighter until we are called home. Beware of anything that fogs up Jesus reflections in your life. Often it is something good that will fog up the reflection of Jesus. Keep yourself open to God and to others. Don't let your goals, your desires, your work, your hobbies, your friends, even your family crowd out your relationship to God and others. We must guard against a hurried lifestyle or we will crowd out the voice of the Lord. This is elementary but it is the most difficult lesson we will ever have to learn.

Paul writes in the next chapter, II Corinthians 5:16-18 NIV, "Though outwardly we are wasting away, yet inwardly we are being renewed day by day. For our light and momentary troubles are achieving for us an eternal glory that far out weights them all. So we fix our eyes not on what is seen, but on what is unseen. For what is seen is temporary, but what is unseen is eternal."

Lord Jesus, my desire is to love you with all my heart, soul, mind and strength. Other things, good things, crowd out your best for me. Forgive me. Help me put my relationship with you first. Enable me to love others more than myself. Amen.

October 7

Don't Buy the Lies

John 8:44 NIV

"When he lies, he speaks his native language, for he is a liar and the father of lies" (John 8:44 NIV).

Satan will do his best to keep your mouth shut about Jesus. He will whisper lies to you so you come up with the following excuses:
1. I really don't know them well enough.
2. They are too busy. Now is not the time. Just build relationships a little longer.
3. They need to see Jesus in my life before I can talk to them.
4. If I share the Gospel they will reject me and reject Jesus.
5. My life is not consistent with my message anyway. They won't believe me.

Compare this with Paul's words to the Corinthians.

"That's why we work urgently with everyone we meet to get them ready to face God. God alone knows how well we do this but I hope you realize how much and deeply we care" (II Corinthians 5:11 Msg).

Why does Paul say he works urgently with everyone to get them ready to face God? Verse 10 says, "Sooner or later we'll all have to face God, regardless of our conditions. We will appear before Christ and take what's coming to us as a result of our actions, either good or bad. That keeps us vigilant. It's no light thing to know that we'll one day stand in the place of judgment."

Jesus' brother Jude didn't buy these lies. He writes that we must snatch our friends from the fire and save them. (See v. 23). *The Message* Bible reads: "Go after those who take the wrong way. Be tender with sinners, but not soft on sin. The sin itself stinks to high heaven."

A vivacious second grade teacher was gloriously saved. She came into my study and said, "I don't understand what is wrong with me. In the teachers' lounge I can talk about anything but when it comes to sharing Jesus I clam up." The devil is there every time to tell us they don't want to hear our witness. Don't buy his lies!

Lord Jesus, make me bold. Give me the courage I need to follow your Spirit in sharing Jesus with my friends and neighbors. Amen.

October 8

Remember Those in Prison and Those Mistreated

Hebrews 13:3

"Remember those in prison as if you were their fellow prisoners, and those who are mistreated as if you yourselves were suffering" (Hebrews 13:3 NIV).

Jesus says to those sheep on his right hand: "I was sick and you stopped to visit, I was in prison and you came to me" (Matthew 25:36 Msg).

In our world where multitudes of Christians are suffering because of their witness for Christ we must ask ourselves, do we care? Do we care enough to intercede for them? These scriptures make it clear that we are to remember them and to identify with them. For persons like myself who have never been imprisoned for sharing Jesus it is not always easy to identify with them. May those of us who live with freedom to worship and speak about Jesus pray with a heart of compassion for those who are persecuted. Pray for God's grace to keep them strong in the faith and to deliver them. Pray for their families who suffer with them and for their churches that are torn apart with persecution.

While Daniel may not be speaking of our contemporary situation the verses in Daniel 11:33-35 (Msg) are relevant. "Those who keep their heads on straight will teach the crowds right from wrong by their example. They'll be put to severe testing for a season: some killed, some burned, some exiled, some robbed. When the testing is intense, they'll get some help, but not much. Many of the helpers will be halfhearted at best. The testing will refine, cleanse, and purify those who keep their heads on straight and stay true, for there is still more to come."

"Anyone who wants to live all out for Christ is in for a lot of trouble; there's no getting around it. Unscrupulous con men will continue to exploit the faith. They're as deceived as the people they lead astray. As long as they are out there, things can only get worse" (II Timothy 4:12-13 Msg).

Lord Jesus, be near to comfort and sustain those who are suffering persecution for your name. Provide special grace for their families. Use their suffering to advance your Kingdom. Amen.

October 9

Remember

Deuteronomy 5:15

"Remember that you were slaves in Egypt and that the Lord your God brought you out of there with a mighty hand and an outstretched arm" (Deuteronomy 5:15 NIV).

Jesus in the upper room with his disciples, just before his crucifixion, "Took bread, gave thanks and broke it, and gave it to them, saying, 'This is my body given for you; do this in remembrance of me'" (Luke 22:19 NIV).

"Remember" or one of its forms appears nearly 50 times in the Psalms and nearly 300 times in the Bible. In Moses' final sermon recorded in Deuteronomy he tells the people to remember at least sixteen times. The New Testament tells us to remember at least 55 times. I confess that I have not always appreciated history. I am future focused. But I need roots. I would not be here without my parents. I would have no future without my past. I would have no hope except faithful witnesses passed on the message of Christ to me.

Our faith is rooted in history. It is based on facts—the facts recorded in the Scriptures. God revealed himself in many ways (Hebrews 1:1) but supremely in his Son, the Lord Jesus. We must go back to those facts for the foundation of our faith.

When a child is leaving home the parents say, "Remember who you are." In other words, remember what you have been taught and act appropriately. God is saying the same to us over and over in the Scriptures. That's why Paul writes in II Timothy 3:15-17 Msg, "There's nothing like the written Word of God for showing you the way to salvation through faith in Christ Jesus. Every part of Scripture is God-breathed and useful one way or another—showing us truth, exposing our rebellion, correcting our mistakes, training us to live God's way. Through the Word we are put together and shaped up for the tasks God has for us."

Paul reminds us to remember we were separated from Christ, without hope and without God. (See Ephesians 2:12-13) Remembering our past state will help us appreciate the new life we have in Christ.

Lord Jesus, thank you for parents and others who passed on their faith to me. Amen.

October 10

Why Don't I Share My Faith?

Revelation 2:4

"You have forsaken your first love." Revelation 2:4 NIV.

Why don't we share our faith? Some surveys claim that only about ten to thirteen percent of Christians are actively sharing their faith. Why might this be true? There are many reasons. Let me share a few today as well as others in the next reading.

1. We have lost our first love. (See Revelation 2:4). Pray for the zeal and the spirit of Peter and John: "We can't keep quiet about what we have seen and heard" (Acts 4:20 Msg).

2. We don't relate to unchurched people. We don't have unchurched friends. The longer you are a Christian the more likely it is that you have very few relationships with those outside Christian circles. Jesus, our example, gave much of his time to those who were not his disciples. We need to intentionally go into the world. (See Matthew 18:12-14.)

3. We are uncomfortable bringing people to our church. Do you hesitate to invite people to Jesus because you know if they receive him they need a family to welcome and nurture them? Is your church family a welcoming place? If you are not enthusiastic about your church you will be greatly hindered in your witness. Bringing a Christian into new life without a family is like a women giving birth to her baby in the hospital but as they leave the hospital she lets the baby in the street.

4. Satan wants us to be quiet. He will whisper lies to you such as: "They don't want to hear what I have to say. They are too busy." "You can't talk." We need to say, "Get behind me Satan!" and claim God's Holy Spirit's power. "You will receive power when the Holy Spirit comes on you; and you will be my witnesses beginning at home, or across the street,…" (See Acts 1:8.) We must take Jesus to the workplace, to the schoolroom and our communities.

Lord Jesus, forgive me for making excuses. Help me to be obedient to your Holy Spirit as I seek to share Jesus with my friends and neighbors. Amen.

October 11

Why Don't I Share My Faith? Part II

I Corinthians 2:1-5

1. Intellectualism robs us of our zeal. Often the more education we have the more reasons we come up with, not to share our faith. Worldly "smarts" (wisdom) often flies in the face of Holy Spirit wisdom. Paul puts it this way: "When I first came to you I didn't use lofty words and brilliant ideas to tell you God's message. For I decided to concentrate only on Jesus Christ and his death on the cross. I came to you in weakness—timid and trembling. And my message and my preaching were very plain. I did not use wise and persuasive speeches, but the Holy Spirit was powerful among you. I did this so that you might trust the power of God rather than human wisdom" (I Corinthians 2:1-5 NLT).

2. Obnoxious approaches by others have turned us off. Just because someone uses an inappropriate approach does not mean we should stop sharing our faith. "We reject all shameful and underhanded methods. We do not try to trick anyone, and we do not distort the word of God. We tell the truth before God, and all who are honest know that" (II Corinthians 4:2 NLT).

3. We don't really believe our good neighbors are lost. Many Christians today don't believe a loving God would send anyone to eternal judgment. I find it helpful to remember that we send ourselves there when we reject the truth. Romans 1:18 NLT, "God shows his anger from heaven against all sinful, wicked people who push the truth away from themselves."

4. We don't know how to relate to people. We are afraid. Perhaps we use the excuse that we are introverts. God will use the witness of everyone. Remember Francis of Assisi's famous statement: "Witness 24/7, if necessary use words." It's necessary to use words. Jesus had to tell us who he was so we need to eventually explain that our good deeds are because Jesus has been so good to us.

Lord, whenever I am tempted to make excuses for not sharing my faith help me to hear your voice and say what you want me to say. Empower my words and actions to bring people to you. Amen.

October 12

Stir Up the Gift

II Timothy 1:6-7

"I remind you to fan into flame the gift of God, which is in you through the laying on of my hands. For God did not give us a spirit of timidity, but a spirit of power, of love and of self-discipline" (II Tim. 1:6-7 NIV).

Various translations use different wording for "stir up;" fan into flames, keep your gift ablaze, made full use of the gift, rekindle the gift, stir up the inner fire, and keep alive the gift. Timothy was timid. (See II Timothy 1:7). So many Christians are timid especially when it comes to obeying the great commission. Remember the Great Commission is a commandment for every Christian. It is not the great suggestion!

Paul writes: "Exercise daily in God—no spiritual flabbiness, please! Workouts in the gymnasium are useful, but a disciplined life in God is far more so, making you fit both today and forever" (I Timothy 4:7 Msg). The NIV says, "Train yourself to be godly."

In the New Testament, believers are described as being bold or encouraged to be bold twice as often as they are told to be humble. The disciples were timid, and lacked courage before the resurrection. Compare that to Peter's boldness on the day of Pentecost. Look at how the early church turned the world upside down. As the Christians were scattered they went everywhere preaching the word. (See Acts 8:4.) "The righteous are as bold as lions" (Proverbs 28:1 NIV).

The devil has de-passioned us. He has robbed us of our power. We must stir up the gift of the Holy Spirit in us. Pray for God to give you eyes to see opportunities. Pray for boldness to take the risk to follow through. It may not feel comfortable at first. Learn to go with the flow of the Holy Spirit. Life becomes exciting as you bear fruit for our Lord.

Lord Jesus, I will fan into flame the gifts you have given me. I will move out in faith as the Holy Spirit leads me. Amen.

October 13

Experience the Best Teacher?

Psalm 106:43

"Over and over God rescued them, but they never learned—until finally their sins destroyed them" (Psalm 106:43 Msg).

"Lord, teach me lessons for living so I can stay the course" (Psalm 119:33 Msg).

If you have worked on a job for forty years you don't necessarily have forty years experience. You have forty years of time on the job but that is different than forty years of experience. We don't learn from our experience but we do learn if we reflect or meditate on our experience and make changes in our practice. We may have many years of work but very few years of experience.

Experience is not the best teacher if we don't learn from our experiences. The Israelites did not learn from their experience. "Over and over God rescued them, but they never learned—until finally their sins destroyed them." Are we learning from our experiences?

Notice the relationship between experience and maturity. "The testing of your faith develops perseverance. Perseverance must finish its work so that you may be mature and complete not lacking anything. If anyone of you lacks wisdom, he should ask God, who gives generously to all without finding fault, and it will be given to him. But when he asks, he must believe and not doubt, because he who doubts is like a wave of the sea, blown and tossed by the wind. That man should not think he will receive anything from the Lord, he is a double-minded man, unstable in all he does" (James 1:3-8 NIV).

We can learn from other's experiences as well. That's why teachers have an important role. We need to learn from them. "A wise friend's timely reprimand is like a gold ring slipped on your finger" (Proverbs 25:12 Msg). Reflect on your experiences and ask the Lord for insight and grace to apply what you observe from your experiences. You will grow from one degree of glory to another. Life will be exciting.

Lord Jesus help to be learn from my experience so I can serve you more effectively as I move toward maturity. Amen.

October 14

Perfect Love Drives Out Fear

I John 4:18

"There is no fear in love. But perfect love drives out fear, because fear has to do with punishment" (I John 4:18 NIV).

Are you fearful of sharing God's love with those around you? Ask God to fill your heart with his love for them. Claim this Scripture from the love chapter of the Bible: Love never gives up. Love cares more for others than for self. Love doesn't force itself on others. It doesn't keep score of the sins of others. It takes pleasure in the flowering of truth, and puts up with anything. It always trusts God. It always looks for the best, but keeps going to the end. (Adapted from I Corinthians 13:4-8 Msg).

Most of us have experienced fear when it comes to sharing our faith. If God has given us a passion driven by his love for those we are witnessing to we can claim his promises. We don't force ourselves on others. He cares more for them than we do. We don't focus on their sins or mistakes. We delight in sharing the Good News of Salvation. We put up with most everything the person does. Love perseveres and leaves the results to God.

"Use your heads as you live and work among outsiders. Don't miss a trick. Make the most of every opportunity. Be gracious in your speech. The goal is to bring out the best in others in a conversation, not put them down, and not cut them out" (Colossians 4:5-6 Msg).

When you get to heaven will someone run up to you and say, "Thank you for what you did for me. I am here because you kept loving me and sharing the Good News with me?" Can you imagine the joy of meeting people who you helped to get there? Jesus said, "There is more joy in heaven over one sinner's rescued life than over ninety-nine already saved people in no need of rescue" (Luke 15:7 Msg).

The salvation of one person is more important than anything you will ever achieve in life. People last forever.

Lord Jesus, when I draw back from sharing the Good News, help me to remember that perfect love overcomes any fear I may have. Amen.

October 15

World Class Christian or Worldly Christian

Psalm 67:2 and Matthew 24:14

"Send us around the world with the news of your saving power and your eternal plan for all mankind" (Psalm 67:2 LB).

Worldly Christians are basically self-centered. God is primarily there for personal fulfillment. They go to church, to seminars, but you will not find them at prayer meetings or mission conferences because they are not interested. They want to know how God can make them more comfortable. As Rick Warren says, "They want to use God for their purposes instead of being used for his purposes."

I believe this Scripture could well apply to many worldly Christians: "I know your deeds, that you are neither cold nor hot. I wish you were either one or the other! So because you are lukewarm—neither hot or cold—I am about to spit you out of my mouth. You say, 'I am rich; I have acquired wealth and do not need a thing. But you do not realize that you are wretched, pitiful, poor, blind and naked'" (Revelation 3:15-17 NIV).

On the other hand, World-Class Christians know they are saved to serve. They know they are sent by Jesus into the world for the purpose of witnessing to their neighbors. Fully alive people have confidence, joy and enthusiasm that is contagious as they see lives being changed. They know they are making a difference.

God invites you to be a World-Class Christian. Email, internet, and high-speed travel have made it easy for the whole world to be at your fingertips. We can pray and communicate with people around the world. Let's hasten the day of Jesus return as every nation of earth receives the Good News. "This Gospel of the kingdom will be preached in the whole world as a testimony to all nations, and then the end will come" (Matthew 24:14 NIV). [iv]

Lord Jesus, make me a World-Class Christian. Amen.

October 16

World News

Acts 1:8

"You will tell everyone about me in Jerusalem, in all Judea, in Samaria, and everywhere in the world" (Acts 1:8 CEV).

When you watch the news do you feel overwhelmed with all the needs? Try to watch the news through the eyes of Jesus. He wept over Jerusalem. (See Luke 19:41.) Jesus' most common emotional response was compassion!

Jesus saw people as sheep that had been bruised, beaten, and thrown about. Rather than being filled with disdain, He was filled with love. "When he saw the crowds, he had compassion on them, because they were harassed and helpless, like sheep without a shepherd. Then he said to his disciples, (that's you and me), 'The harvest is plentiful but the workers are few. Ask the Lord of the harvest, therefore, to send out workers into the harvest field'" (Matthew 9:36-38 NIV).

Wherever there is conflict, God can use these conflicts to bring people to him. People are usually more receptive to God when they are under tension or in transition. Pain and change usually help to make people more receptive to the Gospel, for example: marriage crisis, divorce, birth of the first child, death of a family member or close friend, loss of a job/financial setback, sickness, a move, child in trouble, accidents, graduations, etc. Since the rate of change is increasing that means more people are open to hearing the Good News now than ever before.

Their need is the door for God to use you to bring them to Jesus and to build a nurturing relationship with them. When there is conflict at the office pray for the Lord to open your eyes to how you can be a person of Christ's peace. Listen to their pain. Don't be afraid to ask questions. Jesus asked 150 questions. Why? He wanted to hear what was in their heart. Try to stay away from "why" question because "why questions" make us defensive and build walls rather than bridges.

Lord, help me to respond to conflicts with compassion. Give me a discerning heart to know how to help. Amen.

October 17

The Long Range View

II Corinthians 4:18

"We fix our eyes not on what is seen, but on what is unseen. For what is seen is temporary, but what is unseen is eternal" (II Corinthians 4:18 NIV).

So much of what we spend our time on will not matter a year from now. This world will soon be destroyed. Peter writes: "The day of the Lord's return will surprise us like a thief. The heavens will disappear with a loud noise, and the heat will melt the whole universe. Then the earth and everything on it will be seen for what they are. Everything will be destroyed. So you should serve and honor God by the way you live. You should look forward to the day when God judges everyone, and you should try to make it come soon. On that day the heavens will be destroyed by fire, and everything else will melt in the heat. But God has promised us a new heaven and a new earth, where justice will rule. We are really looking forward to that!" (II Corinthians 3:10-13 CEV).

"Time is of the essence. There is no time to waste, so don't complicate your life unnecessarily. Keep it simple—in marriage, grief, joy, whatever. Even in ordinary things—your daily routines of shopping, and so on. Deal as sparingly as possible with the things the world thrusts on you. This world as you see it is on its way out" (I Corinthians 7:29-31 Msg). What will matter? Our relationship to God and to people is what will matter.

Jesus said, "No procrastination. No backward looks. You can't put God's kingdom off till tomorrow. Seize the day" (Luke 9:62 Msg).

Why did God let us here after we accepted him? In heaven we can worship, fellowship, sing, pray and hear God's Word, but we won't be able to win people for Jesus and make disciples. We are here to win people to Jesus and make disciples!

Lord, help me to keep first things first. Give me a heart of compassion, a mind filled with wisdom, and the energy to do what I know you want me to do. Amen.

October 18

Salvation is a Miracle

John 6:44

"No one can come to me unless the Father who sent me draws him, and I will raise him up at the last day" (John 6:44 NIV). "He (the Father) draws people to me—that's the only way you'll ever come" (John 6:44 Msg).

It is impossible for a person to become a Christian unless this great miracle happens. We cannot persuade them or argue them into the kingdom of God because their problem is not an intellectual one. They cannot change their behavior and become like Jesus because they are born with a selfish nature. Only Jesus can bring about the new birth, the new life and the new Godly nature. They are spiritually dead (See Ephesians 2:1-2). The devil has taken them captive to do his will. (See II Timothy 2:26).

The forces that hold people captive are far more powerful than we are in our own strength. There is not the slightest possibility that we can lead anyone to the cross unless Jesus is drawing them. The good news is that we can be absolutely sure that Jesus will help us to reach the lost. The word of God says, "God isn't late with his promise as some measure lateness. He is restraining himself on account of you, holding back the End because he doesn't want anyone lost. He's giving everyone space and time to change" (II Peter 3:9 Msg).

On the day of Pentecost the Holy Spirit was poured out on the disciples. Peter preached under the power of the Spirit and they cried out, "What shall we do?" Peter replied, 'Repent and be baptized, everyone one of you, in the name of Jesus Christ for the forgiveness of your sins. And you will receive the gift of the Holy Spirit'" (Acts 2:37-38 Msg).

We need the Holy Spirit to witness. (See Acts 1:8.) We need the Holy Spirit to be born into God's Kingdom. (See John 3:5.) We cannot do anything apart from the Spirit. (See John 15:5.)

Holy Spirit, guide me in my witness for you today. Amen.

October 19

Success Without a Successor Is Failure

II Timothy 22

"The things you have heard me say in the presence of many witnesses entrust to reliable men who will also be qualified to teach others" (II Timothy 2:2 NIV).

One of the great challenges of life is to pass on to the next generation the faith that has become so precious to us. Notice the passion of these Biblical writers: Moses writes: "These are all the commands, laws, and regulations that the Lord your God told me to teach you so you may obey them…and so you and your children and grandchildren might fear the Lord your God as long as you live. …You must love the Lord your God will all your heart, all your soul and all your strength. …Repeat them again and again to your children. Talk about them when you are at home and when you are away on a journey, when you are lying down and when you are getting up again. Tie them to your hands as a reminder, and wear them on your forehead. Write them on the doorposts of your house and on your gates" (Deuteronomy 6:1-9 NLT).

The Psalmist Asaph writes: "I will teach … stories our ancestors handed down to us. We will not hide these truths from our children but will tell the next generation about the glorious deeds of the Lord. We will tell of his power and the mighty miracles he did…He commanded our ancestors to teach them to their children, so the next generation might know them… that they in turn might teach their children. So each generation can set its hope anew on God, remembering his glorious miracles and obeying his commands. Then they will not be like their ancestors—stubborn, rebellious, and unfaithful, refusing to give their hearts to God" (Psalm 78:2-8 NLT).

David writes: "O God, you have taught me from my earliest childhood, and I have constantly told others about the wonderful things you do.… Let me proclaim your power to this new generation, your mighty miracles to all who come after me" (Psalm 71:17-18 NLT). Someone has said, "Success without a successor is failure." We are responsible to pass on our faith to the next generation.

Lord, help me to pass on to the next generation the faith that is so precious to me. Amen.

October 20

Declaring God's Glory All Day Long

Psalm 71:8

"O Lord, you alone are my hope. I've trusted you... from childhood. Yes, you have been with me from birth; from my mother's womb you have cared for me. No wonder I am always praising you! My life is an example to many, because you have been my strength and protection. That is why I can never stop praising you. I declare your glory all day long... I will praise you more and more. I will tell everyone about your righteousness. All day long I will proclaim your saving power, for I am overwhelmed by how much you have done for me.

"I will praise your mighty deeds, O Sovereign Lord. I will tell everyone that you alone are just and good. O God, you have taught me from my earliest childhood, and I have constantly told others about the wonderful things you do. Now that I am old and gray, do not abandon me, O God. Let me proclaim your power to this new generation, your mighty miracles to all who come after me. Your righteousness, O God, reaches to the highest heavens. You have done such wonderful things. Who can compare with you, O God? You have allowed me to suffer much hardship, but you will restore me to life again and lift me up from the depths of the earth. You will restore me to even greater honor and comfort me once again.

"Then I will praise you with music on the harp, because you are faithful to your promises... I will sing for you with a lyre... I will shout for joy and sing your praises, for you have redeemed me. I will tell about your righteous deeds all day long..." (Psalm 71:5-24 NLT).

David's life was focused on praising God continually (vv. 6, 8, 24) to everyone (vv. 15, 16). Even in his old age he asks God to help him proclaim his power to the new generation (v.18). His life is an example to many (v.7). He is a witness to everyone with musical instruments, with his voice as he sings and shouts praises to the Lord who redeemed him (vv. 22-24).

Lord, I want to be like David, praising you continually to everyone with my life, my songs and my voice. Amen.

October 21

Eliminating Walls

John 4:3-7

"He (Jesus) left Judea to return to Galilee. He had to go through Samaria on the way. Eventually he came to the Samaritan village of Sychar,.. Jesus, tired from the walk, sat wearily beside the well about noontime. Soon a Samaritan woman came to draw water and Jesus said to her, 'Please give me a drink'" (John 4:3-7 NLT).

Was Jesus provincial? He was the opposite. He was focused on the world. He came to take down the walls. "He has broken down the wall of hostility that used to separate us. By his death he ended the whole system of Jewish law that excluded the Gentiles. His purpose was to make peace between Jews and Gentiles by creating in himself one new person..." (Ephesians 2:14-16 NLT).

"God so loved the world that he gave his only Son, so that everyone who believes in him will not perish but have eternal life..." (John 3:16 NLT).

David writes, "May your ways be known throughout the earth, your saving power among people everywhere. May the nations praise you, O God. Yes, may all the nations praise you...You direct the actions of the whole world" (Excerpts from Psalm 67 NLT).

We tend to build walls—walls between husband and wife, parents and children, extended family walls, walls with our neighbors, walls with Christians in other congregations, walls with people of other cultures. Jesus came to do away with walls. He touched the lepers. He spoke with women and treated prostitutes with respect. He ate with the tax collectors who were looked upon as traitors. He healed Roman citizens. He associated with the poor and the rich, the religious and those who claimed no religion or a different religion. There were no walls with Jesus. He chose Simon the Zealot whose passion was to eliminate the Romans. Jesus chose Levi the tax collector who cooperated with the Romans. With his great love and wisdom he was able to help them to forget their differences so they could work together. Do all you can to eliminate walls.

Lord, your love extends to all people. Enable me to express your love. Push me out of my comfort zone empowering me to relate to those whom I have been avoiding. Amen.

October 22

You Have to Have It to Share It

Acts 4:20

"There's no question—we can't keep quiet about what we've seen and heard" (Acts 4:20 Msg).

A radio speaker I heard today asked, "Why don't we share our faith?" Maybe we don't have enough training. Training is helpful but that is not the crucial reason. Maybe we don't know the unchurched. Last time I checked there were unchurched everywhere. Surveys say that less than fifteen percent of the U.S. population goes to church each week in any given community. There is no county in the continental U.S. where the Christian population is growing. Are we afraid people may reject us? That could be the case.

The point the speaker was making was, we don't share our faith because we don't have it to share. You have to have it to share it! Apostles Peter and John had it and they couldn't help but share it. (See Acts 4:20.) If we have it we will want to share it. That is our priority.

The Muslims share their faith. Why, because they believe their way is the only way to heaven. They say, "We accept your Jesus, why can't you accept our Mohammad. He is more recent than Jesus."

Have we lost our zeal to share our faith because we are not sure that Acts 4:12 is really true: "Salvation is found in no other name under heaven given to men by which we must be saved." (NIV). *The Message* Bible reads: "Salvation comes no other way; no other name has been or will be given to us by which we can be saved, only this one." If we truly believe Acts 4:12 we will find that Acts 4:20 will be a reality for us.

As a young man, Billy Graham, like all of us, had doubts about the authority of Scripture. He told the Lord that he accepts the Scripture by faith as God's divine Word. From that moment forward he had a new confidence and power.

Lord Jesus, I accept the authority of your Word. Restore to me the excitement of a renewed faith in you. Help me to share it. Amen.

October 23

Jesus—Yes: Church—No?

Hebrews 10:25

"Let's see how inventive we can be in encouraging love and helping out, not avoiding worshiping together as some do but spurring each other on, especially as we see the big Day approaching" (Hebrews 10:23-25 Msg).

The belief in "solo" Christianity or "lone ranger" Christianity is spreading. Too often I hear, "You can be a Christian without participating in a church." That's about the same as saying, "I want to be a football player or baseball player but I'm not interested in joining a team." You can't play by yourself. There is no such thing as being an effective Christian in isolation. Sometimes we hear: "My faith is personal, it's none of your business what I believe. I have my own personal walk with God."

We need to have a personal faith in God but we are part of the body of Christ. Americans are individualistic. I believe there is a direct relationship between our individualism and the breakdown of the home as well as the disunity in our churches. The more we isolate ourselves the more we will fight discouragement and depression. We need each other. The church is a body.

Our churches are not perfect. The church needs to be a hospital for sinners not a rest home for saints. Churches need to be a place of acceptance, love and healing. People will go where they feel at home. Why do bars keep prospering? You never see a beer commercial with one person drinking alone. People go to the bar and are free to let their hair down. They find acceptance with people who listen without condemning them. They find someone who understands. To be understood is to be loved. Let's make our churches a place where people can come and experience acceptance. This doesn't mean we accept sin.

The church must be relevant to the community. Many churches could close and the community would not even notice. People drive past them for years and have no idea why they are there. We must become outward focused meeting needs in the lives of our neighbors and making an impact on our communities.

Lord, enable me to help my church become a transforming community reaching people in our neighborhood. Amen.

October 24

Serving or Loving

Matthew 22:37-39

"Jesus replied, 'You must love the Lord your God with all your heart, all your soul, and all your mind.' This is the first and greatest commandment. A second is equally important; 'Love your neighbor as yourself.' All the other commandments and all the demands of the prophets are based on these two commandments" (Matthew 22:37-40 NLT).

How do we prove our love for God? Our culture is production and goal oriented. We must produce. The bottom line is what counts. We tend to prove our love for God and for people by our works, by serving them. If a husband wants to prove his love for his wife, what does he do? He often tries to prove his love by working long hours to provide for the family. While this is good she wants more. She wants a loving intimate relationship. She wants to know he cares about her, he loves her. She wants a loving relationship, not only service.

Many of us have observed a marriage breakup that caught us unaware. We thought things were great between husband and wife. He provided for her, what more could she want? She fell in love with another man who showed her affection by listening to her heart and spending time with her. She was drawn to his ability to enter into her feelings. That's a much deeper level than providing food, housing and transportation.

When Jesus summarized the law and the prophets he said that love from our hearts is what he wants. We often find it much easier to serve and work for Jesus than to develop an intimate relationship with him. Mary chose to sit at Jesus' feet while Martha was focused more on service. (Luke 10:38-42) We cannot truly serve him until we love him.

Let's remember that relationships takes precedence over service. That's especially difficult for most men. We will need to pray and ask Jesus to give us that heartfelt love for him. We must learn to draw near to God and he will draw near to us. (See James 4:8.)

Lord, help me to love you from my heart, to enjoy spending time with you, listening to your voice and thanking you for your grace, your kindness and goodness to me. Amen.

October 25

Knowing God

Philippians 3:10

"Everything else is worthless when compared with the priceless gain of knowing Christ Jesus my Lord. I have discarded everything else, counting it all as garbage, so that I may have Christ and become one with him... For God's way of making us right with himself depends on faith. As a result, I can really know Christ and experience the mighty power that raised him from the death" (Philippians 3:3-10 NLT).

I have the privilege of ministering to persons from many different nationalities. Culture, as you know, has a great influence on our relationships. In premarital counseling sessions it became apparent that the groom did not love his fiancé. To him love was not important. It will come later. He had no concept of marrying for love. In his culture the parents picked the spouse so for him love was far from the most important criteria for marriage. He looked upon his fiancé as one who would do the house work and be the mother of his children.

How would you describe the marriage relationship where the couple's main ambition was to produce children? Intimacy would occur only for the purpose of producing offspring. There would be no interest in knowing each other personally.

How different is this from our desire for God to use us to bring people to Him when we ourselves don't have an intimate relationship of love and fellowship with our Lord? When we have a loving relationship with God, we will reproduce the way he intends. "Those who remain in me, and I in them will produce much fruit. For apart from me you can do nothing" (John 15:5 NLT).

Moses said, "Teach me your ways so I may know you and continue to find favor with you" (Exodus 33:13 NIV). David says, "My soul thirsts for you" (Psalm 63:1 NIV). Paul said, "I want to know him and the power of his resurrection and the fellowship of sharing in his suffering" (Philippians 3:10 NIV).

The men and women who desire to know God more than anything else stay faithful to Him, finishing the course He set before them. Seeking Him above everything else they live close to the heart of God.

Lord, above everything else, I want to know and love you. Amen.

October 26

Include International People

Revelation 7:9

"I saw a large crowd with more people than could be counted. They were from every race, tribe, nation, and language, and they stood before the throne and before the Lamb" (Revelation 7:9 CEV).

In my fifty years of pastoral ministry I was blessed with many wonderful relationships with people from many nations. I miss the cultural diversity when there's only one nation, culture, sex or race present in a group. Heaven is pictured as an international community all focused on Jesus.

Make a special effort to build relationships with people of different races and nationalities in your life and in the life of your congregation. Your Bible studies will be energized. Your concept of God will be enlarged. Your diet may even be enriched! One thing sure is your worship will become a foretaste of heaven.

Jesus made no mistake when he created diversity. Let's embrace, encourage and promote it. I am greatly grieved and embarrassed that Sunday morning is the most segregated hour of our week. We need to intentionally break down those walls that divide us.

"Christ brought us together through his death on the Cross. The Cross ends the hostility. Christ came and preached peace to you outsiders and peace to us insiders. He treated us as equals, and so made us equals. Through him we both share the same Spirit and have equal access to the Father" (Ephesians 2:17-18 Msg).

Jesus is our model. In John 4:4 and 9, he went through Samaria even though the Jews had no dealings with the Samaritans. He chose to go this route to break down the barriers between the Jews and Samaritans. Jews usually avoided Samaria by crossing the Jordan and traveling on the east side to get to Galilee. Jesus was intentional. We too must be intentional to overcome these barriers. Welcome international persons into your life and church. Churches that make this effort are being revitalized. Include international people and empower them. International people will teach us new levels of faithfulness to our Lord.

Jesus, forgive me for being so provincial. Help me go out of my way to develop friendships with those of different cultures and nationalities. Amen.

October 27

Praise

Psalm 134:1

"I will praise the Lord at all times. I will constantly speak his praises" (Psalm 34:1 NLT).

One reason David is known as the man after God's heart is because he was continually praising the Lord. The word "praise" appears in the Psalms approximately 180 times. That's more than the word appears in the remaining 65 books of the Bible.

Praise is sometimes translated "Hallelujah." George Frederick Handel in composing "The Messiah" repeats the word "Hallelujah" approximately 150 times. It has been said that when he finished composing he wept for some time because he'd seen the face of God. Praise puts us into the presence of God. The Lord inhabits the praises of his people. (See Psalm 22:3 KJV.)

David's final Psalm (150) includes eleven commands to praise the Lord. He says we are to praise him for his acts of power, and his surpassing greatness. We praise him with the trumpet, harp, lyre, tambourine, strings, and symbols. We praise him with the dance. Everything that has breath is instructed to praise the Lord.

When we first encounter Jesus we want to praise him for his gift of salvation. As time passes we tend to lose our first love. We need to discipline ourselves to praise him. To practice his presence, we need to praise him. David says, "I will constantly speak his praises." Praise affects our attitude. Attitude affects our relationships and productivity.

Praise propels us into his presence. There will be many times when you don't feel like praising God. Feeling must not control us. When praise becomes a discipline you learn to praise him even in times of adversity.

Praise invites his presence into your life—into the seemingly impossible situations. That's when you know Jesus is present, putting the situation in a totally different perspective.

Lord Jesus, you are worthy to be praised, I choose to praise you continually. Amen.

October 28

Weeds

Hebrews 12:1-2

"Let us throw off everything that hinders and the sin that so easily entangles, and let us run with perseverance the race marked out for us. Let us fix our eyes on Jesus, the author and perfecter of our faith, who for the joy set before him endured the cross, scorning its shame, and sat down at the right hand of the throne of God" (Hebrews 12:1-2 NIV).

When working in the lawn one has to deal with weeds. You have several options: you can let them grow and spread, cut them off, spray them to hopefully kill them, or pull them—uprooting them.

In dealing with sin you have several options as well. You can resist sin by redoubling your determination to have more willpower to overcome it. You can take the advice of a psychologist who coaches you to relax and let go of your moral scruples, and give a deaf ear to the nagging voice of your conscience that's causing you guilt and discomfort. After all, you will be told, you are basically a good person, not nearly as bad as many others... And the psychologist may ask, "who can live up to such high expectations." There's no need to be neurotic. Just do what brings you fulfillment and works...

Jesus, however, would truly transform us! Come to Him in genuine repentance and let him forgive your sin so you can live according to the new resurrection nature he gives you. With resurrection power he replaces hate with love, resentment with forgiveness, and worry with peace. He deals with the root of the problem. (See Galatians 2:20.)

When we come to Jesus he purifies us from all unrighteousness but temptation is still there. The winds of the world blow weed seeds into our minds. We need to decide what we'll do with those weed seeds. Paul asks, "We died to sin; how can we live in it any longer?" (Romans 6:2 NIV). Does this mean we never sin? "If we claim to be without sin, we deceive ourselves and the truth is not in us. If we confess our sins, he is faithful and just and will forgive us our sins and purify us from all unrighteousness" (I John 1:8-9 NIV).

Lord, thank you for the victory you provide when we come to the cross and receive your cleansing. Amen.

October 29

A Missionary God

Acts 1:8

"You will receive power when the Holy Spirit comes on you; and you will be my witnesses in Jerusalem, and in all Judea and Samaria, and to the ends of the earth" (Acts 1:8 NIV).

A bishop brother opened my eyes to what was a new interpretation of these final words of Jesus. He said we need to consider interpreting this verse: "You will witness Jesus being a missionary God. When the Holy Spirit comes you will see me in Jerusalem, in Judea, in Samaria and to the ends of the earth. Jesus is already present wherever we go. He is already present in the people with whom we will be sharing Jesus."

Doesn't that make it much easier? This is basically saying we work with Jesus since he is already there, more than we work for Jesus. Let's pray for the Holy Spirit to open our eyes as we are relating to people so we can see where He is already working in and through them, preparing their hearts for his entrance. This not only makes it much easier to witness, it raises our faith level, increasing our confidence and boldness.

Our spiritual eyes can become 20/20. We begin to see people as Jesus sees them. Jesus saw people as sheep that had been bruised, beaten and confused. Rather than being filled with distain, he was filled with love. "When he saw the crowds, he had compassion on them, because they were harassed and helpless, like sheep without a shepherd" (Matthew 9:36 NIV).

As our spiritual maturity increases, our love and our approachability increases. The more we grow in seeing God at work in the world the more we are willing to open our hearts and our arms to hurting people. This gives the Holy Spirit the freedom to work through us. People feel God's love through our works and our demeanor.

Lord, we thank you that wherever we go you are already present preparing hearts to receive you. Lord, give me eyes to perceive you at work in every person and boldness to declare the Good News. Amen.

October 30

Church to Outsiders

John 4

"Jesus, tired as he was from the journey, sat down by the well. It was about the sixth hour (noon time)" (John 4:6 NIV).

How can we take the gospel to our neighbors instead of waiting for them to come to us? Jesus entered the space of the Samaritan woman crossing ethnic, religious, and gender barriers to reveal the life of God. The well was a space for two different people from different backgrounds to safely interact with one another.

The banquet that Matthew, the tax collector, throws for his friends became a space allowing Jesus to interact with others whom the Jews would generally not associate. (See Matthew 9:9-13).

Jesus was passing through Jericho. The chief tax collector, Zacchaeus, was desperate to see Jesus. He was short of stature and could not see Jesus because of the crowd. This wealthy man put aside his pride and climbed a tree so he could see Jesus. "Jesus looked up and said to him, 'Zacchaeus, come down immediately, I must stay at your house today'" (Luke 19:6 NIV). "Everyone who saw this incident was indignant and grumped, 'What business does he have getting cozy with this crook?'" (v.7 Msg). Bringing outsiders to church is often not appreciated by church folks if it interferes with their style of worship.

When Peter had his vision of the unclean animals he was led by the Holy Spirit to enter the house of a Gentile to preach the gospel. (See Acts 10). The home of Cornelius was uncomfortable for Peter but he was compelled by the Spirit to enter this space to share the Good News.

Where is God asking you to go to share the Good News? Over a family meal? Might it be the bowling alley, the lunch room at work, the bar, the community park, the town mall, or a community soccer league? Why not invite them into your family circle?

Lord, enable me to take the Good News to people in their space. Banish any fear of criticism from other Christians. May your Spirit empower me and guide me today. Amen

October 31

Ministry

Matthew 25

"The King will reply, 'I tell you the truth, whatever you did for one of the least of these brothers of mine, you did for me'" (Matthew 25:40 NIV).

Ministry flows from an intimate relationship with God. There is no substitute for time spent with him. Maintaining intimacy is important.

Many Christians find it hard to be disciplined to have a regular time with God. Many carry guilt because of this. One way many Christians feel close to God is through serving. The Good Samaritan models this for us. As we help people who are facing life's extreme difficulties we feel close to God.

Jesus said, "Whatever you did for one of the least of these brothers of mine, you did for me." As we feed the hungry, give drink to the thirsty, provide a room for the homeless, give clothes to the shivering, visit with the sick and those in prison we are ministering to Jesus.

If parents love their children and there is a good relationship between parent and child there is a closeness between them. When we obey our Father we have a good relationship too.

"If anyone has material possessions and sees his brother in need but has no pity on him, how can the love of God be in him? Dear children, let us not love with words or tongue but with actions and in truth. This then is how we know that we belong to the truth, and how we set our hearts at rest in his presence whenever our hearts condemn us. For God is greater than our hearts, and he knows everything" (I John 3:17-20 NIV).

How do we know that we belong to the truth? We live in truth by sharing our material possessions. Doing this, John says puts our hearts at rest in his presence. Ministry and intimacy with God are closely related. If you are feeling distant from God ask God to show you who is in need and then ask him to help you meet that need. You will begin to feel close to Jesus. Don't forget to thank him for using you to be Jesus to this person.

Lord, help me to be Jesus to someone in need today. Amen.

November 1

Passion for God

Ephesians 3:17-19

"I pray that you, being rooted and established in love, may have power, together with all the saints, to grasp how wide and long and high and deep is the love of Christ, and to know this love that surpasses knowledge—that you may be filled to the measure of all the fullness of God" (Ephesians 3:17-19 NIV).

Our passion for God will never exceed our understanding of his passion for us. This is a statement I read that turned a light on for me. Why is it that we can go to church all our lives and not have a passion for God? Why can seminary students study the Scriptures every day for years and still not have a passion for God? They graduate, enter the pastorate and all too often they are not disturbed if lives are not being transformed. They have knowledge but no passion. The Holy Spirit needs to reveal God's extravagant love to us and make it alive in our hearts. When we know the word but do not put it into practice it is a dead work. Hebrews 6:1 reminds us we must repent from dead works.

Jesus said we are to love God with all our hearts. Just as your heart is the key to understanding your spouse so your heart is the key to understanding God. Intellectual understanding of God and his plan of salvation is not enough. Belief alone is not enough. It is true that Paul writes, "Believe in the Lord Jesus, and you will be saved" (Acts 16:31 NIV). However, the Greek word for believe is always an action word. Believe means that we trust in, cling to and rely upon the Lord Jesus. Believe is more than a head trip.

Paul prays in Ephesians for the church to grasp the indescribable love of God. "God is love" (I John 4:16 NIV). Jesus longs for us to grasp his love and his passion for us. God delights in us! "There is no fear in love. But perfect love drives out fear, because fear has to do with punishment. The one who fears is not made perfect in love. We love because he first loved us" (I John 4:18-19). "Go after a life of love as if your life depends on it" (I Corinthians 14:1 Msg). It does!

Lord Jesus, I want to grow in love. Open my eyes afresh to your love for me. I desire a greater passion for you. Amen.

November 2

Eagles' Wings

Isaiah 40: 29-31

"He gives strength to the weary and increases the power of the weak. Even youths grow tired and weary, and young men stumble and fall; but those who hope in the Lord will renew their strength. They will soar on wings like eagles; they will run and not grow weary, they will walk and not be faint" (Isaiah 40:29-31 NIV).

There comes a time when the mother eagle pushes her young from the nest. Sometimes God takes our lives and pushes us out of our comfort zones. Millions were shocked when the banks had to be bailed out in 2009 and their retirement funds were cut in half. Medical tests may reveal shocking news of a major health problem. Marriages that seem secure disintegrate. Your life may be as you wanted it, but things changed.

Why would God push you out of your nest? Is it because he no longer loves you? No, as the eaglets would never learn to fly unless pushed out of their nests, so it is with us. God has to push us out of our lethargic mind sets so we learn to trust him and soar to new heights. God is at work in those painful changes. We were not made to grovel in the dust; we were made to soar in the heights.

Our world is going through rapid change. The more rapid the changes the more people are open to considering God in their equation of life. They realize their once secure nest is no longer secure. This means they are often more open to consider other options. The door is open for Christians to introduce God into their equation of life. When the foundations shake, it may be God who is shaking them.

Take the initiative and introduce people to the foundation of life that is solid and secure. "No one can lay any foundation other than the one already laid, which is Jesus Christ" (II Corinthians 5:11 NIV). As I look back over my life it was the times that God pushed me out of my nest that I grew the most.

Lord Jesus, thank you for pushing me out of my nest so I can soar to new heights. Amen.

November 3

God-given Dreams

Genesis 37:5-11

"Joseph had a dream, and when he told it to his brothers, they hated him all the more" (Genesis 37:5 NIV). "Joseph had another dream and he told it to his brothers" (v. 9).

Joseph's brothers didn't appreciate their seventeen year-old younger brother, the favorite son of their father, informing them of his dreams that he was going to rule over them. From our perspective it would seem better if he had kept his dreams to himself.

Has God given you a dream or a passion to follow a particular path in life? Joseph's dreams got him into trouble because he told them to his brothers. I suspect if the brothers were spiritually mature they could have accepted his dreams without feelings of hatred or jealousy. I have had dreams from my boy-hood. Some I have shared, others I have kept to myself. Perhaps some were more self motivated than God motivated, time will tell.

A dream often has to be planted as a seed in the dark earth. It remains there to germinate—sometimes for years. Does that mean we do nothing? No, we weed, fertilize, cultivate, water, that is, we walk in obedience before the Lord. We practice living in the fruit of the Spirit. We buy up every opportunity to share our faith as the Holy Spirit directs us. We practice self-discipline and make every effort to work out our salvation.

God will cause that seed to sprout, break through the soil and grow in his time. Our part is to abide in his will. If you are faithful, he will be faithful. Those aspects of our dreams that were from the Holy Spirit will be fulfilled.

We cannot ask God for too much if our hearts are pure, earnestly believe, continue to pray in line with his will, and act on our belief. "God can do anything, you know—far more than you could ever imagine or guess or request in your wildest dreams! He does it not by pushing us around but by working within us, his Spirit deeply and gently within us" (Ephesians 3:20-21 Msg).

Lord, thank you for the dreams you have given me. Help me to do my part in fulfilling those dreams. Amen.

November 4

Harvest Time is Now!

Ephesians 2:13

"But now in Christ Jesus you who once were far away have been brought near through the blood of Christ" (Ephesians 2:13 NIV).

"Now is the time of God's favor, now is the day of salvation" (I Corinthians 6:2 NIV).

"Do not say, 'Four months more and then the harvest'? I tell you, open your eyes and look at the fields! They are ripe for harvest. Even now the reaper draws his wages, even now he harvests the crop for eternal life, so that the sower and the reaper may be glad together" (John 4:35-36 NIV).

Now is the time to pray for workers. Jesus commands his disciples: "The harvest is plentiful, but the workers are few. Ask the Lord of the harvest, therefore, to send out workers into his harvest field. Go! I am sending you out like lambs, among wolves" (Luke 10:2-3 NIV).

Ed Steltzer writes, "We've jazzed up the music, spiced up the sermons, and spruced up the buildings but the wheat still isn't harvesting itself." How true! Jesus says we are to pray for more workers. The problem is not the harvest. The harvest is everywhere. We bump into the harvest every time we go to the supermarket, service station, dental office, post office, or a football game. The harvest is work peers or classmates. Be conscious of the harvest every time you see the U-haul truck in your neighborhood, every time a new house is being built. God loved the people of the world so much he sent Jesus to give eternal life. We are called to give our lives for them as well.

Ask the Lord to give you his passion 24/7. Pray throughout the day for the Holy Spirit to guide your heart and mind so you can point people to Jesus. Eventually many will be brought into the wonderful harvest of eternal life. How blessed we are today to have the privilege of introducing people to the Good News of eternal life through Jesus Christ our creator and savior.

Lord, help me to remember that today is the day of salvation, now is the time to offer the Good News to those we meet. Give me a passion for the harvest. Amen.

November 5

Do You Believe in Heaven and Hell?

John 14:2-3

"In my Father's house are many rooms; if it were not so, I would have told you. I am going there to prepare a place for you. And if I go and prepare a place for you, I will come back and take you to be with me that you also may be where I am" (John 14:2-3 NIV).

"When Christ, who is your life appears, then you also will appear with him in glory" (Colossians 3:4 NIV).

"God didn't let the rebel angels off the hook, but jailed them in hell till Judgment Day…He knows how to hold the feet of the wicked to the fire until Judgment Day" (II Peter 2:4 & 9 Msg).

One of the battles we are facing is the question of the reality of eternal hell. If Satan can get us to question this he will have succeeded in taking the edge off our passion for the lost.

Most people believe there are consequences to their actions, what we sow we reap. (See Galatians 6:7). On the other hand the concept of a loving God allowing someone to be punished for eternity seems unjust. Since God is a just and loving God he will do what is right. Abraham challenged God concerning the destruction of Sodom, "Far be it from you to do such a thing—to kill the righteous with the wicked, treating the righteous and the wicked alike. Far be it from you! Will not the Judge of all the earth do right?" "The Lord said, 'If I find fifty righteous people in the city of Sodom, I will spare the whole place for their sake.'" (Genesis 18:25-26 NIV).

Since God is love, (I John 4:16), just, (Romans 3:26), and all wise (Psalm 139:1-18), we know he will do what is right. Let's remember he doesn't send anyone to hell we send ourselves there when we reject his love.

Lord, thank you for proving your love for us so we can have an abundant and eternal life. Give me your passion to share the love of Jesus. Amen.

November 6

Why Don't I Do What I Know is Right?

Romans 7:14-8:2

"I know all of God's commands are spiritual but I'm not…I'm full of myself…I decide one way, but then I act another, doing things I absolutely despise. …I obviously need help! I realize that I don't have what it takes. I can will it, but I can't do it. … I'm at the end of my rope. Is there no one who can do anything for me?... He (Jesus) acted to set things right in this life of contradictions where I want to serve God with all my heart and mind, but am pulled by the influence of sin to do something totally different. With the arrival of Jesus, … that fateful dilemma is resolved. Those who enter into Christ's being-here-for-us no longer have to live under a continuous, low-lying black cloud. A new power is in operation. The Spirit of life in Christ, like a strong wind, has magnificently cleared the air, freeing you from a fated lifetime of brutal tyranny at the hands of sin and death" (Romans 7:14-8:2 Msg).

What wonderful news! Why should I witness to my neighbor? I want to witness to my neighbor because what I want to do I am doing through the help of Jesus. The fruit of the Spirit is self-control. (See Galatians 5:23). What my neighbor wants to do they can't do because they don't have Jesus. I don't always do what I know God wants me to do but I have experienced his power and victory often enough to know it works.

If I am not convinced Jesus is the answer then I don't have the answer for my prebelieving neighbor. Therefore one of the keys to effective witnessing is to know for sure, not only intellectually but from experience, that Jesus is the answer. At the same time we must humbly admit that we do not always allow Jesus to be our answer. Whenever we become self-absorbed, and self-centered we cancel his power in our live but that never negates the fact that Jesus is the only solution to life's problems.

Lord, give me boldness to share the news that you are the only one to deliver us from our self-absorbed, defeated life. Thanks for your resurrected life lived through me. Amen.

November 7

You Are a Rescuer?

I Corinthians 9:19

"I have become a servant of everyone so that I can bring them to Christ" (I Corinthians 9:19 NLT).

Jesus left heaven. Can you imagine leaving your residence and living in a refugee camp or on the edge of a dump, or in a roach-infested apartment in one of the high-crime areas of our cities? Those pictures come to my mind as I think of the contrast Jesus must have experienced when he left heaven and came to live on earth. Why did he come? He came because he loved us. He knew he could save those who were willing to be rescued from their hopeless condition.

Jesus wants us to be a rescuer of men and women. When Jesus called Peter and John, he called them to fish for men. (See Matthew 4:19). Jesus' brother Jude informs us that we should snatch people from the fire and save them, or rescue them. (See Jude 23). Jesus in the parable of the heavenly banquet informs us that we are to make them come to the banquet or as two versions read, force them to come to the banquet. (See Luke 14:23.) This is a priority. It is a matter of life and death!

Have you lost your passion to rescue people from death? I encourage you to pray: "Father you gave your only son because you loved me. Give me your passion so I can love them as you loved me. Jesus, you were willing to suffer and die for me, give me your passion so I can love my lost neighbors. Holy Spirit you left heaven and came to live in my sinful heart now made holy by your transforming grace, give me your passion for my lost friends."

Just as Jesus came to take many sons and daughters to glory so we too can choose to be on his team to rescue people. Jesus makes us fishers of men and women. We are his representatives. "God has given us the task of reconciling people to him" (II Corinthians 5:18 NLT).

Lord, help me to rescue those who do not have a hope of eternal life. Amen.

November 8

The Mission Field Begins at Home

Deuteronomy 6:5-6

"You must love the Lord you God with all your heart, all your soul, and all your strength. And you must commit yourselves wholeheartedly to these commands... Repeat them again and again to your children. Talk about them when you are at home..." (Deuteronomy 6:5-7 NLT).

Husbands and wives submit to one another out of reverence for Christ. (See Ephesians 5:21.)

We can witness at work and to our neighbors, but if we are not faithful in living for Jesus at home we have lost the battle. We can be successful in business, in the community and in church but if our home is in disrepair we have failed.

I have been exceedingly blessed to have parents who were not perfect but who lived their Christianity at home. My parents had mottos on many of our walls. These are short statements that express a principle for enriching our lives. Two of the mottos that impacted my life were: Your life will soon be past only what's done for Christ will last.

Say nothing you would not like to be saying when Jesus comes. Do nothing you would not like to be doing when Jesus comes, and go nowhere you would not want to be when Jesus comes.

My mother read the Bible each evening before we went to bed and made sure I said my prayers. Perhaps more importantly I observed them kneeling beside their bed in prayer before they retired for the night. They taught me by modeling the value of prayer.

Even though my dad has been deceased for many years I can still hear him whistling hymns as he worked. Let's bring whistling back.

When there was a needy family, especially among relatives who lost a mate, my parents offered assistance. They were modeling the importance of loving and serving others. When one farmer was short on hay, my Dad delivered a wagon load of hay to him. That was years ago but the farmer talks about it to this day. Live your faith beginning with your family.

Lord, enable me to be a faithful disciple expressing love to my spouse, children and extended family. Amen.

November 9

Don't Hide Your Light...Let It Shine

Matthew 5:14-16

"You are the light of the world. A city on a hill cannot be hidden. Neither do people light a lamp and put it under a bowl. Instead they put it on a stand, and it gives light to everyone in the house. In the same way, let your light shine before men, that they may see your good deeds and praise your Father in heaven" (Matthew 5:14-16 NIV.)

Don't be bashful about your good deeds. Tell people what you are up to. Not that you are arrogant or a braggart but we are here to bring out the God-colors in the world. (See Msg.) When people see our acts of kindness many of them will thank us. Point them to God with statements like, "God has been good to me, I enjoy sharing his love with you." Or "God has blessed me with health and a good job I want to share his blessings. I enjoy passing his blessings around."

As the Spirit directs, use these statements as a springbroad to a conversation about faith in God. You may ask if they have faith in God. Or you might say, "After what you have been through perhaps God seems pretty distant." Their need provides a bridge to walk across to introduce them to Jesus.

Jesus says we are not to hide our good deeds. Sometimes Christians allow the devil to tempt them into keeping their mouths shut by whispering: "talking about your works is bragging." If we know that everything we do is only because of Jesus that's not being proud. Paul puts it well: "I can do everything through him who gives me strength" (Philippians 4:13 NIV).

It will be a great day when Christians are known for good works rather than for what they are against.

Lord, I pray that people will see my good works and thank you. Help me to hear your Holy Spirit's voice to say what you want me to say and boldly witness for you. Amen.

November 10

Barnabas the Encourager

Acts 4:36-37

"There was Joseph, the one the apostles nicknamed Barnabas (which means 'Son of Encouragement'). ...He sold a field he owned and brought the money to the apostles for those in need (Acts 4:36-37 NIV).

When Paul arrived in Jerusalem following his conversion they thought his story was a trick for him to capture more Christians. Barnabas convinced them otherwise. Barnabas encouraged Mark to go along on Paul's first missionary journey. Part way through the journey Mark left for home. Later Paul was upset with Mark and would not take him along but Barnabas took him and encouraged him, and he became one of our Gospel writers. (See Acts 15:36-41.)

Nearly every time we read about Barnabas he is encouraging someone. Growing up on a dairy farm in the 1950's, I did not have time to participate in after-school sports. I was a stuttering kid with an inferiority complex. During my freshmen year the junior varsity team was not doing well so the coach approached me about coming to practice. While I was not able to join the team, the coach will never know what encouragement he was to me.

Spot gifts and talents in other people and encourage them. Ask God to open your eyes, especially to people who are hurting and on the margins, to give wisdom to discern how you can encourage them. While I was in seminary someone sent me an anonymous gift of money. I was encouraged by their faith in me and appreciated greatly their financial help. Paul writes: "Encourage each other and build each other up" (I Thessalonians 5:11 NLT). In verse 14 he says, "Encourage those who are timid."

Best of all is the truth in II Thessalonians 2: "May our Lord Jesus Christ himself and God our Father, who loved us and by his grace gave us eternal encouragement and good hope, encourage your hearts and strengthen you in every good deed and word." (vv.16-17 NIV).

Father, I thank you for your eternal encouragement. Enable me to encourage someone today. Amen.

November 11

Not Ashamed

Romans 1:14-17

"Everyone I meet—it matters little whether they're mannered or rude, smart or simple—deepens my sense of interdependence and obligation. And that's why I can't wait to get to you in Rome, preaching this wonderful good news of God. Its news I'm most proud to proclaim, this extraordinary Message of God's powerful plan to rescue everyone who trusts him, starting with Jews and then right on to everyone else! God's way of putting people right shows up in the acts of faith" (Romans 1:14—17 Msg).

As I meet people I frequently pray, "Lord what do you want me to say?" It's exciting, it's fun and it's amazing how God answers that prayer.

Paul is proud to proclaim the Message! He's not intimidated in going to the capital of the world. Why? Because his message is extraordinary. It has power to change lives, power to transfer people from one kingdom to another. No wonder he was not ashamed of the Gospel. I believe one reason so many in the U.S. are not sharing the Gospel is because they have not experienced this powerful transformation. Perhaps their transformation was so gradual they forget how Jesus has changed them.

If you found a great doctor, a mechanic you could really trust or even a terrific diet, you probably would tell your friends about it. Since you've found the One who forgives sin and gives you a new life, don't you think that's something you ought to share?

Don't be discouraged if people don't respond immediately. Some studies indicate that it usually takes many contacts before a person comes to Jesus. I have worked in phone evangelism for years. I call new movers for six months and then say to them, "I don't want to waste your time or mine. I am going to take you off my phone list unless you prefer that I continue to call you." It is amazing how many people say, "Continue to call."

Lord, help me to tune into your Holy Spirit's voice to hear how and what to share concerning the powerful plan of salvation to someone today. Amen.

November 12

In the Name of Jesus

John 14:14

"You may ask me for anything in my name, and I will do it" (John 14:14 NIV).

"You did not choose me, but I chose you and appointed you to go and bear fruit—fruit that will last. Then the Father will give you whatever you ask in my name" (John 15:16 NIV).

"I tell you the truth, my Father will give you whatever you ask in my name" (John 16:23 NIV).

"In that day you will ask in my name" (John 16:26 NIV).

There is something about praying in the name of Jesus that connects us to the heart of God. It is so easy for me to allow this phrase, "In the Name of Jesus" to become mechanical. We dare never use Jesus' name as a magical formula. There is a fragrance in Jesus' name that appeals to the Father. There is power in Jesus' name when we sincerely pray from our hearts.

If I go to a bank and give them a check in my name they will cash it as long as I have the money in my account. If my account is depleted they will not cash it. If a wealthy depositor gave me a signed check they would cash it. It's like going to the bank of heaven when I go to God in prayer and ask in Jesus' name. Jesus has unlimited credit. He wants you to use it!

"…He will give you" (John 16:23). Jesus said that because of my name my Father will respond to your prayers. When we pray in the name of Jesus the Father sees us and honors us the same as he does his son. The challenge is to remain in Jesus, to be one with him, so our requests are in line with the thought, motives and desires of Jesus. These prayers the Father will answer.

There is truly power in the name of Jesus.

Jesus, thank you for the privilege of asking in your name, knowing your bank is more than adequate for withdrawals in line with your will. Thank you! Amen.

November 13

A Bondservant of Jesus

Galatians 2:20 NIV

"I have been crucified with Christ and I no longer live, but Christ lives in me. The life I live in the body, I live by faith in the Son of God, who loved me and gave himself for me" (Galatians 2:20 NIV).

"I identified myself completely with him. Indeed I have been crucified with Christ. My ego is no longer central. It is no longer important that I appear righteous before you or have your good opinion, and I am no longer driven to impress God. Christ lives in me. The life you see me living is not 'mine,' but it is lived by faith in the Son of God, who loved me and gave himself for me. I am not going to go back on that" (Galatians 2:20 Msg).

My independence is gone. My rights are gone. It is not my goals, my life; it is Jesus' life and his alone that counts. I must surrender my life to him. No one can do this for me. I must decide this myself. This is a daily decision. Jesus said we must deny ourselves and take up our cross daily and follow him. (See Luke 9:23). *The Message* Bible states (vv. 23-24): "Anyone who intends to come with me has to let me lead. You're not in the driver's seat—I am. Don't run from suffering, embrace it. Follow me and I'll show you how...Self-sacrifice is the way, my way to finding yourself, your true self."

Say to Jesus, "Whatever you want to do with me is fine, I want your will above everything else." If I need to go through the valley of the shadow of death to be broken before you, that is what I want. You know what I need to be crucified with you. When you reach that point immediately the supernatural identification with Jesus takes place in you.

The passion of Christianity comes from knowingly and intentionally signing away your own rights and becoming a bondservant of Jesus Christ. Until you do that you will not be a true disciple of the Lord.

Lord, first give me a vision of what you want me to do with my life, then break me until that vision is totally yours, not mine. Heal me and use me to extend your reign. Amen.

November 14

God's Passion Burning Inside Me

II Corinthians 11:2-4

"The thing that has me so upset is that I care about you so much—this is the passion of God burning inside me! I promised your hand in marriage to Christ, presented you as a pure virgin to her husband. And now I'm afraid that exactly as the Snake seduced Eve with his smooth patter, you are being lured away from the simple purity of your love for Christ" (II Corinthians 11:2-4 Msg).

In order for Paul to compare his own ministry with the false teachers who invaded the church at Corinth, he had to speak about himself. He has God's passion burning within him. How we need people with God's passion burning within them. Do you pray for God's passion to burn within you?

Paul was the one who led the Corinthians to Christ. He promised these Christians to Christ, the bridegroom and now they are opening their hearts to another groom. Their new groom was the legalism of Judaistic teaching. These false teachers brought a spirit of bondage, fear and worldliness instead of freedom, love, joy, peace and power. It was a different gospel which was no gospel at all. It was bad news, not good news. They were tolerant of these deceivers in their midst.

As Paul was upset, so we are upset when those who accept Christ turn and follow a different gospel. Just as we need to be direct and confront our children when they take a path that leads to death we must be direct with those who walk down the path of legalism. Paul reminds them how he brought the Gospel to them without remuneration. Now they are turning their backs on him and following those who impose burdens on them. While this is not an approach we take with people every day there are times when we need to confront those who are in danger of leaving the true gospel of Jesus for another gospel of good works which is no gospel at all.

Lord, may your passion burn within me, your divine jealousy motivate me to do all I can to bring back those who are being seduced by Satan to follow another gospel. Enable me with wisdom and courage to warn them with your spirit of truth and grace. Amen.

November 15

Spring of Water

John 4:13-14

"Whoever drinks the water I give him will never thirst. Indeed, the water I give him will become in him a spring of water welling up to eternal life" (John 4:13-14 NIV).

Jesus is picturing a vigorous fountain. Other translations read: a perpetual spring, living water or an artesian spring within, or a gushing fountain of endless life. The water leaps up. Jesus is speaking of vigorous, abundant life. (See John 10:10). He is using water as a symbol of the Holy Spirit. (See John 7:39). We are commanded to be filled with the Spirit, literally "keep on being filled" with the Spirit. (See Ephesians 5:18).

If you find that the fountain of life is not springing up from within you blessing the lives of others—something is blocking the flow. Could it be that the flow has stopped or is only a trickle because you are not passing it on? Are you a dead sea? A dead sea produces nothing of life.

Learn to pass it on. Jesus' life in you becomes a fountain that overflows, spilling out on those you meet. This river passes through you to others. Jesus said, "If anyone is thirsty, let him come to me and drink. Whoever believes in me…streams of living water will flow from within him" (John 7:37-38 NIV). (See also John 4:10.)

If you are not living in the Spirit, God has so much more for you! Stay true to him. Be obedient in every detail and you will experience the water that becomes a spring gushing up and overflowing to others.

Keep paying attention to the source. Remain in Jesus and you will bear much fruit. No one can block a river indefinitely. It will overcome every obstacle. Others may throw rocks in its path or try to dam it up but it will overflow to them.

Father, I thank you for your Holy Spirit. Thank you that I never need be thirsty again. Help me to overflow to the many thirsty people around me today. Amen.

November 16

All Things New

Isaiah 42:9

"I'm announcing the new salvation work" (Isaiah 42:9 Msg.)

Jesus said, "No one sews a patch of unshrunk cloth on an old garment, for the patch will pull away from the garment, making the tear worse. Neither do men pour new wine into old wineskins. If they do, the skins will burst, the wine will run out and the wineskins will be ruined. No they pour new wine into new wineskins, and both are preserved" (Matthew 9:16-17 NIV).

Most churches think if they just keep doing the things they have been doing they will fulfill God's design for the church. If your church hasn't baptized a new adult believer for a year are you fulfilling the Great Commission? We can't keep doing the same thing over and over and expect different results.

Doing new things usually means dropping the old things. Someone quipped: "Everyone is in favor of new things as long as they are exactly like the old things." Most older congregations are afraid of trying new things. They are more comfortable staying the same size even though they know Jesus calls us to fish for men. They would rather give to missions in another part of the world than give to reach their neighbors across the street.

If your church is not reaching anyone in the community or hasn't baptized an adult that is serious. If the Lord calls you to be a witness to that congregation, that is your mission. However, if year after year they do not hear your cry to pray for and give priority to reaching the lost in your local communities you need to shake the dust off your feet and move to where the Spirit is moving. We need to love the wine and not the wine skins.

Jesus said the harvest is ripe. He also said you will receive power when the Holy Spirit comes upon you to witness. Has the Holy Spirit lost his power or have we lost the power of the Holy Spirit? Jesus said, if we abide in him we will be faithful—faithful yes, but also fruitful.

Lord Jesus, give me the courage to go with the powerful wind of your Holy Spirit. Amen.

November 17

How Did Jesus Keep the Disciples on Track?

Matthew 10:2-4

"These are the names of the twelve apostles:...Matthew the tax collector; ...Simon the Zealot" (Matthew 10:2-4 NIV).

How could Jesus keep Simon from killing Matthew? The zealots were a patriotic party that resisted the Roman aggression. They degenerated into a body of assassins. Matthew, on the other hand, cooperated with the Romans to collect taxes. The tax collectors were considered traitors. They were hated by the Pharisees as well as most of their Jewish brothers. The tax collectors could charge whatever they wanted as long as they provided Rome with its allotted funds.

Imagine having these two men in your same small group of twelve. The difference between Republicans and Democrats is no comparison. Maybe a terrorist and a conservative Republican is a better comparison. How did Jesus keep Simon and Matthew from fighting each other and constantly upsetting the group? At least part of the answer is that Jesus' mission was so focused and so intense that they were caught up in the vision of helping him fulfill the mission of calling people to follow him. Statements of Jesus like those in Luke 9:23-26 NIV gripped their hearts and changed their whole philosophy of life: "If anyone would come after me, he must deny himself and take up his cross daily and follow. For whoever wants to save his life will lose it, but whoever loses his life for me will save it. What good is it for a man to gain the whole world, and yet lose or forfeit his very self? If anyone is ashamed of me and my words, the Son of Man will be ashamed of him when he comes in his glory...".

They obviously took Jesus seriously when he said, "If you forgive men, when they sin against you, your heavenly Father will also forgive you. But if you do not forgive men their sins, your Father will not forgive your sins" (Matthew 6:14-15 NIV). When we take the word of God seriously and keep our focus on the mission of the church we will not have time to disagree in our Christian gatherings.

Lord, help me to stay focused on the Great Commission. Enable me to forgive others who sin against me. Use me as an instrument in extending your Kingdom. Amen.

November 18

Overflow with Hope

Romans 15:13

"May the God of hope fill you with all joy and peace as you trust in him, so that you may overflow with hope by the power of the Holy Spirit" (Romans 15:13 NIV).

Prisoners can endure indescribable suffering as long as they have hope. Those who don't know Jesus, Paul describes as being "without hope and without God in the world." (Ephesians 2:12 NIV). In First Thessalonians he writes of those "who have no hope" (4:13 NIV).

The Scriptures were written to give us hope: "For everything that was written in the past was written to teach us, so that through endurance and the encouragement of the Scriptures we might have hope" (Romans 15:4 NIV). If you are discouraged let the Scriptures build you up and give you hope. Meditate on Psalm 23, or 9:18, 25:3, 119:43, I Corinthians 6:14, and 15:19.

C. S. Lewis wrote: "We try to be our own masters as if we had created ourselves. Then we hopelessly strive to invent some sort of happiness for ourselves outside of God, apart from God. And out of that hopeless attempt has come human history . . . the long, terrible story of man trying to find something other than God which will make him happy."

"We who have run for our very lives to God have every reason to grab the promised hope with both hands and never let go. It's an unbreakable spiritual lifeline, reaching past all appearances right to the very presence of God where Jesus, running on ahead of us, has taken up his permanent post as high priest for us,..." (Hebrews 6:18-20 Msg).

You may remember the gospel song written by Edward Mote in 1834: My hope is built on nothing less than Jesus' blood and righteousness. I dare not trust the sweetest frame, but wholly lean on Jesus' name. When he shall come with trumpet sound, oh, may I then in him be found, dressed in his righteousness alone, faultless to stand before the throne. On Christ the solid rock, I stand; all other ground is sinking sand.

Father, help me to overflow with hope by the power of your Holy Spirit. Amen.

November 19

O Mighty Warrior!

Judges 6:12

"The angel of God appeared to him (Gideon) and said, 'God is with you, O mighty Warrior!'" (Judges 6:12 Msg).

When God called Gideon he was hesitant to respond. He questioned God's presence since the Israelites were hiding in caves and dens for fear of Midian, their oppressor. Gideon asked, "Where are all the miracles our fathers told us about?" God said, "Go in the strength that is yours. Save Israel from Midian. Haven't I just sent you?" (6:14 Msg). Gideon responded, "Me, my master? How and with what could I ever save Israel? Look at me. My clan's the weakest in Manasseh and I'm the runt of the litter" (v.15 Msg).

After the Lord gave Gideon several miraculous signs of his presence, "God's Spirit came over Gideon" (verse 34). With God's Spirit he defeated the enemy.

You have God's Spirit. He is with you. "You will receive power when the Holy Spirit comes on you; and you will be my witness in Jerusalem, and in all Judea and Samaria, and to the ends of the earth" (Acts 1:8 NIV).

You have God's commission: "Just as the Father sent me, I send you" (John 20:21 Msg). "In the same way you gave me a mission in the world, I give them a mission in the world" (John 17:18 Msg). (See also Matthew 28:18-20.)

Since we have God's Spirit in us and since we are sent by Jesus, God's Son we too will conquer the enemy. "The Spirit in you is far stronger than anything in the world" (I John 4:4 Msg).

Let's enter the world knowing that Jesus' Spirit is in us. We are commissioned by Jesus. We will overcome the enemy. "'Not by might, not by power, but by my Spirit,' says the Lord Almighty" (Zechariah 4:6 NIV).

Lord Jesus, enable me to remember who I am in you. Since you are in me and commissioned me, I will conquer the enemy through the power of your Spirit. Amen.

November 20

Good News for Today and Hereafter

John 10:10

"I came that they may have and enjoy life, and have it in abundance—to the full, till it overflows" (John 10:10 AMP).

Unbelievers today look for relief more than truth. The younger generation wants not only good news for themselves but for their world. They want to know whether Christianity will make our world better. The Good News for them is a full and meaningful life today and for eternity. Although we desire to be part of a perfect world with no sin awaiting us in heaven, most young people in our postmodern world are more excited about a meaningful life in the present context.

"Be relaxed with what you have. Since God assured us, 'I'll never let you down, never walk off and leave you,' we can boldly quote, 'God is there, ready to help; I'm fearless no matter what. Who or what can get to me?'" (Hebrews 13:5-6 Msg).

Jesus makes all the difference here and now. Listen to these truths. I'm chosen by God and adopted as his child. (See Ephesians 1:3-8, John 1:23). I'm forgiven and live in right standing with God. (See Romans 5:1). I am free of condemnation. (See Romans 8:1). I am confident that God will complete the good work He started in me. (See Philippians 1:6). I am a citizen of heaven. (See Philippians 3:20). The evil one cannot touch me. (See I John 5:18). Jesus is my friend. (See John 15:14).

Since Jesus arose from the dead he is more powerful than any situation I will ever encounter. (See Ephesians 1:18-23 & 2:6). As we work with him he will give us wisdom to deal with the huge global problems of poverty, starvation, AIDS, trafficking of children, global warming, racism, sexism, disease, war, and drugs.

"His divine power has given us everything we need for life and godliness through our knowledge of him" (II Peter 1:3 NIV).

Lord Jesus, I thank you that you came to walk with us and provide all we need for life and godliness. Amen.

November 21

God Can't Use Them or Can He?

Judges 11:1

"Jephthah the Gileadite was one tough warrior. He was the son of a whore" (Judges 11:1 Msg).

Jephthah's half-brothers, born to his father's wife, had kicked him out of the family so he would have no part in the inheritance. Time passed. When the Ammonites began fighting Israel, his half-brothers remembered Jephthah being a mighty warrior. They approached him asking him to lead them into battle. Jephthah agreed provided they promised to make him their leader (v.9). Jephthah tried to reason with the Ammonies but they refused to listen to a word that he said. "God's Spirit came upon Jephthah… God gave them to him. He beat them soundly" (vv. 29 & 32).

Look at a few of Jesus' ancestors. Tamar deceived Judah in retaliation for his neglect in giving her his third son, Shelah, for a husband. Rahab was a prostitute. David was a murderer and adulterer. Rehoboam abandoned the worship of God and allowed idolatry to flourish. Asa responded with rage when confronted about his sin. Uzziah tried to perform priestly duties in direct disobedience to God. Ahaz sacrificed some of his children in Baal worship. Manasseh sacrificed his children to idols.

God works through people whom we are inclined to reject. If you feel like a failure, remember that Jephthah, and many in Jesus' linage were people of poor reputation. No matter what our background, God can use us. It doesn't matter where you were born, or who your parents and ancestors were, God can use you. Are you open to allowing God to bring unchurched people into your church and walk together with them as they become Christians? As they mature in faith will you be willing to move them into leadership or hold them back indefinitely because of their past life of sin?

I like the question, "Is your next pastor saved yet?" In other words do we have the faith to believe that God is transforming the prebelievers into believers who are being discipled and can become workers and leaders in "our" church? That needs to happen.

Lord, you are not a respecter of persons. Thank you for accepting me with my background. Enable me to accept everyone you accept. Amen.

November 22

Make Love Practical

Romans 15:7

"So reach out and welcome one another to God's glory. Jesus did it; now you do it!" (Romans 15:7 Msg).

Nothing destroys unity among Christians more than extra Biblical rules and regulations. It is the Holy Spirit's work to convict us of sins that are not clearly stated in Scripture. The Bible clearly sets forth behavioral expectations for Christians. "The acts of the sinful nature are obvious: sexual immorality, impurity and debauchery, idolatry and witchcraft; hatred, discord, jealousy, fits of rage, selfish ambition, dissensions, factions, envy, drunkenness, orgies, and the like. (See Galatians 5:19-21 NIV.)

The Bible condemns acceptance or rejection based on external patterns that go beyond specific spiritual statements. We are to accept one another just as Christ accepted us. (See Romans 15:7.) We are to accept those whose faith is weak without passing judgment on disputable matters. (See Romans 14:1). Paul illustrates this with the issue of eating meat offered to idols. Some knew the idols were mere idols and they had no influence over them so they could eat meat. Others were emotionally tied to their past. It bothered their conscience to eat so Paul advises them not to eat this meat. He further advised, "The man who eats everything must not look down on him who does not, and the man who does not eat everything must not condemn the man who does, for God has accepted him" (Romans 14:3 NIV). We are not to judge each other in areas that are not specified as sin. Each one is to be convinced in his own mind. (See v.5).

To those who could eat meat offered to idols Paul warns them to not offend their weaker brother by eating meat because you may cause them to sin. "We who are strong ought to bear with the failing of the weak and not to please ourselves" (Romans 15:1 NIV). Mature Christians will care about the weaker ones. If these attitudes are operating in our churches, unity will emerge. Those who are weak will become strong as they understand the freedom Jesus has provided for them. Those who are strong will become even more mature.

Lord Jesus, deliver me from a judgmental spirit and grant me patience with those who have a weaker conscience. Enable us to reach out and welcome one another to God's glory. Amen.

November 23

Jesus is More Powerful Than Our Worse Condition

Mark 5

"When Jesus got out of the boat, a man with an evil spirit came from the tombs to meet him. This man lived in the tombs, and no one could bind him anymore, not even with a chain. For he had often been chained hand and foot, but he tore the chains apart and broke the irons on his feet. No one was strong enough to subdue him. Night and day among the tombs and in the hills he would cry out and cut himself with stones" (Mark 5:2-5 NIV).

After Jesus healed the man he begged to go with Jesus but Jesus sent him to witness to the people who knew him. (See vv. 18-20). Too often we have sinful habits in our lives that we need to overcome. Paul explains for us how deliverance can take place.

"If God himself has taken up residence in your life, you can hardly be thinking more of yourself than of him. ...For you who welcome him, in whom he dwells—even though you still experience all the limitations of sin—you yourself experience life on God's terms. It stands to reason, doesn't it, that if the alive and present God who raised Jesus from the dead moves into your life, he'll do the same thing in you that he did in Jesus, bringing you alive to himself? When God lives and breathes in you (and he does, as surely as he did in Jesus), you are delivered from that dead life. With his Spirit living in you, your body will be as alive as Christ's!

"...We don't owe this old do-it-yourself life one red cent. There's nothing in it for us, nothing at all. The best thing to do is give it a decent burial and get on with your new life...

"This resurrection life you received from God is not a timid, grave-tending life. It's adventurously expectant, greeting God with a childlike 'What's next, Papa?'... We know who he is, and we know who we are; Father and children. And we know we are going to get what's coming to us—an unbelievable inheritance!... If we go through the hard times with him, then we're certainly going to go through the good times with him!" (Romans 8:9-17 Msg).

Father, thank you for the resurrection life that delivers us from sinful habits. Amen.

November 24

Raise Up Leaders

Titus 1:5

"The reason I left you in Crete was that you might straighten out what was left unfinished and appoint elders in every town, as I directed you" (Titus 1:5 NIV).

Paul and Barnabas appointed elders for them in each church and with prayer and fasting, committed them to the Lord, in whom they had put their trust" (Acts 14:23 NIV).

The Message Bible says that Paul and Barnabas handpicked leaders in each church. Did these leaders have an opportunity to say, "No?" They were willing. What has happened in our churches today? We often find it difficult to find willing leaders. One bishop with tears in his eyes shared with me his heartbreak for a church established for decades but it could not raise its own leaders. This is true for large churches as well as smaller ones. A church that can't reproduce its own workers and leaders is not a healthy church.

Only Jesus, working through the church can change the world. Business, government, military or even education cannot change hearts. We may invent new technologies but people live in fear, perhaps more than at any time in history. Jesus can use the church to change the hearts and lives of people who in turn can change the world. The church needs leaders.

Jesus instructed us to pray for workers (See Luke 2:10.) When Paul, Barnabas and Titus appointed elders it appears no one said, "We will not do this." Do we get that response today? Perhaps we have tapped the wrong person and they should say "no" but more likely we have raised carnal Christians who are not willing to serve Jesus and his church in leadership responsibilities.

Do we prepare our children to serve our Lord wholeheartedly or do we encourage them to get an education to make big money to live for themselves and later retire in ease and pleasure. Pray for willing, dedicated workers and leaders. Our churches will only be as strong as its leaders.

Father, I pray for workers. Help me to encourage young men and women to give themselves to church leadership so our churches can be agents of redemptive change. Amen.

November 25

Practical Ideas for Witnessing

Acts 8:4

"Forced to leave home base the Christians all became missionaries. Wherever they were scattered, they preached the Message about Jesus" (Acts 8:4 Msg). If you have a passion to obey the Great Commission under the Holy Spirit's direction, pray for opportunities to share Jesus. My wife suffers with four chronic medical conditions. She lives with pain but is known as an encourager. When she walked into the physical therapy room she was greeted with, "Here comes inspiration." She witnesses by encouraging others. Prayer is the key behind her life.

Use your gift to share Jesus. Invite others to dinner. Go to a ball game or a musical drama together. Visit the park with your children. Children make great missionaries. Get to know the non-believers, and prayerfully seek opportunities to speak about Christ.

Get involved in the community. Community involvement should be an outreach opportunity. What are the possibilities? The parent/teacher association; the chamber of commerce; community softball leagues; a bowling or golf league; the neighborhood association; the Kiwanis Club; hobby groups. In rural communities farm shows, ball teams or school events are often popular attractions where you can relate to your unchurched neighbors. Join groups, seeing every relationship as an opportunity to witness. Intentionally pray for non-believers by name. (See Rom. 10:1.) Encourage each other by praying in groups for the unchurched. Pray for the Lord to open blinded minds (II Corinthians 4:3-4), to free them from the enemy's power (Acts 2:18), to transfer them from the Kingdom of darkness to the kingdom of Jesus Christ (Colossians 1:13), and for the Holy Spirit to make them a new creation (II Corinthians 5:17).

Something happens to you when you pray for others. God redirects your focus, changes your thinking, and moves in your heart. Start praying for non-believers and watch what God does as you connect with those who need to hear the Good News.

Jesus, I promise to begin praying for my unbelieving friends by name and to trust you to open doors for me to build bridges so they can hear the Good News of eternal life. Amen.

November 26

Who Do You Relate to?

Luke 15:1

"By this time a lot of men and women of doubtful reputation were hanging around Jesus, listening intently. The Pharisees and religion scholars were not pleased, not at all pleased. They growled, 'He takes in sinners and eats meals with them, treating them like old friends'" (Luke 15:1 Msg). "Tax collectors and other notorious sinners often came to listen to Jesus teach" (Luke 15:1 NLT).

Jesus saw Levi at his tax collection booth and invited him to follow. "That night Levi invited Jesus and his disciples to be his dinner guests, along with his fellow tax collectors and many other notorious sinners. (There were many people of this kind among the crowds that followed Jesus.) But when some of the teachers of religious law who were Pharisees saw him eating with people like that they said to his disciples, 'Why does he eat with such scum?' When Jesus heard this, he told them, 'Healthy people don't need a doctor—sick people do. I have come to call sinners not those who think they are already good enough'" (Mark 2:15-27 NLT).

What was it about Jesus that sinners liked to be with him and listen to him? Was it because they knew he understood them, accepted them rather than condemned them? Was it because he condemned religious hypocrisy? Was it because they saw the miracles?

Jesus was comfortable with sinners. He came: to seek and save the lost. (See Luke 19:10). He came not to call the righteous but sinners. (See Mark 2:17). That was his life's purpose and it must be ours. We accept unbelievers because Jesus accepted them. (See John 3:17.)

Did he condone their sin? No, but he accepted them as persons—persons who were valuable, people worth understanding. He related to them by entering into their life, talking and eating with them. (See Matthew 19:5.) We will not win people for Jesus in our Christian ghettos. We must take Christ to the workplace. For salt to do its work it has to get out of the salt shaker. Jesus instructs us to let our light shine for people to see our good works and glorify God.

Lord Jesus, help me to love sinners—to understand them, to build bridges to them. Amen.

November 27

Never Thirst Again

John 7

Jesus said to the woman at the well, "Everyone who drinks this water will be thirsty again, but whoever drinks the water I give him will never thirst. Indeed, the water I give him will become in him a spring of water welling up to eternal life" (John 4:13-14 NIV).

Jesus is not taking about H2O. He is talking about spiritual water. Concerning spiritual water he says we will not thirst again. Do we believe this statement of our Lord? Are we satisfied with what he has done and is doing in our life? He is able to do more than we can ask or imagine. (See Ephesians 3:20-21). Why do we limit him? But you say I have this deep hurt. Can he not heal that hurt? You forget he is the Lord Almighty! He can heal every hurt. He can quench every thirst.

David said his soul thirsts for God. (See Psalm 42:1.) In the New Testament we have the invitation of Jesus, if we are thirsty to come to him and drink. If we drink, streams of living water will flow from us. (See John 7:37-38.) James reminds us if we draw near to God he will draw near to us. (See James 4:8.) Jesus says we are to come to him and he will give us rest. (See Matthew 11:28.) Again he invites us to hunger and thirst for righteousness and we will be satisfied. (See Matthew 5:6.)

With so many straightforward promises from Scripture you have no excuse for not living a victorious life. Don't forget the Almighty One is living in you? Do you not recognize that God, the creator of the cosmos as well as the one who raised Jesus from the tomb is the same Almighty God whose Spirit dwells in you?

We must abandon ourselves and surrender to Jesus. He says, "He who believes in me will never be thirsty" (John 6:35). God has so much more for us. Look to him and drink deeply from him. Isaiah 49:10, Revelation 7:16-17, 21:6 and 22:1, 17 all remind us of the water of life in Glory. He desires for you to drink today.

Lord, whenever I am dry and thirsty, help me to come to you the fountain of living water. Thank you for quenching my thirst. Amen.

November 28

Remember Who You Were

Ephesians 2:12-21

Remember you were without hope and without God. (v.12) "Because of Christ—dying that death, shedding that blood –you who were once out of it altogether are in on everything.... He tore down the wall we used to keep each other at a distance.... Instead of continuing with two groups of people separated by centuries of animosity and suspicion, he created a new kind of human being, a fresh start for everybody. Christ brought us together though his death on the Cross. ... He treated us as equals, and so made us equals. Through him we both share the same Spirit and have equal access to the Father. ... You're no longer strangers or outsiders. You belong here, with as much right to the name Christian as anyone. God is building a home... He's using you, fitting you in brick by brick, stone by stone, with Christ Jesus as the cornerstone that holds all the parts together" (Ephesians 2:13-21 Msg).

In Christ the walls are gone. There are walls everywhere. What walls do we keep in our minds to keep others out? There are walls of race. Sunday morning is the most segregated time of the week. There are economic walls. We can often tell the economic status of a person by the denomination or church they attend. There are walls of prejudice passed down from one generation to another.

Paul says remember we were on the outside, without God and without hope, separated from those who knew Jesus. If we were raised in a Christian home our separations do not seem as dramatic as those who were raised where God was not recognized. Let the Holy Spirit reveal our self-centered, self-absorbed and carnal hearts. Until we see how far we are from Christ's commandment to love the Lord with all our hearts and love our neighbor as ourselves we will have a difficult time appreciating the tremendous work of Jesus in removing these walls.

Jesus treats us as equals. The ground is level at the cross. We have the same Holy Spirit and the same access to the Father. We are no longer divided. We are part of the same building. We fit in with others just as one brick fits with another since we are all build on the foundation stone of Jesus Christ.

Lord, remove the walls between myself and my brothers and sisters. Help me to build my life on you—the one who holds us all together. Amen.

November 29

I Make the Most of My Ministry

Romans 11:13-14

In speaking of his ministry to the Gentiles Paul writes, "I lay great stress on this, for I want to find a way to make the Jews want what you Gentiles have, and in that way I might save some of them" (Romans 11:13-14 NLT).

Paul is determined to see as many of his Jewish brothers and sisters enter God's kingdom as possible. He makes as much of his ministry as he can. The Amplified Bible reads: "I lay great stress on my ministry and magnify my office. In the hope of making my fellow Jews jealous—in order to stir them up to imitate, copy and appropriate –and thus managing to save some of them."

Do you make much of your ministry? Do you tone down or belittle your ministry so no one can accuse you of being proud? Let's not be afraid to glory in the cross, to magnify Jesus and the fulfilling and abundant life he gives to all who come to him. Let's thank him personally and publicly for the joy of serving him in the ministry he has given to us.

"I have an obligation to discharge and a duty to perform and a debt to pay. So...I am willing and eagerly ready to preach the Gospel to you also who are in Rome" (Romans 1:15-16 AMP).

Let's not grow weary in fulfilling Jesus' commission to us. Paul reminds the Corinthians, "So, my dear brothers and sisters, be strong and steady, always enthusiastic about the Lord's work, for you know that nothing you do for the Lord is ever useless" (I Corinthians 15:58 NLT). To the Thessalonians: "I say to the rest of you, dear brothers and sisters, never get tired of doing good" (II Thessalonians 3:13 NLT). And to the Galatians he says almost the identical admonition: "Don't get tired of doing what is good. Don't get discouraged and give up, for we will reap a harvest of blessing at the appropriate time. Whenever we have the opportunity, we should do good to everyone, especially to our Christian brothers and sisters" (Galatians 6:9-10 NLT).

Father, infuse me with your Holy Spirit's power and enthusiasm to share the Good News in both word and deed so others want to come to you. Amen.

November 30

Overcoming Spiritual Dullness

Hebrews 6:10-12

"For God is not unfair. He will not forget how hard you have worked for him and how you have shown your love to him by caring for other Christians… Our great desire is that you will keep right on loving others as long as life lasts… Then you will not become spiritually dull and indifferent. Instead, you will follow the example of those who are going to inherit God's promises because of their faith and patience" (Hebrews 6:10-12 NLT).

"The more you grow…, the more you will become productive and useful in your knowledge of our Lord Jesus Christ… Work hard to prove that you really are among those God has called and chosen. Doing this you will never stumble or fall away. And God will open wide the gates of heaven for you to enter into the eternal Kingdom of our Lord and Savior Jesus Christ" (II Peter 1:8-11 NLT).

These writers remind us that if we work hard at caring for others we will not have a dull and indifferent Christian life. God will reward us by opening wide the gates of heaven. On the other hand, carnal, self-centered Christians don't work hard for the Lord and don't reproduce. Their works will be burned up.

"If any man builds on this foundation (Jesus Christ), using gold, silver, costly stones, wood, hay or straw, his work will be shown for what it is, because the Day will bring it to light. It will be revealed with fire, and the fire will test the quality of each man's work. If what he has built survives he will receive his reward. If it is burned up, he will suffer loss; he himself will be saved, but only as one escaping through the flames" (I Corinthians 3:12-15 NIV).

"I discipline my body like an athlete, training it to do what it should. Otherwise, I fear that after preaching to others I myself might be disqualified" (I Corinthians 9:27 NLT). It's only God's pure self-less love flowing through us that can reach others and overcome spiritual dullness and dryness.

Lord, by your grace I will work hard to show love to everyone. Let your love flow through me to others today. Amen.

December 1

Unity Can Happen

Colossians 3:12-14

"As God's chosen people, holy and dearly loved, clothe yourselves with compassion, kindness, humility, gentleness and patience. Bear with each other and forgive whatever grievance you may have against one another. Forgive as the Lord forgave you. And over all these virtues put on love, which binds them all together in perfect unity" (Colossians 3:12-14 NIV).

A church split. Why? It was discovered it began at a banquet when an elder was served a smaller piece of ham than the person beside him. While it is hard to keep from either laughing or crying, it is all too true that the smallest slights can begin a root of bitterness and in this case a church split.

A person once admitted to me that he would not attend business meetings at church because he cannot keep his cool. He had a root of bitterness, probably existing for years. Some Christians call this bearing it in love; however, if we bear something in love we don't carry any resentment. True forgiveness holds no grudges.

Do we stuff our deep hurts inside only to have them surface later? In the meantime, this root of bitterness robs us of being an effective Christian servant and makes it impossible to reproduce healthy offspring. One writer says we Christians have more trouble with this than secular organizations because we have high moral standards but are short on grace. We must learn to extend grace. Since God forgave us for so much, we must learn to forgive others. The church is the only organization that kills its wounded.

When there are unresolved hurts and wounds we often take vengeance. Paul reminds us that vengeance belongs to God. He will take care of the avenger. (See Romans 12:19.) Vengeance usually causes the avenger to commit the greater evil. Come to the cross and let Jesus heal you of your hurt. Learn to confess your hurts to each other so you can be healed. (See I John 1:9 & James 5:16.)

Father, forgive me for carrying hurts in my heart. I bring them to you for healing. Thank you. Amen.

December 2

Holy Compassion

Philippians 3:18

"As I often told you before and now say again even with tears, many live as enemies of the cross of Christ. Their destiny is destruction, their god is their stomach, and their glory is in their shame. Their mind is on earthly things. But our citizenship is in heaven. And we eagerly await a Savior from there, the Lord Jesus Christ" (Philippians 3:18-20 NIV).

At the Congress on World Evangelism in London someone commented it was easy to tell who the Americans were. After the evening session the Americans asked where they could find the nearest restaurant, while many from other countries asked where they could find a room for prayer.

Are we more concerned about getting to the restaurant following church than to spend time in fellowship and in encouraging each other?

A Christian brother was concerned about his young banker who did not know the Lord. For eighteen months, every time he went to the bank he asked the young man to meet with him so they could study the Bible together. The young man refused. To get him off his back he finally agreed. They studied together and the young man accepted Christ. Today the young banker has a dramatic testimony and is as persistent and zealous as the Christian who led him to the Lord.

Paul says he told the Christians repeatedly with tears that many people are enemies of the cross. Why the tears? Because the destiny of these people is destruction. Their god is their stomach. All they think about is earthly things.

When a group of international persons left America to return to their home country they were asked what impressions they will take with them. Their response was the many obese people and all the food that is thrown into the garbage. Is our god our stomach? Do we Christians glory in how much we eat? (See John 4:32.) What will it take for us to discover a passion for the lost souls of our neighbors?

Lord Jesus, forgive me when my stomach is more important than my desire to pray and witness to the lost people I know. Amen.

December 3

Rescue the Wanderer

James 5:19-20 and Matthew 18: 12-14

"My dear friends, if you know people who have wandered off from God's truth, don't write them off. Go after them. Get them back and you will have rescued precious lives from destruction and prevented an epidemic of wandering away from God" (James 5:19-20 Msg).

James instructs us to rescue those who wandered away from God and thus keep them from destruction as well as the many they will take with them. Can you imagine what joy you will have now as well as in glory when you meet those you rescued from the path of destruction?

James says, "You prevented an epidemic of people wandering off!" We never know the influence of one person and how one person's change of direction impacts multitudes. Who had the greater influence, Billy Graham, or the person who led Billy to faith in Jesus?

Jesus said, "If a shepherd has one hundred sheep, and one wanders away and is lost, what will he do? Won't he leave the ninety-nine others and go out into the hills to search for the lost one? And if he finds it, he will surely rejoice over it more than over the ninety-nine that didn't wander away! In the same way, it is not my heavenly Father's will that even one of these little ones should perish" (Matthew 18:12-14 NLT).

God has called you to be a rescuer of wanderers. Hopefully most people in your congregation have a good foundation. But as happens in every congregation some grow cold and wander away. Jesus is asking you to rescue and save them from destroying others in the process.

Join the coast guard for Jesus. "Brothers and sisters, we urge you to warn those who are lazy. Encourage those who are timid. Take tender care of those who are weak. Be patient with everyone" (I Thessalonians 5:14 NLT). Ask the Lord to give you eyes to see those who are in need of encouragement to move from lukewarm to hot.

Lord Jesus, enable me to be a rescuer for those who are wandering, an encourager for those who are timid and patient with everyone. Amen.

December 4

Shine Like Stars and Beacon Lights

Daniel 12:3

"Those who are wise will shine as bright as the sky, and those who turn many to righteousness will shine like stars forever" (Daniel 12:3 NLT).

Picture yourself as a shining star. "You are to live clean, innocent lives as children of God in a dark world full of people who are crooked and stubborn. Shine out among them like beacon lights holding out to them the Word of Life. Then when Christ returns how glad I will be that my work among you was so worthwhile" (Philippians 2:15-16 LB).

Picture yourself as a beacon light in this dark world. "You are the light of the world—like a city on a mountain, glowing in the night for all to see. Don't hide your light under a basket! Instead, put it on a stand and let it shine for all. In the same way, let your good deeds shine out for all to see, so that everyone will praise your heavenly Father" (Matthew 5:14-16 NLT).

Picture yourself as a light on top of the mountain. "You are all children of the light and of the day; we don't belong to darkness and night" (I Thessalonians 5:5 NLT).

"As you have the light, believe in the light. Then the light will be within you, and shining through your lives. You'll be children of light" (John 12:36 Msg).

"The Lord is my light and my salvation—whom shall I fear?" (Psalm 27:1 NIV). *The Message* Bible reads: "Light, space, zest—that's God! So, with him on my side I'm fearless, afraid of no one and nothing."

"For though your hearts were once full of darkness, now you are full of light from the Lord, and your behavior should show it" (Ephesians 5:8 NLT).

Lord, enable me to remember that your light is shining through me. It is a reflection of your glory for everyone to see. Let me shine like the stars in the universe. Thank you Jesus. Amen.

December 5

Everything We Need

II Peter 1:3

"His divine power has given us everything we need for life and godliness through our knowledge of him who called us by his own glory and goodness" (II Peter 1:3 NIV).

He provides salvation/deliverance from sin. "This is how much God loved the world: He gave his Son, his one and only Son. And this is why: so that no one need be destroyed; by believing in him, anyone can have a whole and lasting life" (John 3:16 Msg).

He provides a right standing with himself: "Since we have been justified through faith, we have peace with God through our Lord Jesus Christ, through whom we have gained access by faith into this grace in which we now stand" (Romans 5:1 NIV).

He provides a seat beside himself: "God raised us up with Christ and seated us with him in the heavenly realms in Christ Jesus" (Ephesians 2:6 NIV).

He provides status: "I assure you, of all who have ever lived, none is greater than John the Baptist. Yet even the most insignificant person in the Kingdom of Heaven is greater than he is!" (Matthew 11:11 NLT).
He provides a purpose and direction:
- "You will be my witnesses…" (Acts 1:8 NIV).
- "God has given us the task of telling everyone what he is doing. We're Christ's representatives. God uses us to persuade men and women to drop their differences and enter into God's work of making things right between them. We're speaking for Christ himself now. Become friends with God, he's already a friend with you" (II Corinthians 5:20 Msg).
- "As the Father has sent me, I am sending you" (John 20:21 NIV).
- "If you know of people who have wandered off from God's truth, don't write them off. Go after them. Get them back and you will have rescued precious lives from destruction and prevented an epidemic of wandering away from God" (James 5:19-20 Msg).

Lord Jesus, you provide everything I need. I gladly receive your provisions and claim them for my daily living. Amen.

December 6

Early Church Believers

Acts 12:2

"He (King Herod) had James, the brother of John, put to death with the sword" (Acts 12:2 NIV).

The early church believers were passionate to the point of being willing to die for their faith. How the scene in most of our churches has changed. Too often witnessing to others is not worth stressing a relationship. Society and our culture have bought into the myth that everyone goes to a better place when they die. This negates the need for salvation. Why bother to recue people from eternal suffering if we are not sure Jesus really meant what he said about hell or even if there is a hell?

Our culture decided that Jesus is only one path among many to reach eternal bliss. Too often church members agree with society that Jesus is the better way among many ways to God. Then it is not long until we decide that our friends, neighbors, and world have far more pressing needs to address than coming to know Jesus. Conversion is not necessary for those who believe that Jesus is simply a better way, not the only way to God.

The next step focuses on delivering people from physical suffering. We feed the hungry, provide clean water for the thirsty, clothe the shivering, eradicate diseases which is what Jesus taught us to do but these works often take precedence over sharing Jesus, even to the point where we forget why we minister to human suffering.

For many Christians it is much easier to meet physical needs than minister to the spiritual needs. This can result in neglecting evangelism. Compassion is viewed as essential to evangelism but often becomes the only side of evangelism that matters. In Mark 2:5 Jesus met the spiritual need before he met the physical need.

The apostles died for sharing their faith. Are we willing to risk straining a relationship with our unchurched friends to bring them to Jesus saving them from eternal destruction?

Lord, help me not only to give to the physical needs of people but to share the Good News even when I sense it may strain a relationship. Amen.

December 7

One Thing You Can't Do in Heaven

Matthew 28:18-20

Why did God let us here after we accepted him? In heaven we can worship, fellowship, sing, pray and hear God's Word, but we won't be able to win people for Jesus and make disciples. Let's not forget why we are here.

I was talking with a father of two children. It was close to Halloween. He was spending time and money on building a casket for his ghost which was built so that the ghost periodically appeared as the casket opened and then descended into the casket as it closed. All this took place directly across the street from a church. This father believes we humans are no different than dogs, if fact he says dogs are more sensible than people. There are times when I would have to agree dogs seem more sensible.

When this account was reported to a small group at church, the response seemed to be: we are here, our doors are open, you can't change people, we're not responsible. Shake the dust off your feet, and put your head on your pillow and enjoy your sleep. Don't worry about them; you can only do so much. This congregation is in decline.

In a survey of eighty adults in another congregation only nine percent of the members said that concern for the unchurched should be one of the three most valued aspects of their congregation. As we might expect, that same congregation, reported that only five percent have a sense of excitement about their future.

Paul writes: "I pray that you may be active in sharing your faith, so that you will have a full understanding of every good thing we have in Christ" (Philemon 6 NIV). When we lose our passion for reaching people for Jesus we lose one of our main purposes for living.

Lord, thank you for the privilege of being your ambassadors in sharing our faith so others can experience eternal life in heaven. Amen.

December 8

The Most Quoted Scripture By American's College Students

Matthew 7:1

"Do not judge, or you too will be judged" (Matthew 7:1 NIV).

A few years ago the most quoted Scripture by any group in America was John 3:16, "For God so loved the world that he that he gave his one and only Son, that whoever believes in him shall not perish but have eternal life." (NIV).

Today the most quoted Scripture is "Judge not and you will not be judged."

Call "wrong doing" a sin and get people's reaction. To help us deal with this attitude all we need to do is read on a few verses later where Jesus said, "Do not give dogs what is sacred; do not throw your pearls to pigs. If you do, they may trample them under their feet, and then turn and tear you to pieces" "Matthew 7:6 NIV". We need God's wisdom to judge.

Jesus described for us how to judge. "Why do you look at the speck of sawdust in your brothers' eye and pay no attention to the plank in your own eye? How can you say to your brother, 'Let me take the speck out of your eye, when all the time there is a plank in your own eye? You hypocrite, first take the plank out of your own eye, and then you will see clearly to remove the speck from your brother's eye" (Matthew 7:3-5 NIV). We must always look at our own lives first. We extend grace. Our judgment must match God's and not condemn things where the Scripture is silent. We must not judge the unsaved by Christian standards. That's God's job. We hate the sin and love the sinner. Only by God's grace is this possible.

In every area of life we know that some things are right and some are wrong. In our culture, tolerance is king. Morality is relative, and everyone is right no matter what you do or believe, but the Christian needs to call sin, sin.

Lord, help me to remove the log from my own life first. Enable me to love the sinner and hate sin. Amen.

December 9

Hearing God's Call

Psalm 37:23

"The steps of a good man are ordered by the Lord and he delights in his way" (Psalm 37:23 JKV). How do I know God's will for my life? Is his will specific for me? When do I stop praying and use my own judgment?

First, as your study the Scriptures you see how God worked in the lives of different people. This gives you some indication of how he will work in your life. "By your words I can see where I'm going: they throw a beam of light on my dark path" (Psalm 119:105 Msg).

Secondly, there is wisdom in Godly counselors. "Without good direction, people lose their way; the more wise counsel you follow, the better your chances" (Proverbs 11:14 Msg).

Thirdly, what energizes you? What have you enjoyed doing in the past? What do you desire to do today? "Delight yourself in the Lord and he will give you the desires of your heart" (Psalm 37:4 NIV).

Fourthly, what experiences have you had that prepared you to serve God presently? "The Lord who delivered me from the paw of the lion and the paw of the bear will deliver me from the hand of this Philistine" (I Samuel 17:37 NIV).

Fifthly, where has God placed you presently? Your situation may be the door God is opening for you to walk through. God frequently uses circumstances to guide us. "His (Joseph's) brothers pulled Joseph out of the cistern and sold him for twenty pieces of silver to the Ishmaelites who took Joseph with them down to Egypt" (Genesis 37:28 Msg).

Sixthly, learn to hear his voice. "He (Jesus) goes on ahead of them; and his sheep follow him because they know his voice" (John 10:4 NIV). "If anyone hears my voice and opens the door, I will come in and eat with him and he with me" (Revelation 3:20 NIV).

Finally, stay close to Jesus. He will give you his peace. (See John 14:27).

Lord Jesus, I desire to be close to you; to be obedient in all things. Thank you for guiding my life into meaningful and joyful service. Amen.

December 10

Any Means Possible

I Corinthians 9:22

"I have become all things to all men so that by all possible means I might save some" (I Corinthians 9:22 NIV).

As far as results are concerned the most effective method for me in reaching people for Jesus is using the phone in calling new movers and welcoming them to the community. Various companies provide names of new movers for a small fee. When newcomers answer the phone, I introduce myself and welcome them to the community and then state that if they have not found a church since they moved could I have their permission to send them a flier inviting them to worship with us some Sunday. Many people respond by saying it is ok to send the flier.

Hand address the envelope using first class mail. Then call back in a week or so and if possible speak to the person you spoke to originally and ask them if they received the flier? Next ask if there is a possibility they may come and worship with us some Sunday. Don't say, "this Sunday" because they may have an excuse and then it is difficult to move the conversation forward.

At this point many will ask a question which opens the door to building a relationship. Often they state why they can't come. More often than not the reason is one that you could pray for so I simply pray a short prayer asking God to work in meeting the need that they shared. I do not ask them if it is ok to pray with them. I simply pray. Frequently, I can tell they are deeply touched by the prayer. Ninety-seven percent of Americans believe in prayer.

Next I call back in a couple weeks and ask how things are developing since we prayed two weeks ago. It's truly amazing how God answered those prayers. Some are moved by the Holy Spirit and eventually come to church and bring others with them. New people bring new people. They become your evangelists, some even before they make a commitment to Jesus.

Lord Jesus I thank you that whatever gift you give to us you can use to reach people for you. Show me how I can use my gifts and give me the courage to trust you to bring people closer to you through my efforts. Amen.

December 11

Who Will Be in Charge?

Romans 7:18-20

"I know that nothing good lives in me, that is, in my sinful nature. For I have the desire to do what is good, but I cannot carry it out. For what I do is not the good I want to do; no, the evil I do not want to do—this I keep on doing. Now if I do what I do not want to do, it is no longer I who do it, but it is sin living in me that does it" (Romans 7:18-20 NIV).

We have two levels of processing going on in our lives. On the conscious level I desire to do what is right but there is the subconscious old nature who wants control. As God's child we choose to live on the conscious level.

We must consciously focus on Jesus' Holy Spirit power at work within us to overcome the subconscious messages. For example, I don't want to raise my voice at my wife or children but if I am tired and stressed when they do something that irritates me my subconscious voice automatically causes me to speak in an angry voice. My subconscious tells me they should know better than to bother me now, or answer all their questions because I had a difficult day.

When I pause to pray, "Lord help me respond as you would respond, then I can overcome the subconscious message and respond appropriately." When we fail, and we fail many times, we come to the cross, die to self, repent and ask God for his strength to do better next time.

Paul continues: "In my inner being I delight in God's law; but I see another law at work in the members of my body, waging war against the law of my mind and making me a prisoner of the law of sin at work within my members. What a wretched man I am! Who will rescue me from this body of death? Thanks be to God—through Jesus Christ our Lord!" (Romans 7:22-25 NIV).

Lord Jesus, help me to be aware of the power of your Holy Spirit's power continually giving me the ability to respond as you would in every situation. Thank you. Amen.

December 12

Think Positively

Philippians 4:8

"Summing it all up, friends, I'd say you'll do best by filling your minds and meditating on things true, noble, reputable, authentic, compelling, gracious—the best, not the worst; the beautiful, not the ugly; things to praise, not things to curse" (Philippians 4:8 Msg).

Paul was in prison when he wrote these words. How could he fill his mind with good thoughts in prison? Perhaps Proverbs 23:7 JKV helped him understand the importance of thinking good thoughts: "For as he thinks in his heart, so is he." Paul had learned that positive thoughts are more profitable and God honoring than negative thoughts. Studies have shown that negative thoughts linger longer and make a deeper impression in our minds than positive thoughts. It's a good practice before giving a negative statement to another person to precede it with several positive compliments.

Jesus says, "You have minds like a snake pit! How do you suppose what you say is worth anything when you are so foul-minded? It's your heart, not the dictionary that gives meaning to your words" (Matthew 12:34-35 Msg).

The more you think negative thoughts about a person the more you have trouble loving them. Sometimes we hear we are to love the sinner and hate the sin. Is that possible? If we determine by God's grace to think positive thoughts about a person whom we naturally do not appreciate it will help us to accept and love him or her. We begin to see the person through God's eyes. With the Holy Spirit's power we can love them knowing Jesus loves them and died for them. This helps us separate the person from their evil acts.

"Whatever is true, whatever is noble, whatever is right, whatever is pure, whatever is lovely, whatever is admirable—if anything is excellent or praiseworthy—think about such things" (Philippians 4:8 NIV).

Jesus, I join the psalmist David in his prayer:, "Search me, O God, and know my heart; test me and know my anxious thoughts. See if there is any offensive way in me, and lead me in the way everlasting" (Psalm 139:23-24 NIV).

December 13

Welcome

Romans 15:5-9

"May our dependably steady and warmly personal God develop maturity in you so that you get along with each other as well as Jesus gets along with us all. Then we'll be a choir—not our voices only, but our very lives singing in harmony in a stunning anthem to the God and Father of our Master Jesus! So reach out and welcome one another to God's glory. Jesus did it; now you do it! Jesus, staying true to God's purposes, reached out in a special way to the Jewish insiders so that the old ancestral promises would come true for them. As a result, the non-Jewish outsides have been able to experience mercy and to show appreciation to God" (Romans 15:5-9 Msg).

It happened again today. My consulting takes me to different churches. I entered the building and received a program or a bulletin. There was no recognition that I was new. This was a small congregation of 75 so everyone knew everyone else. I had to ask where the Sunday School classes met. No one informed me where the restrooms were located. There were refreshments in the basement where some had gathered but no one made any effort to inform me concerning the refreshments.

I chose a class and sat down in a circle of twenty chairs with ten of them occupied. The teacher made no attempt to welcome me. I have experienced such cold shoulder treatment in other churches as well.

Verse 7 above says, "So reach out and welcome one another to God's glory. Jesus did it; now you do it." Our churches should be places of warm fellowship reaching out to those we don't know. "Love cares more for others than for self" (I Corinthians 13:4 Msg). Someone said, "A church not reaching out passes out."

Jesus left heaven to welcome us. When will we learn to intentionally reach out to others to welcome them? To stay in our own little cliques is inexcusable. God's Kingdom will never expand unless we have love in our hearts that intentionally reaches out to others.

Lord, help me to be sensitive to new people who come so they feel God's love and respond in worship to him. Amen.

December 14

Times are Desperate But the Church is Not

Matthew 24:11-14

"Lying preachers will come forward and deceive a lot of people. For many others, the overwhelming spread of evil will do them in—nothing left of their love but a mound of ashes. Staying with it—that's what God requires. Stay with it to the end. You won't be sorry, and you'll be saved. All during this time, the good news—the Message of the kingdom—will be preached all over the world, a witness staked out in every country. And then the end will come" (Matthew 24:11-14 Msg).

The church is too often wrestling with internal problems when it needs to be focusing on its main purpose—to seek and save the lost and to make disciples. When this Gospel of the Kingdom is preached to the whole world then the end will come.

Jesus final words to the church were: "The Holy Spirit will come upon you and give you power. Then you will tell everyone about me in Jerusalem, in all Judea, in Samaria, and everywhere in the world" (Acts 1:8 CEV). The Holy Spirit has come which means the power to tell everyone is in us. Let's move out in that power sharing the Good News. "Never be lacking in zeal, but keep your spiritual fervor, serving the Lord" (Romans 12:11 NIV).

Let's hasten the Lord's return by sharing the Good News. Is reaching the lost at the top of our prayer list? Do we spend more time watching ball games on TV than we do building relationships with our unsaved neighbors? Are our church programs focused on the ninety-nine who are in the fold while we neglect the ones outside? Does our church budget and our personal budget reflect the priority of sharing the Good News?

There is more fear in our world today than at any time in history. This should spur us to action. Perfect love for Jesus removes our fear (I John 4:18). Some fear in witnessing is normal, but as we witness in fearfulness we will overcome this fear through the power of the Holy Spirit.

Lord, these are desperate times. Help me to be faithful until the Good News is heard in every nation. Amen.

December 15

When People Don't Return

Luke 14:23

When first-timers don't return to church, people inevitably blame the first-timers. You hear such statements as: "They were looking for a different kind of church," "They haven't been to church for so long. It will take time to develop the habit," "They are not our kind of people," "Their children don't know how to sit still in church," or "Our kind of music is not what they appreciate."

Why not ask ourselves what we can do to make it easier for them to return? (1) Ushers and greeters need to be hospitable, but it is even more impressive when persons who are not official greeters come and extend a warm welcome. They can develop meaningful conversation; introduce them to others and to their pastor. (2) Give them a gift such as a book and literature describing the activities of the church. A coupon for the Christian book store is appropriate. (3) Lead them on a tour of the facility. (4) Take them to the snack bar where they can meet other attenders. (5) Show them the church mailboxes. Take the mail from your own box and give them your mail. (6) Walk them to the car. If possible, provide Sunday lunch either at a restaurant or in your home.

That week the pastor sends a letter thanking them for their participation. It is most appropriate for one of the elders whom they met to give a phone call later in the week. If they do not return the next Sunday or two, send them a weekly program. If they are not present the third Sunday call them again. Thank them for coming and check to see if they found a church or if they are open to returning again to worship with you. (See I Peter 3:14-15.)

Jesus said, "Go out to the roads and country lanes and make them come in, so that my house will be full" (Luke 14:23 NIV). If we are polite and sensitive to where they are concerning their relationship to Jesus and the church they will not be offended. We need to do all we can: "make them come in, so my house will be full."

Father, enable me to be assertive in welcoming those who come to church. Amen.

December 16

Cut Out the Word Impossible

Matthew 19:26

Jesus said, "With man this is impossible, but with God all things are possible" (Matthew 19:26 NIV).

"Jesus looked hard at them and said, 'No chance at all if you think you can pull it off yourself. Every chance in the world if you trust God to do it'" (Matthew 19:26 Msg).

A young ruler ran to Jesus and asked, "What good thing must I do to get eternal life? Jesus responded: "Why do you ask me about what is good?" "Why do you call me good?" "No one is good except God alone. If you want to enter life, obey the commandments" (See vv. 16-17).

The ruler declared that he kept the commandments and asked, "What do I still lack?" (v.20) Jesus replied, "If you want to be perfect, go, sell your possessions and give to the poor, and you will have treasure in heaven. Then come follow me" (v.21).

He went away very sad, because he was a man of great wealth. Jesus said, "How hard it is for the rich to enter the Kingdom of God" (v.23). In fact Jesus explained that it's easier for a camel to go through the eye of a needle than for a rich man to enter the kingdom of God. The disciples responded, who then can be saved? vv.24-25. Then the punch line from Jesus, "With man this is impossible, but with God all things are possible" (v. 26).

With God, all who humble themselves and turn to Christ can be saved no matter how hopeless they seem from our perspective. No matter how terrible our circumstances God will never leave us or abandon us. He will take us through the valley of the shadow of death. (See Psalm 23:4.)

Take the word impossible out of your vocabulary. God has a purpose for your life, find it. Don't focus on what you don't have. Focus on what you have and use it. "Nothing is impossible with God" (Luke 1:37 NLT).

Lord Jesus, thank you that with you all things are possible since I am in you and you are in me. Amen.

December 17

How You Can Help Your Pastor

Ephesians 6:19-20

"Don't forget to pray for me. Pray that I'll know what to say and have the courage to say it at the right time, telling the mystery to one and all, the Message that I, jailbird preacher that I am, am responsible for getting out" (Ephesians 6:19-20 Msg). "Brothers, pray for us" (I Thessalonians 5:25 NIV).

There is always a need for pastors and congregational leaders. How can we help our pastors?

1. Pray. Pray for wisdom, strength and God's grace to rest upon the pastor and his family! Prayer unlocks the devil's grip on people's hearts and the evil forces over our communities.
2. Encourage the pastor to delegate responsibilities.
3. Encourage others in the congregation to step up to the plate in carrying out their ministry.
4. Take training to increase your ministry skills.
5. Be assertive in asking the pastor how you can assist him/her in working under the pastor's direction.
6. Affirm your pastor by verbal and written notes of appreciation. Point out specific things you appreciated in their messages. Affirm and encourage him or her in other appropriate ways.
7. Be a listening ear for the pastor.
8. Be a friend to the pastor's spouse and children.
9. Offer to help him/her with household tasks.
10. Surprise the pastor and family with an occasional gift.

Encourage your pastor to follow Ephesians 4:11-13 Msg, "He handed out gifts of apostle, prophet, evangelist and pastor-teacher to train Christians in skilled servant work, working within Christ's body, the church, until we're all moving rhythmically, and easily with each other, efficient and graceful in response to God's Son, fully mature adults, fully developed within and without, fully alive like Christ." So often in our churches pastors have to do it all. The Scripture makes it clear that others have gifts to help build up the body of Christ.

Father, I pray for our pastor and his family today. I pray for wisdom, for physical strength but more importantly, strength of character. I pray that others will use their gifts along with his/hers so we can grow to maturity. Amen.

December 18

Cultural Things Do Matter

I Corinthians 9:19-22

"I have voluntarily become a servant to any and all in order to reach a wide range of people: religious, nonreligious, meticulous, moralists, loose-living immoralists, the defeated, the demoralized—whoever. I did not take on their way of life. I kept my bearings in Christ—but I entered their world and tried to experience things from their point of view. I've become just about every sort of servant there is in my attempts to lead those I meet into a God-saved life" (I Corinthians 9:19-22 Msg).

Too often community people have no idea what goes on inside the church. They see the church as irrelevant. To be irrelevant is irreverent. It is inexcusable. Jesus gave us the opposite picture of who we are to be: the light that can't be hid and the salt that changes the flavor of the community. (See Matthew 5:14-16.)

When I ask congregations what the main purpose of the church is they usually respond by saying, "worship and fellowship." The main purpose of the church is the same purpose Jesus had, namely, to seek and save the lost. (See Luke 19:1). The main purpose of the church is to fulfill the Great Commission. (See Matthew 28:18-20.)

How do we build bridges to our communities? Some examples are: (1) we participate in the community activities: sports teams, school programs, hosting block parties, etc. (2) We become servants to the communities: feeding the hungry and helping to meet needs of the less fortunate, providing after school programs, or volunteering in the hospital and schools. (3) We try to fit in culturally by maintaining a neat and clean property.

Jesus fit in with the culture by how he dressed. On different occasions he slipped through the crowd. He was able to do this because his attire was no different from theirs. If the culture is casual dress, we wear casual dress rather than a suit and tie. If we live in a community where everyone has a late model car, it is helpful to have a car that is not ready for the junk yard. It's important to be conscious of the culture so as to build bridges to the unchurched.

Lord, help me to relate well with the unchurched so I can be an effective witness for you. Amen.

December 19

Lord Teach Me to Pray

Luke 12:2-4

"One of his disciples said, 'Master teach us to pray'…So he said, 'When you pray, say, Father, Reveal who you are, Set the world right. Keep us alive with three square meals. Keep us forgiven with you and forgiving others. Keep us safe from ourselves and the Devil'" (Luke 11:2-4 Msg).

Eight different times Luke refers to Jesus praying. If prayer is that important for Jesus, God's Son, how much more do we need Jesus to teach us to pray?

Jesus' pattern begins with praise and is followed by requests. We call God "Father." God is majestic and transcendent yet loving and intimate. We pray for his name to be revealed and honored in our lives and in our world. We pray for his rule in our world. We are also praying for more and more people to enter God's kingdom. It is a missional prayer. It is a prayer for evil to be overcome and destroyed. It is a prayer for heaven to invade earth. We pray for personal needs. Bread can be both physical and spiritual. We must depend on God for both. We depend on him for each day's needs. When we think we have all our needs met for the future we tend to neglect our relations with God.

Forgiveness is always necessary because we are not perfect. Just as God forgives us we must forgive others. If we are not forgiving it is obvious that we do not understand how badly we need God's forgiveness.

We pray for God not to lead us into temptation. (v.4 NIV). The Greek word for "temptation" means to test or entice us. God never tempts us. (See James 1:13). "The Lord's Prayer affirms the will of God ('your will be done'), then asks for relief and delivery from trials. In the garden, Jesus asked the Father to remove the cup of trial while immediately declaring his willingness to cooperate with his Father's will. …This sentence… is a reminder of the importance of testing, even though believers seldom desire it. Jesus, fully knowing that the Father will do what is best, both taught and modeled a freedom in prayer that dared to ask almost anything." [v]

Lord, teach me to pray. Amen.

December 20

Persistence in Prayer

Luke 11:9-13

Jesus said, "I say to you, Ask and keep on asking, and it shall be given to you; seek and keep on seeking and you shall find; knock and keep on knocking, and the door shall be opened to you. For everyone who asks and keeps on asking receives, and he who seeks and keeps on seeking finds, and to him who knocks and keeps on knocking the door shall be opened....If you then, evil-minded as you are, know how to give good gifts... to your children, how much more will your heavenly Father give the Holy Spirit to those who ask and continue to ask him!" (Luke 11:9-13 AMP).

Persistence is an indication of faith. If you are to do great things for God you must persist. When your prayers are not answered in the way you desire God wants you to continue to cry out to Jesus. "Anyone who comes to him must believe that he exists and that he rewards those who earnestly seek him" (Hebrews 11:6 NIV). "You will seek me and find me when you seek me with all your heart" (Jeremiah 29:13 NIV). Sometimes God does not answer our prayers as we desire. But if we are praying according to God's will we will receive his best.

Pet dogs, when their master is eating, sit by their master waiting for food. As we stare in the face of God day after day, diligently seeking his will and his power to carry out the great commission, God will answer.

Jesus told a parable of the persistent widow who came to the judge. The judge finally gave her what she asked for. Jesus concludes that God will surely answer those who cry out for him day and night. Then he asks: "When the Son of Man comes, will he find faith on the earth?" (See Luke 18:7-8 NIV). The challenge for you and me is to persist in faith even when we don't understand what God is doing. He has bigger things in mind than the answer to our immediate prayer.

Lord, enable me to persist in prayer for your Kingdom to come more fully into my life and in the lives of others. Amen.

December 21

Dead Church

Revelation 3:1-3

"I see right through your work. You have a reputation for vigor and zest, but you're dead, stone dead. Up on your feet! Take a deep breath! Maybe there's life in you yet. But I wouldn't know it, by looking at your busywork; nothing of God's work has been completed. Your condition is desperate. Think of the gift you once had in your hands, the Message you heard with your ears—grasp it again and turn back to God" (Revelation 3:1-3 Msg).

Some churches are busy but dead. There is no fruit. Activities are focused inward. When our knowledge of God's truth no longer translates into our life we die. We need to stir up ourselves and overcome our fears.

"I remind you to fan into flame the gift of God, which is in you through the laying on of my hands" (II Timothy 1:6-7 NIV). The *Amplified Bible* talks about rekindling the embers, fanning the flame and keeping the inner fire burning (v.6). We do this by sincerely praying the prayer I have used several times in these readings: "Father give me your passion—the passion of giving your only Son for this lost world, Jesus give me your passion—the passion you had when you died on the cross for this lost world. Holy Spirit give me your passion –the passion you have in leaving heaven in all its splendor and coming to dwell in sinful humanity, now made holy by your work.

"For God did not give us a spirit of timidity—of cowardice, of craven and cringing and fawning fear—but [He has given us a spirit] of power and of love and of calm and well-balanced mind and discipline and self-control" (v. 7 AMP). Claim this verse as you enter your day. Claim this verse every time you meet another person who does not know Jesus.

Living out these two verses will transform your church and your witness from death to life, from busywork to fruitful work that remains.

Lord, enable me to stir into flame the gifts you have given me—to move from fear to power, from death to life. Amen.

December 22

The Son Reveals the Father

Luke 10:22

"No one knows who the Son is except the Father, and no one knows who the Father is except the Son and those to whom the Son chooses to reveal him" (Luke 10:22 NIV).

The good news is that Jesus has chosen to reveal the Father to us. "Anyone who has seen me has seen the Father" (John 14:9 NIV). We come to the Father through Jesus (see John 14:6). Jesus reminds us: "You did not choose me, but I chose you and appointed you to go and bear fruit –fruit that will last. The Father will give you whatever you ask in my name" (John 15:16 NIV). Since he appointed us to bear fruit we can ask the Father and he will respond to our prayers.

What wonderful truths! Jesus reveals the Father to us. We come directly to the Father. (See Matthew 6:9.) The Father answers our prayers. (See John 16:26-27.) I am justified—given a right standing with God—through faith. (See Romans 5:1.) Jesus intercedes for us. (See Romans 8:34.) The Spirit intercedes for us. (See Romans 8:27.) We are God's children. (See Romans 6:16.) Jesus is our brother. (See Hebrews 1:11-12.) We receive the same inheritance Jesus receives. (See Romans 8:17.) I am a friend of Jesus. (See John 15:14.) I am united with Jesus and one with him in spirit. (See I Corinthians 6:17.) I am a member of Christ's body. (See I Corinthians 12:27.) I am complete in Christ. (See Colossians 2:9-10.)

Let me continue: I have been translated from the dominion of darkness and transferred into the kingdom of Jesus Christ and I have been redeemed and forgiven of all my sins. (See Colossians 1:13-14.) I have direct access to the throne of grace through Jesus Christ. (See Hebrews 4:14-16.) I am free from condemnation and cannot be separated from God's love. (See Romans 8:1 and 31-39.) I am confident that God will complete the good work He started in me. (See Philippians 1:6.) I have been born of God and the evil one cannot touch me. (See I John 5:18.) I am secure. (See John 10:28.) I am a citizen of heaven. (See Philippians 3:20.) I can do all things through Christ. (See Philippians 4:13.) I am his minister and ambassador. (See II Corinthians 5:17-21.)

Father, your promises are beyond my comprehension. Enable me to make each one a reality in my life. Amen.

December 23

Living For Others

I Corinthians 10:32-33

"So whether you eat or drink or whatever you do, do it all for the glory of God. Do not cause anyone to stumble, whether Jews, Greeks or the church of God—even as I try to please everybody in every way. For I am not seeking my own good but the good of many, so that they may be saved" (I Corinthians 10:32-33 NIV).

Paul lives to glorify God in everything. He is not seeking his glory but God's. Why does he do this? So people may be saved. Paul was always conscious that the unsaved were watching him. I try to silently pray for wisdom as I meet people. I want to say and do only what the Lord wants me to say and do so they can be saved. That was the purpose of Jesus' life and it must be our purpose.

Paul writing to the Christians in Thessalonica says: "Make it your ambition to lead a quiet life, to mind your own business and to work with your hands, just as we told you, so that your daily life may win the respect of outsiders" (I Thessalonians 4:12 NIV). Our daily life's work needs to be above reproach as a witness to those who do not know Jesus.

Paul again writes: "Teach slaves to be subject to their masters in everything, to try to please them, not to talk back to them, and not to steal from them, but to show that they can be fully trusted, so that in every way they will make the teaching about God our Savior attractive" (Titus 2:9-10 NIV). We make Jesus attractive by how we live so that people will want to become a follower of Jesus.

Paul had a clear purpose for living: to glorify God and call people to salvation in Christ. His purpose must become our purpose if God's Kingdom is to expand in our local communities.

Lord Jesus, help me to live faithfully obeying you in everything at home, at work and in my community so others will be attracted to you and become your child. Amen.

December 24

Choked Messages

Mark 4:7,18-20

"Other seed fell among thorns, which grew up and choked the plants, so that they did not bear grain" (Mark 4:7 NIV).

Many Christians find the pastor's message meaningful the moment they hear it, but by Wednesday studies indicate they forget at least 95% of what they heard. How much of the 5% we remember do we put into action? Suppose we had one Sunday a month when we hear the message, the next Sunday we process the message, the third Sunday we apply the message to our lives, and then the fourth Sunday we report how we applied it? We would move from infancy to maturity more rapidly than our present church structure seems to allow.

In this parable Jesus pictured four kinds of soil. Many Christians are in group three which is good soil but thorns choke out the crop. Jesus explained this in vv. 18-19. These hear and accept the message but it is choked out by the worries of this life, the deceitfulness of wealth and the desire for other things.

(1) Are the worries of this life causing us to be unfruitful? Faith and worry can't exist together.
(2) Are we preoccupied with all the things we want to acquire? Are we over concerned about having enough money for tomorrow? "Godliness with contentment is great gain" (I Timothy 6:6 NIV).
(3) Are we full of selfish desires?

These three fruit robbers are with us every day. When you catch yourself worrying confess your sin of worry. Ask God to forgive you and give you faith. "Cast all your anxiety on him because he cares for you" (I Peter 5:7 NIV). When your mind is focused continually on gaining more wealth confess the sin of covetousness and focus on your blessings. When you have selfish desires pray for grace to love the Lord with all your heart, soul, mind and strength.

If we, by the Spirit's power, remove these three thorns we will reap a huge harvest of thirty, sixty or even a hundred fold (v.20).

Lord, these thorns are too often in my life. I confess I need your power to remove them so I can reap a harvest pleasing to you. Amen.

December 25 (Christmas Day)

Good Tidings of Great Joy

Luke 2

"The angel of the Lord appeared to them (the shepherds), and the glory of the Lord shone around them, and they were terrified. But the angel said to them, 'Do not be afraid. I bring you good news of great joy that will be for all the people. Today in the town of David a Savior has been born to you; he is Christ the Lord'" (Luke 2:8-11 NIV).

The *Message* Bible reports that the angel announces a great and joyful event that is meant for everybody, worldwide: A Savior has just been born...a Savior who is Messiah and Master. (v.11)

What a wonderful privilege and obligation we have to spread "Good tidings of great joy" this Christmas! The Savior, Jesus, is born in the hearts of more and more people each day. Consider these statistics from: http://christianity-about.com/od/denominatons/p/christiantoday.htm. In the unevangelized world, there are 20,500 full-time Christian workers and 10,500 foreign missionaries. In the evangelized non-Christian world there are 1.31 million full-time Christian workers. In the Christian world, there are 306,000 foreign missionaries to other Christian lands. Also in the Christian world, 4.19 million full-time Christian workers (95%) work within the Christian world.

Approximately 83 million Bibles are distributed globally per year. There are approximately 6 million books about Christianity in print today. And the most impressive statistic is that 171,000 Christians worldwide are martyred for their faith per year. This Christmas pray earnestly for the families and churches of those who were martyred. Pray for God to make them strong in their faith. Pray for their physical needs to be supplied. Pray that those who took their lives will be convicted of their sin and come to Jesus for forgiveness and transformation.

Pray that our home congregations will be zealous so the Gospel can go to the ends of the earth. Jesus says, "Because of the increase of wickedness, the love of most will grow cold. But he who stands firm to the end will be saved. And this gospel of the kingdom will be preached in the whole world as a testimony to all nations, and then the end will come" (Matthew 24:12-14 NIV.)

Lord Jesus, this Christmas day may I appreciate your birth, life and death enough to share this good news with others. Amen.

December 26

Solomon's Prayer

I Kings 8:59-60

Solomon prays that God will meet each day's need, "So that all the people of the earth may know that the Lord is God and that there is no other" (I Kings 8:59-60 Msg).

"Honor the prayers of the foreigner so that people all over the world will know who you are and what you're like and will live in reverent obedience before you just as your own people Israel do; so they'll know that you personally make this Temple that I've built what it is" (I Kings 8:43 Msg).

Solomon's prayer is humble as, on his knees, he asks for the Lord to meet each day's needs. His passion comes through in the use of exclusive language concerning Jehovah God. "The Lord is God and there is no other." He is missional as he entreats God for "all the people of the earth" (v.60) and "all people all over the world" (v.43). His sincerity is indicated by his sacrificing a hundred and twenty thousand sheep, and twenty-two thousand cattle (v. 63).

He emphasizes obedience (v.43). His honesty is remarkable as he confesses their sin and recognizes God's inevitable punishment for their sin entreating God for his forgiveness. "When they sin against you—and they certainly will; there's not one without sin!—and in anger you turn them over to the enemy and they are taken captive to the enemy's land, whether far or near, but repent in the country of their captivity and pray with changed hearts in their exile, 'We've sinned; we've done wrong; we've been more wicked,' and turn back to you heart and soul in the land of the enemy who conquered them, and pray to you toward their homeland,... Listen from your home in heaven to their prayers desperate and devout and do what is best for them. Forgive your people..." (I Kings 8:46-50 Msg).

His prayer is bold but humble. It gives God his rightful place. It is missional. It is passionate.

Lord Jesus, thank you for this model prayer of Solomon. Teach me how to pray as Solomon prayed. Amen.

December 27

Taking Inventory

Galatians 5:22-23

"What happens when we live God's way? He brings gifts into our lives, much the same way that fruit appears in an orchard—things like affection for others, exuberance about life, serenity. We develop a willingness to stick with things, a sense of compassion in the heart, and a conviction that a basic holiness permeates things and people. We find ourselves involved in loyal commitments, not needing to force our way in life, able to marshal and direct our energies wisely" (Galatians 5:22-23 Msg). Most versions list the fruit of the Spirit as love, joy, peace, patience, kindness, goodness, faithfulness, gentleness and self-control. Let's compare these with the Message Bible translation and ask ourselves these questions:

Love: Do I have affection for others? Jesus commands us to love others as we love ourselves. (See Matthew 22:39).

Joy: Am I exuberant about life? Paul reminds us to be joyful and to rejoice in the Lord always. (See I Thessalonians 5:16 and Philippians 4:8).

Peace: Do I radiate serenity. Peter reminds us to cast all our anxiety and care on Jesus. (See I Peter 5:7).

Patience: Am I willing to stick with things or do I become irritable and angry? Philippians 2:14 reminds us to do all things without bickering or arguing.

Kindness: Do I posses a compassionate heart?

Goodness: Do I have a conviction that a basic holiness permeates people. Everyone is created in the image of God. (See Genesis 1:27).

Faithfulness: Am I trustworthy and loyal? Do I keep my word?

Gentleness: Can I work along with those who think differently or do I insist on having my way?

Self-Control: Am I able to marshal and direct my energies wisely.

Choose one or two that you need to develop and then pray: *Lord Jesus, it is only by your Spirit that I can live as you desire. Enable me to walk in the Spirit's power to please you in all things. Amen.*

December 28

Now!

Ephesians 2:12-22

"Remember… you were separate from Christ…, without hope and without God in the world. But now in Christ Jesus you who once were far away have been brought near, through the blood of Christ. For he himself is our peace, who has made the two one and has destroyed the barrier, the dividing wall of hostility, by abolishing in his flesh the law with its commandments and regulations. His purpose was to create in himself one new man out of the two, thus making peace, and in this one body to reconcile both of them to God through the cross, by which he put to death their hostility. He came and preached peace to you who were far away and peace to those who were near. For through him we both have access to the Father by one Spirit" (Ephesians 2:12-18 NIV).

Before we were Christians we were without hope and without God in the world. But NOW through Jesus' blood we are brought into God's family. The walls of hostility are gone. Take the walls down between you and your extended family. Remove the walls that divide your church members, remove the walls between you and Christians who don't agree with you, between you and your unfriendly neighbor, between you and the enemies of our nation.

"If it is possible, as far as it depends on you, live at peace with everyone. Do not take revenge…'It is mine to avenge, I will repay,' says the Lord. On the contrary, 'If your enemy is hungry, feed him; if he is thirsty, give him something to drink… Do not be overcome with evil, but overcome evil with good" (Romans 12:18-21 NIV).

Jesus said, "Blessed are the peacemakers" (Matthew 5:9 NIV). "Peacemakers" remove walls. "Peacekeepers" may keep the walls but we are to be proactive and remove walls. Jesus again says, "If you enter your place of worship and… remember a grudge a friend has against you, abandon your offering, leave immediately, go to this friend and make things right. Then… come back and work things out with God" (Matthew 5:23-24 Msg).

Lord, enable me to remove walls in my family, in my workplace, in my church and in my community. Amen.

December 29

Can't Keep Quiet

II Corinthians 4:12-15

"We are not keeping this quiet, not on your life, just like the psalmist who wrote, 'I believed it, so I said it,' we say what we believe. And what we believe is that the One who raised up the Master Jesus will just as certainly raise us up with you, alive. Every detail works to your advantage and to God's glory: more and more grace, more and more people, more and more praise!" (II Corinthians 4:13-15 Msg).

The message of the Gospel is so vital that it demands an evangelistic declaration. We can't keep it quiet. The more trials Paul had the more Jesus shone through him. His opposition and persecution rather than deterring him, embolden him. He understands that God's grace working through his hardships brings more and more people to Jesus.

The cost of communicating the Good News for Paul is expressed in verse 12, "Our lives are in constant risk for Jesus' sake, which makes Jesus' life all the more evident in us. While we're going through the worst, you're getting in on the best!" Is Christ and his life being expressed through you?

Our lives must be like a rug. We lay our lives down for people so they find comfort and help in Jesus. We must say "no" to every demand that our flesh makes for recognition, approval, or vindication. There is no way the light of Jesus can shine through us if we haven't been to the cross.

Jesus said, "If any of you want to be my follower, you must put aside your selfish ambition, shoulder your cross daily, and follow me" (Luke 9:23 NLT).

The principle of the world is "self-glorification," and the principle of the Christian is "self-crucifixion." The principle of men is greatness, pomp, and show; the principle of the cross is death. If we are to be a channel of Christ's light then there must be a constant submission to the cross.

Lord, I come to the cross and lay my life down. Cleanse me from every sin. Make me bold to speak and live for you. Amen.

December 30

Heal Our Land

II Chronicles 7:14

"If my people, who are called by my name, will humble themselves and pray and seek my face and turn from their wicked ways, then will I hear from heaven, and will forgive their sin and will heal their land" (II Chronicles 7:14 NIV).

God asks four things of his people: (1) humility, (2) prayer, (3) seeking his face, and (4) turning from their wicked ways. Then he will respond: (1) He will hear from heaven, (2) forgive their sin, and (3) heal their land.

Are you and I humbling ourselves before the Lord? Are we saying an unconditional "Yes" to Jesus in every area of our lives? If there is one "little" area where we have not given over to the Lordship of Jesus he is not Lord and we are not walking in the power of the Spirit.

Are you and I praying people? Ask the Lord to send a spirit of prayer into your life. (See Zechariah 12:10). Ask him to teach you how to pray. Until we make prayer a priority in our lives and in our churches we will be ineffective and fruitless. Paul writes, "Prayer is essential in this ongoing warfare. Pray hard and long. Pray for your brothers and sisters. Keep your eyes open. Keep each other's spirits up so that no one falls behind or drops out" (Ephesians 6:18 Msg).

Are we seeking his face? The Amplified Bible translates "seek my face" as: "crave and require of necessity my face." David writes: "As the deer pants for streams of water, so my soul pants for you, O God. My soul thirsts for God, for the living God" (Psalm 42:1-2 NIV).

Are we turning from our wicked ways? Have we said "no" to the world and the acts of the sinful nature? (See Galatians 5:19-21).

When we do this God has promised to (1) hear from heaven, (2) forgive our sin, and (3) heal our land.

Lord God, our land needs healing. We are so far from you. Forgive our sin. Give us grace and strength to cast aside our selfish and sinful ways. Come into my life with the fullness of your Holy Spirit and use me to be an instrument of healing in our land. Amen.

December 31

Sharing Jesus Without Fear

I Corinthians 2:3-5

"I...felt totally inadequate—I was scared to death, if you want the truth of it—and so nothing I said could have impressed you or anyone else. But the Message came through anyway. God's Spirit and God's power did it, which made it clear that your life of faith is a response to God's power, not to some fancy mental or emotional footwork by me or anyone else" (I Corinthians 2:3-5 Msg).

The Great Commission is a command to Christians to obey, not an option for our consideration. James 4:17 NIV reminds us that, "Anyone...who knows the good he ought to do and doesn't do it, sins." If we have not been sharing our faith we are guilty of the sin of silence.

It's a privilege and a joy to share our faith. After all, the Gospel is Good News. All we are called to do is share it. We can't bring a person to faith, that's the Holy Spirit's work. Jesus promised to be with us. (See Matthew 28:20.) Are we afraid of not knowing enough? If so, share your testimony. People can't argue about what you know is true in your experience. If they reject you, Jesus says they are rejecting him. Don't fear rejection.

Pray for God's love to come through you. Enlist the help of brothers and sisters to pray for the Holy Spirit to give you words you can share and expect God to answer. Jesus used a different approach for everyone he met. The following approach may help you get started.

Some questions can help you move a conversation toward spiritual concerns:

1.Do you believe in God? 2. Who is Jesus to you? 3. Do you think there is life after death? 4. The Bible says that we will die and after death we face the judgment of God. God loves you so much that he gave his Son Jesus to die on the cross to pay for our sin. Are you ready to accept the gift of eternal life that Jesus gives to everyone who trusts in him.

Father, I confess I do have fear in sharing Jesus. Forgive me and empower me to be bold for you. Thank you. Amen.

Endnotes

[i] Myer, Everett. *Coming to Jesus For Life* (Lulu.com.), p. 15.

[ii] Kroll, Woodrow. *Taking Back the Good Book* (Wheaton, Ill.), p. 90.

[iii] Chambers, Oswald. *My Utmost for his Highest* (Oswald Chambers Publication, April 24, 1992).

[iv] Chambers, Oswald. *My Utmost for His Highest.* (May 16).

[v] Montgomery, Jim. "I'm Gonna Let It Shine," p. 147.

[vi] Scott, John. "The Living God is a Missionary God," Quoted in *Crossman, Perspectives Exposure*, p. 14.

[vii] Yun, Brother. *Living Water* (Zondervan, 2008), pp.42-43.

[viii] Hattaway, Paul. *Back to Jerusalem* (Waynesboro, Ga.: Gabriel Pub., 2003), p. 68.

[ix] Meyer, Joyce, *The Confident Woman* (N.Y., N.Y.: Warner Faith, 2006), pp. 23-24. From "The Journal of John Wesley," www.ccel.org/ccel/wesley/journal.toc.html.

[x] Carmichael, Ralph, *The New Church Hymnal* (Lexicon Music, Inc., 1976), p. 74.

[xi] *Life Application Bible* (Grand Rapids, Mich.: Zondervan Pub., 1991). Notes of Matthew 5:13-16.

[xii] www.cfointernational.org/pdf/TheGame_Minutes.pdf.

[xiii] "Go, Labor On," by Horatius Bonar, 1843, music by Lowell Mason, 1850. *The Mennonite Hymnal* (Scottdale, Pa.: Herald Press, 1969), #431.

[xiv] Montgomery, Jim. *I'm Gonna Let it Shine!* (Colorado Springs, Colo.: Dawn Ministries, 2001), pp. 28-30.

[xv] *The New Church Hymnal* (Lexicon Music, Inc., 1976), p. 302.

[xvi] Thomas, Gary. *Sacred Pathways* (Zondervan, 1996), p.18.

[xvii] Ibid., p. 9.

[xviii] Warren, Rick, *The Purpose Driven Church* (Zondervan, 1995). pp. 20-21.

[xix] Chambers, Oswald. *My Utmost for His Highest* (Grand Rapids, Mich.: Discovery House, 1992), January 14.

[xx] Chambers, Oswald. *My Utmost for His Highest (*Oswald Chambers Pub., 1992), May 27.

References

[i] Yohn, Rick. *Discover Your Spiritual Gift and Use it* (Wheaton, Ill.: Tyundale House Publishing, 1974).

[ii] Stezter and Putman, *Breaking the Missional Code* (Nashville, Tenn.: Broadman and Holman Publishers, 2006), p.51.

[iii] Adopted from Noah Kaye's blog. Pastor noah@blogspot.com Sept. 9, 2009.

[iv] Much of this reading was adapted from Rick Warren's *The Purpose Driven Life*, chapter 38. (Zondervan, 2002).

[v] *Life Application Bible Commentary, Luke* (Wheaton, Ill.: Tyndale House), p. 290.

Scripture Index
For Living With Godly Passion

Genesis
- 1:27 = 12/27
- 2:2-3 = 9/30
- 2:15 = 9/30
- 2:18 = 7/23
- 5:24 = 4/6
- 6:1-3 = 4/6
- 6 = 6/4
- 12:3 = 2/19
- 18:25-26 = 1/17, 11/5
- 18:32 = 1/28
- 22 = 8/12
- 22:17 = 1/17
- 32 = 5/8
- 37:5-11 = 11/3
- 37:28 = 12/9
- 41:4 = 9/13

Exodus
- 3:11 = 4/20
- 4:10-13 = 4/20
- 6:12 = 4/20
- 7-8 = 8/13
- 18:17-27 = 9/13
- 20:1 = 4/27
- 27:20 = 5/12
- 31:1-11 = 9/24
- 35:30-35 = 9/25
- 32:32 = 1/31

Numbers
- 6:25-26 = 2/18

Deuteronomy
- 1:22 = 10/1
- 5:15 = 10/9
- 6:1-9 = 10/19, 11/8
- 6:4 = 6/8
- 10:18-19 = 2/26

Judges
- 6:12-15,34 = 11/19
- 11 = 11/21

I Samuel
- 17:37 = 12/9

II Samuel
- 12:19 = 8/4

I Kings
- 3:16-28 = 9/4
- 4:32 = 9/25
- 8:43-60 = 12/26
- 19:4,10-12 = 4/20, 8/10

II Kings
- 6 = 4/18
- 6:16-17 = 8/22
- 7:3-10 = 4/16
- 19:35 = 1/28

I Chronicles
- 15:19 = 9/25
- 16:11 = 4/28
- 21 = 3/1

II Chronicles
- 7:6 = 9/25
- 7:14 = 12/30
- 29:26-30 = 9/25
- 34:12 = 9/25

Ezra
- 3 = 5/9

Nehemiah
- 8;10 = 8/18
- 8:19 = 1/11

Esther
- 4:14 = 4/13

Job
- 13:15 = 3/16
- 31:1 = 7/24

Psalm
- 2:8 = 1/16, 8/24
- 6 = 8/15
- 6:6-7 = 1/12
- 9:18 = 11/18
- 16:5 = 2/21
- 16:8-11 = 1/3, 2/11, 4/17, 5/19, 8/18
- 18:29 = 1/12
- 22:3, 6 = 5/19, 10/27

23 = 1/6, 11/18
23:1 = 6/13, 8/7
24:1 = 6:14
25:3 = 11/18
27:1 = 12/4
27:4 = 2/21
32:8 = 6/22
34 = 8/15
34:1 = 9/25
34:7 = 8/14
37:4-6 = 7/1, 12/9
37:23-24 = 5/17, 10/2, 12/9
39:5 = 6:15
42:1-2 = 1/4, 22/27, 12/30
42:3 = 9/25
42:25 = 1/12
46:10 = 10/3
53:2-3 = 5/12
56:3 = 5/26
56:8 = 1/17, 4/23
67 = 10/21
67:2 = 10/15
71:2 = 1/12
71:5,8,17-18,24 = 10/19
73:15 = 2/21
77 = 2/2
78:2-8 = 10/19
85:1 = 1/12
90:12 = 1/26, 6/15
91:11-12 = 8/14
92:14-15 = 1/26
103:7 = 4/11
106:43 = 10/13
111 = 2/2
119:20 = 1/5, 2/2, 9/25
119:33 = 10/13
119:37 = 1/6
119:39 = 2/2, 2/21
119:40 = 9/25
119:43 = 11/18
119:55 = 7/17
119:81 = 9/25
119:97-100 = 1/5
119:105 = 1/5, 12/9
119:111 = 2/2
126:5-6 = 4/23
127:1 = 6/12
131 = 2/2

134:1 = 10/27
139: 1-18 = 11/5
139:1-4 = 1/17, 4/13
139:13 = 4/26
139:23-24 = 2/18, 7/12,
    7/17, 8/4, 12/12
139:7 = 1/9
140:13 = 5/19
146:8 = 2/6
147:4 = 1/17
150 = 10/27

Proverbs
11:14 = 12/9
17:17 = 1/8
16:18 = 3/1
18:24 = 1/8
19:27 = 2/2
21:23 = 5/15
23:4 = 12/16
23:7 = 12/12
24:14 = 2/2
25:12 = 10/13
28:1 = 6/28, 10/12
29:18 = 4/8

Ecclesiastes
11:4 = 5/26

Isaiah
6 = 5/25
11:6 = 2/24
12:2 = 5/26
29:13 = 8/7
35:5 = 2/6
35:7 = 7/1
40:29-31 = 11/1
42:9 = 11/16
49:10 = 11/27
55:1-2 = 3/29
55:8-9 = 1/17
58 = 8/17
61:1-2 = 2/16, 4/29
61:10 = 4/30, 6/5

Jeremiah
5:1-2 = 1/28, 5/12
17:9 = 2/10, 3/1, 7/16, 8/4
19:23 = 2/18
29:13-14 = 1/4, 1/9, 2/18,
    5/25, 12/20
32:20 = 9/28

Lamentations
  3:23 = 1/9
  3:19-27 = 2/11 3/27
Ezekiel
  3:17-20 = 8/27
Daniel
  1-12 = 5/12
  6:22 = 8/14
  9 = 9/19
  11:33-35 = 10/8
  12:3 = 12/4
Jonah
  1:1 = 7/21
  1:2-3 = 3/21
  1:5 = 7/19
  1/12-14 = 7/20
  4:1-2 = 7/21
Micah
  7:2 = 5/12
Habakkuk
  3:17-19 = 1/30, 6/1,
Zechariah
  4:6 = 2/27, 11/19
  8:16-17 = 8/4
  12:10 = 7/22, 12/30

Malachi
  4:5-6 = 6/19
Matthew
  1:21 = 1/23, 4/26
  4:18-22 = 7/3
  4:19 = 5/22, 10/5, 11/7
  5:3 = 5/8, 7/24
  5:3-12 = 4/27
  5:6 = 4/29, 6/5, 11/27
  5:7 = 9/15
  5:8 = 5/21, 7/16
  5:9 = 12/28
  5:10-12 = 1/3, 7/13
  5:13-16 = 4/8, 4/19, 5/13,
      8/17, 8/28, 11/9, 12/4,
      12/18
  5:17 = 1/20
  5:20 = 6/5
  5:23-25 = 9/9, 12/28
  5:36 = 2/27
  5:44 = 7/22
  6:10 = 2/12, 6:14,

6:9-15 = 6/18, 9/19, 11/17
6:22-23 = 7/24
6:25-34 = 4/14, 6/13
6:33 = 2/21
7:1-6 = 8/20, 12/8
7:17-20 = 3/15
7:21-23 = 8/13
8:12 = 5/11
9:9-13 = 10/30
9:16-17 = 8/2, 11/16
9:29 = 1/17, 8/6
9:35-36 = 1/23, 2/1, 3/10,
    10/5, 10/29
9:36-38 = 7/7, 10/16
10:1 = 3/25
10:2-4 = 11/17
10:11-13 = 5/31, 5/13,
10:30 = 1/17
10:40-42 = 1/19, 4/15,
    4/12, 5/23
11:11 = 1/10, 12/5
11:22 = 3/24
11:288-29 = 5/2, 11/27
12:34-35 = 12/12
13:9 = 4/22
13:13-25 = 7/31
13:42,50 = 5/11
14:31 = 2/12
15:18-20 = 7/16
16:15-18 = 1/18, 4/28, 5/24
16:24-25 = 3/14, 6/11, 8/9
17:17 = 2/12, 3/15,
18:4-5 = 3/15
18:9 = 7/24
18:10 = 8/14
18:12-14 = 10/10, 12/3
18:23-35 = 3/7
19:5 = 11/26
19:7 = 7/22
19:20-26 = 12/16
20:28 = 5/6, 6/9
22:10 = 1/13, 8/20
22:14 = 4/20, 5/25
22:25-26 = 8/19
22:33-39 = 7/21, 12/27
22:37-39 = 1/20, 3/24, 4/17,
    5/1, 5/2, 5/29, 7/29,
    10/24

23 = 2/14, 5/2, 7/10
23:5 = 7/10
23:13-14 = 7/20
23:25 = 7/16
24:11-14 = 4/21, 12/14, 12/25
24:14 = 10/15
24:24 = 8/13
25:14-30 = 7/8
25:36-40 = 1/19, 4/30, 9/17, 10/8, 10/31
25:41 = 5/11
26:37-38 = 1/12
28:18-20 = 1/7, 1/15, 2/3, 3/12, 3/16, 3/20, 3/21, 3/23, 4/2, 7/8, 12/7, 12/18, 12/31

Mark
1:38 = 1/23
2:1-12 = 3/2, 5:20,
2:3 = 3/3
2:4 = 3/4
2:5 = 12/6
2:12 = 2/28
2:15-27 = 11/26
2:17 = 5/31
2:15-16 = 7/4
3:17 = 1/25
3:20 = 5/2
3:33-35 = 1/8
4:3-5 = 3/3
4 = 5/31
5 = 11/23
5 = 5/13
6:3 = 9/24
6:4-7 = 3/25, 8/6, 9/27
7:33 = 9/27
8:20 = 2/25
9:1 = 12/18
9:30-31 = 5/1
10:45 = 2/20, 9/7
11:19 = 4/24
11:22-25 = 2/12, 5/28, 9/18
11:27 = 2/4
12:30 = 2/10
12:43-44 = 9/10
13:32 = 3/17
14:3-9 = 9/11

Luke
1:1-4 = 9/2
1:37-38 = 3/31, 12/16
2 = 12/25
2:10 = 22/24
3:23 = 1/25, 9/24
4 = 7/21
4:1-14 = 4/30
4:1-2 = 3/25, 7/9
4:7,18-20 = 12/24
4:14 = 3/25, 7/9
4:18-19 = 1/6, 2/16, 4/18, 4/30
4:24-29 = 7/13
4:32 = 2/16
4:42 = 9/19
5:13 = 7/29
5:16-17 = 3/25, 7/9, 9/19
5:27 = 7/1
5:28-29 = 6/26, 7/22
6:12 = 5/2, 9/19
6:32 = 5/3
7:9 = 8/6
8:24-25 = 2/12
9:23-26 = 5/8, 11/13, 11/17, 12/29
9:48 = 1/19
9:62 = 10/17
10:1-12 = 2/24
10:2-4 = 2/23, 2/26, 3/16, 8/24, 11/4
10:5-6 = 2/25
10:8-10 = 2/22, 9/27
10:16 = 1/19, 4/15, 6/30
10:17-20 = 1/3, 1/7, 2/23, 2/27, 2/28, 5/26
10:22-24 = 1/10, 12/22
10:25-37 = 9/15
10:33 = 7/22
10:38-42 = 3/9, 4/11, 10/24
11:2-4 = 12/19
11:9-13 = 2/14, 3/5, 8/23, 12/20
11:34 = 1/6
13:3-5 = 1/28
13:34-35 = 1/23
14:23 = 5/2, 6/11, 6/30, 7/3, 11/7, 12/15
14:33 = 6/11,

14:26 = 2/21
14:23 = 2/8
15:1 = 11/26
15:3-24 = 1/1, 3/27
15:5-7 = 1/31, 10/14
15:17-20 = 7/22, /25
16:22-31 = 5/27, 7/26
17:21 = 2/22
18:1-8 = 5/28
18:22 = 8/30
19:1-10 = 6/18, 10/30, 12/18
19:10 = 1/16, 1/23, 2/3, 2/15,
    7/8, 11/26
19:41 = 1/23, 10/16
19:45 = 5/2
22:19 = 10/9
23:50 = 9/10

John

1:9 = 5/25
1:23 = 11/20
1:40-41 = 6/30
1:45-46 8/2
1:47-49 = 8/4, 9/3
3:5 = 6/8, 10/18
3:8 = 1/20
3:16-17 = 1/19, 1/23, 3/6, 6:10,
    10/21, 11/26, 12/5
3:27 = 2/13
3:30 = 6/2
4 = 2/25, 5/13, 7/4, 10/30
4:3-7 = 5/2, 5/31, 10/21, 10/26
4:9-10 = 1/29, 11/15
4:13-14 = 11/27, 11/12, 11/15
4:16-19 = 9/3
4:23-24 = 1/9, 1/19, 3/9, 3/29,
    4/1, 4/11, 6/8
4:32 = 12/2
4:34-38 = 2/24, 5/10, 11/4
4:39-40 = 1/5, 3/29
4:50 = 9/27
5:4 = 2/27
5:15-16 = 3/24
5:19 = 5/17, 7/9
6:7-11 = 3/28
6:30 = 5/27
6:35 = 3/30, 11/27
6:37-40 = 3/31, 11/27
6:44 = 10/18

6:63 = 6/2
7 = 11/27
7:24 = 9/22
7:37-38 = 1/4, 1/29, 4/21,
    6/17, 11/15
8:32 = 7/29
8:44 = 10/7
9:4 = 2/24, 8/27
9:7 = 9/27
9:25 = 6/27
9:39 = 1/23
10:3-4 = 1/21, 12/9
10:10 = 4/14, 4/22, 11/15, 11/20
11:18-19 = 3/11
11:28-29 = 3/29
12:32 = 3/30, 4/1, 6/2, 8/16
12:36 = 12/4
12:47-48 = 1/23
12:49-50 = 5/17, 7/9, 8/10
13 = 8/21
13:14 = 8/21
13:34-35 = 7/6, 8:8
13:58 = 3/25
14:1-3 = 2/7, 6/14, 6/23,
    9/30, 11/5
14:6 = 5/14, 12/22
14:12-14 = 6/13, 6/17,
    9/28
14:15-17 = 1/21, 6/7, 6/8
14:19 = 10/2
14:23 = 6/23, 8/18,
14:27 = 1/14, 6/5, 6/6, 7/11,
    12/9
15 = 1/27, 5/22
15:2 = 2/13, 7/9
15:4 = 6/17
15:5 = 1/7, 5/5, 6/17, 10/25
15:7-8 = 2/20, 5/17, 5/28
15:11 = 5/5, 5/17, 5/19, 6/7,
    8/18
15:14-15 = 4/11, 5/6, 11/20,
    12/22
15:16 = 2/20, 5/17, 11/12,
    12/22
16:13 = 1/20
16:22-24 = 5/19, 6/7, 11/12
16:26-27 = 12/22
16:33 = 6/5, 6/6

17 = 2/19, 7/4, 8:26
17:11 = 5/19
14:15-17 = 7/15, 8/28
17:18-19 = 1/16, 2/9, 2/20,
　　3/11, 3/12, 4/9, 4/20,
　　5/21, 7/8, 8/21, 11/19
17:21-22 = 1/8, 5/17, 6/4,
　　7/6, 8/8, 8/24
18 = 2/15
20:19-23 = 2/9, 2/28, 3/5,
　　3/6, 3/18, 3/19, 3/25,
　　7/11, 7/11
20:21 = 1/16, 2/20, 4/9, 4/20,
　　5/8, 8/21, 12/5
20:22 = 2/5

Acts
1:4-8 = 3/17, 3/25
1:8 = 1/7, 1/24, 2/20, 3/12,
　　3/16, 3/18, 3/19, 3/21,
　　4/9, 6:8, 7/9, 7/15,
　　7/28, 9/16, 10/4,
　　10/10, 10/16, 10/29,
　　11/19, 12/5, 12/12
1:9 = 6/3
2:4 = 3/25, 9/29
2 = 7/11
2:17-18 = 7/1, 7/23, 11/25
2:23 = 6/28
2:37-47 = 6/3, 6/4,
2:38 = 3/23, 10/18
2:41-42 = 4/24, 6/28
2:44-45 = 9/11
4:12 = 8/27, 1/5, 10/22
4:13-16 = 8/3
4:18-20 = 8/3, 10/10, 10/22
4:36-37 = 11/9
5:3 = 7/15
5:1-11 = 9/22
6 = 2/7
6:15 = 1/30
6:14-15 = 2/25
7 = 1/30
7:60 = 9/21
8:4 = 4/9, 6/24, 10/4,
　　10/12, 11/25
8:4-18 = 2/29
8:26-40 = 5/31
8:35 = 9/16

9:1-19 = 2/29
9:15 = 9/20
9:36 = 6/25, 9/10
10:1-46 = 9/29, 10/20
10:1-2 = 5/13
10:11 = 2/25
10:20-31 = 9/22
10:38 = 1/23, 6/9
10:44-45 = 3/25
11:1-3 = 4/2
11:14 = 2/25
12:2 = 12/6
12 = 8/14
12:6-10 = 8/14, 9/21
13:8 = 9/8
13:22 = 7/13
14:23 = 11/24
15:2 = 9/4
15:12-21 = 9/4
15:36-41 = 11/10
15:41-42 = 9/21
16:6-7 = 7/15
16:14 = 5/13
16:15,30-31 = 2/25, 6/5, 11/1
16:25 = 9/21
18:8 = 2/25
19:1-6 = 9/29
19:9 = 6/29
19:11 = 3/12
20:1-2 = 3/13
20:14 = 6/15
20:19 = 4/23
20:25 = 9/10
20:31 = 3/20, 4/23, 6/12
21:8 = 9/16
22 = 6/27, 10/4
26 = 6/27, 10/4
24:27 = 1/21
27:23-37 = 1/28, 5/30, 8/27

Romans
1:10-13 = 3/11, 7/23, 8/24
1:14-17 = 4/5, 6/9, 11/11, 11/29
1:16 = 5/31
1:18-20 = 5/25, 10/11
3:23 = 2/10,
3:26 = 11/5
5:1 = 2/18, 11/20, 11/22, 12/5
5:2 = 2/7

5:3-5 = 3/14, 4/3, 4/25
5:15 = 5/25
6:2 = 10/28
6:16 = 12/22
7:14-8:2 = 11/6
7:18-25 = 12/11
8:1-4 = 1/22 7/11, 7/15,
    7/16, 7/29, 11/20, 12/22
8:9-17 = 11/23
8:9 = 4/30
8:11 = 6/8
8:14 = 7/15
8:16-17 = 1/16 6/8, 12/22
8:23 = 4/20
8:26-27 = 6/8, 12/22
8:28 = 6/16
8:29-30 = 2/13, 4/21, 5/7, 8/15
8:31-39 = 12/22,
9:1-3 = 1/31, 4/23, 5/2, 5/19
10:1-2 = 3/2, 11/25
10:14-19 = 5/13, 9/20
10:17 = 3/15, 8/5
11:13-14 = 11/29
12:3-6 = 4/8, 7/27, 9/17,
12:8 = 9/15
12:10 = 8/21
12:11-12 = 2/7, 4/21, 6/24,
    7/31, 12/14
12:19-21 = 8/22, 12/1, 12/28
14:1 = 11/22
14:17 = 6/5, 6/6, 6/7, 8/18,
15:4 = 11/18
15:5-9 = 12/13
15:7-11 = 7/26, 8/26, 11/22
15:13-14 = 8/21, 11/18

I Corinthians

1:2 = 5/21
1:8-10 = 8/15
1:22-28 = 7/14
1:30-31 = 3/24, 4/29, 6/5, 7/14
2:1-5 = 10/11
2:2 = 3/4, 6/2
2:4-5 = 6/2, 12/31
2:16 = 1/7
2:9-14 = 2/7, 6/8
3:1-3 = 5/20
3:5-8 = 2/27
3:6-11 = 3/4, 5/2, 6/12

3:12-15 = 11/30
4:7 = 8/9
4:29 = 9/17
5:1, 8-20 = 7/27, 8/22
5:58 = 7/31
6:2 = 11/4
6:14 = 11/18
6:17 = 8/28, 12/22
6:19 = 6/8, 7/15
7:32-34 = 9/23
8:1-3 = 2/2, 3/10
9:19 = 5/3, 11/7
9:20-23 = 4/5, 4/27, 6/4, 6/20
9:24-27 = 5/3
9:7 = 2/17
9:19-22 = 7/10, 8/26, 12/10,
    12/18
9:27 = 11/30
9:29-31 = 10/17
10:12 = 3/1
10:13 = 1/11
10:31-33 = 9/23, 12/23
11:17 = 8/6
11:29-30 = 4/6, 9/27
12:1,7, 9,11, 28, 30 = 8/29,
    9/27
12:1-6 = 8/31
12:4 = 7/15
12:10 = 9/29
12:14-17 = 9/1
12:22-23 = 9/8
12:17 = 12/22
13 = 5/6
13:1-3 = 3/10
13:4-8 = 4/27, 10/14, 12/13
14 = 9/28
14:1 = 11/1
14:4, 18 = 9/29 9/29
14:32-33, 39 = 9/17, 9/25 9/28
15:1-6 = 7/6
15:9-10 = 2/10, 7/22
15:19 = 11/18
15:58 = 11/18
16:17-18 = 7/23

II Corinthians

1:4-5 = 5/1
2:4 = 4/23
2:14-16 = 3/26

3:1-4 = 6/14
3:10-13 = 3/13, 10/17
3:16 = 6/23
3:17 = 7/29
3:18 = 1/5, 1/10, 2/7, 10/6
4:2 = 10/11
4:4 = 2/6
4:5-12 = 4/7, 10/2
4:8-10 = 4/3
4:11-12 = 3/11
4:13-18 = 2/17, 3/27, 10/6, 10/17, 12/29
5:10-11 = 5/11, 10/7, 11/2
5:17-21 = 1/10, 1/22, 2/7, 8/11, 8/22, 8/27, 10/6, 11/7, 11/25, 12/22
5:20 = 4/11, 4/12, 6/2
6:9-10 = 1/3, 4/17, 5/19, 8/18
8:2-7 = 9/10
9:7 = 9/10
9:15 = 1/10, 5/4, 7/25, 9/15
10:1 = 5/2
10:4-5 = 4/21, 6/23,
11:2-4 = 11/14
11:14-15 = 9/22
12:4 = 2/7, 6/14
12:9-10 = 3/14, 9/23
12:7-10 = 4/4
12:15 = 4/5, 6/21
12:20-21 = 2/14
13:5-6 = 7/17

Galatians
1:6 = 2/14
2:20 = 1/13, 4/14, 6/30, 8/1, 8:25, 10/28, 11/13
3:19 = 5/1, 8/14,
4:13 = 4/30
5:1-2 = 3/23
5:7-8 = 7/29
5:13-14 = 3/23, 5:6, 5/29, 8/21
5:13-21 = 8/16
5:16 = 7/29
5:19-21 = 11/22, 12/30
5:22-25 = 2/20, 3/10, 5/19, 6/8, 6/11, 8/3, 8/10, 11/6, 12/27
6:7 = 4/6, 11/5
6:9-10 = 7/31, 11/29

6:12 = 8/21
Ephesians
1:4 = 3/24
1:3-8 = 6/2, 8/25, 11/20
1:13-14 = 6/8
1:18-23 = 1/2, 4/10 , 4/12, 11/20
1:27-29 = 1/18 9/5
2:1-3 = 9/5, 9/19, 10/18
2:6 = 1/2, 1/3, 3/6, 4/10, 11/20, 12/5
2:8-9 = 6/22, 9/18
2:10 = 2/13, 5/29
2:12-13 = 11/4, 11/18, 12/28
2:11-22 = 8/21, 8/16, 10/9, 10/21, 10/26, 11/28
2:20 = 1/22, 7/30
2:13 = 5/13
3:8 = 2/10, 7/22
3:16-19 = 1/15, 1/29, 2/11, 6/23, 7/23, 9/24, 11/1
3:20-22 = 2/5, 2/12, 9/30, 11/3, 11/27
4:2 = 8/21
4:7,11-13 = 1/24, 4/9, 6/25, 8/6, 12/17
4:15 = 8/28
4:17 = 6/25
4:25 = 8/4
4:28-32 = 7/15, 7/18, 8/10
5:1 = 5/7
5:8 = 4/12
5:12 = 8/21
5:15-17 = 6/15, 8/11
5:18 = 2/11, 3/3, 3/10, 3/25, 4/30
5:19 = 11/15, 12/4
5:19-21 = 3/25, 6/16, 6/19, 8/6, 9/25, 11/8
6:2-3 = 1/26
6:4 = 9/17
6:10 = 2/5
6:12 = 8/24
6:18-20 = 9/16, 12/17, 12/30
Philippians
1:6 = 11/20, 12/22
1:8 = 5/2
1:12-13 = 1/21

376

1:21-22 = 2/23
2:3-4 = 5/29, 9/26
2:5-8 = 2/15, 9/27
2:12-13 = 4/19
2:14-16 = 7/28, 12/27
2:15 = 2/13, 4/17
2:17 = 4/30
2:12-13 = 6/22
2:15-16 = 12/4
2:19 = 7/23
2:26-27 = 9/27
3:8-9 = 2/21
3:10 = 1/7, 2/21, 4/25, 10/25
3:18-20 = 11/20, 12/2
4:4 = 8/18
4:8 = 1/6, 4/27, 12/12, 12/27
4:11-13 = 1/11, 1/14, 6/13,
    8/7, 8/9, 8/20, 11/9, 12/22
4:19 = 6/13, 8/7

Colossians
1:13-14 = 1/21, 6/9, 7/14,
    11/25, 12/22
1:18 = 5/24, 6/12
1:28-29 = 5/30, 6/12
2:3 = 2/18
2:8-10 = 12/22
2:18 = 8/14
3:1-17 = 3/23
3:1-4 = 4/14, 6/14,
3:3-4 = 1/21, 11/5
3:12-14 = 12/1
3:5-17 = 7/5, 7/17, 9/25
4:2-6 = 2/3, 4/24, 6/15,
    8/11, 8/24, 10/14

I Thessalonians
2:11-12 = 3/13, 6/19,
2:19 = 8/10
3 = 8/5
4:12 = 5/23
5:11-17 = 1/27, 3/13, 5/19,
    8/15, 8/21, 9/6, 11/10
5:16-17 = 4/24, 9/19, 12/3,
    12/27
5:19 = 8/10
5:20-21 = 9/17
5:25 = 12/17

II Thessalonians
2:9 = 8/13

2:16-17 = 3/13, 11/10
3:1-3 = 8/24
3:5 = 2/17
3:13 = 7/31, 11/29

I Timothy
1:6-7 = 2/5, 7/2
1:16-17 = 9/8
2:5 = 5/14
3:2 = 9/9
3:4-5 = 6/19, 9/16
4:7 = 7/29, 7/30
4:16 = 2/17
4:20 = 9/27
5:23 = 4/30, 9/27
6:6 = 12/24
6:11 = 6/5

II Timothy
1:6-7 = 4/21, 8/6, 10/12
1:16 = 7/23
2:2 = 10/19
2:3-5 = 7/28, 7/29
2:26 = 3/18, 10/18
3:5 = 8/5
3:6 = 7/30
3:15-17 = 1/20, 5/27, 10/9
4:7-8 = 6/20
4:12-13 = 10/8
4:20 = 4/20
6:12 = 4/21

Titus
1:5-9 = 9/19, 11/24
2:9-10 = 12/23
2:13 = 2/7

Philemon
6 = 12/7

Hebrews
1:1 = 10/9
1:11-12 = 12/22
1:14 = 8/14
2:2 = 8/14
2:1-13 = 5/7
2:11-13 = 1/8, 3/6,
3:12 = 7/16
4:13 = 7/12
4:14-16 = 4/17, 5/1, 12/22
5:7-8 = 4/23, 4/25, 7/9,
5:11-16 = 5/18, 9/22
6:1 = 8/19

6:10-12 = 9/7, 11/30
6:18-20 = 11/18
7:26 = 7/16
10 = 8/25
10:19-20 = 5/6
10:24-25 = 3/13, 7/23, 8/6, 10/23
10:29 = 7/15
11:1 = 8/5, 9/18
11:6 = 3/15, 7/10, 8/5,
    9/18, 12/20
12:1-2 = 6/21, 10/28
12:1-4 = 7/28
12:4-6 = 2/13, 4/25, 9/6
12:7-10 = 9/15
13:2-3 = 9/9, 10/8
13:5-6 = 1/15, 1/17, 2/18, 11/20

James
1:2-4 = 2/2, 2/17, 4/11,
1:5-8 = 5/15, 9/4, 10:13
1:13 = 12/19
1:22 = 5/18
1:26 = 7/18
3:2 = 3/22
3:26 = 3/22
4:7-8 = 4/17, 5/17, 8/18, 10/24
4:17 = 12/31
5:13-20 = 2/22, 7/12, 9/27,
    12/1, 12/3, 12/5

I Peter
1:4-5 = 1/10, 6/22
1:7 = 12/27
1:10-12 = 1/10, 3/3, 8/14
1:18-19 = 3/7
2:9 = 4/13, 10/4
2:12 = 3/11
2:16 = 7/29
2:21-3:1 = 9/27
3:11 = 6/22
3:14-16 = 7/30, 8/11, 12/15
3:18 = 8/19
4:1 = 2/29
4:10-11 = 2/15, 4/8, 8/6,
    8/29, 9/1
4:12-13 = 4/25
5:7 = 12/27
5:20 = 12/24

II Peter
1:3-5 = 1/10, 6/5, 7/12,
    7/30, 11/20, 12/5
1:8-11 = 11/30
1:10 = 6/22
1:15 = 5/6
1:17-20 = 5/4, 5/6,
2:4, 7-9 = 4/6, 11/5
3:9 = 3/18, 3/21, 3/24,
    5/25, 10/18
3:14-16 = 3/22, 6/22
3:18 = 2/10, 4/4, 5/21, 7/22

I John
1:7-9 = 1/21 5/16, 7/17,
    8/10, 8/25, 12/1
1:8-9 = 2/9, 3/22, 4/21,
    7/6, 7/12, 10/28
3:17-18 = 1/19, 5/18, 10/31
4:4 = 1/17, 6/23, 11/19
4:16 = 11/1, 11/5
4:18 = 5/26, 7/25, 12/14
5:3 = 7/29
5:14-15 = 1/29, 3/21
5:18 = 11/20

III John
4 = 7/3

Jude
14-16 = 4/6
22-23 = 4/6, 5/11, 7/3,
    10/7, 10/14, 11/7

Revelation
2:2 = 7/31
2:4-5 = 4/21, 6/24, 10/10
3:1-3 = 12/21
3:5 = 4/26
3:15-17 = 4/22, 6/24, 10/15
3:20 = 4/22, 6/23, 12/9
7:9-12 = 2/19, 4/1, 8/8,
    8/26, 10/26
7:16-17 = 11/27
9:20 = 6/15
13:13 = 8/13
14:6-12 = 8/14
16:14 = 8/13
19:20 = 8/13
20 = 8/14
21:6 = 11/27
22:1, 17 = 3/29, 11/27